WHAT'S WRONG
with
MY CHILD?

*How to Understand and Raise
a Behaviorally Difficult Child*

Ruth Gattozzi, Ph.D.

Foreword by Lendon H. Smith, M.D.

McGraw-Hill Book Company

New York St. Louis San Francisco Auckland Bogotá Guatemala
Hamburg Johannesburg Lisbon London Madrid Mexico Montreal
New Delhi Panama Paris San Juan São Paulo Singapore Sydney
Tokyo Toronto

1 2 3 4 5 6 7 8 9 DOCDOC 8 7 6

ISBN 0-07-038781-8

LIBRARY OF CONGRESS CATALOGING IN PUBLICATION DATA

Gattozzi, Ruth.
What's wrong with my child?
1. Minimal brain dysfunction in children.
2. Minimal brain dysfunction in children—Patients—Care and hygiene.   I. Title.
RJ496.B7G38 1986   618.92'685'89 85-6715
ISBN 0-07-038781-8

BOOK DESIGN BY PATRICE FODERO

For all the Claudes

There but for the grace of God goes anyone's kid.

—A Hinckley neighbor in Evergreen, Colorado

In the beginning there was the slow, tortured recognition that Jennie's world was different, and it was not the world I would have for her.

—Anonymous parent, Churchill Forum (winter 1982)

Acknowledgments

Special thanks are due Shela Barker, Rosine DeCervantes and Dr. Lendon Smith, two parent friends and one celebrity author who trusted my awkward beginnings.

Contents

PART TWO

PART THREE

Preface

Smiling paternally, the chief of obstetrics and gynecology at the New York Hospital–Cornell Medical Center turned to the group of residents, all of them white-coated young men, hovering anxiously behind him. "*They* claim they can feel fetal movements at sixteen weeks, but naturally *we* know this isn't possible before twenty weeks." His grin broadened.

Easing my feet out of their icy stirrups and shrinking inside the sheet of paper draped across the examining table, at that moment I entered unknowingly into a nightmare of bias, prejudice, and pain which was to last for over ten years. If I did not recognize the ominous intricacies and machinations of those collective smiles that morning, the months and years to follow would teach me their tragic meaning only too well.

The question I had just been asked—the response to which provoked a round of quiet chuckles—was whether, approximately four months pregnant, I could as yet feel my unborn baby's movement.

The truth was that I had been able to feel inner activities, some weak as whispers and some not so faint, for at least the preceding two or three weeks. While watching television in the evening, I could even lie on the couch in the living room and look down at the grapefruit of shiny, stretched skin at my navel tossing from side to side like a tiny boat shipwrecked in a storm.

It was midsummer and cindery hot in the city, and by the mythical date of twenty weeks, when it suddenly becomes acceptable to begin to feel inward stirrings, I was too embarrassed to go into the stores without a coat to cover the unruly waves that moved visibly across my belly, wrinkling and lifting the fabric of my summer dresses.

Since this was not my first pregnancy, I was hardly unfamiliar with the events of a normal pregnancy. In this sense, the doctors were correct—the premature jarrings that I was experiencing, that pitched me out of bed in the mornings and caused me to cross my arms while waiting in supermarket or bank lines, were definitely *not* part of the course of a typical gestation. They had not happened to me before, nor were they happening to any of my pregnant friends.

Even the four years of study I had just completed for my doctorate in clinical psychology had not prepared me for the subtle implications and nuances of my baby's prenatal life. Nineteen seventy-five was the heyday of the psychogenic hypothesis, and class after class and seminar after seminar had concentrated on the theoretical stages of child development according to Freud, Erikson, or Piaget (none of whom, I might add, had experienced even one pregnancy, let alone multiple pregnancies).

All along, the entrenched belief had been hammered home that if something went wrong—should a baby or child turn out to be be-haviorally deviant or slightly "off center"—such a cruel outcome was due either to deliberate or unwitting environmental damage. In a word, Mother. Never was the child's own physical functioning implicated as the culprit or the source.

The premature movement should have been the first indication that something in my pregnancy was possibly not normal. Instead, my honest answer had been met with derision simply because it did not fit with the stages of embryonic and fetal development delivered up in the medical textbooks. (And this was at one of the leading hospitals for obstetrics in the nation.) To the everlasting sorrow of thousands of parents, these manuals are all descriptive of *normal* pre- and postpartum stages. The text on the stages of *abnormal* pregnancy and fetal development has never been written.

And yet, there are many subtle or "soft" signs that go unrecognized, by the wayside—mine, and others to be described in this book—which, if read correctly at the start, could lead to a far different outcome than the usual explosion into family tragedy when the facts of a child's behavior handicap are finally known, often six or seven or more years too late.

But even had I known for certain back then when I was disengaging myself discreetly from those stirrups that my baby would not be normal—even if the medical experts had at least been willing to consider the validity of my inner experience—could anything have been done at that early stage to alter the course of the subsequent tragic years?

I have since learned that the answer is a resounding yes. There is much that can be done, if not yet in the months of prenatal development—although even here, giant strides are being made—then most certainly within the first days and weeks of postnatal life.

I would not be writing today if I did not now know this. Nor would I be writing if I did not know that my own painful experience is paralleled, and perhaps exceeded, by thousands of similar stories.

Out of my own years of struggle, groping from misdiagnosis to misdiagnosis in an effort to comprehend my child's "oddness"—and from the similar experiences of hundreds of parents I have met through the California Association for Neurologically Handicapped Children and other parent groups—I have learned that the greatest regret of these parents, many of whose lives have been broken irreparably, is that neither they nor the professionals they consulted recognized their child's problem, in all its heart-wrenching ramifications, sooner.

This book is aimed at helping those individuals who know a child most intimately (and care the most) in early detection of behavioral and developmental difficulties. It is meant not only as a preventive tool, but also as a confirmation of the parental reality that a child is somehow "different" from the start. For I have never once met a parent who, whether or not she (or he) had other children, did not apperceive or *sense* when something was wrong with her baby. If not prenatally, then very soon thereafter.

Millicent, a friend and colleague, illustrates the usual case in a dramatic way. Only because she is a strong, mentally healthy woman with a good deal of life experience behind her, she managed to hold steadfastly to her inner conviction that Amble, her green-eyed, red-headed firstborn, was not quite "right," in an important but maddeningly elusive way, through all her own mother's denial and protests that there was nothing wrong with this beautiful little granddaughter except that she, Millicent, was making the child neurotic by dragging her around to all those specialists.

In spite of this resolve, even she began to waver under the onslaught of the professional advice: Stop worrying so much—relax and enjoy your baby; stop playing doctor with your child; some babies bang their heads and some don't—it's not important; it's just a phase, she'll grow out of it; our own son wouldn't breast-feed as a baby and he's perfectly fine today. And the most heinous advice of all, given when Amble was barely one week old: Don't feed her for three or four days—she'll *have* to breast-feed.

Only when this aggressive, superactive and oddly developing little girl drowned a family of pet hamsters in the toilet bowl, one by one, at age 3 and, a year later, clawed her baby brother's eye to the extent that he required surgery did the doctors (and Grandmother) come round to conceding that perhaps her development was not proceeding so averagely after all.

Echoes of those early professional smiles. Every parent of a minimally handicapped child knows many more pat formulas and statements of faith—just as every parent remembers the day when he or she knew irrevocably that this unordinary and incomprehensible child would not in fact "grow out of" his difference in the normal course of events.

What is not covered here are the more recognizable developmental disabilities such as Down's syndrome, mental retardation, or infantile autism which are generally diagnosed at very early ages. This book is addressed, rather, to that more subtle, but no less tragic, group of deviations or behavior handicaps variously known in the medical literature by more than fifteen different names; minimal (not to be equated with "trivial") brain dysfunction, attention deficit disorder, learning disability, hyperactivity, maturational 'lag," sensory deficit, and perceptual or central processing dysfunction are a few of the currently most popular.

These are the offbeat, disruptive, mildly to moderately neurologically impaired children who constitute approximately 15 to 18 percent of the child population, and who constitute as well the most common reason for referrals to pediatricians and mental health counselors from school systems.

They make up the frustrating, heterogeneous group which professionals find so difficult to diagnose, especially at early ages, since they look deceptively normal, usually have average or superior (but far from even) intelligence, and in fact behave normally under certain conditions—such as the half-hour slice of life when they are seen in the doctor's office. They are frequently misdiagnosed as neurotic, psychopathic characters, behavior disorders, or victims of parental neglect or failure to "structure" and "limit." ("Today's Abused Child Is Tomorrow's Thunder," proclaims a flyer for one southern California school for neurologically handicapped children.)

Picture those difficult-to-place children of all races and ethnic groups smiling their hesitant, gap-toothed smiles out of the pages of the *National Enquirer*. Along with a plea for a permanent adoptive home—"Can You Give Cheerful, Energetic Leonard a Loving Home?"—the article which accompanies the picture will most likely also mention a learning disability and related social-behavioral problems. Since they require supernormal understanding, perseverance and patience, they are the children most often placed for adoption or shunted away in growing numbers into foster homes and into the residential treatment centers springing up like crops of mushrooms across the nation.

If through monumental efforts by the parents these children do not end up in an institution, their fate is to become the hard-to-handle or "impossible" youngsters rejected by their teachers and normally developing peers and by just about everyone else in the neighborhood. Oddball loners, they are painfully aware of the anger directed at them from every side, and soon succumb to feelings of depression and hopelessness which often escalate later into suicidal ideation. Neither they nor anyone else can make sense of their difference, which seems so minimal, to judge only by appearance, or fathom why they cannot be made to conform despite massive amounts of discipline or punishment.

Sometimes earlier, but almost always by school age, their self-esteem plunges to a low from which it seldom recovers completely. Although a child may have been protected by parental tenderness and affection in the first few years, and/or by strenuous efforts to engineer the environment in order to avoid frustrating or conflictual situations, school is the point at which the child *must* become aware of his difference in relation to his peers; and by deduction, the shattering recognition of his unfitness for survival in the world as he is and it alters his perception of himself and his world forever.

They are the children that one distraught parent wished "could wear braces on their heads" for all the world to see. And thereby, presumably, to be educated toward compassion.

Their vulnerability and pain, I am convinced, is greater than that of their mentally retarded or autistic second cousins because of their keen awareness and intelligence.

As the parents of such children, we have all written this book together, through our shared suffering and years of fighting to hold onto the belief that our children are worthwhile though different. And through a ready and gratifying willingness to respond to requests for information and interviews.

The early indicators of behavior handicap described in the subsequent chapters are based on the introspective reports of over eighty parents gathered in questionnaire data and personal interviews. Though these reports are supplemented by a number of talks with pediatricians, teachers, and other specialists, this book is mainly the collective experience of the parents.

In a few cases, the reports are based on the observations of relatives or friends. For it is almost a certainty that even if we do not have our own "unusual" child, most of us know or have known—or will know—at least one of these children. Parts Two and Three are devoted to the basics of survival for both the hurting parents and their children; they contain home methods and techniques for interrupting and relieving the various conditions of odd growth and development. The methods have been culled from a combination of readings in the literature of child development, professional meetings, special education curricula, and general behavioral principles (conditioning and reinforcement methods). They also include adaptations of techniques that have proved useful in other medical and psychological conditions as well as some original techniques for helping children I either hammered out intuitively or stumbled on in my own moments of desperation.

Most of all, though, when all is said and done, this book is written for Claude, that rambunctious fetus of eleven years ago, in the hope that he will one day find in it an answer to that haunting question he has asked in times of anguish after a suspension from school, a rejection by still another friend, or exclusion from a community activity: Why was I ever born?

Postscript: If, at first, I had some second thoughts about the need for this book, trusting wishfully that perhaps the great damage and injustice caused by misunderstanding and misdiagnosis of atypical children are changing in our more enlightened times, that illusion was dispelled once and for all just last evening as I watched the nightly news.

There in front of me, wiggling, squirming, writhing and then whirling round and round in his courtroom swivel chair, was Jaimie Means, a blond, blue-eyed seven-year-old who had just become the youngest criminal trial defendant in California history.

As Jaimie orbited reflexively and obliviously, an impressive procession of teachers and school counselors took the stand to testify that the slightly built first-grader had always been "strange," had "no conscience" nor any notion of right or wrong. To a person, they voiced their certainty that this diabolical child—this modern-day "Rosemary's baby"—was headed straight for a life of crime.

By the end of the three-day trial in the Ventura courtroom, these ominous prophecies had turned into truths as this child was convicted of two counts of malicious mischief and one count of petty theft. The camera cut to a shot of Jaimie with his head now plunged into his seat and his feet in the air.

Closing on a note of obvious satisfaction, the news anchorperson reported that several times during the day's solemn proceedings, Superior Court Judge Charles McGrath had been forced to halt the testimony while he ordered young Jaimie to stop his damnable fidgeting. "He's a distraction," McGrath winced sourly. ...

Foreword

For years I have addressed the problems of hyperactive or "impulse directed" children. These children's responses are very individualized. For instance one of them will act wild and crazy because he wants marshmallows for breakfast, while another might be set off by seeing a dog while walking to school. They are all sensitive and ticklish. They notice everything. There are common traits that should indicate to parents that they have "one of those" in their midst.

Dr. Gattozzi gives useful guidelines to help alert parents to potential problems such as attending school. Just the fact of *attending* school and watching other children do things that seem impossible is enough to bring the hyperactive child's self-esteem down a few notches.

This book will show you how to "read" your child's own very unique capabilities. How to be understanding instead of critical. How to be a support system instead of another negative. The parent's role is, after all, to make the child's life easier, not harder. This book will show you how to spot signs of minimal brain dysfunction in your child (it just means the child cannot do as well as his age would indicate) so you may help your child cope with all frustrations and fears that go with this diagnosis. You will also learn to deal with your own feelings and prepare for the special problems that go with rearing such a child.

But most important, this book shows that you are not alone in your feelings, sorrows, and challenges in rearing a child so touched. Remember, the doctor does not live with your child; the doctor sees the child only on exam days, and all the subtle difficulties that a parent is aware of are usually not glaring out at the doctor like pneumonia or a broken leg.

Dr. Gattozzi's questionnaire is a powerful diagnostic tool. You should take this with you if you have a skeptical doctor. Take heart—there are a number of things you can do to smooth the path. The ideas in this book can actually make life at school and home a little saner.

My wife and I were guilt-ridden because some of our children were noncompliant, had mood swings, wet the bed, talked back. How relieved we were when we discovered milk allergies, screwy brain waves, pinworms, hyperactivity, and calcium deficiencies to explain these defiances! How relieved we were that it was not our fault!

Trust your instincts. If you feel something is wrong in your household, something probably *is* wrong.

The world has long needed what Dr. Gattozzi has done here, and I like the way that she has done it. Every parent should have this book. Parents are the ones who are in the best position to diagnose their children. Support systems for parents of the child who does not fit in are sorely needed. This book will be the bible for those parents and those groups. It is human, humane, and encouraging.

—Lendon H. Smith, M.D.

Introduction:
Why Parents Aren't
to Blame

Such is the heady progress of science as a great unfolding detective story that while this book has been in the making, a number of important new discoveries about the human brain have come to light. They illuminate in sharp relief the separate biological inheritance of males and females shaped by the billions of years of our evolutionary past. Really, like most scientific revolutions, it's been a slow coming-together of an enormous amount of research: a solidifying of the bits and fragments of evidence gathered in clinics and laboratories all over the world in the last fifty years.

Tracing its clues painstakingly through a labyrinth of suggestive glimmers and whispers, the "new" brain science draws its inferences from many diverse sources—animal studies, cultural anthropology, "accidents of nature" such as chromosome and glandular abnormalities, electrical recordings of brain activity, observations and testing of mental patients and psychopathic criminals, genetics, endocrinology, neurochemistry. And it has yielded up a clearer picture than we have ever had of what goes wrong in the innermost neural snakings and brain whorls of children with developmental disorders like learning disability and hyperactivity.

It's a necessary oversimplification of the recent breakthroughs, but briefly, brain scientists have spotlighted a critical stage in prenatal development when the two hemispheres of the brain separate out, roughly symmetrically, from the glutinous swelling of brain tissue and are sculpted and organized in different directions under the control of the sex hormones. There's more: a wealth of evidence points dramatically to a special vulnerability to the hormonal environment in the womb—particularly, to circulating levels of the main male sex hormone, testosterone—at the heart of developmental disorders.

Here, in crossroads where the sex hormones, brain development, brain anatomy, and behavior meet, a surprising number of the once jumbled pieces of the behavioral puzzle interlock into a vivid first picture—the fact, for instance, that boys more often than girls are afflicted with developmental disorders, mental retardation, hyperactivity, delayed speech, stuttering, childhood allergies, asthma, dyslexia, infantile autism, sterotyped movement and tic disorders, and schizophrenias of early onset, or that boys show more left-handedness, weaker immune systems, and less verbal (left hemisphere) control over the emotional impulses originating in the right sides of their brains, including aggression, violence, and sexual deviance.

The link between all of these natural misfortunes is that an oversupply of testosterone slows down the growth of the left hemisphere in the fetal brain. The common result is that "left-brain" processes such as language and reasoning ability are suppressed.

The revelations trickling back from the new frontier of brain physiology make a good deal of instant and intuitive sense. For years, parents, educators, therapists, and other adults whose life or work brings them close to deviant children have noted that these youngsters, usually boys, appear strikingly similar in their behavior patterns: like "throwbacks" to an earlier evolutionary age. Slowly and reluctantly, the realization dawns in conscientious and well-intentioned parents and child workers. Alley Oop is the painful but persistent image.

The primitive tooth-and-claw displays, the sensation seeking, explosiveness, boundless energy, vengeance, antisocial attitudes, and irrationality, and the lonely, seemingly territorial fight for dominance with which antagonistic children approach the world, *regardless of their upbringing*, push us finally into this disquieting association. And clashing head-on with the towering orthodoxy of psychology and sociology—which for the last quarter-century has heralded that any inequalities or differences between children *must* be caused by their environment—it first jolts and then stills our senses.

So just what the "new" science is finding to be chemically and physiologically true fits smoothly, and even a little eerily, into the slots of long and bitter parental experience. As more and thinner spider-threads of the great mystery of brain science unravel, it's turning out to be the fact, and no longer merely the figment of an alleged alarmism in parents, that *some children have taken a different path from the normal during their embryonic development*—a step or two backward in evolution, if you will.

The cruel thing about all this is that the traits and abilities laid down in the child's brain before birth—specifically, the exaggerated right-brain functions like visual-spatial sharpness, which has been linked to aggression and a keyed-up "fight-flight response"—were once adaptive, the very means of survival in a long-ago hunting and gathering way of life when men had to be fierce competitors for sex and dominion over the planet. But emerging full-blown and overdeveloped in some children at the time of their birth into the modern world, as many parents can attest, these traits are excruciatingly maladaptive.

The long-range future of science lies in the direction of chemical and genetic technology. But it's still years off (and some hope never) before biogenetic engineering and the repairing of defective genes become a practical fact of life. Even as they approach that day, scientists will be faced with the thorny, and perhaps insoluble, problem of finding a technique of gene selection that would preserve the often *superior* specific talents of children with behavioral and learning disability.

Obviously, none of this will come to pass in your child's lifetime, and so it may seem at first to matter very little, except on a hazy intellectual plane, that science has now "caught on" to what makes some children so maddeningly nonconformist and nonresponsive. Understandably, you may be wondering what is the practical meaning, if any, of the new biological findings to your everyday life with your child.

What good, in other words, is knowing that a hypersensitivity to his hormonal world, genetically programmed by the sex genes, was very likely responsible for your youngster's deviance, or that the sex hormones were dramatically involved in the formation of his violent attributes and behaviors? How will the new information about brain-behavior relationships filter down into the home, and what effect will it really have there? Or should it have?

The most far-reaching change may well lie in your general attitude toward your misfit child. Knowing with the authoritative backup of science that your youngster's academic and behavioral failure are not, and never were, his choice or his "fault" should make a real difference. For a state of internal vulnerability, and the skewing of the whole functional relationship between the two halves of the brain, surely cannot be something any child ever asked to carry through life.

An expansion of your feeling of love and compassion for your child may follow—a softening of your response to his peccadilloes, floundering, and ineptness. A forgiveness. And if you are inclined as are many scientists to believe in the subtle but compelling influences of prenatal emotional life on behavior, including behavioral "imprinting," and in the the responsivity of the fetus to sensory impressions, then the implications of a chemical imbalance during the molding of brain tissue in the womb are nothing short of astounding.

Another timely effect of the new delineation of biologically caused deviance, which is delivering up fresh insights almost daily, may be to help relieve hurting parents of their crushing burden of guilt—the dark side of parenting we all carry inside us as the progenitors of oddly developing children, no matter what our level of education, how rich the fund of knowledge at our fingertips, or how high our status in life, and no matter how many parenting seminars we may have attended or given.

Until now, this rain cloud has always existed in us alongside the incongruous realization that, whatever our human failings, we wished our child well—we did nothing deliberately or knowingly to produce his or her massive behavioral damage. A little green monster that won't go away perches perpetually on our shoulder, spilling over into every area of our lives, spoiling our proud moments.

Science is now moving over rapidly to the side of parents in anguish as it proclaims, loudly, that the enigmatic obstinacy of many children is the end result of a distinct biological inheritance over which neither parent nor child had a wisp of control.

But if you have any lingering doubts about the potency of the sex hormones as determinants of behavior, you need think no further than on the harrowing stress and storminess which is the "normal" experience of adolescence in America. Most parents, including, it may seem, everyone you know, are fortunate enough to float through relatively trouble-free years in which they feel in control of their lives—up to the time when their child reaches adolescence. At that time, the abrupt change in their child's "colors," under the direction of the sex hormones, offers them their first experience of real parental agony.

Thousands of other, not-so-lucky parents, for whom this book is written, face a tidal wave of insurrection and formidable barriers to physical and social communication from the moment of their child's birth—and sometimes even before. What the new science is shouting, in brief, is that the scripts of children's personalities, including their skills, abilities, and social behaviors, if not already written to conclusion before their births, are *strongly biased* in certain directions: organized, "tuned up," and preadjusted for precise functioning along definite behavioral grooves, all before our odd children ever see the light of day.

This book is about deflecting the frightening, heart-freezing course which seems to be the fate of the "differently" developing child, and about all the new and old ways we have as parents to do this. It's about offsetting the biological damage of special children and helping them to live out what should be their normal span of years. For it's a well-known statistic that not only are more of the aggressive and impulsive children placed in foster care, psychiatric hospitals, and group homes or adopted out, but their lives are often actually foreshortened as they enter in disproportionate numbers into childhood crime and delinquency, become early alcoholics and drug addicts, and die prematurely in automobile accidents or violent brawls.

Recently, in a restaurant a few miles from where I live, an argument over a tamale that apparently wasn't hot enough led to a shooting death. "Man Killed over Tamale" read the small headline in the back pages of the newspaper. Complaining that his corn snack didn't have enough chili in it, a male customer jumped behind the counter and threw a beer can. The counterperson, another young man, responded by pulling out a gun and shooting him. Two formerly pugnacious and impulse-ridden children—walking "time bombs"? More than likely. Senseless and preventable? Absolutely.

And since heaven can wait for both you and your child, this book is also about holding yourself together during your child's periods of rampant wildness.

Human nature, in the not very human ways it's often expressed, should tell us that despite the new scientific enlightenment, parents will be around and needed for a long time to come. Also tragic but true, it should reveal that the secondary (psychological) damage to the "different" child's self-esteem will still go on, perhaps always. In recent memory, we've had many examples to stamp in this sad lesson, ranging from the history of scapegoating and the treatment of minority groups (and of the animal families who share our earth) to the ongoing conflict between conservationists and those industrialists who would destroy the resources and beauty of the planet.

At this moment, then, the only real way to assure your deviant child of the future which is his or her birthright lies in detecting differences as early as possible and stepping in to arrest and ameliorate damage by the techniques described in this book and other books, and by strategies you may discover on your own. For the tens of thousands of parents and slightly dysfunctional children whose pain is driving them to think of ending their lives (or the lives of others), who don't want to live with the many hurts inside of them, tomorrow may be much too late.

And in all of us, young and old alike, who have lived through the experience of behavior difference and reached the other shore, there's a trapped core of feeling, often a searing but sometimes a singing, that cries out for our stories to be heard today.

PART
ONE

1

Cradles of Heartache

The Bette Davis Story

It was the winter of 1951. Holding her newly adopted infant, an appealing baby girl named Margot, screen goddess Bette Davis smiled for publicity photographs which Twentieth Century-Fox would distribute to *Modern Screen*, *Photoplay*, and the other popular fan magazines of the day.

Little Margot, who had been adopted when five days old, not only appeared to be a healthy, normal, and perfect baby, but also breezed through a series of preadoptive medical examinations with no obvious problem. She had been named Margot for sentimental reasons. Bette and her actor husband, Gary Merrill, first met and began their romance while making *All About Eve*, a picture in which Bette played the role of Margo Channing. "It is so typical of Bette that the information she gave about the new baby is very meager," bemoaned one Hollywood gossip columnist.

To all appearances, the adoption indicated how strongly Bette believed in this marriage, her fourth; at the time, there truly seemed good reason to be optimistic. Even before the marriage took place, it was whispered that Bette Davis had finally met her match. And over the

3

years Bette had always insisted to the newsmongers, between puffs on her close-smoked cigarette, that she wished Barbara, her four-year-old daughter, could have a playmate, since she believed that an only child leads a lonely existence.

Two years later—at the beginning of what Bette would call, with her famous nervous hand gesture and a slight shudder, "my ten black years, one tragedy after another"—Margot began displaying mystifying behavior problems: bouts of violence and destructiveness in which she would lift and throw pieces of heavy furniture, sometimes through upstairs windows, with little apparent effort.

Margot's first two years had revolved around famous movie star parents with fast-paced, hectic schedules involving much moving, traveling, and motel stopping. Although it would mean that their careers would recede into the background, the Merrills soon made a determined effort to give Margot and their two other small children a stronger sense of security and stability in their home life. They packed off the whole family—which included servants, nurses, and pet French poodles—all the way across the country, to the rocky and rural coast of southern Maine, where they began a period of concentrated domestic life in a handsome stone and wood house open on all sides to the ocean, at cape Elizabeth, just outside the city of Portland. According to a regional manager of National Van Lines, the furnishings that were loaded into two moving vans for the cross-country trek weighed in at more than 35,000 pounds, as contrasted with the average household's 3,000 to 4,000 pounds of furniture. They named the new seaside house Witch-Way ("Because we didn't know which way we were going, and a witch lived there—guess who?").

The newspaper articles of the day expressed surprise at the sudden voluntary exile to Maine, in order to roast chestnuts and join the PTA, of the woman who had long reigned over dramatic films. "In the beginning I must have shocked my Maine neighbors," Bette chuckled to a reporter from *Collier's* magazine. "When they came to call, they were expecting gold lamé and 10 servants, I'm sure. Instead they found me running around with a broom or cleaning a bird cage." The new household included an amphitheater of a kitchen and a king-sized menagerie of cats, dogs, goats, ducks, chickens, and even a donkey. A sprawling sun porch with a striped awning overlooked a pond, a barbecue oven, stacked lobster pots, and lawn chairs.

Margot's disturbing symptoms did not go away by themselves, either with time or in the idyllic new setting. She began having strange screaming fits at night, and she had to be tied down in her bed with a protective device to prevent her from hurting herself. Spells of lethargy would sometimes fill the spaces between the violent episodes. She was very restless—"almost as if she was possessed by a demon," Bette said retrospectively to the *Collier's* reporter; Margot was a child "who could not put on the brakes."

The Merrills tried hiring a private nurse for Margot whose main responsibility was to look after her and restrain her, but most of the women who signed on for this job would leave after a week or two. Cuddling, rocking, walking the floor—all the usual infant remedies—failed to comfort this odd child. Her older sister Barbara (B. D.) once remarked to a friend, "My sister has a broken head." With this new stress added to the strain of Bette's interrupted career, the frustrations in the Merrills' marriage that have been described by the grown-up B. D. in her account of this domestic period must naturally have increased manyfold. According to the account, screaming matches in which the two seasoned and temperamental performers vented their painful parental guilt and argued over which of them was to blame for Margot's troubles broke the tranquility of the pastoral setting that was supposed to have given all of them a saner atmosphere.

A thorough medical examination at Presbyterian Hospital in New York City eventually revealed that Margot was not simply showing the symptoms of an emotional disturbance brought on by an unstable family situation, for which the prognosis would have been more optimistic; she had apparently been brain-damaged at or before birth. Like all conditions of brain trauma, her illness was invisible but incurable. Her extraordinary feats of strength were probably a form of physical compensation for her gross intellectual inadequacies. The doctors advised that the wisest course of relief for both Margot and her family was to institutionalize her as soon as the arrangements could be made. Since Margot could no longer be handled at home by her parents or nurses and the disruptive effects of her condition on the other children in the family were beginning to tell, placing her in a school equipped to deal with her special disabilities would be the kindest, as well as the most unselfish, act. Here, she could be brought along slowly with children of her own capabilities.

Finally Bette had to admit that "what we had vaguely suspected now became a reality," and she also said, "It was a bitter blow and an enormous heartbreak to Gary and me." Three years old, dressed in a sailor suit and hat, Margot left for a new lifetime adoptive home, a residential facility in upstate New York called the Lochland School.

"If Bette Davis, the fightingest star in Hollywood," gushed Hedda Hopper in her nationally syndicated column, "is great in the fights she can do something about, she is equally great in the lost cause. The baby she and Gary Merrill adopted shortly after they married developed into a retarded child. 'Margot has to be away at school,' she told me. 'She can't be kept with our other two children. She is a 60 IQ, really the most tragic thing because only one-half of the brain functions due to a birth injury. I feel that talking about this may help some other mothers.'"

With Margot's sad departure, an unaccustomed quiet settled over the big picture-windowed downstairs living room that was comfortably furnished with flowery chintz sofas and chairs, antique tables and floor lamps, a braided rug, and alcove bookcases in which Bette kept her two Oscars. Bette, who was also at this time recuperating from surgery on her jawbone, sensed that she needed to return to Hollywood, "my town," to ease her psychological distresses, but at first she hesitated, filled with many self-doubts after an absence from working in films of three years. "All sorts of questions kept running through my mind," she said of this difficult time. "Could I still remember lines? Was my acting ability a tenuous thing that now was gone forever? Would my mouth bother me? The numbness had not completely disappeared even now." On her first day back at work shooting *The Virgin Queen*, she managed to get through the rehearsal. "Action," boomed the director. As she began to roll out her lines on cue, she knew with relief that the enormous concentration and emotional intensity that her work demanded had rescued her.

Eighteen years passed. Margot was now twenty-one, and, in a calm and accepting mood, Bette wrote: "Margot has improved yearly. Lochland has been her second home. She is a beautiful, loving child, able to cope with her limitations. It, of course, has been a heartbreak for all of us, but thank God we found the school, for her sake and for ours."

Soon after her initial placement at Lochland, it would be confirmed by the official psychological tests that this strangely developing little girl was indeed mentally retarded. But in the intricate and labyrinthine world of neurological symptoms, most investigators envision a continuum of nervous system dysfunction which ranges from states of severe retardation and infantile autism, at the one pole, to milder conditions of attentional disorder, minimal brain dysfunction, cerebral palsy, and learning disability, at the other.

With this concept in mind of a continuous sequence of behavior and symptoms, it becomes possible to draw some pointed parallels between the history of Margot and the early lives of the multitudes of more subtly brain handicapped children.

Chiefly, the Bette Davis or Margot Merrill story illustrates the stubborn and enigmatic resistance of the disturbing behavior to efforts at modification by the parents and other concerned adults, the wide mood swings and overemotionality of the afflicted children, the violent frustration of the children's efforts to compete and keep up with normal children, and the children's exasperating—and ultimately tragic—failure to improve their biologically based "bad girl" or "bad boy" behavior with experience, discipline, or time.

A similar sadness unfolded a few years ago in the Los Angeles mansion of Sylvester Stallone. The slow discovery over a period of three years that his young son was afflicted with autism, a still puzzling and little understood brain disorder, led the actor with the rugged, unbeatable image to remark with a certain grimness that he now knew that reality, rather than dark glasses and box-office success, was the main event in the ring of life.

As in little Margot's case, a specific cause for the vulnerability of a child's nervous system to trauma will likely never be known, and a parent would do well to accept our present state of medical ignorance at the start. (There are a few exceptions to the prevalent lack of medical knowledge—for instance, premature birth is known to be a strong risk factor in cerebral palsy, and reduced oxygen supply to the fetus during labor and delivery is known to increase the risks of mental retardation.) But in general, the medical consensus is overwhelmingly that these various aberrations in neurological makeup begin during embryonic and fetal development, and that *all the related disorders, from slight to severe, are associated with a chemical disturbance or deficiency deep in the base of the brain or brain stem.*

The distractibility, the short attention span, the poor short-term memory, and the inability to organize input from the environment that are shared by the diverse syndromes are functions of certain areas in the brain stem collectively called the reticular formation. These are the areas most commonly implicated as the site of the trauma or chemical imbalance. The reticular regions have direct connections to the cerebral cortex, the thinking and integrative department of the brain. They also funnel impulses into a structure almost hidden from sight between the cortex on top and the spinal cord below known formally as the limbic system and informally as the "animal" or old reptilian brain.

The importance of the limbic system in human emotion is that it acts as a filtering or "taming" device to modulate the intensity of the stimuli that come to it from all the sense organs. The ability to inhibit or withhold emotional responses is also largely a limbic function, so that a poorly operating limbic system may lead to excessive arousal and activation (too great an "energy" of feeling relative to a source) and poor control of impulses such as violent, uncontrolled aggression and rage reactions.

Childhood Disturbance in Eminent Persons

Scores of professionals in medicine, psychology, and teaching swear that the phenomena of minimal cerebral dysfunction, learning disability, and hyperactivity are increasing in a geometric progression—virtually exploding—among their young charges. They cite as probable causes our prevalent junk food diet, the proliferation of premature and brain-damaged infants who survive nowadays into childhood, and such reliable realities of modern life as lead and other poisons in our atmosphere, along with insatiable drug and alcohol use by so many young parents.

Granted that the incidence of deviant children among us may well be rising, the syndrome itself and its associated night-follows-day behavior problems are hardly new. They have existed since the dawn of recorded time, until very recently as merely a variant of normal behavior.

For instance, which of us has not known a seemingly incorrigible, Tom Sawyer-ish boy like this mid-nineteenth-century individualist:

The seventh pregnancy of a middle-aged and exhausted mother had resulted in a difficult birth in the middle of a severe winter. The large size of the infant boy's head had especially caused complications in the delivery; the village doctor thought he probably had "brain fever." As the boy grew, his frail body never seemed quite adequate to support that odd, oversized head with its broad forehead, deep-set eyes, and downturned mouth.

His early years were plagued by physical ailments—constant colds, bronchitis, and ear inflammations. His older sister sarcastically called him Rinckey. At the age of twelve he complained to his mother, "Ma, I'm a bushel of wheat. I weigh just sixty pounds."

The town of Milan, Ohio, bordered on the Huron River a few miles south of Lake Erie. From the start, the boy had an above-average propensity to get into scrapes in the thriving waterfront community of farmland, grain warehouses, and canal basins. Indefatigably adventuresome and mischievous, he was forever peering into bees' nests and climbing up the grain elevators in the local flour mill. One time he fell into a pit of spilling grain and nearly smothered. Unseen hands rescued him at the last possible minute.

His father, Sam, was driven to his wits' end by his small son's unruliness and incessant "foolish questions," and could not conceal his disapproval and disappointment in him. Scoldings and birch switchings, to the point where the bark wore off, had no noticeable effect. At the age of six, while experimenting with a small fire, he burned his father's barn to the ground, and Sam then administered a whipping in the village square, which he advertised in advance to the public.

An excessive craving for sweets surfaced early and became a focus of never-ending conflict with his mother, Nancy, who tried in vain to keep him from stealing the sugary treats with which she stocked the cookie jar.

Some of his misdeeds made his frustrated father fear he must be lacking in ordinary good sense. One afternoon while playing in a neighbor's barn he gathered a nest of goose and chicken eggs, which he sat on until deep into the evening in an attempt to hatch them. As usual, no one knew where he had disappeared to on this occasion, and so his family had to set out on one of their frequent late-night search parties.

Far more serious was the time he went exploring and swimming in a creek on the outskirts of town with a playmate, the son of a prosperous town shopkeeper. It was already dark when he realized that his friend had drowned. Frightened and not knowing what else to do, he went home and slipped quietly into bed. He said nothing until he awakened in the middle of the night to a burst of lantern light and was interrogated by the boy's frantic family.

At the age of eight, he lasted a scant three months in a one-room schoolhouse run by the Reverend and Mrs. G. B. Engle. The stern and severe frock-coated Reverend Engle did not spare his cane or leather strap on his pupil's arms and buttocks, but even with the backup of the trusty canings and whippings refused to allow him back when he returned to school after a bout with scarlet fever. According to the Reverend, he was hopelessly inattentive and "addled."

What he carried away from his school experience was a lasting distaste for mathematics, rote learning, and the oppressive discipline of formal schooling. As he put it long afterwards, "To see for myself, to test things myself for one instant was better than learning about something I had never seen for two hours." What his father got out of the ordeal was the advice to "keep him in the streets for he would never make a scholar."

Even his short stay had had a disastrous effect on the whole school. One morning, for instance, he lowered a fishhook out a second-story window, caught a squawking chicken, and yanked it up to the window before a crowd of screaming, appreciative children. But despite several such moments of supreme popularity, his puniness and lack of coordination in games made him an object of rejection around other children.

Years later, he recalled his brief schooldays in a newspaper interview: "I remember I used never to be able to get along at school. I don't know what it was, but I was always at the foot of the class. I used to feel that the teachers never sympathized with me and that my father thought I was stupid, and at last I almost decided that I must really be a dunce. My mother was always kind, always sympathetic, and she never misunderstood or misjudged me. But I was afraid to tell her all my difficulties at school for fear she too might lose her confidence in me."

With his academic career a fading memory, he largely withdrew from the other children and created a solitary world in the cellar of the family home, where he pursued his fascination with chemistry experiments, batteries, and engines. His mother had moved him there because of the impossible mess and disorder he created in his bedroom. Of this time his father said, "He spent the greater part of his time in the cellar. He did not share to any extent the sports of the neighborhood. He never knew a real boyhood like other boys."

He still had at least one friend in the chore boy his father had been forced to hire to help out on the farm. (Though he was restless and active, he personally abhorred any form of physical labor and would go to great manipulative lengths to avoid it.) On one occasion he persuaded his playmate to drink large quantities of an effervescent, gaseous drink he had concocted. He had reasoned that if the principle of inflation worked for balloons, then a person could be made lighter than air in the same way. Why would anyone then need a balloon in order to be airborne? This ingenious experiment ended when the hapless young hired hand became violently ill.

He would often stay up past midnight after he and another friend built a half-mile telegraph line through the woods between their houses. The project was exceedingly resourceful, if unsightly: stovepipe wire strung along crudely fashioned insulators, which were small glass bottles nailed to trees. But with this primitive device, amazingly, the friends could actually send and receive messages quite efficiently.

Throughout his life, he was to retain his love of pranks and practical jokes such as the "rat paralyzer" he invented by employing battery circuits and two metal plates to electrocute rats, and a similar gadget to shock cockroaches on their ascent up a wall—as well as human onlookers. The schemes were always fantastic and visionary, but the remarkable thing is that they often worked.

His first job at thirteen hawking newspapers and candy on a train ended dismally when he accidentally set fire to a wooden train car with some phosphorus chemicals with which he had been attempting to set up a laboratory on wheels. In the subsequent years of earning his living as a teletype operator, he was fired from one job after another because of his penchant for experimenting with the company equipment and his strong resistance to the office rules and protocol. Over the next decade, he became variously known as a hustler, a drifter, a dreamer, and a ne'er-do-well.

This boy was Thomas Alva Edison—or young Al, as he was known as a child.

The family legend has it that when Hermann Einstein asked a headmaster for advice on what profession his son Albert should follow, the answer was curt: "It doesn't matter; he'll never make a success of anything." It was hardly a secret that Hermann and his wife, Pauline, agonized over the future of their alternately detached, alternately rebellious young son.

What worried them the most, understandably, was the abnormally late age at which Albert learned to speak: when he was around five years old. His childhood difficulties included hesitancies of speech, slowness to respond to questions, a poor memory, a generally slow intellectual development, and an obsession with "droll ideas." To add to his parents' alarm, he seemed withdrawn into himself, immature, shy, and cut off from the world of other children. He was also troubled by dizziness and tired easily.

Not one of his teachers ever recognized a spark of genius or held out bright hopes. In fact, just the opposite, as Einstein described in a letter in 1940: "When I was in the seventh grade at Luitpold Gymnasium (and thus about fifteen) I was summoned by my home-room teacher who expressed the wish that I leave the school. To my remark that I had done nothing amiss he replied only 'your mere presence spoils the respect of the class for me.'"

The military mentality and the dull, mechanized methods of teaching of the day were sources of great stress throughout Albert's school years. "The teachers in the elementary school," he remembered years afterwards, "appeared to me like sergeants and in the Gymnasium (secondary or high school) the teachers were like lieutenants."

After his expulsion from high school, he went on to fail his entrance examinations for the Swiss Federal Polytechnic School, a prestigious university in Zurich where he had planned to study engineering. During a year of private study at the Cantonal School at Aarau that he hoped would prepare him to pass the rigorous screening tests, he wrote his parents that he felt like a dunce having to return to secondary school when he had planned instead to enter a university.

A fellow student at Aarau portrayed him in equivocal terms: "Sure of himself, his gray felt hat pushed back on his thick, black hair, he strode energetically up and down in a rapid, I might almost say, crazy, tempo of a restless spirit which carried a whole world in itself."

Many years later Einstein, now famous and deluged with mail, replied to a student who had complained that she was below average in mathematics and had to work at it harder than her friends, "Do not worry about your difficulties in mathematics; I can assure you that mine are still greater."

And in an interview during his last years in Princeton, he pondered openly, "I sometimes ask myself how did it come that I was the one to develop the theory of relativity. The reason, I think, is that a normal adult never stops to think about the problems of space and time. These are things which he had thought of as a child. But my intellectual development was retarded, as a result of which I began to wonder about space and time only when I had already grown up. Naturally, I could go deeper into the problem than a child with normal abilities."

The Dyslexic Society lists Einstein as one of the famous persons who suffered in childhood from a form of reading disability often equated today with minimal brain dysfunction or learning handicap. Michelangelo,

Hans Christian Andersen, Leonardo da Vinci, and Niels Bohr, the Danish physicist, are other examples of larger-than-life individuals who the Society claims overcame the disability of dyslexia.

Surely the details of their biographies make one wonder if physical and emotional misery must always, to a greater or lesser degree, accompany genius.

In times closer to our own, there is a similar lore surrounding the turbulent early lives and careers of Nelson Rockefeller and General George Patton—among other celebrated persons whom we may or may not particularly admire, according to our personal tastes, values and philosophies.

On a recent Phil Donahue television show, Olympic decathlon athlete and actor Bruce Jenner appeared along with Dr. Harold Levinson, a New York City specialist in dyslexic diagnosis and treatment. Before the vast television audience, Jenner described the trauma of his early school years when he was ostracized and taunted by the other children because of his "difference" and was held back in the first grade for two years by angry teachers.

The greatest fear he has ever felt, Jenner reminisced—more agonizing than the anxiety before an Olympic contest—was being called on to get up to read before the class. And even today, in spite of years of private tutoring, "I don't read as well as I should," and reverberations of this early humiliation course through his body. He tries futilely to hide from the cameramen and script girls his painful inability to read the cue cards held up in front of him. Instead, when he is acting, he has to laboriously memorize every line of dialogue before he arrives at the studio each day.

Meanwhile, on a competing network, singer Phoebe Snow was pouring out to an enthralled talk show host and studio audience the many problems involved in raising her autistic daughter Valerie. She disclosed the sense of utter hopelessness and despair she sometimes feels, which has carried its disruptive effects over into her career.

As illustrious as the roster of persons with probable minimal brain dysfunction is, musing on these anecdotes of long-suffering parents and their errant but brilliant children provides at best a momentary solace. The narratives illuminate but a tantalizing potential, a glimpse of light at the end of a long and far tunnel.

Provided, that is, that the parent of a behavior-skewed child can even make it through to tomorrow or next week, or get through the current school year without falling apart completely. For the sad fact is that in our day-to-day dealings with the hard-to-handle or different-wavelength child, the successes of others, however dramatic and taut with hope, seldom make us feel much better inside for very long.

What will then? Almost every parent who responded to the "For Parents Only" Questionnaire[1] agreed that the true means of salvation for both the different child and his family lies in the earliest possible detection of the soon-to-unfold behavior handicap and the earliest application of the various interventive, preventive, and remedial techniques.

If the professionals will not help us, if they are too immersed in their own biases or personal histories—whichever—to see the proverbial forest for the trees, then we have no choice except to help ourselves.

And in doing so, help each other.

Ordinary People: An Overview of the Research

For several years after my own son was diagnosed as having an attentional disorder, I was struck by the similarities in the early histories and behavior symptoms of slightly neurologically impaired youngsters, regardless of their specific diagnostic label or their environmental circumstances, similarities that parents would recount over and over again. After a while it began to sound as though we all had given birth to the exact same child—with some minor variations in size, skin, and hair color. And indeed, after several experiences of exchanging babysitting duties with these parents, it actually started to seem to me as though the children *were* interchangeable.

From my talks with other parents—really, informal "therapy" sessions among the huddles of them in the corridors of lecture halls and at school meetings and in the hotel bedrooms at large conferences late at night—I devised the items in the parent checklist and some of the items in the questionnaires of Chapter 3 empirically, by a combination

---

[1] This research instrument appears separately in Appendix I. I named it the "For Parents Only" Questionnaire when I discovered the large number of special education teachers, school psychologists, and other interested specialists who attend both the small, regional meetings and large, statewide conferences of the various chapters of the Association for Children and Adults with Learning Disabilities (ACLD). This organization was originally founded by a few desperate but energetic parents as a self-help group and political lobby, but as the need soared has rapidly expanded into a sizable international membership.

of note-taking and memory. The personal interviews and anecdotal material that run through the book are the experiences mainly of friends and eager-to-talk acquaintances who had reared, or were struggling to rear, deviant children.

And by one of those fortuitous quirks of fate, my job at that time as a psychologist in a California state prison offered me the unique opportunity to observe firsthand the connection, which most of the parents lived in dread of, between early behavior problems and violent crime. The stories in Chapters 6 and 8 are compilations of the lives of the numerous incarcerated individuals, including some mothers, I have known. It was therefore not one source, but several sources of material, that comprised the contents of my research. In gathering it, I set out to provide the book that I had needed so badly, but that had not been there, when my own son was young.

The eighty-three participants in the study who completed the "For Parents Only" questionnaire were drawn from a number of sources: the Colorado Association for Children with Learning Disabilities, the California Association for Neurologically Handicapped Children, and two private special education schools. A few additional parent respondents were contacted through a public school special day class in the Van Nuys, California, Unified School District.

The data from all the sources were tallied collectively to yield a composite picture or "personality profile" of the infant and young child most likely to demonstrate later behavioral and adjustment problems. While the mean age for the children in the sample was 12.6 years at the time, the questions were directed primarily at the early ages, years 0 to 3.

Statistically, the ratio of 6:1 in favor of boys over girls agrees with most previous research, which has generally placed this proportion at approximately 6 or 7 to 1. A large majority (nearly three-fifths) of the 111 children included in the study had blue, green, or hazel eyes, but it seems important to note that this finding, which receives some support in the medical literature, may nevertheless be due to sampling or bias error—since most of the parents and children were Caucasian middle-class urban or suburban Americans.

Among the youngsters with right-handed parents and close relatives, there were a fair number of nonfamilial left-handers (slightly over one-sixth of the children), a divergence which has long been recognized as a key "soft" neurological sign. Even more striking was the prevalence of at least one known minimal brain dysfunction or learning disabled adult in the family—often an uncle or grandfather or, in many cases, a parent. That the prototypal bloodline adult turned up more frequently on the father's side of the family provides some limited verification for the unproven but rampant verbal reports that these nervous system anomalies are transmitted through the paternal lineage. (The exact genetic mechanism and pattern of this transference, though, still remains a matter of speculation.)

It was also quite common, in 26 percent of the cases, for a multiple-child family to have produced more than one behaviorally deviant child—some further evidence for a genetic link. On the other hand, birth order, fetal position, average length of gestation, birth weight within normal limits, and obstetrical method of delivery including the use of anesthesia did not appear, at least in this sample, to be significant correlates of the syndrome.

Over and over again, parents used such adjectives to describe their infants as "cranky," "colicky," "irritable," "frantic," "temperamental," "extremely demanding," "whiny," "sleepless," or "supercharged," or said their children had come into the world "fighting mad."

Sometimes the unusually strong reactivity to environmental input and stimulation noted in the first few weeks in 68 percent of the infants was depicted in a graphic way. According to one mother, her child immediately became a "prune face" in the rain while the other babies in carriages and strollers around them slept on unperturbed. And the infants were felt to have unusually large startle reflexes and to "jump out of their skin" in reaction to everyday noises such as a vacuum cleaner, a door slamming, or construction noises in the street outside the window.

This hyped or super response to the environment frequently showed up in sleep difficulties—trouble falling or remaining asleep and/or erratic and confused cycles of waking and sleep (76 percent of the children). A number of children were pictured as having gotten through their infancies only in various states of overtiredness, which were echoed in the exhaustion of their bleary-eyed parents.

The following description is especially vivid: "When Ricky would finally fall asleep, he would somehow manage to look disorderly, thrashed, jammed up in a corner, and a shambles even in sleep. By then he was so worn out he would snore loudly and sometimes stop breathing for alarmingly long periods."

Along with night wakefulness through the first year—"nights pock-marked by screams," according to one father—nursing difficulties and excessive crying were the second and third most frequently reported physical symptoms of early infancy, occurring in 65 percent and 62 percent of the children, respectively.

Over half of the infants seemed to be particularly hungry and hunger-driven children who experienced either poor sucking or swallowing or some other overload of frustration during breast- or bottle-feeding which prevented them from getting enough to eat at any given time. They had to be nursed every hour or two and responded very early, with what one parent termed a "lightning reaction," to small amounts of "filler" foods such as cereal or strained fruit—not usually advised by the pediatrician, but given anyway by desperate, sleep-deprived parents and grandparents after the first few weeks.

Sixty percent of the babies were reported to have had chronic or recurrent digestive system disturbances including constipation, diarrhea, vomiting, gas, or colic, along with "one cold after another" during the first year which in 45 percent of the affected children usually terminated in bronchitis, croup, and/or ear infections.

"For the first two years of Cathy's life," wrote one mother, "she had so many ear infections that the refrigerator was always stocked with those pink bottles of Ampicillan, which is a sweetened, chalky form of children's penicillin. I sometimes think sarcastically that this is how Cathy got so hooked on sweets in the first place."

A number of other investigators have also noted the foreboding but little understood link between infantile ear infections and childhood manifestations of behavior or learning disability. Sometimes a history of "harmless" ear infections—despite their ostensibly rapid healing or clinical disappearance—has been associated with central nervous system "lags" and reading disability. Recurrent ear problems have also been identified as possible allergic reactions and related to motion sickness, vertigo, disorientation, and poor balance at later ages.

An approximately equal number of infants (43 percent) showed an unusual skin sensitivity in the form of tenacious rashes, eczema, and boils, or chronic bouts of impetigo and other pustules which sometimes left scarred bottoms, fingers, or faces.

Behaviorally, a large group of the infants, over two-thirds, were described as having been, from just about the first waking moment, highly demanding, excessively impatient, and easily frustrated babies who seemed to be plunged into a life-or-death urgency over the slightest delay in food or sleep, or over being held or put down.

While a minority group (23 percent of the infants) were characterized as underreactive or "tuned out" to the environment—appearing, on the contrary, to be withdrawn, listless, and apathetic—it sometimes turned out on further probing that this excessive passivity and fearfulness developed only *after* the child had been subjected to some rather harsh disciplinary measures—most often, being ignored and left to "cry it out" for hours on end by a relative, a babysitter, or even a parent.

The most typical "nutshell" personality description of the minimal-brain-dysfunction child in his first few weeks, then, was an infant with an extreme reaction to hunger, tiredness, wetness, cold, and other physical states of disequilibrium, mirrored on the outside by an equivalently profound response to external events or changes in the environment.

In keeping with a sizable body of carefully conducted research, whether an infant was breast- or bottle-fed did not directly emerge as a significant factor in delineating the syndrome. Rather, the important factor seemed to be whether or not an individual infant received an adequate amount of touching and other forms of physical closeness and contact comfort during nursing—an interpersonal situation which, in turn, was partially dependent on the degree to which the infant himself was more or less resistive to feeding, cuddling, and other bonding behaviors.

The group of bottle-fed babies, though, did show a moderate tendency toward more frequent outbreaks of skin irritations, gas, diarrhea, noisy breathing, and ear infections—supporting the notion that these symptoms may well be related to food allergies or intolerances. At least one change in formula due to suspected allergies or food sensitivities (usually to cow's milk) was reported in 36 percent of the bottle-fed infants.

The problem appeared circular, and to have no easy solution, in that the children who were most suspect of being allergy-prone were often those very same infants who violently resisted the frustrations of breast-feeding in the first few postnatal weeks.

Social responsivity in the form of smiling and recognizing familiar adults appeared to occur normally in the babies around six to eight weeks of age. At the same time, a fair number of the infants (24 percent) were reported to have shown an earlier-than-normal separation anxiety and fear of strangers—well before the usual age of six months, and sometimes as early as two months—along with great apparent fear of new places and unfamiliar persons such as babysitters introduced into the early social environment.

Many also appeared unusually ticklish, touchy, or "goosey" babies, as well as perseveratively responsive to bodily stimulation (unable, for example, to "turn off" their reactiveness to pleasurable forms of touch and physical play). Forty-four percent of the parents reported unusual difficulties in diapering and dressing their children, who seemed especially resistant to outside interference with their bodily "structure" and led their parents on a bare-bottomed scramble over the bed. (One couple went back to smoking cigarettes after an abstinence of two years over the daily hassles of dressing their exceptionally squirmy daughter.)

In addition, 22 percent of the infants appeared unusually stiff in bodily stance or postures and more or less refractory to cuddling—or, in a few cases, even "paranoiacally insulated" against the other person—with definite and rigid preferences for certain body positions. Another 12 percent seemed "floppy" rag doll children, with poor muscle tone and insufficient muscular rigidity. Eight percent were claimed to have mostly avoided eye contact from the beginning—as though looking into a parent's eyes were too unbearably overstimulating.

With only very few exceptions, then, a baby destined for behavioral difficulty showed his bodily discomfort—his incompatibility with the normal everyday world, as it were—in one significant physical way or another within the first two months of life, such as through the skin or musculature, or through the digestive tract or the intestinal pathways.

For the majority of cases, it is accurate to say that the child's troubles in adapting to his human environment were instantaneous. (Three of the children were even born with broken arms or legs.) *But only in 5 percent of the cases was any medical problem ever noted in the first year.*

In a personal communication, pediatric consultant and author Dr. Lendon Smith has noted: "The doctor cannot seem to help as he needs to see or feel the disease. There has to be some pus somewhere or a shadow in the X ray." And so for years Smith has been "encouraging the world to do some of their own diagnosing by *reading the body.*"

The first step in solving the "body problems" lies in correctly interpreting and responding to those seemingly mysterious states of sudden purpling or reddening of the infant's face, persistent dry patches or rashes on the cheeks or body, prolonged digestive symptoms, sleeplessness, irritability, and noticeable over- or underreactivity to sensory stimulation.

It may well turn out that the early maladaptation to the physical environment is not lasting and the baby goes on to develop quite normally in spite of the presence of several of these warning symptoms or "cues" in infancy. If so, so much the better. But for the approximately 18 percent of all American parents and children whose futures will not turn out so fortunate, a parent can give her child (and herself) no greater head start and gift of love than this kind of fingertip sensitivity to what his body is saying to her via its unique but universally decodable language—a skill, incidentally, most of us can acquire, or else there would be no reason for this book.

Oftentimes, if we can but read the signs, our vulnerable infants are literally crying out to us.

One summer afternoon a five-year-old sibling nicknamed Poncho burst into the room where her mother was quietly reading. She was screaming: "There's something wrong with Peanut!" As the mother rushed into the children's room, there indeed was one-year-old Peanut kneeling in his crib, forcefully but without apparent pain, banging his head against the wooden slats.

After the age of five or six months, highly dramatic indicators of neurological difficulty such as head-knocking, rocking, and other obsessive, ritualistic behaviors were present in approximately one-fourth of the children. While that is a substantial proportion of the total population, these "dead giveaways" were perhaps not so common as a strict and obsessive diagnostician might wish for.

Far more prevalent was the *subtle pattern* of difficulties in brain-behavior relations described above—early nursing problems along with an apparent inability to tune out the environment showing up especially in a strong resistance to sleep, often to the extent that a parent had to pounce on a baby and almost smother him with the bottle or breast before he would settle down to sleep.

About a third of the babies displayed an earlier-than-usual motor precocity in activities such as holding up the head (35 percent before five months), crawling (32 percent before seven months), standing (38 percent before eight months), or walking (15 percent before eleven months). But for approximately half of the sample children, these early motor milestones fell within the range of the normal. And there was only a slight trend, in 12 percent of the cases, wherein a baby failed to demonstrate creeping, crawling, backward crawling, pulling up to a standing position, or other sensorimotor precursors to ambulation.

Many infants in the more motorically energetic or advanced group appeared unusually accident-prone. Even with vigorous safety measures which included constantly monitoring the environment and removing physical objects in the child's path, it was not uncommon for these baby gangbusters to have had two or three sets of stitches in the emergency room and countless bangs, bruises, scrapes, and cuts before their second birthday.

They were the children who seemed to fall out of cribs, topple backwards out of high chairs, stumble haplessly against table edges, and capsize strollers and shopping carts, almost on a daily basis. Fourteen percent of this same group also showed a propensity for ingesting strange substances such as plaster, paint, cigarette butts, and so on.

With some notable exceptions in which a baby appeared "phobic" or tuned out to the environment (23 percent of the cases), a large majority (approximately three-quarters of the children) shortly became incessant "touchers"—babies who reached for, mouthed, and physically manipulated, dismantled, and often lastingly destroyed, any and all objects within range.

Probably the urge to touch started out normally as the infant's earliest developed modality of sensorimotor learning. But what stands out as odd is that this tactile predisposition did not appear to lessen or to become integrated into other sensory channels of information (such as the visual or auditory pathways) in the normal manner, over the passage of time.

At somewhat later ages, the ingrained drive to always be touching and manipulating objects was carried over in a strong resistance to social control and family routine. Over and over, parents reported an acute response in their babies, a franticness or an "explosiveness," to physical curbing or thwarting of an ongoing pursuit. Frequently the toddler became a tantrum thrower.

No-no's lamented like a broken record and other conventional methods of discipline or restraint seemed to elicit no response in this child as he went on recklessly dashing in the path of swings in the playground and touching stove tops and other forbidden and dangerous objects at home. His stance was noticeably an oppositional one long in advance of the traditional and socially expected "terrible twos."

The children simply did not appear to develop gradual inhibitory controls over their behavior and impulses at the same ages as their normally developing peers and siblings. At such early and relatively uncomplicated developmental stages, it is easier than it will ever be again to separate the "can't" of the child's actions from the "won't"—a distinction which causes a great deal of confusion, misunderstanding, and injustice at later ages. For in these initial phases of a child's physical and perceptual growth, it is clear that he *cannot* control his undesirable or obstreperous behavior, rather than that he *will not*.

It was as though these babies craved the *sensory surety* and the sense of psychological "rightness" that touching provides in order to orient and locate themselves in what could only be their surrounding chaos. Often, too, in addition to the need to sensuously ground themselves by constant touch, the children soon became collectors of junk or odd objects, their pockets and fists bulging with bits of string, old spark plugs, and the like—once again as if their sense of security in the world depended on the sameness of objects within the physical environment.

The difficulty the children have in adapting to a changing world and shifting patterns is nicely illustrated by one two-year-old baby who clung to his heavy winter jacket all summer long. "As we prepared to go out, Ralphy would grab for his 'wooly' and insist on wearing it zipped up to his neck just as he had during the winter months. After a while it became too much of a daily struggle to try to wrest it from him, with him screeching and kicking and resisting, so we ended up going out that way no matter how sweltering the day—with him hugging his plaid wool coat and people on the street in shorts and T-shirts staring at us—and one elderly woman once accusing me of child abuse."

Another mother made the innocent mistake of changing the curtains in her daughter's room overnight. She was rudely awakened the next morning to shrieks of, "Hurry, hurry, Mommie! The world is gone!"

Akin to the strong need to touch, which seemed irrepressible or at least very difficult to suppress in them, many of the children appeared unusually rash and impulsive (64 percent of the sample). And in over half of the cases, the parent felt that her child somehow lacked a natural sense of physical danger or normal foresight in his interactions with the environment—and, in some instances, the basic ability to connect simple cause and effect events.

"No matter how many times Adam saw me go to the refrigerator and take out his bottle, he never seemed to learn that his hunger was about to be satisfied. He would go on screaming like a banshee. The situation never appeared to register and he just did not seem to 'get it.'" This kind of child may need more than one dramatic, experiential lesson in the first two years such as, "If I stick this (hairpin, paper clip, etc.) in the light socket, I will be shocked."

Another key behavioral indicator of possible organic difficulties demonstrated by over 60 percent of the children in the first year or year and a half was an untempered and peak reaction to mild or moderate frustration. Everyday events and disappointments such as having to leave the playground, a broken or misplaced toy, or a balloon bursting—no matter how many times they would happen—immediately turned into full-blown traumas and prolonged howling sessions.

The babies also appeared to "fall apart" suspiciously easily, and with an unnatural devastation, over minor variations in the environment such as a change in the parent's habitual appearance, even from regular eyeglasses to sunglasses, or, in one memorable, histrionic case, a new checker in the supermarket.

Along with their excessive emotionality, the children appeared never satisfied or satiated in any one activity. A parent could push the child on a swing or hold him up in the air endlessly, until her arms felt about to fall off, and he would go on screaming hysterically for more. Nothing ever seemed to go quite right for them—and therefore for their families. Early on, the temperature or bath water was too hot or cold, the park was too stimulating, or the stroller outing too long or too short, and so on.

Later, if the child got a battery-operated toy, the batteries would not fit in the compartment properly or would burn out too quickly, or the train cars would not stay on the track just right. Anything and everything would precipitate an explosion of emotion which could not be easily relieved. And often his great frustration would cause him to smash or break the offending toy or object.

The third most common behavior precursor of future trouble which emerged in the period of middle infancy (approximately eight months to one year), noted in 55 percent of the cases, was that in spite of a good deal of frenzied and random activity, the youngster appeared paradoxically to lack the normal stamina and physical endurance of his age-mates.

In the playground, for instance, he would at first respond vigorously to the surrounding stimulation, with distractible and overwrought behavior (called the "cocktail party syndrome" in adults), but then would tire more easily and quickly than the other toddlers. In spite of his overactivity, this child would stand out as physically weak or fragile, and could seldom sustain an interest in one activity or toy as long as the other children could.

A baby with this rather common pattern of cycles of lethargy or neurasthenia alternating with random excitability seemed to a number of parents to have an "inborn knowledge" or wisdom that he could not keep up with the others, and a violent emotional reaction to his limitation.

There were numerous instances of psychomotor "lapses," reported in 22 percent of the cases, in which in the midst of play or some other activity a child would suddenly stare off into space and seem dazed for a minute or two. Usually it was not possible for a parent to relate the child's breaks in ongoing behavior, speech, or mood to causative changes in his environment.

By their first birthday, most of the children seemed noticeably younger and less mature than their age-mates, and to be fixated on very early sources of gratification such as blankets, thumb-sucking, rocking, or "bye-bye" and "peek-a-boo" games—often along with repetitive, obsessive types of behaviors (endlessly manipulating electrical cords, fitting pieces or old pipe together, and so on). Or a child would still be dismantling everything he could get his hands on, including radios and vacuum cleaners—a pastime which often proved, to the chagrin of his parents, not so much an early sign of genius as a forerunner of later destructiveness and behavior disorganization. (This very early intense interest in manipulating and taking things apart that so many of the children share seems to begin as a way for them to screen out the too-painful stimulation around them and therefore to be a compensatory form of behavior, but if a child's self-esteem holds up in other areas as he grows and if his curiosity is encouraged, it *can* become the source of a later specific talent, in mechanics, electronics, or other technological pursuits.)

A fair number of the children (28 percent) showed a deficient awareness of bodily space or boundaries. Before his childhood was over, such an intrusive baby might well give his mother or babysitter a couple of broken ribs with his incessant pouncing and jumping on her.

Perhaps related to this lack of a normal sense of physical limits were later problems in sequencing ability, which showed up in difficulties in remembering the words of simple songs or nursery rhymes, and still later in remembering the order of the days of the week or months of the year.

Often spatial and temporal confusion or disorientation—difficulties with the concepts of up/down, over/under, inside/outside, top/bottom, etc.—accompanied the sequencing difficulties. As one four-year-old girl explained her predicament: "I don't like to wear my pajamas to bed because it's too hard to put them on again in the morning."

Late in the questionnaire, most parents would single out social relations as the area of greatest vulnerability to damage as well as resistance to change. According to a majority of the respondents, once a child blundered his way into social troubles, this area of functioning continued to be ridden with agonizing, far-reaching, and long-term problems which usually lasted into middle childhood.

But before a susceptible child got this far along, the most outstanding stumbling block in his higher mental and integrative functioning after the age of one—which was reported in 77 percent of the children and appeared much less variable than physical development—was some degree of disturbance in the development of language.

While the average age for the first spoken word for the group of child subjects was thirteen months (which places this milestone in the range of the normal), the mean age for the first two- and three-word sentences was a surprisingly late 2.8 years. The significant clue in early language behavior, then, appeared not so much the initial age at which a child spoke his first words, as the abnormally large gap between one-word and two- or three-word utterances. This phenomenon has been widely reported by parents for many years, but up to now has received almost no recognition in the professional literature.

In addition, about half of the children, once they did begin to speak, were described as having mostly unintelligible speech—and sometimes idiosyncratic enunciation, pronunciation, or inflection amounting to a "word salad" or a gibberish à deux understood only by a child and his parent—for an unusually long period into the second, third, or fourth year.

In contrast, the area of *receptive* speech, which develops prior to *expressive* or spoken language and enables a young child to understand what is said to him and obey a simple command, showed no matching lag or deficit. Even if a child could not yet speak single words at the age of one or one and a half, most had no apparent difficulty in pointing to or signifying a common household object named for them by an adult ("Show me the . . .").

After the age of eighteen months, language was undisputedly the area of greatest concern for the parent and difficulty for the child. And this seemed to hold true regardless of whether or not a parent had happened to notice earlier sensorimotor clues such as a child's failure to establish the notion of permanent objects by approximately five or six months, or to begin searching for lost objects by about eight or nine to eleven months.

The slightly older child typically has difficulty in using his fingers and hands with skill, ease, or steadiness (fine motor incoordination, found in 67 percent of the cases) and/or awkwardness in moving his arms, legs, or body (gross motor incompetence, reported in 45 percent of the children).

At preschool ages, the child will show the former impairment in such activities as building towers of blocks, which he will be unable to do consistently at two or even three years of age; drawing; printing; stringing beads or manipulating other small objects; buttoning his shirt; lacing his shoes; holding and using pencils or crayons; and copying circles, squares, and other simple geometric figures or designs. (He will also often put his shirt and pants on backwards and/or inside out.)

Along with odd objects and collages of junk and miscellanea, large cars, vans, and trucks will tend to be this child's favorite toys. His first reaction to a line of blocks or puzzle pieces laid out invitingly on a nursery school table will likely be to sweep the lot of them violently onto the floor.

Gross motor incoordination will turn up in troubles in pumping a swing, riding a tricycle, balancing, throwing, hopping on one foot, skipping, walking a straight line, or running. A child may even have a visible tremor when asked to hold his arms straight out from his body.

On the basis of their motor difficulties, children with neurological problems are often noted to be unable to play like other children. Their outdoor activities frequently consist of nothing more than motoric fallout—running every which way, pushing, shoving, throwing, dashing, and hitting without purpose. They may literally have to be *taught* to play in one-on-one sessions with an adult.

Sometimes a child will also appear slow to develop cerebral "dominance," and will still use both hands alternately for the same activity after two years (30 percent of the children). Or he may show signs of "cross dominance" or mixed brain laterality—preferring his right (or left) hand to throw a ball, his left (or right) foot to kick, and his left (or right) eye to sight a far object.

Often he will show jerky, unstable eye movements (reported in 38 percent of all cases). Later, when he attempts to read or write, this imbalance will cause blurring and scrambling of letters; changes in word size; difficulties in fixation, tracking, and mental concentration; and reversal and rotational tendencies. And sometimes a child also finds it impossible to close one eye while keeping the other open.

Most school-age youngsters can control their vision (and their nervous system) through their fine motor skills, but not this child. His visual system controls and restricts him so he cannot follow a moving object or scan pages like the others. Despite the new shoes, first-day-of-school clothes, and notebooks and other supplies, he will soon find himself lost in the world of school. Later, the school psychologist will say that the child has poor eye-hand or visual-motor coordination and will probably label him "dyslexic" or learning disabled.

A lesser number of children (18 percent of the sample) showed closure or assimilation difficulties in auditory discrimination—failures to distinguish word endings or to differentiate between similar-sounding words (for example, "bad" and "bed," "pat" and "pet," respectively).

But by whichever perceptual or motor pathway the syndrome manifests itself, the child who is not identified and helped during the early stages is already on his way to almost certain loss of self-regard and, by school entry, personal and social failure.

An interesting incidental piece of information reported in nearly 80 percent of the cases was a swift and intense reaction on the child's part to the first tastes of sweet—usually given in the form of cane sugar or corn syrup added to milk, cereal, or strained vegetables. It even seemed to some parents as if their child became instantly "hooked" and showed a craving for, and a whining after, sugars ever afterwards.

Since this "addictive" behavior occurred at such an early age, an explanation of the sugar "blues" in terms of the biochemical imbalance basic to the child's organic pattern seems the most reasonable—as though he had accidentally stumbled precociously early upon his "drug of choice" that immediately made his body feel better. The psychoanalytical hypothesis that the craving for sweets represents a psychological regressive dynamic in which a child returns to primitive forms of emotional satisfaction via sweets—as in a similar way he comes later to prefer the company of younger children—does not take into account the earliness and instantaneousness of the phenomenon.

Possibly linked to this predisposition for "junk foods," 22 percent of the sample children showed a mild but persistent anemia (deficiency in red blood cells or hemoglobin) after the age of eighteen months. Over 40 percent were described as "picky" eaters with highly developed food preferences and resistance to new foods and/or hard-to-chew foods such as meat or raw vegetables by one year.

Often only sweets would seem to satisfy a young child who held out against other foods for disturbingly long periods—until his distraught and anxious parent "gave in" by providing the ravenously coveted foods, whereupon the child would dig into his meal with gusto so globs of frosted cornflakes or sweetened fruits would wind up on the walls, floor, and ceiling, or on the appliances set innocently across the room.

As time passed, the early disturbance in sleep patterns which is indicative of the underlying problem in "filtering"—or handling a normal amount of stimulation—tended to persist in such nighttime symptoms as fear of the dark, nightmares, bed-wetting, or sleepwalking. One or more of these disturbances were found in an impressive 72 percent of the children.

Even if the child went to bed at midnight, he would be unable to adjust or "normalize" his quota of sleep and would be up and doing as usual by 5 or 6 A.M. He showed no more moderation in the biologically based cycles of waking and sleep than in any other area of functioning.

During the day, he was also likely to react to fears with an exaggerated emotional and physical response which was often carried over into night terrors. For example, one two-year-old baby associated a parent who had mildly corrected him earlier in the day with certain scary animals he had seen on a visit to the zoo. That night he cried pathetically over how the gorilla he could "see" in the shadows at his window had angry brown eyes just like Mommie's.

As a group, the children tended to wean late and only with great difficulty, as though they "sensed" their inordinate need to cling as long as possible to primitive forms of satisfaction and early molds. But the fact that toilet training was accomplished relatively easily in most of the children around the age of two or shortly thereafter is another proof—a revelation, in fact—that the relationship with the parent is really *not* the source of the problem at very young ages.

Like the infant's early, quite ordinary social responsivity, this timely toilet training is telling evidence for the development and proliferation of normal bonding and interactive behaviors *before the larger world—with which this child will surely clash—creeps in and destroys the inner reality of both parent and child.*

In spite of the alarming nature of some of the gross infantile symptoms if taken at face value, a staggering 87 percent of all parents portrayed their children just after the period of infancy (roughly beyond the first year) as happy, cheerful, enthusiastic toddlers. Frequently these children would break into deep belly laughs or robust chuckles which strangers on the street would sometimes stop to notice and remark on.

They seemed lively and alive children with a zest for living and—provided a parent was close by to give them a base of security and confidence—a supernormal alertness, curiosity, and thirst for learning.

Until, that is, they reached the social age.

In the social domain, only a small number—approximately one-eighth of the children—displayed an abnormal aggression and violence in early infancy amounting to an almost "feral" quality. The behaviors in this class included persistent biting and scratching of other people (usually the parent), excessive amounts of hair-pulling, wanton and unprovoked attacks on other children with metal trucks or other toys, and sometimes cruelty toward animals.

"My first impression of him straight off in the delivery room was that he looked like a Viking," one mother wrote. "His thatch of red-blond hair and sea-blue eyes and transparent, parchment skin made me think of that. Unfortunately, right from the start, his obstreperous and abusive behavior proved me right."

Perhaps this unusually unruly minority may have been the more neurologically aberrant or cortically inadequate children or, alternately, those with the highest constitutional levels of aggression-related hormones. A third possibility exists that since the memories of the parents were retrospective, a certain amount of convenient, survivalist forgetting of unpleasant recollections might perhaps have been operative. In this case, the number of organically excitable and combative babies may actually have been *more* than that reported.

For the majority of children, though, the histories showed maladaptive social behavior only *after* a child had been introduced into a peer-group situation such as a play group, nursery school, or day care, where it soon became possible for the child and the adults around him to begin to compare his emerging skills with those of other children.

A number of parents reported that their child would arrive home from nursery school sobbing that he could not run as fast as the other children, or pump a swing or ride a toddlerbike as adroitly as the others. Or the teacher had unwisely and insensitively let him know that compared to the other children, his attempts at drawing were mere "scribble dabbles."

The complaints of early teachers included that the target child could not (or would not) sit still and listen to a story; was unable to use a pencil or crayon, keep within the lines in a coloring book, cut with scissors, or fit together the pieces of a simple puzzle as well as he "should" for his age; and frequently showed erratic behavior and a willful disregard of the school rules such as not changing seats or tables, and a general disorganization (forgetfulness, untidiness, perpetual motion, "wandering" from the task at hand, not putting his toys away after use, and so on).

Seldom were parents informed in concrete and helpful terms that a child's gross or fine motor skills, or his verbal or social development, seemed lagging. Instead, teachers quickly and forever after labeled the child with behavior difference "high-strung," "sullen," "rebellious," "spoiled," "undisciplined at home," or plain "impossible." Through word and attitude, this adult disappointment in his developing skills—and by implication, in him as a person—did not fail to be communicated to, and imprinted in, the child.

In some cases, there were also accusations about a child's swearing and obscene language or physical aggression toward other children, which did not seem to improve with time or discipline but, rather inevitably, grew alarmingly worse as he increased in size and strength. Ultimately, such behavior either got the errant child "eliminated" from the school or, more commonly, caused the embarrassed parent to withdraw him before still more blame and moral indignation could be heaped on her head.

Even such time-honored expedients as isolating the child from the group and having him sit on a brightly painted "disciplinary bench" for most of the day, or in one case hauling him down to the local police station and forcing him to empty his pockets of the miniature cars pilfered from the school toy box, proved of no avail. Time and again, teachers would lament that they were "at the end of their rope," and did not know what more they could do with (or to) this strangely nonconforming child.

Dropping the child off or picking him up at nursery school—which *should* have represented a joyous experience in early learning for their child as it appeared for most other children—shortly became a routine of nightmare for some parents. One mother reported that as she drove up in the afternoons, she could hear the teacher yelling from a block away. From afar, she sensed that this degree of hostility could only be directed at her child. And she was right.

To add to a parent's distress, many of these children displayed an abnormal and prolonged dependency and, in line with their general overemotionality and resistance to change, an extreme reaction to separation. As the mother prepared to leave, they would cry uncontrollably.

One parent described the agony she felt watching the other children disembark from cars and run happily into the neighborhood "Kiddie Kollege" while her own son clung piteously to her leg, his face dirty and disfigured by tears. This reaction did not lessen with time, and as she observed the other children separate with ease each day, she began to wonder on the spot where she had already gone so wrong.

A lesser number of children (just under one-third) did not act out their fear or anger at being abandoned, but instead became phobic and almost catatonically immobile in the school setting so that great effort was required to coax them into an activity for even a short time. But since these subjects did not behave aggressively or disruptively or call attention to themselves, they were not considered problems—only somewhat backward, or slow starters. Their subsequent school histories showed a record of meritorious but false "social promotion," indicating that they were recognized as "good" children for all the wrong reasons.

Interestingly, they were the very same children who at home appeared alternately hyperactive and, for equally long periods, withdrawn or "spaced-out." They tended to suck their thumbs, endlessly twirl a lock of hair, or cling to unwashed "security" blankets or decrepit stuffed animals well into late childhood. The "phobic" children also appeared to come from homes in which the parents were more strict and unbending disciplinarians than those of many of the other children in the sample, whose early environment provided somewhat more room for "acting-out," rather than "acting-in," types of responses to stress and frustration.

Barring some fortunate circumstance such as a knowledgeable and sympathetic teacher or child care worker, which seemed rare, as the weeks and months of preschool progressed, the damage to a child in constant criticisms and put-downs gradually took its toll. By the time he had "graduated" into kindergarten, he not only had learned that he was "different"—meaning inferior to and less desirable than his peers—but despite his poor skills he had usually also been able to infer that fundamental equation in our blithely wholesale democracy: since he is different, he is automatically, by definition, bad or "all wrong."

Those of us who do not share the problem of abnormal body chemistry can only begin to imagine the shattering effect on a child's fragile, embryonic self-esteem when he recognizes that he cannot do what others around him seem to do with ease. For him, the classroom is a jungle of shapes, edges, sounds, colors, symbols, and spatial boundaries which have no integrated meaning—indeed, perhaps even no *match* in the reversed or rotated engrams or impressions on his cerebral cortex.

Yet for reasons which do not make sense to him, he finds himself trapped in a carnival house of mirrors with no escape. And as surely as a small, quivering animal cornered by a large, fang-toothed predator, he is about to meet his social fate.

Here in the "magic castles," "sugar plum lands," and "great rock candy mountains" across the nation, those seemingly happy places of childhood with their regulation jungle gyms and sandboxes, the stage is being quietly and treacherously set for later trouble. For even if a susceptible child undergoes the same experiences as his nondisabled age-mates, you can be sure that he will not *perceive* or *process* these experiences in the normal way. For example, he may not be learning the joys of sharing so much as the message, "The teacher and the other children are all against me."

He has no outside resources as do most adults to buttress him when he feels violated. He cannot call up a friend to console him at the end of a crazy, chaotic day or mix himself a soporific cocktail. He cannot even at his rudimentary stage of cognitive and verbal development put his anxiety into words which might soothe his weakened ego. The anxiety is locked inside his small body, which shortly begins to struggle—thrash about and strike out randomly—in its aborted "fight-flight" urge.

The different child is attacked very early on at least three separate fronts. To add to his own growing awareness of his "inadequacy," there are his teacher's anger and disapproval of him, and the disparaging taunts of his peers, who, in good time, begin to sense his oddness and join in the conspiracy against him relentlessly as though pursuing a wounded animal. In "Wonderland," he is stigmatized with labels amounting to cruel name-calling which he will often wear for a lifetime.

Even if his parents remain affectionate, loyal, steadfast, and sympathetic at home, the day will come inexorably when their love will not suffice to override his growing awareness of his unfitness for survival in the world as it is and he is. And once a young child no longer trusts in his future, the world will never again appear the same to him.

In some cases, the degree of a child's school trauma seemed, a bit ironically, to be related to the amount of early protection and acceptance he had enjoyed at home. About the worst prognosis for social adjustment derived from the combination of a highly nurturant single-child home with a very early or premature and hasty introduction into an established social group (before the age of $3\frac{1}{2}$). Conversely, regardless of early background, whether heavily protective or more perfunctory, a child appeared to have a greater chance of social success if he had grown up in a home with other children.

A Catch-22 situation existed, then, wherein a firstborn or only child of sensitive and caring parents who had experienced few babysitters and limited contact outside his family appeared at high risk for social disaster. Such a child seemed the least prepared of all for the stark, cold realities of the world beyond his immediate family. If this child did not vanish into his school surroundings altogether, he was likely to draw on the very strength of character his early environment had given him to become the toughest and most die-hard resister of social rules and school tyranny.

One mother wrote feelingly of the almost tangible break in her son's development at the age of five, "In this connection, I have a dim memory which is fading around the edges like an old snapshot, of a happy-go-lucky little preschool boy with a tumble of unruly curls who had a zest for whatever was around the next bend in life, and used to chortle a lot. I have not heard Craig laugh—really spontaneously, joyfully laugh—in four long years. The teachers and the principal were implying that it was *me* who was damaging my child, and I would have given anything or done anything—I still would—to bring back that laughter if I could."

A lawyer father who was suing his school district for supplementary educational services they were unwilling to provide described his similar experience in a slightly different way: "There have been many innuendos along the way that I somehow feel it's me, not my child, who is 'special'—i.e., superior to the public school system—and enjoy being so. Nothing could be further from the truth. Why else would I give anything on earth just to hear my daughter's voice outside the window, among the voices of the other children at play? As it was, I was standing by watching everything that I had ever wished for my child go slowly up into smoke."

On closer scrutiny, it almost always turned out that it was the abruptness of the separation and placement outside the home more than anything else—and the lack of a period of preparation for this profound transition—that precipitated the school refusal or "phobia," and the associated behavior symptoms. The techniques in later chapters, which take this child's special vulnerability into account, are aimed at preventing these very failures in his social and school life.

Almost inevitably, atypical children grow up loners, losers and lonely. For even if a child starts out on the right foot by enjoying the company of other children, as many do, his peers soon come to symbolize his rejection in an especially vivid and painful way, and he will begin to withdraw or otherwise turn against them. If he does attempt to find friends, he will tend imprudently to gravitate toward other disruptive, usually younger, children as though by a secret radar. It might be he feels more secure and on safer ground—out of harm's way for the moment—if he acts like a small child. After all, no one will expect very much of him then.

To add to his difficulties, he will often show parallel play, rather than more socially advanced, interactive types of play, well beyond the age of 3—a situation which may cause him to be misjudged and written off in his teacher's mind as "stupid" or "dull" while she goes on hurtfully showering praise and positive attention on her more conforming—and hence more personally rewarding—charges.

Besides the obvious conclusions to be drawn that behaviorally un-usual children do not profit from repeated experience or consequences, even severe ones, in the normal manner and that their social-emotional development is considerably slower than the average, this investigation of early social behavior should teach us another key lesson by deduction.

Though we may be understandably reluctant to accept this warning, and may even decide to go against it out of necessity or choice, we should never lose sight of the basic reality: *Children with behavior difference are in fact often simply not ready for the next stage in development at the expected or statistical age.*

If we accept this wisdom, which has implications for virtually every facet of development, then it should come as no surprise when—unlike their siblings, their cousins, or the neighbor's children across the street—these overlively and distractible children are unprepared for nursery school at the average age of $2\frac{1}{2}$ or 3, or even 4.

Perhaps the outstanding general discovery to emerge from the reports of parental experience is that in spite of a rankling sense of their child's divergence from the normal most parents have from early on, actual confirmation of the syndrome is usually a gradual unfolding—a slow sinking-in which calls to mind novelist Mary McCarthy's pithy insight that "a truth is something that everyone can be shown to have known, as people say, all along."

The steps in this corroborative process bear a resemblance to the stages of dying identified by Elisabeth Kubler-Ross in her early writing. She described in compassionate terms how a person moves from initial shock and denial, through a period of grieving mixed with a good deal of resistance and anger at the fates, to eventual acceptance.

An interesting departure from this collective experience in the case of parents of deviant children is the great sense of relief and unburdening most say they feel when the basic biological, as opposed to environmental, origin of the difficulty is finally recognized. And they feel this way even though organic dysfunction is widely believed to be less treatable than emotional disturbance.

Since no statistical study or list of behaviors can ever substitute for the separate human dramas *behind* the statistics, we turn now to some individual accounts of the process of awakening to the different child's need. We live in an age when most of us are denied the long-headed wisdom, strength, and shelter of Grandmother or Aunt Sarah to support us in our need and help us make sense of what we must endure. United, the members of the extended family were able to absorb any loss or trauma, however cataclysmic, within their fold.

These stories of our contemporaries perhaps come closer than anything else to providing a measure of the personal assistance, guidance, and support lacking in our modern-day isolation—which for many parents of nonconforming children is tantamount to being adrift in a private hell.

Without this support, without this most intimate of all sharing as a foundation, it is all too easy for us to become lost—as parents and as human beings. Lost as our desperate children.

2

The Parental Experience: Three Letters

Tucked in among the completed questionnaires were a number of letters expressing an unexpected gratitude at having the opportunity to communicate fears, anxieties, and other feelings that had sometimes remained secret for years. One parent sent a box of tapes into which she had poured the otherwise silent suffering of over fourteen years.

Several of these letters are so remarkable and articulate in their depiction of the slow and gradual discovery of a child's behavior handicap that I know of no better way to illuminate this process than to quote from these personalized messages.

The first letter is from Mary, who lives in half of one of those old sprawling brick duplexes which are a staple of midwestern cities. Her house, nestled under a fan of elm trees, faces a park of small lakes in downtown Denver.

"I named him Brian after my brother who was killed in Viet Nam a few months before he was born, but from the beginning he was B. J. Right after he was born, the nurse put him in the incubator for a little while—he wasn't premature and weighed a few ounces over eight pounds, but it was the standard procedure at that hospital. Twice, he kicked off the blanket and burst the tape on his diaper because he was thrashing and struggling so much. The nurse commented sternly that she had never before seen anything like it. After the second diaper she took him out before he was supposed to come out.

"So right away, before he was even five minutes old, people were making concessions and changing their normal routines to accommodate him. He didn't fit into the hospital structure, which I sometimes think of as his first 'school,' and he hasn't fit into any other to this day.

"From the beginning, there in rooming-in, I would say that he was erratic and unpredictable. Usually he was up every hour screaming the loudest of all the babies, but on the third day he slept mysteriously for a stretch of eleven straight hours before the nurse finally got frightened and woke him up.

"I used to look around at the other babies all breast-feeding so docilely and feel an embarrassment because putting B. J. to my breast was a horrible struggle right from the start. He'd fuss and scream and wouldn't nurse, but would wait for the night nurse to come round with the formula she fed each baby around midnight. He'd gobble that down so voraciously that I knew it wasn't that he had poor sucking but he was actually, by some rudimentary smarts, holding out for the easier nipple.

"All those books I'd read, mostly by male doctors, singing the praises of breast-feeding came flooding back to haunt me. I started to feel inadequate—and like there was already some deep disturbance in our relationship—before we ever left the hospital. But back then I was convinced something was wrong with me. I hadn't wanted my baby badly enough, or I secretly wanted to lose weight and not stick to those long lists of foods you're supposed to eat when you're nursing. Just some subconscious, negative emotions operating in me that I had no control over but my wise baby sensed.

"B. J. was examined by the staff pediatricians and obstetrical residents any number of times while we were in the hospital, which was a big teaching hospital, and pronounced normal and healthy by all. One doctor even mentioned his exceptionally good color. But when we got home the struggle over breast-feeding continued with B. J. frantically refusing and resisting, and me feeling more and more like a failure. And worse, trying to hide my failure from my relatives and friends, even from my husband, and having to live with this agonizing knowledge that somehow I had managed to ruin my baby's life before he was even a week old.

"Then suddenly, during the second week at home with him, this feeling began to spill over into everything else. The lights started looking eerie and sort of like elongated flashes, the furniture appeared shadowy and alien, and I was depressed because the baby things I had managed to get by scrimping and saving—the white wicker bassinet and the plastic vaporizer I got on S & H trading stamps—began to look cheap. I was morose over the shopping bags of hand-me-downs a neighbor had given me—even though the clothes, which had belonged to her son, were very expensive, and some of them had never been worn.

"And one evening when I spotted a cockroach in the bathtub I felt that this prehistoric bronze crawler was a sign that all the preparations I had made to welcome B. J. home had just not been good enough.

"By the time he was ten days old, I was desperate going through the thankless struggle of trying to get him to nurse many times each day and then, after Paul left for work or when he fell asleep at night, sneaking out the commercial formula furtive as a criminal and feeding B. J. a fast six or seven ounces. He would swallow it down like a starving animal, his sly, glassy eyes seeming to reproach me all the while. Afterwards, when he'd sleep, were the only peaceful moments I knew, but even those times were spoiled by guilt.

"One bad morning I tried calling the local chapter of the La Leche League. The woman who answered seemed cold and unsympathetic, like she too was blaming me for what had gone wrong. She stated flatly that the only thing I could possibly do now to salvage the situation was not feed B. J. for a few days. She used words like 'botched' and 'damage.'

"That morning, I got through four or five hours with B. J. screeching at the top of his lungs the whole time before I thought suddenly, 'Oh hell, nothing is worth this.' I went out and bought a case of infant formula with iron.

"After that, with B. J. guzzling those little bottles all day, we got along better and things settled down into a routine. I began taking him out in the stroller every day while I shopped for groceries or went to the laundromat.

"I'll never forget one day when we were in the drugstore. The saleswoman, who had become sort of a friend during my pregnancy, peered down over the countertop at B. J. sleeping like an angel in his folding stroller and commented on how attractive he was with his fair, transparent skin and long eyelashes. As he opened his eyes then and shifted them quickly from side to side, she remarked on how bright and alert he seemed.

"I'll never know what made me say it, but it leapt out of some deep knowledge in me—an impression I couldn't trust at the time, and in fact it took me a full seven or eight years to really learn to trust my own instincts. I just started to shake my head. I told her that in spite of appearances to the contrary, I *knew* there was something wrong with this baby. Only I didn't know what it was then, so I told her I felt he might be mildly retarded.

"She looked at me with horror, then quickly made the sign of a cross over the carriage. She told me I should never say that—or even think that—again. After that, for a long time, I didn't. I never let on to anyone, not even Paul, my anxiety that something elusive but all too real was wrong with B. J.

"As I think it must be for every parent of a subtly handicapped child, there were enough good moments early on—slices of eternity, I call them—to keep the hope going that perhaps he was normal after all. Like one was the memory of his pale, peaceful face with the sun falling on it as we piled into the taxi the day we came home from the hospital.

"Plus he was such a gorgeous baby with huge blue eyes and one of those big, fuzzy, well-shaped, mostly bald heads. People would come up to me in the streets to compliment me. One elderly lady who had spotted B. J. from afar rushed up and said, 'My dear, if you can have such beautiful babies, you are a person who should have six children.' And a black woman strolled by while we were sitting in the park and exclaimed that B. J. was beautiful as a Siamese cat. They were moments of motherly pride that kept me going in spite of the fears about his 'difference' gnawing at me inside.

"So when things were going well, I began to think maybe those mother instincts were just smokescreens for my own feelings of inadequacy or not wanting him enough. I even thought maybe the breast-feeding had been his way of getting back at me for the resentment I was harboring about the hard physical work I hadn't anticipated in taking care of a baby!

"I can smile about it now, but some of the books by those doctors actually teach you to think that way—that your infant has all these pure feelings and insights, and with no overlay of negativism, he is really your superior in simple, unspoiled emotion. Even if you can manage to hide you neurosis from other adults, he can zero in on it like a laser beam. That sort of thing.

"As I said, after the struggle over feeding, things settled down and we got through the next few months pretty smoothly. The woman at the drugstore in fact appeared right—B. J. seemed an unusually alert and intelligent baby. He would devour the surrounding sights of the city on our walks, and from the beginning was eager to touch and mouth everything in sight.

"Though he was my first baby, I had plenty of opportunity to compare his growth and the new things he did each week with the other babies I saw just about daily in the park. A group of us with infants around the same age would gather each afternoon on a bench across from the lake. B. J. was much earlier than the other babies in a lot of motor things like reaching for objects, holding up his head before he was four months, and starting to crawl backwards by five months.

"But before he could even hold up his head, something happened one day to confirm my worst fears. I had propped him up on my bed with his head resting against the headboard so he could look around while I was dressing. He couldn't hold up his head, but was squirming around and fidgeting and then there was a sound of soft thuds. B. J. was bouncing his head, rhythmically and systematically, against the planking.

"The alarming thought shot through my mind that this must be some kind of self-stimulation. I didn't know quite what that meant but froze there a moment while the idea sank in. The next minute I rallied and started to blame myself again, this time for not having provided him with enough stimulation.

"Maybe the walls in the bedroom were too bare of pictures, maybe I should get a more interesting mobile for his crib, maybe I was just too boring a person so we were a hopeless mismatch. I snatched B. J. up and held him against me. At that moment his usually soft and moldy body seemed rigid and stiff as a board. Those early fears I had almost forgotten in the last two peaceful months came rushing back.

"In those days we couldn't afford a private pediatrician so I was taking B. J. to the well-baby clinic at the hospital where he was born. On our next appointment, I told the Korean resident who examined him about his head-banging a few weeks before. He just shrugged and dismissed it as not worth his time or interest. He said it wasn't important because a lot of babies did this.

"Instead, he seemed more concerned with advising me that my baby would shortly be moving around on his own and getting into things, and when he started to touch things like light sockets, I should slap his hand. Then with an ingratiating Cheshire cat grin, he left the examining room. Once again, I was alone with the doubts and worries that wouldn't go away, that surrounded me like shadows.

"About this time, when B. J. was around three and a half months old, I noticed he had these extreme responses to noise and movement which didn't diminish with time or familiarity. When I'd try to use the blender in the next room, he would almost literally jump out of his skin. And when he was only a *little* hungry or a *little* tired, he wasn't just cranky or fussy but he'd go out of control with yelling and kicking and flailing his arms. Nothing would help except to drop whatever I was doing and run to satisfy his demand. I guess you could say B. J. conditioned me early because I was truly afraid of his excessive reactions which soon went into head-knocking whenever he was the least bit frustrated.

"One night we had a dinner guest, a friend who had been living in Morocco for the last year. She was our first evening guest since B. J. had been born, and his reaction to another person in the apartment after dark seemed odd.

"No matter what I did, I couldn't settle him down. For over an hour we took turns pushing him in the baby swing nailed up over the doorway in the living room. Usually this gentle back and forth motion made him drop off to sleep right away, but that night it only seemed to increase his fitfulness and trap him in his bodily agitation. It was as though his body had become a motor that couldn't be switched off.

"Carol and I had wanted to spend the evening talking, and by midnight she was really getting annoyed with the situation. I remember she groaned, 'Can't you do *something* to push his sleep button?' B. J. had been up for ten hours straight and was still going strong.

"By five months, he was either climbing or falling out of his crib regularly. A lot of mornings when I would first enter his room, I'd find him fast asleep on the floor. Shortly, I'd find him in other rooms as well (we always left his door open). Once it took me a good ten minutes, with panic mounting all the while, to finally locate him wedged into a narrow space between the bed and the bureau in my room. I hadn't even known that he had wandered in.

"I took him to the hospital often because he was forever falling against a table edge or swallowing coins and wooden kitchen matches. Since he was usually a mass of bruises and cuts and scrapes, I began to feel uncomfortable telling my latest misadventure to the doctors in the emergency room. Though nothing was ever mentioned, I felt they suspected me secretly of child abuse.

"When B. J. was barely eight months old, I was still asleep one morning when he suddenly appeared at my bed. He was holding onto the nightstand and staring at me eye level and distinctly saying 'mu-mu' (mama). He said it two or three more times that day, but after that, except for saying 'flure' (flower) at around a year, he didn't talk again for almost three years.

"Rather, he had become 'a man of action' who climbed out of the infants' seats in shopping carts and reached over and knocked down whole shelves of displays with one swoop of his hand. He would run madly up and down the darkened aisles of the theater at the library where they showed children's cartoons on Thursday afternoons. He became an indefatigable cat and pigeon chaser. When he did finally start to talk, his speech was soft and garbled and indistinct for the next two years.

"I hate to say it because I don't like the image, but B. J. fit the description of those chimpanzees that are reared in families along with children. They start out precocious and outstrip the children in early motor activities like walking and climbing stairs, but then quickly fall behind in more human behaviors like language and reasoning.

"The winter B. J. was two, Paul got laid off from his construction job and we were forced to go on public assistance for five months. B. J., who was by now a wild and willfull toddler, made the experience even worse by dashing frenziedly around the waiting room in the social services office. If I even turned my back on him for five seconds, I'd have to run after him and retrieve him from one of the private offices.

"By this time, I had discovered on my own a number of ways to handle his obstreperousness. I would only take him to stores or the bank during the slow times of day, and I purposely made the shortest possible visits to relatives or friends. But with the public welfare system, long waits and long lines were unavoidable. It was excruciating with all the clerks and the other recipients giving me dirty looks.

"Although public assistance was for the most part a grueling experience, something happened there in the office one day that was the start (or the first articulation, really) of a contradiction that was to haunt me for years, and still does.

"The moment is imprinted in my brain. I was carrying B. J. off on my hip from a side office he had just streaked into when I passed an intelligent-looking, bespectacled male official on my way back to the waiting room. Because he was staring hard at us, I smiled my apologetic smile and offered my usual lame excuse, 'I don't know what's wrong with him today.' Looking directly at me, this man said, 'There's nothing wrong with him, lady. It's you and me.'

"Saying that, he confirmed what was maybe the most painful reality of all. For side by side with the knowledge of B. J.'s 'difference'—which is to say his handicap because they are the same thing in our society— there was also a realization from deep within me that a lot of B. J.'s 'mis-behavior' like the bodily resistance, the struggling to be free of restraint or tight clothing, and even his behavior in our nursing disaster wasn't pathological in the least, although it would soon be diagnosed as such.

"Even though B. J. carried things to an extreme, a secret part of me saw his obstinate, rebellious actions as a strong and healthy fighting for himself against a world that did its best to change him, to strenuously mold him into 'same' rather than 'different,' simply because there is just no room and no allowance in the world as it is for difference.

"I'm certain he has long since forgotten us, but I'm as sure I will never forget that county worker—his kind face, and the flood of relief and recognition I felt when he said that.

"To this day, that contradiction is locked inside me—the dread on the one hand that B. J. is hopelessly maladjusted to life, and the belief on the other side that he is unusually clever in sheer survival because he has *had* to be.

"Just last week there was an instance of this. We had gone on an outing to a lake in the mountains with a waterslide. At first it was a catastrophe because the first thing B. J. saw, and headed straight for, was this long snaky rope at the top of the slides from which adults were swinging down into the middle of the lake.

"The next thing I knew, B. J. had scrambled to the top of the hill and was suspended over the lake with his little body thrashing in the air like a miniature Tarzan. He let go and dropped down right beside a sign stuck up in the water—'Danger: Deep Water'—but of course B. J. at ten still doesn't read. The teenage lifeguard had to jump in and pull him out and then sit with him till he caught his breath.

"After he recovered in a few minutes, he was back climbing to the top of the slide again. Streams of children with plastic Donald Duck see-through rafts were filing up the paths on each side, but B. J. was the only kid walking in his lone wolf style straight up the middle between two of the slides.

"I knew he would have a reason when I asked him about it on the way home. It turned out that he had not one but two reasons and although they were unusual, they were not lacking in intelligence. He said, because it was the shortest path to go up the middle rather than along the sides, and because it was less rocky and didn't hurt his feet.

"But you asked about early signs of behavior handicap, in the first year or two. In retrospect, there were many others: B. J.'s forehead was always bruised from banging his head on the ground over the merest mishap; he would greet playmates by whacking them over the head with the nearest object; he continued to eat sand and cigarette filters long after the other babies in the park had stopped; and in the midst of his manic sandbox activity, he would suddenly have these strange lapses where for a minute or two he would stare off into space and seem lost. He also never had a proper sense of physical danger or really any 'commonsense.' I sometimes think B. J. was the exception to those infants and baby animals in the studies of 'visual cliffs' who all have an inborn sense of danger which stops them from crawling over the edge.

"All this time, the only thing the doctors at the baby clinic ever wrote down in his record as possibly abnormal was a notation of 'delayed speech' when he was three and a half.

"This year B. J. and I celebrated our birthdays together, last month in May. I'm thirty-two now and he has just turned ten.

"B. J. at ten is still a bundle of problems. Because of his unacceptable behavior he has had to be changed from school to school. (At one private school he lit two fires.) I still can't let him loose in the neighborhood even to ride his bicycle because although he is intelligent (in spite of his learning difficulties, his IQ tests as superior), he feels so awful about himself that he constantly taunts and teases and puts the other children down. Especially older boys because he just can't stand their superior skills or domination. Then they gang up on him and retaliate with their fists for his mouthiness. The usual advice of talking to him about alternate behaviors has always been all but useless.

"He can't even go alone to the pet shop on the corner where he runs into other kids in an unsupervised situation. Since they all dislike him, and for good reasons, there's always a clash and I get a call from the store owner to come and get him out of there.

"He is highly reactive to sweets and junk food, which he will nearly kill for, and still goes berserk when the least bit hungry or tired. B. J. is always the skinny, messy kid with the shredded pantslegs and the cardboard cartons and the tin cans tied to the back of his bike. Right now he is about to begin a summer program at a new school, and has gone back into some of his old symptoms of school fear like sleepwalking and nightmares.

"Because he has spent so much time alone, he has developed talents in a number of non-academic areas which have become like compensatory pockets of richness in his loneliness. Like he excels in model car building and carpentry. He builds birdhouses and fish tank stands, which he then paints, and constructs whole cities out of toothpicks.

"Even with these interests, B. J. still spends long stretches dreaming over Radio Shack catalogs or old issues of *Boy's Life*. His biggest dream is to belong to a club. He draws plan after plan for building clubhouses in trees and makes up long lists of imaginary members. So this tells me that the feeling of loss, the world of friends and fun which is closed to him, is always very much with him.

"Yet, after ten torturous years, I can see some of the hyperactivity, impulsivity and belligerence slowly beginning to fade. We still have stormy days when B. J. falls apart over and over again and nothing will work for him, but starting to notice signs of improvement and maturity at long last feels like a ray of light at the end of a dark tunnel. [The message of hope that Mary is sending can actually be expanded. Many people who were troublemakers, fighters, and "impossible" as young children seem to settle down or "burn out" and discontinue their patterns of aggressive and dissocial behavior as they mature physically and neurologically. Fifteen or sixteen is the most common age for these welcome changes to occur—leading some professionals to link them with internal hormonal changes—but, as we see in Mary's situation, relief may come even sooner.]

"Recently, he has become curious about girls, and interested in cars and motorcycles. These are about the first normal interests he has had at the right age, and in these things he is even a little ahead of his peer group. I can trust him around matches now and to stay alone for a couple of hours during the day. I thought that day would never arrive, but it has, and it signifies that in all likelihood, other days and other milestones will come, too.

"He plays mostly with a couple of four-year-olds on the next block. With them he can be a hero, and their parents, who are related, love him dearly and invite him on overnight campouts in their backyard. They are about the first people who have genuinely liked him and not felt he was just loud, untidy and obnoxious, and they go out of their way to include him. Needless to say, I'm enormously grateful. About my worst fear now is that one of them will move away.

"It has come about recently, through these same neighbors, that B. J. has joined a church and is excited about spending a week this summer at a bible camp on an Indian reservation. Joining the church was his own decision, and because it goes against my own agnostic beliefs, and

Paul's, I consider it long overdue vindication for the many times over the years when professionals, who don't have one of these oddball kids themselves, have called me 'overprotective.'

"It is living proof that all along I could have let go of B. J. if not for the physical danger he gets into, and would have had I not *had* to protect him so much up to now. Even a mother bear senses when she has an errant cub and devotes more attention to it and keeps it closer to her than the rest. Though I won't be there with B. J. in church and he knows this, I am able to wish him well in his new life.

"Since this is a decision with many repercussions, and B. J. has felt free to make it at the tender age of ten, I wonder further what this would tell the doctors about their second major error, which was blaming me all the time for the way he is. (Their first mistake, of course, was in not diagnosing him as neurologically immature soon enough, but letting things slide until they were almost beyond redemption.) Or would they just now say that I was being perfunctory or indifferent?

"B. J. has even asked for a suit and tie (which he calls a 'tuxedo') to wear to church. One way or another, though money is really tight right now, I'm determined to buy them for him.

"Not to belabor the point or beat it into the ground, but this new development is also evidence for something else I've felt all along in my heart, which goes back to the contradiction and was the reason for moving from place to place and searching for the 'right' school like a cancer patient looking for a Laetrile clinic.

"Surrounded in the Sunday school by well-supervised groups of children who he knows will not attack him first (at least not in those circumstances) and with whom he doesn't have to defend against his 'backwardness,' B. J. feels safe, comfortable and at home. Poignantly, for the first time, like a 'nice kid' himself.

"I'm looking forward to returning to work shortly, in an office to start with but then getting into freelance photography, which is my consuming interest. I'm really savoring the expectation of going out into the world again, as a person on my own, not just functioning in the restricted role of mother as I've had to for the last ten years.

"Because of B. J.'s problem and the expense of private education, plus the special high-protein diet, we decided early not to have any other children. I've gotten over a lot of the feeling of inadequacy because by now I know for a fact what I only sensed early on—that the difficulties between B. J. and me, and between B. J. and everyone else, come from his peculiar body chemistry, something he was born with, and not from any lack of love or nurturance or failure to want him on my part.

"In closing, I guess about the best advice I can give any parent of a similar child is what I needed to know years ago but didn't. In retrospect, it's extremely simple. Stick to your guns, insist on the validity of your own instinct, insist on getting the earliest possible help no matter what anybody tries to tell you.

"Over the years, I've been laughed at, ignored, ridiculed, maligned, accused of being a doormat and of being a rejecting and abusive monster behind closed doors. I've been called negligent and overcontrolling in the same breath, and labeled symbiotic, manic-depressive and schizophrenogenic. B. J. has been diagnosed a lot, too, and some of those labels are blatantly contradictory. It's been really hard to take, not so much the handicap, as what everyone else is throwing at you out of their own bias or their personal trauma, or a mixture of both.

"And when I say some of it is at last receding and B. J.'s behavior is becoming more moderate and under control, I don't know for sure but I think this is probably not a unique happening. So if their experience is anything like mine, above all else I would want the parents of other B. J.'s to hold on through the hard years as best they can, with everything in them if need be.

"Because I'm convinced that there is an element of mercy somewhere in the universe, operating like a safety-valve, which makes the pain at last finite."

Virginia is a 55-year-old parent of an adopted perceptually handicapped son. The family's sprawling canyon house, which has been featured in the *Home* magazine section of the *Los Angeles Sunday Times*, sits on a wooded acre in the exclusive Mount Helix neighborhood east of San Diego. A brook trickles audibly in between the steel caissons which buttress the foundation, and families of raccoons troop to the back door at night to feed at an outdoor trough.

But even having had ample money for the finest medical care and private schools, and having known about Ted's problem from the beginning, Virginia still felt the same need as other, less financially well-off parents to write at length of her experience.

"To tell the truth, until I embarked on this project for your study, I had blocked out a lot of what happened in those early years. At sixteen,

Ted has outgrown so many of those old painful symptoms that I thought well, the sooner forgotten, the better for all of us.

"In fact, it was amazing to me just a short time ago when we were involved with someone with speech problems. I learned that Ted had no recall of the fact that he was unable to talk even at age three, that he required a speech therapist for almost two and a half years, and as he began to put two and three words together, he went into secondary stuttering.

"We thought it would most likely be a problem for the remainder of his life, but as it turned out it wasn't, and Ted has no recall that he was ever a stutterer. And so I've recently gone into some of his old papers that I kept in the event that they should be necessary for his future. I'm going to bring out some of them now so maybe I can remind myself of what the problems were back then.

"Now the reason why we were made so very much aware of any of this was that Ted is an adopted child. There was a question in the mind of the doctor who handled the delivery, and later with the adoption bureau, as to whether we should really make this commitment.

"The questions seemed minimal enough at birth. The doctor was a little concerned about the size of Ted's head, which was slightly larger than normal, and the fact that his ears seemed to be a bit lower than normal.

"There were certain physical signs that made him question what the problem was, and so that entire first night he waited for Ted's cry. He said he wanted to hear the baby's cry for himself. The next day he indicated to us that it might be absolutely nothing, but we have no way of telling at birth. We can't predict to you what the future of this child will be, only there are certain things that we would like you to watch for.

"Ted was born up north in Oregon, and we brought him down three days later. He was in an incubator for a couple of days because, among other things, his natural mother was Rh-negative. I've since heard that she has lost every subsequent child which makes me think the only reason Ted survived was he was her firstborn. He was born cesarian section which may or may not have been part of the cause for his problem. They don't know. Nobody knows. The delivery seemed absolutely normal in every respect, but maybe there wasn't enough oxygen. Or she may have attempted to take drugs or abort—we just don't have any history.

"But we were less preoccupied as to the why. It didn't seem to matter very much anyway. It still doesn't matter what the reasons were, but the doctor did send a letter down to the pediatrician that I had prepared to take Ted to asking him to watch for certain symptoms since there were questions in his mind. Let me see if I can find that letter somewhere, or some other reference to it.

"Here it says that Ted's mother, who was sixteen years old, had mild anemia when he was still in utero. There's some indication that the maternal grandmother had an organic problem and a paternal uncle was possibly mentally retarded, but no real family medical history.

"The worst problem in the early days was that Ted was unable to eat except for one teaspoon of cereal or one ounce of milk at a time. It was all the food he could seem to absorb at one sitting, and so for the first year he had to be bottle-fed every hour. After eight months of insomnia and exhaustion, I pleaded with the pediatrician to let me increase his Pablum.

"I remember he told me, 'Mother, don't think of yourself. Think of what your baby needs.' Right then and there, I made myself into a martyr. The only reason I was ever given was that Ted was tiny and 'too nervous to stay with the bottle very long.'

"I wouldn't say that Ted was a very socially responsive baby, but people smiled at him because he was cute and he'd smile back. I would say, though, that he developed a very early separation anxiety—maybe because he had his own bedroom from the age of five days?

"Ted's developmental skills were mostly acquired at a slower than average rate. He didn't walk until he was twenty months old, and he would chatter incessantly and nonstop, but it was only a mumble-jumble of words with no real speech. He didn't say any clear words until he was three and a half.

"He also never crawled. He would maneuver and pull himself around by his elbows, though. He apparently had no strength in his legs but would scoot over to the wall on his elbows and bang his head against it.

"Just about everything was a distraction and a source of frustration for him. It was almost insane how he couldn't crawl but would yank himself around so fast and manage to knock over everything in sight—pull everything off all the tables and out of the cupboards and drawers, in his random and rapid-fire way—so the house was always in shambles. Finally I had to lock everything up.

"People would tell me, 'Just tell him no,' or, 'You're not being firm enough with him.' It's incredible to me now how easily I fell victim to those kinds of criticisms.

"The doctors told me he had a mild hearing loss in one ear, motor perception difficulties, delay in the acquisition of speech patterns—I'm reading now—'rigidity,' 'intensity,' and so on, but none of them ever told me in plain English what was wrong or what to expect next. Or what I could *do* about any of it. It was just going from pillar to post.

"They never could do a valid IQ test on him because in some areas he scored mentally retarded and in others he was superior. The two sets of scores would cancel each other out and Ted would always end up in the range of normal which he obviously wasn't.

"During one examination, a specialist diagnosed him as 'intractably hyperactive, with lagging development' and advised me ominously not to ever put him in public education unless I absolutely had to. All he said by way of explanation was that Ted would just never make it in a regular school.

"By then, at age four, Ted was a mass of tension and anxiety. He bit his fingernails and toenails down to the quick, and was a bedwetter.

"And he would go from tic to tic. He'd play with his eyes and cross them while daydreaming, and he had other facial tics, then a nervous throat-clearing all the time, and as soon as one would pass he would go on to more and more embarrassing tics like constantly scratching his backside or masturbating in class. One neurologist said that his constant foot-tapping might be a tic equivalent and probably an assistive effort to speech, but like all the other explanations, this one wasn't very helpful either.

"All this time, Ted seemed so unaware of life around him and lived within himself to such an extent that there were very few things that we could hold out as rewards for improving his behavior.

"As he was growing up, his greatest frustration was his realization that his sister, who is fourteen months younger and also privately adopted, was more advanced. He could see that and was angry about it. Karly was always covered with sores and scratches from Ted's jealousy and rage to the point where we don't have even one picture of her growing up where her face isn't bloody.

"When we took Ted for counseling about his treatment of Karly, he told the doctor, 'It's sugars. They make me want to kill myself or someone else.' But of course that was only something he had picked up from us, and he had no real insight into his anger.

"As much as I tried to shield him, Ted knew from the beginning that he wasn't like the other children. It was as though he saw other children as belonging to a related, but different, species than himself, and to this day he doesn't have a single friend.

"Most of the time he's isolated and involved with his interest in science fiction and horror movies, which developed early. It's as if he can really identify with the monsters and weird creatures in these comic books and films. I'm afraid that's the real basis of his obsession.

"He didn't even relate to the other children at his own birthday parties. And at nursery school Ted would hit and push and mess up everyone else's work, but in general he didn't seem to care whether the other children were there or not. Because he was so clumsy and distractible, he was a nuisance to everyone else, adults and children alike, and he knew it.

"Now Ted goes on outings with the young people's group at our church, but it's still the same way. They tolerate his being there and so he *participates*, but only in a superficial way, on the sidelines. It isn't like he interacts or is really part of anything. And while he's very, very sensitive and knows he shouldn't be the way he is but doesn't know what to do about it, I wouldn't say that he's actually lonely because he just has no basis for comparison. The psychologist at his present school wrote in a report that although he tries to present an air of confidence and nonchalance, he projects feelings of inadequacy.

"I remember how I used to sit with him hour after hour with these little pictorial charts. I'd put a raisin on each picture so if Ted could name the object in the picture he would get to eat the raisin. The area where we worked had to be absolutely stark because anything and everything would distract him from the book. I had to remove all the pictures and floral patterns in the room and leave only the solid color beige rug we sat on.

"When Ted finally began to speak, at almost age four, it was obvious he was blocked and uncomfortable with expressive language. Here again, I have the awful feeling that he somehow felt he wasn't quite human, and language wasn't *his* kind of communication. What did he need it for anyway since he couldn't really relate or be close to anyone? The things he said did not unfold in any logical fashion, and sometimes they still don't.

"One day we were playing a new language game called Tell-a-Story which his teacher had suggested, where Ted was supposed to dictate a story and I would write it down. I've saved one of those old stories which goes: 'Once upon a time, there was a tiger named Frenalo and he says if I was a little tiger, I was going to be a pussycat on my show.'

Ted was ten years old when he made that up, and it shows plainly the very young, three- to four-year level he was stuck at.

"Usually he was taciturn about his problems at school and didn't complain about being teased or harassed. The only thing he would say when asked is, 'The hardest thing about school is no fun.' About the most I can say for his school progress now is that he's there and seems to listen, but doesn't truly internalize or absorb so that to this day he's unable to make judgments.

"He's the same way at home. With another child I would have been a very different person myself, much more liberal and easy-going, but as I saw what was happening with Ted, how his judgment wasn't developing as it should, I became a fundamentalist out of necessity. I'm determined to induce a lot of healthy guilt and impose a superstructure—a master list of rights and wrongs—to keep his nose clean.

"What happened the other day? It had to do with sex. Our children are both teenagers now and we've been talking a lot about free sex. At dinner, our daughter was telling us how a field trip which was supposed to have included two nights away at a beach had just been canceled by her school. Some of the parents had complained that their daughters might come home pregnant.

"Ted broke into the discussion and asked what difference would it make anyhow if they got pregnant. So I knew then that none of it had gotten through to him.

"On the subject of dinner, I want to add that food has continued to be a problem for Ted. Now he goes at a pace three times that of a normal person and goes through a whole meal before anyone else even starts.

"I can go on with the food thing because when Ted was eleven, he was in a study at UC San Diego where they desensitized him to all foods by permitting him only a food substitute—the name is something like Vivinex—for seven days. It's supposed to be a by-product of oil that the astronauts use. Then they gradually introduce regular foods to test for allergies. One doctor had noticed that Ted had 'allergic shiners' or dark circles under his eyes.

"They found some sensitivity to cow's milk and cane sugar and a couple of other foods and prescribed a diet for him. We followed it religiously and it did seem to help a little, but it had none of the dramatic effects the researchers had led us to believe. Then from time to time, starting at about eight years old, Ted has been on tranquilizers, mostly Mellaril, on an as-needed basis.

"I can't say that we ever had any real behavior problems or acting-out because Ted has always been a cooperative child when he was able to be. Actually, he's too much the other way, not assertive enough. As he was growing up, he would never leave the house or attempt to play with the other boys. He knew he couldn't ride a bike like they could, he knew he was far behind the others, and was always so conscious of his inability that he never even tried to socialize.

"We put him in Cub Scouts and then in Boy Scouts but he didn't make any friends there either. He did excel in hiking, though, when it only involved moving in a forward direction. So long as an activity is straight-line, like hiking or swimming or running, Ted never gets tired because of his false energy level. He was so nervous and hyper he would cover three times the distance the others did at twice the speed, and he could stay under water longer than the instructor.

"Along with his detachment from most people, Ted has enormous dependency needs because of his inadequacy and can be a real manipulator in getting his father or me to drive him here or there, and do this or that for him. Because I've known other neurologically handicapped children over the years with these same annoying, perseverative traits, I've come to believe that they get this way because they sense it's the only way they can make it in the world.

"While we didn't have much trouble with Ted's behavior when he was young, I would say that we are really in for it now and it's going to show up now. It already has. His fondest wish is to take a girl on a date, although his idea of a date is to have his father drive them to Disneyland.

"Some of his behavior, like personal appearance, has changed for the better now that he is very much aware of girls, but he's simply unable to make the right kinds of judgments for this sort of social or sexual situation and makes inappropriate remarks to girls on the street. Ted is showing normal responsiveness for his age, but his mind just hasn't caught up with his body.

"Like a couple of weeks ago he made an inane, intrusive remark to a girl who was with another teenage boy. The boy, who is a neighbor, came to me furious and told me he was ready to beat Ted up. And although I've learned not to always rush into a new situation and try to explain Ted, I did talk to this boy about the way he is.

"Apparently it was futile because the next day he caught Ted up the street and ordered him to get down on his knees and lick his shoes as penance for that tactless remark. Ted got down on his knees. It was one of those times when I alternate between pitying him and being tremendously angry with him.

"I'm very much afraid that Ted may never be able to make these judgments. The masturbating in class went on almost this whole year, and last summer he was involved in a homosexual situation with a younger boy. I hate to even think about this and I'm going to need a lot of guidance in this area, but lately I've begun to feel that he should probably never have children, and a vasectomy might be the best solution as soon as he's old enough.

"I'm so frightened of the consequences of his sexual behavior, which he doesn't seem able to control, and he isn't showing that he's developing a better sense of discretion, not up to now. I haven't mentioned any of this to Ted's father as yet because he just isn't ready to hear it, but though it's sad it's also a reality that he should probably never reproduce.

"Lately it isn't only girls, but Ted has badgered us into letting him take driving lessons. The instructor at Sears, where he goes to driving school, has told us that it will take an exceptionally long time for him to learn to drive, maybe as long as two years.

"But what he doesn't know, and what the Department of Motor Vehicles won't know, is that Ted will be a hazard in the streets. His problem is mainly cognitive—there's a short circuit, a connection missing somewhere in his nervous system where he can't apply what he has learned.

"He knows all the rules and regulations and will be able to follow directions well enough to pass the driver's test, but he won't be able to *apply* the rules to a situation in the street. It's like he can do a math problem which is right in front of him in his book, but he can't transfer a problem from the blackboard into his book. He's doing really well in algebra, yet still can't make change in the stores and has to rely on someone else.

"My husband has mostly stayed out of all of this, especially in the early years. He spent ninety hours a week at work because he couldn't deal with Ted emotionally and up to now has relied wholly on my judgment. The last decision he participated in was when the adoption agency told us that we had six months to decide about Ted and should give it a lot of serious thought. We were given the option of returning him after six months but by then both of us felt that, no matter what the problems, Ted was our baby. We told them, 'No way we aren't going to keep him; we'll do the best we can.'

"I can't say that the doctors were ever much more helpful than his father even though we had the best care that was available for him, both the best doctors and special schools. I remember a really low point when Ted was three and a half and I was telling his doctor that he still didn't say any words.

"In spite of all that was known about Ted's history, that doctor told me, 'Of course, Mother. *You're* doing all the talking for your son. He doesn't *need* to talk.' He referred me to a psychologist because he said *I* was the one who needed the treatment. But fortunately the psychologist called that doctor back after one appointment and told him there was no question that Ted was suffering from an imbalance in his nervous system, not in his environment, and then we got the referral to the speech therapist.

"The one good thing the doctors did was to give me hope that much of his hyperactivity would diminish with puberty. And anyone who knew Ted as an infant simply does not believe him today. He has become a much more acceptable human being than any of us would have thought possible.

"Looking back, I would say that over the last sixteen years I've changed at least as much as Ted. The tight structure I've had to develop, which goes against my natural inclinations, has given me a stronger direction and enabled me to help him. Many times I've wondered if I was doing the right thing by doing so much, but there never seemed to be that choice with Ted because of the way he was.

"Years ago, the social worker at the adoption agency told me that if we hadn't adopted Ted, he would have ended up in an institution. I have no doubt that she was right. Still, there were a lot of times when I thought I should just give up, but then my husband would say. 'Well, Ginny, you saved a person.'

"Probably my biggest regret is that I didn't seek psychological assistance on a regular basis until Ted's most recent school problems. But we were busy for so many years with the physical therapy—eyes, teeth, walking and the rest. We were involved for so long at that level because those were the most noticeable things then and seemed paramount.

"The psychological areas are new to us, and I can't help wondering if therapy would have helped us as parents and helped Ted as well years ago. Then again, maybe not. Perhaps he wasn't ready for this kind of help any sooner.

"What has been hardest on me was that I was so determined at the beginning that I would be able to straighten Ted out. I was determined that one day he would be like other children. It took me many years to realize that this was one thing in my life that no amount of effort, discipline or hard work was ever going to change.

"Ted will always be a 'marginal' person, the kind that others notice right away on the streets or the buses because he walks with this peculiar pumping motion of his arms, one hand always mirroring the other, and holds himself so stiff and moves like a robot.

"He's really a tragi-comic figure of a person, a teenage Charlie Chaplin, only with poor Teddy it's not acting.

"But now I think more realistically. When Ted was still quite young I started a file on possibilities for his future, like trade schools I read about for the learning disabled or apartment complexes where they teach handicapped young adults to live independently—to shop, bank, apply for jobs and everyday things like that. I'm in my fifties and my husband is in his sixties and now I think: If only Ted can function as an adult after we're dead. Somehow. Some way.

"This is all I ask or pray for now, and I can accept that it would be more than enough."

Most of the rearing of their young daughter Margaret fell to Milt, who worked as a computer programmer in the evenings while his wife, Natalie, continued her law studies during the day. Both came to know intimately the early warning signs of behavior and learning handicap in those difficult years in suburban Baltimore.

Still, few of their neighbors guessed the extent of the quiet despair that went on behind the green-shuttered windows and well-trimmed hedges of the family home.

As it turned out, that early hardship did not cushion them from another, similar emotional shock when some of the same symptoms and behaviors showed up in their second little daughter, Alicia.

In his letter, Milt speaks for both himself and Natalie.

"Probably the first time we were aware we had a kid who was different was right after her birth. Margaret was born four weeks early and had a hard time nursing. I don't mean sucking—I mean she didn't appear to be able to get enough to eat. She cried continuously and profusely, and frankly wore us to a frazzle.

"Margaret would never lie on her stomach and always preferred her left side to her right side. During the day she would sleep for very short periods of time, maybe an hour or an hour and a half at the most, so when people told us things like she had her nights and days reversed, I knew that was a lie.

"After a feeding, she would scream and yell with what we could recognize as excruciating stomach pains. Her knees would be drawn up and her stomach hard as a rock. After trying a thousand and one different positions, we finally found that riding her on our hip with the poor little kid's head lopped over was the most comfortable for her.

"Those first months were a zoo. The pediatrician said stuff like Oh, she has to get used to nursing—She's getting enough if she's gained a few ounces—Whatever you do, don't give her any cereal.

"Being the new parents on the block who didn't know any better, we adhered to what the pediatrician said and didn't give her solids. She kept on crying. I spent many, many mornings and many, many afternoons totally wiped out with that baby lying on my stomach till a couple of times I fell asleep and she slipped off onto the floor.

"The doc had said she was probably a little colicky but would outgrow it. Yet after twenty-five bottles of suppositories and putting them in and her shooting them like darts clear across the room, we started to feel there was something more—something strange with this kid that the doctor wasn't picking up on.

"But in those days we still felt that if you were kind, loving parents and did everything right for your child—all that hype—there wouldn't be any problems. We didn't know back then that no matter what you did, there could still be something organically wrong with a baby that you had no control over.

"My mother-in-law is a head nurse at Johns Hopkins and I asked a lot of questions of her and other professionals, but they would always assure me that children develop at different rates, and whatever I was complaining about was no biggie.

"Never once was there anything concrete like Hey, maybe you've got a kid whose neurological makeup is slightly different, or maybe she's a little hyperactive. Either they just didn't recognize it or they turned that possibility off completely.

"Margaret turned over in bed and sat up at a pretty normal age, only she was suspiciously content just to sit there. She would never try to crawl or reach things. By this time, a lot of the crying had ceased, but now she was almost withdrawn into herself, satisfied just to tinker quietly with any object that was near enough.

"We questioned if this was normal because we had seen other children who would attempt to pull themselves up, or at least creep around and get into things. I also questioned that this child wasn't starting to say words, but again everyone assured me that this was normal. Her first word was 'car,' not 'dada' or 'mama,' and she didn't put sentences together for a long time.

"Since I didn't leave for work until around four in the afternoon, I spent a lot of time on the floor helping her play and teaching her to manipulate different objects. When she was well over a year old, she simply pulled herself up one day and walked right off. There was never any creeping or crawling beforehand.

"Another thing that stands out during her infancy was that she had tremendous ear problems—a lot of earaches. You know, with some kids they put tubes in their ears, but that didn't seem to be the problem with Margaret. She seemed to have what we relate now to maybe some allergies or something in the environment that caused the eustachian tube to keep filling up.

"Another thing we noticed very early was that she was hesitant to play with other babies—she'd back off from them. But while she was timid and backward in this way, she was one tough kid in other ways.

"I had to really set the old limits and be more structured with her than I observed other parents being. I had to be very firm in telling her 'no' and consistent, consistent, but even so it took her a long while to learn not to touch things. I even had to smack her hand a couple of times because she was forever trying to chew on electrical cords or touch light sockets.

"Looking back on it, a lot of this was very abnormal, but with her being our first child we didn't realize that. We would talk about it late at night after I got home and end up saying, Well, okay, maybe this is the way kids are. We were hoping, I guess.

"As time went on we started seeing more of the social fear. Like she would cry when I delivered her to a birthday party and didn't even want to be there if I stayed with her. One mother told us that Margaret had sat withdrawn in the bedroom playing with the buttons on the coats and wouldn't participate in any party activities all afternoon long. She was only okay at home, on her own turf, with one of us there.

"She was three and a half by then and I had more and more of a gut feeling that this wasn't normal for a kid not to want to play with other kids. Since Natalie had just become pregnant again, we decided now would be a good time to put Margaret in a nursery school.

"Again she didn't want to go. She didn't cry so much after me, but it was just very hard for the teachers to stimulate her interest-wise.

Natalie tried saying things like Oh, you'll get to do this and you'll get to do that. When I would look in on her at the school, she was always sitting alone at the back of the room, watching the other children but not participating.

"The one thing that stands out that made me think, maybe there's nothing wrong with her, was a two-wheel bike we got her when she was about four and a half. She climbed on it and rode it the first time.

"So the gross motor stuff was definitely intact, but I never realized until I knew what I know now that she couldn't catch a ball, and wasn't interested in any eye-hand coordination kinds of activities—games like Chutes and Ladders or that kind of manipulative eye-hand thing, even though she was exposed to them frequently.

"During this time Margaret had a tendency to get very dirty, like she was always in a mud puddle, and we had tremendous pressure from her grandparents because her shoes were always filthy and she couldn't stay clean. They had a hard time accepting her into their home. They loved her—I definitely believe that—but there was just something different about Margaret.

"She wasn't what I call a plaster-peeler, a kid who is definitely obnoxious and nobody can stand to be around, yet she was active and inquisitive on familiar ground and had a hard time attending to what she was doing or listening to anyone. In a nutshell, if the structure wasn't there, Margaret couldn't handle it.

"Nobody at the nursery school ever said anything to me, but I had a feeling that all was not well there either. During the nine months that she was there, her little face changed completely from a happy face into a sad face. It was absolutely amazing to us that a child could change that drastically, but we've got the pictures to prove it. It was like something inside her that had made her a happy child was suddenly wiped out.

"I'll add at this point that Margaret had only weighed four pounds and some ounces at birth, but now had grown to probably two years above the average size and saw herself as bigger than the other kids. She had a very hard time memorizing nursery rhymes or even caring to attend to anything the least bit academic. Natalie used to love to read to her but she just flat didn't want her to.

"Now Natalie had always been very good in school, an A student, so she anticipated the same thing would happen with her child. I remember all the cute little matching outfits she would lay out each morning, and how the kindergarten teacher would comment, 'Oh, Margaret's a wonderful help—she's the one who picks up all the toys,' and so forth and so on. Never anything but compliments, except that we could see that she wasn't learning her alphabet or numbers.

"At the end of the first year, out of the blue, we were suddenly called into the school for a meeting and informed that although nobody knew what was wrong with Margaret, she just wasn't doing academically what she should be doing. They asked if we wanted to hold her back a year and we said we didn't know because we didn't. The decision ended up to send her to first grade because of her large size.

"I don't believe Margaret was aware at this time that she was failing except she told us that she wanted to stay in the kindergarten class and play with the big dollhouse, so I have a feeling she sensed something was wrong.

"She was also very sad in kindergarten and didn't fit in or relate to her peer group. Sometimes she would try very hard to bring children home which would end up as a total failure because she was so happy to have a friend that she would smother the other kid to death.

"For a while there she tried some acting-out behaviors, but I can be a very hard-nosed person if I need to be. I became her real security because she needed to know exactly where the limits were and if she stepped over them, then she knew what was going to happen to her. I feel that strictness saved her life, and saved her from being identified as a behavior problem or an undesirable child to be around, though it soon became evident that some of our friends thought she was a cute kid and others couldn't stand her. I guess we both blank out some of these things because they're very uncomfortable to think about.

"Margaret was especially rejected and looked at as a behavior problem from my in-laws' standpoint, and it's true that she was more active than the normal. But I've seen lots of hyperactive kids and when I compare them to the way Margaret was, you wouldn't have said automatically she was hyperactive. Then again, maybe we just didn't know what to look for at the time, but she didn't do the horrible things that I've seen some young children do. More subtle kinds of things, okay?

"Anyway, we've since learned that the syndrome isn't all-or-nothing, it's not that simple. At school they finally 'fessed up that Margaret would alternate between wacky, hyperactive kinds of behaviors on the playground and just sitting in the sandbox doing nothing. The whole syndrome, okay?

"It turned out that her first-grade teacher had her own kid with learning problems who was slightly hyperactive, and she explained the gamut of symptoms to us. Natalie started crying immediately. Both of us were feeling pretty rotten because we didn't want to have a child who was different or had problems.

"I'd say we felt that through her whole childhood, that we were stuck with a kid who was different, but I had an opportunity to cover that up and disbelieve it because of what people around me were telling me. She's perfectly normal—There's no problem—Everybody develops differently, etc., etc.

"I think if we had been faced with the reality of Yeah, you have a high-risk child and she's at risk because these kinds of things can occur in the future—and then *listed* them: 1, 2, 3, and so on—we would have been better prepared to understand the problem, and abler to help Margaret. As it was, we were drowning.

"Somehow we made it to first grade without any help, but we were seeing a sadder and sadder face because now Margaret was not only confronted with the alphabet and numbers but words and arithmetic that were far above her ability. When they finally got around to testing her, the school psychologist admitted there was possible neurological damage. Since she never explained this further, we spent the next six months at the library looking up neurological problems, but all we could find were books on brain tumors and diseases of senility that didn't relate.

"The psychologist had recommended Margaret for a special education class at a different school with twelve kids instead of the usual forty or more, but the special class turned out to be full and she was placed on a waiting list with twenty-five kids ahead of her who also needed the same help.

"The psychological evaluation had said we should have a thorough medical examination done on Margaret as well. We looked at each other and said, Oh shit. We didn't know what they were talking about because we took this kid for a regular medical work-up every six months. We called the psychologist and she sort of alluded to a "specialist," but was not comfortable in elaborating any further.

"*Nobody* ever seemed comfortable with this concept of neurological damage. More and more, we were convinced we were the sole people in this world with this weird kid with some weird condition nobody could help, and was it ever lonely.

"By now Natalie had dropped out of law school. She spent the next year and a half crying in the orange armchair in the living room, and eating her way from 125 pounds to 165 out of frustration. Every day

Margaret would come home and ask why she couldn't read or do math, and then the two of them would be crying in the chair together.

"Then the other kids were beginning to pick up on how Margaret was very different, and not at the level that they were, and started really picking on her. And because she had been identified and everybody knew that eventually she was going to get some kind of extra help, the teachers allowed her just to sit in the class and do nothing.

"Within a few months into first grade, her confidence and self-respect had deteriorated to a point where one day she crawled under a desk and wouldn't come out, and nobody knew what to do.

"In the interim, I would call the principal once or twice a month asking about the special program that the psychologist had said Margaret needed. One time he got so angry from me bugging him he told me I was too 'emotionally involved' with my child. I yelled back at him, 'You're damn right I am, you S.O.B. If I'm not nobody is, and what are you going to do to help me?'

"This is about seven years old now. One day Natalie was dropping off our other little girl at her nursery school when she noticed a headline on the bulletin board: The Maryland Association For Children With Learning Disabilities invites you to a meeting . . . The poster mentioned the words 'neurologically handicapped.'

"After we had spent months trying to find out what it meant, we thought Shit, there's that word again. We decided to go together to the meeting.

"Much to our amazement when we arrived, there were some sixty other people in the room with the exact same kind of weird kid. Some with behavior problems, some with learning problems like we had, and some who didn't know what they had. We thought, Holy shit.

"Meeting that group of parents was the best thing that ever happened to us because they took the time to come out to the house and check on us, and talk to us about the kinds of problems that Margaret had. For the first time in this whole mess they all related—everything that had happened in her baby years, her preschool years, even her current school situation. It began to fit together like pieces in a puzzle.

"They told us about a new law called Public Law 94-142, which mandates equal education for handicapped children, and what it says is that if you have a child who is neurologically handicapped, no school district can deny an appropriate education to your child.

"So armed with those few words, I went after the school district—actually started pursuing and haranguing them. Nobody ever mentioned that counseling was available through the school, nobody there admitted to having the authority to *do* anything, and there were no outside agencies—nothing but this little parent group that ever offered us any concrete help.

"Through my aggression and pushing and becoming totally involved with the law and Margaret's rights, I ended up calling the director of special education for the district a stupid cocksucker and threatening to kick his ass. Within a week I got a letter from the district office confirming that Margaret would be placed in the special class that September.

"But it wasn't soon enough because by then I had completely flipped out. Now I have a kid who is in my opinion completely ruined self-image-wise. I've come to school with a beautiful, happy child and I've brought home a rag, an absolute drained rag.

"Margaret would never fight back against the other kids but would always come home crying. With her attitude and behavior, and my frustration in seeing her deteriorate in front of me, I came dangerously close to wanting to smack the shit out of her, just really hurt her because she was causing *me* so much pain.

"I mean, my pain was being felt for her, but Enough is enough, I said—I can't take this anymore. My kid is totally ruined and I don't know what to do about it and look at her, she's acting like an idiot. I never had anything like this before in my life that I couldn't handle or at least get a grip on, and I hated—literally hated—the schools for doing this to my child. I still do to this day because there are still lots of scars and ill effects from that time.

"I was known in the neighborhood as the guy with the weird kid. Can you relate? Parents of regular kids can't begin to imagine what it's like to see your kid, day in and day out, being completely excluded from any activities or games and being called a weirdo and a dummy and whatever else came to mind. I also wanted to smack the living shit out of every goddam kid in that neighborhood.

"Now even in the special education class Margaret did not adjust well, and I know it was because she felt so bad about herself. As a matter of fact, a couple of times she ran home from school which was a distance of over three miles. I can remember this clearly though it's painful to go back and think about it. You know how you close stuff like that out of your mind?

"I would get her all ready for school and when it was getting on the time she had to catch the little yellow school bus, I would have to physically take that child and put her outside the door and insist that she walk to the bus.

"And she wouldn't. She would hide behind the bushes and go into a screaming tantrum you could hear a block away.

"On a couple of occasions the neighbors stopped to stare openly. I *know* they thought I was abusing this child, and in fact one neighbor said she was going to report me. I think if I had been in her shoes I would have probably thought the same thing, but she had no idea how much patience went on in this house, and how we were barely hanging onto our sanity.

"The principal had advised us, Don't go after Margaret, allow her to settle down and walk to the bus by herself. I did some checking around, though, and found out that the kind of harassment that she had gone through the previous year was being done by the kids at the bus stop. You know, now they want to know why she's going to a different school, and harass, harass, harass, so she just didn't have a chance to feel good about herself.

"One morning I found myself hanging over the fence trying to explain the situation to this neighbor who had threatened to report me. This was before I realized that I was wasting my breath talking to people who don't understand—or want to understand—our kinds of kids. Natalie and I both learned the hard way just to go on about our business, do whatever we needed to, and fuck the neighbors.

"I was standing there talking when I heard this piercing scream from a far distance. I mean, a screaming to the top of your lungs. I knew it was my kid and I started to shake.

"And here Margaret came. I could barely see her in the distance, running for all she's worth. Second grade, eight years old, and she's run three miles from school and now she's running down our street. When she fell into my arms, she was almost to the point of exhaustion. I can still remember how little she felt when I lifted her up into my arms.

"Now for the first time in all this shit I'm broken down and crying, too, because now I'm caught off guard. Talk about an emotional level . . . And here's this neighbor lady observing all this and the look on her face was one of shock. You know, like what's wrong with this crazy family?

"Then came the teacher and the principal and the school nurse and the janitor. All these cute little Volkswagen bugs started pulling up to my house and now they're all going to sit inside and lecture my daughter about how she has to go back to school. And I'm yelling the loudest of anyone about how the hell she got off the campus without anybody realizing it.

"I wouldn't allow them to take her back with them like they wanted to. I told them, Tomorrow, if she calms down and we're comfortable around here, then I'll bring her back. Never once did anybody suggest Margaret should see a counselor because she needed to deal with some of her problems. It was just sort of left hanging there.

"Let me note here in the way of a break what I should have mentioned before—that I'm only giving you a quick overview of this whole process. It's actually a spiky thing where we have our highs when we're doing well and feel good about ourselves, and then we have our lows where the bottom seems to fall out of everything.

"There's no rhyme or reason why: I've never been able to relate these cycles to Margaret's medication or to social situations in particular, although I'm sure those things affect it. Only recently her medicine, which she began taking in second grade, had to be increased because she had grown so much and gained so much weight.

"But it simply seems to be a part of the neurological makeup of this child that some days we're really together, and other days are real crappy. One thing that we hold onto is that we never go as low as we did that day when she came running home.

"I think that was her very lowest point. We've never found out what was behind that incident—nobody seemed to have a clue. But Margaret is very verbal and would always say to me, 'Daddy, why is it you're the only one that understands me?' and, 'I'm glad I have you for a friend,' and that kind of thing. I was really her super security blanket.

"Then in sixth grade, last year at the end of sixth grade, Margaret asked on her own to go to counseling. She just said, 'I think you've helped me as much as you can, and I need to talk to somebody outside this family.'

"Her main reason for wanting to go was the social thing. The teasing is still there and she feels isolated, and the social immaturity is quite evident. It's the biggest problem that we've had and continue to have—the reality of how this affects a child's personality and the whole area of social development. She was always convinced that nobody liked her because she was substandard.

"I don't think she ever learned through therapy to deal with the other kids in a social situation. I think she learned more of that through Natalie and me, you know, giving her the right to stand up for herself, giving her that permission, but I do think she learned in counseling how to respond to the adult figures in her life. In other words, to tell them, 'Lookit, this is what's wrong with me and if you don't believe it, I guess I have to accept whatever you give me,' but at least she's able to verbalize it to somebody in authority which she has on a couple of occasions to teachers.

"I haven't mentioned this before, but Margaret's official diagnosis is minimal brain dysfunction with associated attentional deficit. But any parents could give a diagnosis themselves, couldn't they? No problem.

"Whatever you want to call it, the kid can't pay attention in school or direct her attention to get the meaning out of what the teacher is saying. What the Ritalin does is allow her brain to filter out the extra noise around her in school. For that it works fine but it doesn't do a damn for the social problem.

"Going into seventh grade we were so concerned about her self-confidence and her ability to feel adequate that we did an overkill on the drug scene, and now if she even assumes anybody has ever smoked pot one time, that kid is no good. She's just totally inflexible and rigid in her judgment, where a person is either good or bad with no middle of the road. That really hampers social perception.

"She looks like she's sucked on a dill pickle all day when she comes out of school. She's the very first one out the door—she can't wait to get out of the institution. She has two friends now, but can't even say hello or smile at the other kids around her, that's how inflexible she is.

"She's a sensitive soul, a very emotional child who wears her heart on the outside. She cares a lot about animals, her family and people who are underdogs, but most of the time she's still spaced-out. The kind of kid who always opens the car door smack into someone else's fender, you know?

"Now you want to know about Alicia. Alicia has always been the choice of a lot of people to be around, and kids all want her for their friend. As an infant, she ate well, slept well. It sounds like I'm hurrying through the second one, but there were just very few problems.

"Our opinion was that Alicia was a perfect baby. The only thing that was a little different in the milestones was that she was a bit slow in speech. In two years at nursery school she had no problems with social interactions, seemed well-coordinated in all areas and very easy to manage, not at all like Margaret.

"It was like having an angel dropped from above. Natalie was sure when she entered school that this was definitely going to be our

A student, our valedictorian, and that we had been blessed with this child by way of compensation for our previous problems.

"When Alicia got to kindergarten, whoops. Here we go again.

"During the first couple of years of her education, Alicia felt as though she was prettier and brighter than anybody else. She had a false image of her academic performance, and just this year is coming down to earth and coming to realize that she isn't where everyone else is.

"Her disability showed up in a different way. She has almost no short-term memory and her sequencing ability is nil. She is having even more trouble learning to read than her sister.

"Alicia was identified as a special-needs child almost immediately and placed in a small remedial class. So because from the beginning she was in a place where she could fall back and get the one-on-one help she needed, there was never any emotional deterioration like with Margaret.

"Which is exactly what your book is about as I understand it, right?

"Something we would like your readers to know is that because we went through this tremendous hardship the first time around with Margaret, we thought, What the hell, if we have another one, there won't be the same problems because we already know the rungs of the ladder. We were absolutely wrong in this.

"It hit us like a bag of cement and was like starting all over again, and maybe even worse to think now we've got to deal with two of them. Except that we were lucky with Alicia that the social area is intact because she got early help.

"She is that kind of goosey, giggly, ticklish kid that we could hardly diaper, but in general she's meticulous, tidy and well-organized. Anyone would be proud to have her as a daughter.

"We have a few fears about the future when she gets to the point where she has to perform academics without a lot of special help, when it's not as acceptable to fall back on the extra help as it is now in elementary school, and we foresee a few years of helping her get it together later on. But maybe we shouldn't be so apprehensive.

"Weirdest of all is how our children have had such totally different reactions to their handicap, when they became aware of it in relation to other kids, although it's the same basic syndrome. I know that now, and Natalie knows it from the educational advocacy work she has gotten into. It's always the same syndrome but every kid is hit by it a little differently.

"Some of them, when they become aware, become aggressive and take on the world because they feel cheated. Others withdraw and become phobics. It's absolutely amazing that you can almost cut out the pattern, but there will always be something a bit different in every one of them.

"It must be a tremendous frightening thing for these kids to have academic pressures, social pressures, and what have you hit them all at once, usually when they start school, to the point where they could almost explode and don't want any part of anything. It's easy to see why. And it damages the parents' self-esteem too—don't ever let anyone tell you any different.

"It *has* to. You get into the why can't I be a better person than I am, Why do I still get mad at her when I know it's not her fault, kind of thing.

"Since Alicia, too, has attention deficit disorder, it's our gut-level feeling that it's something in the genes, an inherited characteristic, even though research hasn't proven this yet. Natalie's dad has some of these same kinds of problems, and her sister is definitely learning handicapped and sees social situations cockeyed like you wouldn't believe.

"Not just that she's been married four times, but she's strictly a visual learner and had a very hard time with academics. She's a meat cutter who was only able to learn at all through observation and doing, and even at that had to cheat her way through classes to get her apprenticeship license. Evidently though, she's coping, she's making it.

"Back to Alicia. She is proof incarnate of what getting early help can do for a child and what it can forestall. Our experience is once a child loses self-respect, everything else that matters gets lost along with it.

"The moral from all this is that if we can save just one thing in these kids of ours—if they never learn to read or write or do long division—then saving their self-image alone would mean the difference between a tolerable, comfortable life or a living, breathing hell."

3

Parent-Administered Questionnaires

True, all children "act up" or "act out" from time to time, and learn some skills faster than others. It's only when problems are frequent, severe, persistent, and puzzling that there is real cause for concern.

Probably the most accurate global indication that something is wrong—the heart of the problem—is the parent's awareness of an ever-widening gap between his or her child's behavior and that of other children. Despite the cautions not to compare one youngster with another, and all the advice and reassurance you are likely to be getting, the bits and pieces of evidence that your child's development is off the hoped-for course will become increasingly hard to ignore.

Even if both you and your youngster have been unusually lucky during the preschool years, a child with the kinds of problems this book is all about will inevitably stand out by school age as disruptive, withdrawn, or otherwise deviant—an "oddball" at risk for alienation, poor citizenship, and personal unhappiness. But because the behaviors or "clues" are typically variable—occurring in school or with peers but not in the home, or in some other combination of these key situations— they may not be observed directly by the pediatrician, grandparent, or friend doing the heartening and promoting psychological "blinders" for your fleeting peace of mind. (Substitute "sanity" if you have not been so fortunate as some in the early years.)

The checklists in this chapter are groupings of developmental problems and situations that can mean that the red warning flag of potential trouble is up. Most test items are based on everyday behaviors you can easily observe during your child's routine activities. As you progress up the age scales, you will no doubt notice that the telling or giveaway behaviors become more distinctly social and emotional.

First, a couple of preliminary notes:

Children trapped in inadequate, hostile, or chaotic environments may show erratic behavior and an inability to attend or concentrate. In such cases, it may be impossible to determine whether their disorganized behavior is mainly a function of the external or environmental stress, or whether it is due to a basic biochemical difficulty, or both. This is because inattention, impulsivity, and excessive motor activity are not all-or-nothing characteristics, but relatively enduring patterns of relating to the world that span a range from minimal to maximal biological involvement.

These personality traits may be so slight as to require a great deal of school or home stress to produce behavior problems and symptoms. Or they may be so inherently extreme as to spawn a manic, distractible child who falls apart in the bosom of the most peaceable family. The implicit assumption of the questionnaires is that your youngster's home is moderately stable, caring, and free of major parental conflict.

The quantitative score ranges that are given at the end of each scale should be taken mainly as a means of general evaluation, rather than as indelible, hard-and-fast diagnostic "grades". The real purpose is not to add up all the points and then say your child is or is not "abnormal" but to better understand the strengths and weaknesses in his development that combine to make up his unique and special possibilities. The group of parents of special education children (thirty-two of the same parents who completed the "For Parents Only" checklist) who tried out these questionnaires found them to be most helpful in identifying the specific areas of functioning that were problem-ridden for their children. Parents will be able to match the low-ability or problem areas—whether social, educational, emotional, physical, or perceptual—with the techniques in later chapters that are designed to ameliorate the various manifestations of biological and social difficulty.

The content of the items is drawn from the norms of child development that are found in the medical, psychological, neurological, and educational literature, and from parental reports of behavior symptoms.

Because of the restricted range of behaviors that can be assessed in infancy, the first checklist is the shortest as well as the most simply scored.

Generally speaking, babies at risk of becoming problem children and adults are not distinguishable from normally developing children in the earliest and most instinctive stages of their social growth. They seldom show a deficit in initial bonding behaviors—smiling in response to faces, noticing voices, cooing, recognizing and alerting to familiar people, spontaneously reaching for the parent or caretaker when they are to be picked up, participating in social games, showing visual reciprocity, and so on. Most vulnerable infants, though, test divergent (high) on one or more of the dimensions on which this scale is based: sensitivity or irritability; sensorimotor dysfunction; and neurological abnormality, atypical development, or biochemical disturbance.

Details of scoring are given at the end of each test, but, in general, if many checks appear in the right-hand column, you should pay special attention to the techniques for improving your child's early development described in later chapters.

The Infant Development Scale
Ages 0-2

		No	*Yes*
1.	Bleeding or spotting, blood pressure problem, toxemia, or other "high risk" condition during pregnancy	——	——
2.	Previous miscarriage(s)	——	——
3.	Child very active in the womb	——	——
4.	Smoking, drinking, a lot of junk food, or drugs (including prescription medicines) during pregnancy	——	——
5.	Posterior, transverse, breach, or other atypical fetal position	——	——
6.	Labor either rapid or prolonged and difficult with complications—e.g., failure to dilate, irregular or "false" labor, separation of placenta before birth	——	——

	No	Yes

7. Drugs used to stimulate contractions; anesthesia or forceps used in delivery—"head molding" or forceps marks ___ ___

8. Family history of allergies—hay fever, sinus trouble, hives, asthma—and/or learning problems ___ ___

9. Child either a firstborn or large boy, or a premature baby or twin ___ ___

10. Child, if Caucasian, has blue, green, hazel, or light-brown eyes; or child's father has blue, green, or hazel eyes ___ ___

11. Unusual cry—weak, hoarse, or extremely persistent (lasting more than 45 minutes) ___ ___

12. Feeble "rooting" (turning the head toward nipple) and/or grasping reaction (clasping fingers placed inside child's own) ___ ___

13. Weak sucking or difficult swallowing, or problems in breast-feeding ___ ___

14. Child very hungry but showing preference for frequent small feedings ___ ___

15. Gas, cramps, sloppy stools, or feeding disturbance—e.g., regurgitation, vomiting, diarrhea, pyloric stenosis (obstruction in the stomach outlet causing projectile vomiting) ___ ___

16. Doctor diagnoses colic or prescribes formula change ___ ___

17. Sleep apnea (cessation of breathing) or other respiratory problem—wheezing, snorting, croup; mouth or noisy breathing ___ ___

18. Convulsions, twitches, or muscle spasms ___ ___

19. Persistent eczema, skin blotches, red patches, inflammations, or diaper rashes ___ ___

20. Large startle reaction to noise or sudden movement ___ ___

	No	Yes
21. Child either extremely alert or passive and listless	___	___
22. Early surgery for anomalies of the heart, lungs, kidneys, or intestines	___	___
23. Watery nasal discharge or stuffy nose usually present	___	___
24. Definite preference for being propped up after 2 months	___	___
25. Reaching for objects on a table before $2\,^1/_2$ months	___	___
26. More than six colds in first year	___	___
27. Ear infections usually associated with colds—antibiotics prescribed	___	___
28. Anemia, asthma, or food allergies—e.g., dairy products, wheat, eggs, corn	___	___
29. Recurrent infections, dehydration, pneumonia, bronchitis, meningitis, or fever with convulsions	___	___
30. Peculiar posturings; difficulty finding comfortable prone position	___	___
31. Bodily stiffness or rigidity noted on several occasions (child may be upset by cuddling)	___	___
32. Child excessively fussy, whiny, demanding—frantic when hungry, tired, wet, constipated, or when clothing is too tight or movement restricted, etc.	___	___
33. Child floppy, clingy, or uncuddlable	___	___
34. Blank or staring spells	___	___
35. Concussion, head injury, or accident	___	___
36. Child babbles around 3 months but then stops	___	___
37. Precocious motor activity (child sits up before 5 months, crawls before 7 months, walks before 10 months) or excessive activity (climbs out of crib, etc.)	___	___

		No	*Yes*
38.	Early craving for sweets—child may prefer juice to milk; ravenous hunger for sweetened cereal, cookies, colas	____	____
39.	Child resists sleep—struggles, fights, is unable to relax and sleep when obviously tired	____	____
40.	Persistent eating of a nonnutritive substance—e.g., plaster, paint, poisons, cloth, cigarettes	____	____
41.	Child awake and crying during the night after 3 months—in the absence of illness, teething, or nonroutine events such as company	____	____
42.	Child bites, spits, scratches, or pulls hair excessively (you have to wear your hair short, your hands are clawed)	____	____
43.	Self-injurious, repetitive, or stereotyped behavior—rocking, head-banging, head-slapping, biting or hitting self	____	____
44.	Child needs constant restraint to avoid hurting self	____	____
45.	Child tries to feed self with hands before 5 months	____	____
46.	Child extremely stimulated in stores, crowds, or company of others (may cry)	____	____
47.	Either low or excessive spontaneous motility—child very squirmy, difficult to diaper or dress	____	____
48.	Separation anxiety or fear reaction to handling by unfamiliar persons before 6 months	____	____
49.	Child constantly moving, accident-prone, seen for emergency medical treatment (other than illness) more than three times during first 2 years	____	____

		No	Yes
50.	Child hates to chew "hard" foods—meat, raw vegetables, apple, etc.	____	____
51.	Child never satisfied, hard to divert or soothe, cries until exhausted	____	____
52.	Child very ticklish or "goosey"	____	____
53.	Child an "approacher"—touches, destroys, mouths everything in sight	____	____
54.	Child climbs and falls a lot	____	____
55.	Face and hands always dirty	____	____
56.	Child a picky eater	____	____
57.	No sustained interest in toys; child flits from object to object after 9 months	____	____
58.	Child sneezes a lot	____	____
59.	Jerky or wandering eye movements, difficulty focusing eyes	____	____
60.	Periods of calm alternating with fussiness and wakefulness	____	____
61.	Child either clings to you in new situations or leaps in despite obvious danger	____	____
62.	Child runs fever with each new tooth	____	____
63.	Little or no crawling or creeping before walking	____	____
64.	Constant chewing on clothes, blankets, buttons, furniture	____	____
65.	Pacifier very important—child cries when it isn't there	____	____
66.	Child usually sick on holidays when changes in routine occur	____	____
67.	Fascination with water, moving or spinning objects (e.g., fans), intense light, or parts of the body	____	____
68.	Child repeats one word or sound for hours	____	____
69.	Irritable crying; child wants to be held or carried all the time	____	____

	No	Yes
70. Child easily upset, screams, has temper tantrums	___	___
71. Noisy—throws, bangs, dismantles, knocks things off table, etc.	___	___
72. Excessively affected by pain, light, cold, or sound—screams, jumps out of skin, may remember the doctor's office and anticipate visit by crying	___	___
73. Child seems younger than age-mates—more active and distractible, less responsive to verbal commands	___	___
74. First speech a word salad (garbled, unintelligible)	___	___
75. Wild activity and wide "roaming" when placed in walker—child cries in playpen or other confined area	___	___
76. Child difficult to wean from bottle or breast after 1 year	___	___
77. Definite food preferences (likes and dislikes) at 1 year	___	___
78. Child refuses naps by 1 year, or does sleep during the day and stays awake very late at night	___	___
79. By first birthday still unresponsive to "no-no," warnings of "hot," etc.	___	___
80. During first year, often stays awake after 9 P.M.	___	___

	Yes	No
81. Echoes sounds (his own or others), imitates words and inflections of sound by 8 months	___	___
82. Giggling or laughing by 8 months	___	___
83. Shows subtle facial expressions (coyness, attentiveness, etc.) by 8 months	___	___

		Yes	*No*
84.	Pinches with forefinger and thumb in opposition—picks up raisins, crumbs, or other small objects by 9 months	——	——
85.	Plays games (e.g., pat-a-cake) and waves bye-bye by 10 months	——	——
86.	Besides "mama" and "dada," says two or three words at 1 year	——	——
87.	Holds still for dressing or feeding at 1 year	——	——
88.	Releases objects on request or gives a toy if asked at 1 year	——	——
89.	Understands objects out of sight still exist at 1 year	——	——
90.	Rolls a ball back to you at 1 year	——	——
91.	Obeys simple commands at 1 year	——	——
92.	Has concept of personal belonging ("mine") by 18 months	——	——
93.	Scribbles spontaneously with pencil or crayon by 18 months	——	——
94.	Imitates a vertical stroke at 18 months	——	——
95.	Turns pages of a book singly at 18 months	——	——
96.	Points to familiar objects in books by 18 months	——	——
97.	Articulates 10 to 12 words at 18 months	——	——
98.	Takes off coat, shoes, socks, or pants by 18 months	——	——
99.	Pushes and pulls a toy efficiently at 18 months	——	——
100.	Can follow two simple directions at 18 months—e.g., "Come here and show me your shoe"	——	——
101.	Piles three blocks or cubes into a tower by 18 months	——	——
102.	Walks up steps unaided at 18 months	——	——

	Yes	No
103. Combines two different words to make a meaningful phrase (e.g., "want juice," "go out") at 18 months	___	___
104. Pulls on a simple garment, helps in dressing or undressing self at 2 years	___	___
105. Names pictures in storybooks (e.g., dog, cat, horse) at 2 years	___	___
106. Builds a tower of four blocks, lines up three blocks to make a "choo-choo" at 2 years	___	___
107. Opens doors and runs well by 2 years	___	___
108. Forms simple three-word sentences at 2 years (e.g., "Put on coat," "Dada go bye-bye")	___	___
109. Imitates circular scribbling and horizontal strokes at 2 years	___	___
110. Knows several hundred words at 2 years	___	___

	No	Yes
111. Child too messy to feed self with a spoon at 18 months	___	___
112. Unable to sit and listen to a story at 2 years—or disinterested, too busy; tears up books	___	___
113. Ambidextrous at 2 years (no consistent preference for right or left hand)	___	___
114. Has difficulty turning pages of book efficiently at 2 years	___	___
115. Others always advising you "he'll grow out of it"; pediatrician thinks you worry too much or something is wrong with you	___	___

Approximately 30 to 40 checks in the right-hand column of this scale is equivalent to the medical-psychological category of "mild" biochemical or behavior difference. Babies with this level of sensitivity and overreactivity to their surroundings develop normal social attachments and motor and communication skills with few problems during their early years, and often, after the age of four or five, show no deficit in their sensorimotor functioning. In most cases they are not distinguishable from other children except in school when faced with complex perceptual and encoding tasks such as those involved in reading, spelling, or math.

During the primary grades they may profit from special academic classes or educational tutoring for a certain part of the day, but usually by their early teens, if they are reared in a stable and relatively structured and supportive environment, all of the symptoms will have become compensated or will have disappeared completely. This kind of minimally dysfunctional child needs extra attention and direction when he is under unusual social, family, or school stress.

A score between 41 and 75 right-side responses corresponds to the category of "moderate" neurological or behavior dysfunction. Children with this degree of excitability and emotionalism learn to talk, walk, and communicate easily enough, but may encounter special difficulties in meeting the demands of the social or school environment and conforming to the expectations of social rules and conventions.

In the preschool years (ages 0 to 6), such children benefit from training in body dynamics and other sensorimotor practice, and are responsive to specialized techniques that enhance perception, learning, and social behavior (see Chapters IV and V). By school age, they have usually acquired the normal self-help skills and can handle themselves with only moderate supervision, but still need to be protected from too-heavy social or academic pressure.

With more than 75 "right" answers, you need not panic, stop enjoying your baby, turn against your spouse, or sign consent papers for sterilization (unless of course you were already planning this). But a score this high is generally associated with more severe symptoms, including poor motor development, persistent perceptual-motor difficulties, and early delays in speech and language. Because the biological difference is more pronounced, the child with this score will definitely need early intervention and remediation to reach his potential.

Looked at positively, early recognition can give you the impetus and tools that can make all the difference in the world for this youngster, between satisfactory adjustment and the longstanding misery all too frequently brought on by secondary psychological damage when others become aware of his difficulty.

If you have checked fewer than 30 key items, but are still plagued by doubt or an uncomfortable sense that something is amiss in your infant's development, it's advisable to adopt a relaxed but monitoring, wait-and-see attitude.

The dimensions measured at the preschool level include hyperactivity, inattention, and impulsivity; introversion or extraversion; gross and fine motor development; speech and language; and social skills.

A few items on this checklist call for sustained or unusual observation on your part. It's best to approach these items casually—in the guise of a "let's see if you can" game—and space them out over several days. The "yes, no" entries in this scale are scored either 0 or 2.

The Preschool Checklist
Ages 2-6

0—never or rarely   1—sometimes   2—most of the time

		0	1	2
1.	Is overactive—engages in excessive running or climbing, is always "on the go," has difficulty sitting still	—	—	—
2.	Doesn't seem to listen	—	—	—
3.	Is frightened at nursery school when you are not there	—	—	—
4.	Often fails to finish things he starts	—	—	—
5.	If napping during the day, stays awake very late at night	—	—	—
6.	Doesn't spontaneously express tiredness or ready himself for sleep—by lying down with blanket, etc.	—	—	—
7.	Has difficulty skipping, galloping, or jumping	—	—	—
8.	Has trouble pumping a swing, jumping rope, or bike riding	—	—	—
9.	Can't be trusted alone in yard or near street	—	—	—
10.	Lacks confidence in throwing or catching a ball and/or cannot kick a football	—	—	—

		0	1	2
11.	Often trips and falls	—	—	—
12.	Has difficulty buttoning clothes, tying shoelaces, zipping trousers or jacket	—	—	—
13.	Is clumsy, accident-prone, a "bull in a China shop"	—	—	—
14.	Bites, scratches, hits, throws, breaks	—	—	—
15.	Has trouble following directions at home or nursery school	—	—	—
16.	Has difficulty expressing his thoughts	—	—	—
17.	Confuses opposites—up/down, front/back, on/under, come/go, push/pull, etc.	—	—	—
18.	Shows short concentration span, is easily distracted—dashes from one activity to another, gives too much attention to trivial sights and sounds	—	—	—
19.	Is disinterested in food except for sweets, is finicky, refuses to try new foods, avoids fruits and vegetables	—	—	—
20.	Eats on the run—too active to sit at table	—	—	—
21.	Has difficulty jumping from lowest step, walking on tiptoe, or jumping on both feet at $2\,^1/_2$ years	—	—	—
22.	Can't paint or crayon, string beads, or hold a glass in one hand only by $2\,^1/_2$ years	—	—	—

		Yes	No
23.	Toilet-trained by 3 years (boy); by 2 years (girl)	—	—

		0	1	2
24.	Unable to build a bridge of three blocks or cubes at 3 years	—	—	—
25.	Can't imitate a horizontal as well as a vertical stroke at 3 years	—	—	—
26.	Sucks thumb, rocks bed, etc., after 3 years	—	—	—

	0	1	2
27. Has trouble copying a circle at 3 years	—	—	—
28. Has difficulty with sharing and cooperative play after 3 years	—	—	—
29. Can't locate armholes, pull off socks, put on mittens, unbutton clothes, or put on shoes at 3 years	—	—	—
30. Doesn't climb stairs one foot at a time, know age and sex, or count three objects at 3 years	—	—	—
31. Can't make simple declarative sentences, pronounce all vowels, or respond to commands by 3 years	—	—	—
32. Has trouble standing momentarily on one foot or making tower of nine small blocks at 3 years	—	—	—
33. Doesn't draw a man with two parts besides head at 4 years	—	—	—
34. Can't count four objects, tell a story, or execute two-part commands at 4 years	—	—	—
35. Doesn't articulate correctly m, b, d, n, p, f, h, w most of the time at 4 years	—	—	—
36. Can't stand or hop on one foot by 4 years	—	—	—
37. Unsure of eye and hand preference at 4 years	—	—	—
38. Has difficulty throwing overhand at 4 years	—	—	—
39. Confuses colors and shapes at 4 years	—	—	—
40. Unable to copy a cross by 4 years	—	—	—
41. Has restricted vocabulary—can't generate more than short phrases at 4 years	—	—	—
42. Has trouble walking on heels as well as toes at 4 years	—	—	—
43. Can't count to 10 accurately, or dress and undress self without help, at 5 years	—	—	—

	0	1	2
44. Unable to repeat a 10- to 12-syllable sentence at 5 years	—	—	—
45. Doesn't articulate *k*, *t*, *g*, *ng* correctly most of the time at 5 years	—	—	—
46. Has difficulty copying a square at 5 years	—	—	—
47. Skips on one foot but not the other at 5 years	—	—	—
48. Can't identify left or right correctly by 6 years	—	—	—
49. Has difficulty lifting fingers, identifying fingers, or noting differences between them at 6 years	—	—	—
50. Cannot walk heel-to-toe along a straight line, forward and back, by 6 years	—	—	—
51. Has trouble copying a triangle at 6 years	—	—	—
52. No use of future tense by 6 years	—	—	—
53. Doesn't understand qualitative differences (little/big, fast/slow, etc.) at 6 years	—	—	—
54. Doesn't articulate *wh*, *j*, *f*, *l*, *r*, *sh*, *ch*, *s*, *th*, and *v*, know phone number, or repeat five numbers in sequence at 6 years	—	—	—
55. Impulsive—can't wait turn or stand in line, doesn't foresee consequences	—	—	—
56. Has sleep problems—nightmares, night terrors, bed-wetting, sleepwalking	—	—	—
57. Has allergies, asthma, anemia, or strange food patterns	—	—	—
58. Is referred to specialist—allergist, neurologist, audiologist, speech therapist, etc.	—	—	—
59. Has poor auditory perception—can't distinguish "cat" from "cap," "bed" from "bad," "pat" from "pet," etc.	—	—	—
60. Craves sweets—may have early trouble with tooth decay	—	—	—

		0	1	2
61.	Has frequent colds, stuffiness, infections, sore throats, or nosebleeds	—	—	—
62.	Allergic "shiners" or deep circles or puffiness under eyes	—	—	—
63.	Large reactions to insect bites	—	—	—
64.	Diarrhea, constipation, or other bowel problems	—	—	—
65.	Pimples, boils	—	—	—
66.	Speech too fast or too slow or hard to understand	—	—	—
67.	Heart murmur, birth defect, or other physical problem	—	—	—
68.	With authority, is either defiant, stubborn, insolent, or fearful, shy, submissive	—	—	—
69.	Responds excessively to frustration—bangs head, breaks things, attacks others, tears clothes, etc.	—	—	—
70.	Is overexcited by too many playmates at once	—	—	—
71.	Exhibits jerky eye movements (Hold an object such as a colored pen, penlight, or your finger at arm's length in front of your child and move it in circles or diagonals. See if he can follow it with his eyes smoothly without moving his head or body.)	—	—	—
72.	Persistent mispronunciations—e.g., aminal (animal), flim (film), hopsital (hospital), blana (banana)	—	—	—
73.	Failure to understand the order involved in counting or the alphabet	—	—	—
74.	On-and-off memory—child seems to understand letters, words, and numbers one day, then has lost it all the very next day	—	—	—
75.	Excessive thirst	—	—	—

	0	*1*	*2*
76. Constantly fidgeting when concentrating	—	—	—
77. Dizziness, shakiness, or tics	—	—	—
78. Pale, pasty complexion	—	—	—
79. Child is tired, can't keep up, becomes discouraged	—	—	—
80. Suffers from headaches, stomachaches, pains in limbs and/or joints	—	—	—
81. Can't be talked out of fears	—	—	—
82. Is a left-hander in a right-handed family	—	—	—
83. Displays tremor when holding out arms or spreading fingers	—	—	—
84. Awkward in walking or running	—	—	—
85. Unable to make quick stops or sudden changes of direction while running	—	—	—
86. Attracted to wild, unruly, or younger children	—	—	—
87. Unable to draw a straight line on paper within limits or stop and start a line	—	—	—
88. Has difficulty following three oral directions on a short-term basis—e.g., "Put the glass down, shut the door, come over here."	—	—	—
89. Is intrusive—pounces, shows no appreciation of how his own body and position in space relate to other people and objects, doesn't recognize physical harm to self or others	—	—	—
90. Falls off chairs or has difficulty standing or kneeling with eyes closed	—	—	—
91. Can't push or pull objects efficiently	—	—	—
92. Has poor factual knowledge of the body— e.g., doesn't know he has two eyes, two legs, two shoulders joining the arms to the body, or is confused when asked to point to the parts of his body	—	—	—

		0	1	2
93.	Noticeable difference in movement or posture between the two sides of the body	—	—	—
94.	Poor understanding of the reasons for things we do every day—washing clothes, mailing letter, shopping, banking, etc.	—	—	—
95.	Trouble "tuning out" background—e.g., listening to the teacher or parent	—	—	—
96.	Can't sit and watch a children's television program	—	—	—
97.	Can't color inside the lines in a coloring book	—	—	—
98.	Has trouble carrying tunes or remembering the words of songs or nursery rhymes	—	—	—
99.	Can't avoid collisions or hammer a nail with accuracy	—	—	—
100.	Has difficulty standing on one leg or tiptoe	—	—	—
101.	Shows great interest in taking things apart	—	—	—
102.	Rapid eye movements—horizontal, vertical, rotary or mixed shifting—or "lazy" eye	—	—	—
103.	Never satisfied—always wants more, disappointed on birthdays or Christmas	—	—	—
104.	Attached to odd objects—collects bits of string, rubber bands, etc.; insists on always carrying a string or other object	—	—	—
105.	Is reckless, daring; ignores obvious dangers (moving vehicles, heights, etc.); shows poor judgment generally	—	—	—
106.	Can't throw at a target—throws ball or beanbag with no accuracy of aim	—	—	—
107.	Despite constant activity, physical strength and endurance seem below average	—	—	—
108.	Is outstripped by younger children and/or siblings	—	—	—

	0	1	2
109. Is hypersensitive; has crying jags, cries when corrected, overreacts to "normal" cruelty of other children—withdraws or attacks physically	—	—	—
110. Expresses inadequacy ("Why can't I run as fast as Joey?," "The teacher says I'm dumb," "I can't do anything right") or the belief people don't like him	—	—	—
111. Becomes hyped up at bedtime—has difficulty falling asleep, may insist on a fixed sequence of events before going to bed or on someone to stay with him	—	—	—
112. Has vivid dreams	—	—	—

	No		Yes
113. Is right-handed but with a broader left thumbnail or left-handed with a broader right thumbnail	—		—

	0	1	2
114. In nursery school, avoids table activities such as drawing, coloring, pasting, and cutting	—	—	—
115. Has difficulty holding a pencil—holds crayon in fist, scribbles violently	—	—	—
116. Usually doesn't know whether it is morning or afternoon	—	—	—
117. Doesn't adapt activity level appropriately to different situations—e.g., being active on playground or quiet when listening to a story	—	—	—
118. Becomes wild or mean for 2 hours after eating sweets or artificial flavorings or colorings	—	—	—
119. Is very thin	—	—	—
120. Repeats mistakes, apparently doesn't profit from experience	—	—	—

		0	1	2
121.	Bruises easily	—	—	—
122.	Playground activity haphazard, poorly organized, not goal-directed—consists of running without purpose, throwing, pushing, hitting, etc.	—	—	—
123.	Hard to engage in conversation	—	—	—
124.	Avoids eye contact	—	—	—
125.	Shows large reaction to disappointment or everyday mishaps	—	—	—
126.	Use of grammar below age level; peculiarities of pitch or intonation; stuttering, stammering, fumbling for words; or immature articulation or "baby talk"	—	—	—
127.	Uses the pronoun "you" when "I" is the intended meaning	—	—	—
128.	Resists change in routine: is upset if dinner time is changed, becomes hyperactive on holidays, insists on doing things in the same way every time—e.g., putting on clothes always in the same order	—	—	—
129.	Exhibits peculiar posturings, strange hand or finger movements, or odd gait—stiff or lopsided bearing or walking on toes	—	—	—
130.	Has trouble understanding time and distance and/or judges depth and size incorrectly	—	—	—
131.	Has been either asked to leave a school because of behavior difficulties, or held back in same class	—	—	—
132.	Provokes complaints about his appearance, language, or behavior	—	—	—
133.	Exhibits short lapses of attention, daydreaming, or sudden pauses in conversation or movement	—	—	—
134.	Called by teacher bright but lazy, immature, spoiled, or undisciplined	—	—	—

		0	1	2
135.	Shows Jekyll-Hyde behavior—good and bad days	—	—	—
136.	Has temper outbursts or tantrums; demands have to be met immediately	—	—	—
137.	Laughs loudly, cries easily	—	—	—
138.	Complains of mistreatment or "unfairness," blames others, quarrels, sulks, has many gripes	—	—	—
139.	Has difficulty using scissors	—	—	—
140.	Has trouble with large, simple puzzles, or putting shapes into holes on a pegboard	—	—	—
141.	Is overdependent on adults for companionship	—	—	—
142.	Becomes very frightened at the doctor's (may cry), inquisitive (excessive questions and concern about minor procedures), or fidgety—rocks in chair, "flies" paper airplanes in waiting room, etc.	—	—	—
143.	Walks on furniture	—	—	—
144.	Is hard on clothes and shoes	—	—	—
145.	Shows perseverative behavior—is unable to "turn off" or calm down after roughhousing or horseplay	—	—	—
146.	Has no interest in learning new activities at nursery school; may cry or scream if forced into new activity	—	—	—
147.	Is the first one up no matter how late he falls asleep	—	—	—
148.	Fears the dark—calls out, comes into your room at night, sleeps outside door, etc.	—	—	—
149.	Has trouble walking a straight or narrow line	—	—	—
150.	Has difficulty alternating between running and skipping	—	—	—
151.	Cannot close one eye at a time	—	—	—

		0	1	2
152.	Rubs eyes or blinks excessively	—	—	—
153.	Switches lights on and off, flushes toilets, rummages in pocketbooks, opens doors and cabinets, jumps to answer phone or doorbell	—	—	—
154.	Easily gets lost in stores or crowds	—	—	—
155.	Has difficulty showing through gesture how an object is used—e.g., comb, cup, hammer, guitar	—	—	—
156.	Can't make up his mind when presented with a choice (flavor of ice cream, variety pack of cold cereals, etc.)	—	—	—
157.	Approaches strange animals with no caution—has been bitten or clawed by cat, dog, or other animal	—	—	—
158.	Marks up books and walls	—	—	—
159.	Exuberant, noisy, temperamental, spirited, high-strung	—	—	—
160.	Has stuffy nose or postnasal drip, especially after sweets	—	—	—
161.	Disobedient, negativistic, oppositional—discipline or punishment have no effect	—	—	—
162.	Either is light, restless sleeper—bed torn up—or dead to the world (may wet bed)	—	—	—
163.	Constantly chases household pets	—	—	—
164.	A danger to self or others	—	—	—
165.	Has trouble imitating postures, movements, or words, or copying designs with pegs, beads, buttons, toothpicks, etc.	—	—	—
166.	Has difficulty crossing the midline of his body—e.g., is awkward when threading a bead held in his preferred hand onto a wire placed on his opposite side, or has trouble transferring one set of blocks across his body to the other side	—	—	—

		0	1	2
167.	Is out of tune with people around him— can't sense moods or "read" facial expressions or tones of voice	—	—	—
168.	Laces and zippers are always open, shirt on backwards, shoes on wrong feet	—	—	—
169.	At nursery school, either withdraws, or communicates by hitting, pushing, shoving	—	—	—
170.	Doesn't understand games	—	—	—
171.	Tears off clothing, ignoring buttons	—	—	—
172.	Noticeably upset (withdrawn or hyperactive) when parents argue	—	—	—
173.	Has difficulty touching right hand to left ear, or vice versa	—	—	—
174.	Constantly fiddles with objects or buttons	—	—	—
175.	Needs to win; is poor loser	—	—	—
176.	Always wants own way; doesn't give up; is stubborn, resentful; holds grudges	—	—	—
177.	Messy—never puts things away, may soil or wet pants	—	—	—
178.	Appears unready for school (resists prolonged sitting, cooperative activities, etc.), immature or "babyish"	—	—	—
179.	Either frightened of new situations or extremely daring—dashes in headlong	—	—	—
180.	Doesn't like to be read to	—	—	—
181.	Uses right eye to sight, left foot to kick, right hand to throw (or some other combination of eye, foot, and hand preference)	—	—	—
182.	Always underfoot—demands attention, protests when you are with others	—	—	—
183.	Clumsy when walking backwards on heels, or hopping on one foot	—	—	—
184.	Confused when given too many directions	—	—	—
185.	Selfish, possessive, jealous	—	—	—
186.	Too shy or too forward in social contacts	—	—	—

	0	1	2
187. Has dry, itchy skin—rashes, eczema, and/or sensitivity to bubble bath, rough collars, sweaters	—	—	—
188. Difficulty with cause-effect relations—may stick objects in light sockets, touch hot stove, etc.	—	—	—
189. Overstimulated in crowd—touches everything in stores, pushes all buttons in elevator, climbs on escalator	—	—	—
190. Repeats early jokes (pulls down pants, yells "boo," etc.), is attached to blanket or other object, or wants to hear same simple stories over and over	—	—	—
191. Impossible on car trips	—	—	—
192. Has trouble bending, reaching, or touching floor while keeping knees straight	—	—	—
193. Can't avoid the ball in a game of dodgeball	—	—	—
194. Unable to change quickly and smoothly from a lying to a standing position, or vice versa	—	—	—
195. Exhibits mirror motion—when one hand is rapidly turned palm up then palm down, the other hand involuntarily imitates the action	—	—	—
196. Trouble touching fingers rapidly and in sequence with thumb of same hand	—	—	—
197. Accentuated extension of arms when walking on tiptoe	—	—	—
198. With eyes closed, has difficulty identifying individual toes or fingers when they are touched, or is confused about the direction in which they are moved	—	—	—
199. Has trouble knowing when face and hand are touched simultaneously, with eyes closed	—	—	—

0 *1* *2*

200. Can't identify letters or numbers drawn on back ___ ___ ___

201. Trouble perceiving small details—e.g., can the child discriminate among these similar geometric forms? *Yes* *No*

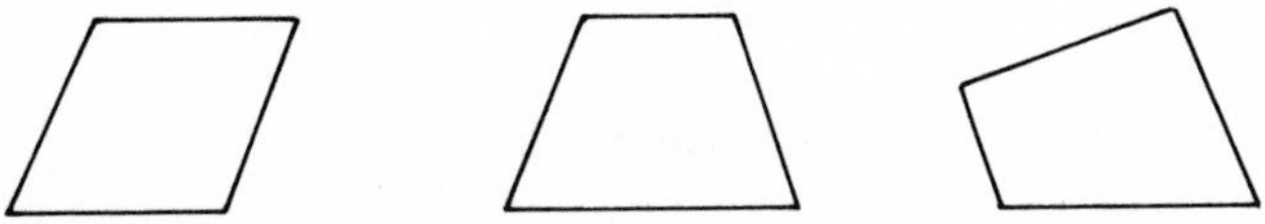

202. Is he able to reproduce these forms from memory in the correct order at 5 years? *Yes* *No*

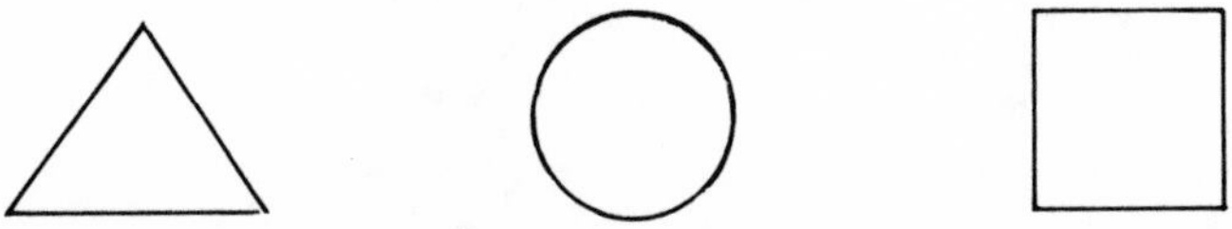

203. Difficulty seeing sameness of a form in varying ways—e.g., can he find all triangles on a page, regardless of color, size, or tilt? Name all objects in a room of one color or shape? Does he see these forms as all squares? *Yes* *No*

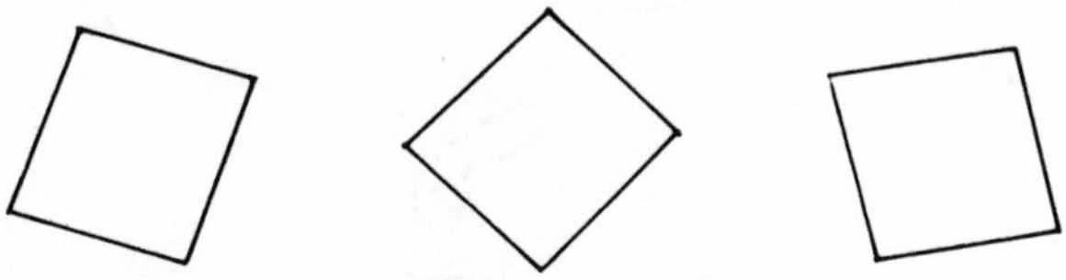

204. Trouble with coding—can he write the appropriate symbol in the empty square below each number quickly and easily at 6 years? *Yes* *No*

1 2 3 4 5 6

4	1	6	3	5	2

205. Difficulty with figure-ground relations—
can he find one or two "hidden figures"
in this form?   *Yes*   *No*

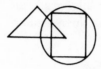

206. Trouble duplicating a dot pattern such
as   *No*   *Yes*

207. Can he guess what these pictures might be
if they were put together?   *Yes*   *No*

208. Does he know what is missing in each
picture?   *Yes*   *No*

209. Can he put the following pictures in logi-
cal order to tell a story?   *Yes*   *No*

     C   A   B

Scores between 100 and 150 points fall within the "mild" category. Generally, these children are nonaggressive, with appropriate social bonds and feelings of guilt and remorse over their misbehavior, but show attentional or perceptual difficulties which can lead later on to social awkwardness or ineptness and/or academic "underachievement"—i.e., performance below the level we would expect on the basis of intelligence and age.

Often the youngster in this category seems to be developing normally in most areas, but reveals a delay or failure in a specific and delimited area, such as language or reading. This slightly out-of-step child should respond well to tailored help from his parent in the areas of sensory and social learning, along with careful attention to routine, planning, and scheduling in his home. A period of home or professional tutoring during the preschool years, if available and affordable, would contribute a good deal to his overall adjustment by giving him a "perceptual head start" in his school life.

151 to 280 points: This score represents the "moderate" category. The primary risk in this group is the child's gradually lowered self-regard. Various undesirable behaviors such as aggression or overactivity may increase as part of his effort to cover the escalating feelings of inadequacy he can only poorly express. Typically, attentional problems become exaggerated for this youngster in groups or stimulating situations such as a classroom, where he may behave as if he were fixated at an earlier developmental stage. With timely application of the techniques for fostering and strengthening self-esteem (see Chapters IV, V, VI and VII), and parental acceptance and consistent management, this child should show significant improvement over time.

More than 280 points: the "severe" category. Difficulties in the home, school, and neighborhood are frequent due to this child's low frustration threshold, quick temper, irritability, defiance, poor peer relationships, and impetuous recklessness. If these behaviors are not recognized and treated, they may prevent him from attending a regular classroom and usher in the painful, long-term problems in personal, social, and vocational adjustment this book is meant to avert. The physical exercises, special nurturant methods, and techniques of environmental engineering described in later chapters are imperative to head off his self-defeating patterns of conduct, undersocialized behavior, and generally poor functioning.

All of the techniques may help, but if there are symptoms requiring immediate attention or treatment (e.g., aggressive behavior, self-mutilation, or excessive anxiety), a highly structured environment with a set routine and a good deal of protection, supervision, aid, and guidance—either in a home situation or a reputable childcare center—is paramount to give this youngster a sense of outer safety and boundedness that will go a long way in counterbalancing his inner stress. Nutritional management, psychological and educational counseling, and environmental manipulation may all have to be tried as well.

The next grouping, covering the school years (ages seven on up), establishes the level of functioning in five general areas: school achievement; ego strength and development; peer relations; aggression and antisocial behavior; and depression, worry, and anxiety.

Personality Inventory for Middle and Late Childhood Age 7 through Adolescence

0—never or rarely   1—sometimes   2—most of the time

		0	1	2
1.	Shows sudden mood swings, is unpredictable, has good and bad days	——	——	——
2.	Has no apparent interest in schoolwork	——	——	——
3.	Is either too aggressive or withdrawn and fearful in new situations	——	——	——
4.	Lacks friends or loses them easily—a loner	——	——	——

		0	1	2
5.	Feels more comfortable playing with younger children	—	—	—
6.	Is bossy around other children, or a bully	—	—	—
7.	Laughs or makes remarks inappropriately	—	—	—
8.	Unresponsive to others' facial expressions, moods, or tones of voice	—	—	—
9.	Noncompliant, stubborn, disobedient, negativistic	—	—	—
10.	Expresses feeling physically—hits when angry, races around when excited	—	—	—
11.	Eccentric behavior or habits	—	—	—
12.	Peculiar hand, face, or body motions	—	—	—
13.	Involuntary motor movements, twitches, or tics	—	—	—
14.	Needs a lot of supervision, can't be trusted	—	—	—
15.	Has stomachaches, headaches, and other pains, especially on school days	—	—	—
16.	Denies wrongdoing, blames others; or tends toward excessive self-blame— "What's the use? Everything I do turns out wrong"; "I might as well be dead"	—	—	—
17.	Usually looks sad, or says he is unhappy	—	—	—
18.	Tense, unable to relax	—	—	—
19.	Needs constant reassurance—always wants to know how book or movie will end, what would happen if . . .	—	—	—
20.	Claims others harass him, pick on him, start trouble	—	—	—
21.	Provokes, teases, hits others, or is excessively critical and sarcastic	—	—	—
22.	Is preoccupied with violence and destruction—explosions, volcanoes, firecrackers, death, blowing things up, maiming, etc.	—	—	—
23.	Is fascinated by fires and sets them	—	—	—

	0	1	2
24. Has excessive difficulty with homework	—	—	—
25. Lacks caution in physical situations— seems a daredevil, likes reckless speed and stunts on bicycle, etc.—you worry about his safety when you are not there	—	—	—
26. Lies, makes up improbable stories, exaggerates exploits and prowess	—	—	—
27. Believes people usually do not treat him fairly or no one cares	—	—	—
28. Shows poor planning and spacing when writing a note—e.g., can't keep on lines of paper, is unaware of edge of paper, may write uphill or downhill—or writes sloppily and illegibly	—	—	—
29. Forms words and letters poorly or squeezes them together	—	—	—
30. Follows words with fingers or a pencil when reading or moves lips while reading—frequently moves and shifts paper around on desk	—	—	—
31. Easily tires of reading	—	—	—
32. Rereads or skips lines, or loses place often	—	—	—
33. Watches television or reads with head either tilted to one side or too close to page or screen	—	—	—
34. Avoids competitive sports and games	—	—	—
35. Speaks well but avoids reading or writing	—	—	—
36. Confuses similar letters or words such as b, d, p, g, q, or "was" and "saw"	—	—	—
37. Guesses constantly when reading	—	—	—
38. Makes many spelling errors—e.g., "dos" (does), "sed" (said), and "cum" (come)	—	—	—
39. Can't build words from letters	—	—	—
40. Cannot match sounds with letters in reading or spelling	—	—	—

		0	1	2
41.	Has extreme difficulty with math	—	—	—
42.	Is attracted to bizarre or irrational thinking—magic, ghosts, ESP, etc.; very interested in esoteric and supernatural phenomena	—	—	—
43.	Is naive—e.g., can't tell when others are obviously lying	—	—	—
44.	Complains of seeing double, says words blur or move while he reads (may cover or close an eye)	—	—	—
45.	Grasps pencil awkwardly	—	—	—
46.	Is easily influenced—picks up "contagious" behavior when around other disruptive children	—	—	—
47.	Persists in negative behavior despite punishment, laughs at discipline—isolation and ignoring don't work, talking to him does no good	—	—	—
48.	Personal insecurity masked in bravura—cocky, chip-on-the-shoulder, world-owes-him-a-living attitude	—	—	—
49.	Feels left out, has no sense of "belonging"	—	—	—
50.	Is discouraged, gives up easily—says "I can't," things often "too hard"—often requests help with schoolwork or other projects	—	—	—
51.	Lacks physical stamina and endurance	—	—	—
52.	Feels stupid, inept, or different	—	—	—
53.	Has poor short-term memory—e.g., studies spelling words and knows them but fails test the next day, has difficulty with multiplication tables, etc.	—	—	—
54.	Relies on pictures or diagrams rather than written instructions—learns best by watching	—	—	—

		0	1	2
55.	Tests average or slightly below average in intelligence	—	—	—
56.	Loses and misplaces things a lot	—	—	—
57.	Is often asked to leave a school or social group on account of unruly behavior	—	—	—
58.	Craves junk foods and sweets	—	—	—
59.	Is impulsive, makes sudden decisions and shows poor judgment	—	—	—
60.	Is overly sensitive—has easily hurt feelings, or is self-conscious or easily embarrassed or humiliated	—	—	—
61.	Stutters or becomes a behavior problem when beginning school—may cry, refuse to go, or develop "phobia"	—	—	—
62.	Is anxious and fearful of change	—	—	—
63.	Is inept and awkward in social situations	—	—	—
64.	Gets poor grades in conduct or "citizenship"	—	—	—
65.	Has "low status" in peer group (wild, mean, withdrawn), the class clown—other children dislike him, often scapegoat, tease, or ostracize him			
66.	Has explosive anger and rage reactions	—	—	—
67.	Responds excessively to frustration or disappointment—or becomes whiny, falls apart with minor stress	—	—	—
68.	Feels cheated or is often jealous	—	—	—
69.	Neglects personal appearance and hygiene	—	—	—
70.	Mismatches clothes or dresses inappropriately for weather or activity	—	—	—
71.	Retaliates, "gets even," makes enemies	—	—	—
72.	Displays precocious sex behavior or preoccupation, or has committed sexual indiscretions	—	—	—

		0	1	2
73.	Saves money for a desired end but spends it on something else	—	—	—
74.	Has trouble telling time	—	—	—
75.	Is highly interested in technological things—machines, mechanics, etc.	—	—	—
76.	Doesn't tell a story so another person can understand what has happened	—	—	—
77.	Is usually either exuberant or down in the dumps	—	—	—
78.	Doesn't appear to know how others feel about him	—	—	—
79.	Remains attached to early objects—blanket, storybook, etc.	—	—	—
80.	Has difficulty after 8 years remembering the days of the week	—	—	—
81.	After 9 years can't name the months of the year	—	—	—
82.	Is excitement-oriented—loves speed, danger, thrills, roller coasters, etc.	—	—	—
83.	Prefers inanimate objects (e.g., cars, trucks) or frisky, high-spirited animals—doesn't play imaginatively with human figures such as dolls or puppets	—	—	—
84.	Interrupts others when they are busy or preoccupied	—	—	—
85.	Is excessively aggressive in defending a friend who has been wronged	—	—	—
86.	Can only attend to one command at a time	—	—	—
87.	Collects string, batteries, or other odd objects	—	—	—
88.	Talks excessively loud and out of turn, too fast or too slowly	—	—	—
89.	Calls out in class, says embarrassing things	—	—	—
90.	Urinates infrequently and at last minute	—	—	—

		0	1	2
91.	Steals, cheats, plays truant from school, threatens to run away from home, or disappears over minor things	—	—	—
92.	Stands too close to or far from others	—	—	—
93.	Anticipates people will not like him	—	—	—
94.	Does not respect property of others	—	—	—
95.	Unaware of time of day or household rhythm	—	—	—
96.	Takes things literally, misinterprets good-natured joking; has poor understanding of social idioms—e.g., "gift horse," "sleeping dogs"; interprets literally proverbs such as "Strike while the iron is hot" or "Look before you leap" after age 12	—	—	—
97.	Can't take criticism	—	—	—
98.	Gets up early—is anxious and impatient to "get going" in the morning	—	—	—
99.	Ticklish	—	—	—
100.	Overreacts to pain, touch, sound, or cold	—	—	—
101.	Throws or breaks things or takes them apart	—	—	—
102.	Spoils family outings	—	—	—
103.	Has difficulty copying words or numbers from blackboard	—	—	—
104.	Can't translate what he knows into speech, writing, or physical activity	—	—	—
105.	Stares or avoids eye contact	—	—	—
106.	Has trouble recognizing differences between similar but slightly different words such as "there," "these," "this," "that," "where," "were," etc.	—	—	—
107.	Lacks sense of fair play, is a poor loser	—	—	—
108.	Won't accept limits, follow rules, or take no for an answer	—	—	—

		0	1	2
109.	Persists in one activity or verbal expression—e.g., draws the same picture over and over or talks about the same ideas	—	—	—
110.	Admires maverick role models and daredevils such as Evel Knievel	—	—	—
111.	Is self-destructive—provokes other children, "begs" to be hurt	—	—	—
112.	An all-or-nothing extremist—can't wait until tomorrow, devastated when things go wrong	—	—	—
113.	Doesn't make rudimentary social distinctions—e.g., uses obscene language frequently and in inappropriate situations, repeats crude playground jokes in adult company, etc.	—	—	—
114.	Talks of killing self or others	—	—	—
115.	Can't shift behavior when problem solving is not successful—goes to pieces, may break furniture or objects	—	—	—
116.	Doesn't show appropriate feelings, such as being sad when others are sick or unhappy, happy when something happens he has looked forward to	—	—	—
117.	Uses gestures or facial expressions incorrectly or rarely uses gestures	—	—	—
118.	Shows poor awareness of social conventions—talks loudly or runs in church or library, phones others at 6 a.m., etc	—	—	—
119.	Gives the impression he isn't listening or hasn't heard what he has been told	—	—	—
120.	Has difficulty organizing and completing work	—	—	—
121.	Does work impulsively and sloppily	—	—	—
122.	Fails to follow through on requests and instructions	—	—	—

		0	1	2
123.	Is restless and impatient—fidgets, wiggles, taps foot	—	—	—
124.	Is well-organized and behaves appropriately one-to-one but becomes dysregulated in a group situation or classroom	—	—	—
125.	Shows personality changes after starting school—may become frightened, irritable, depressed, or more hyperactive	—	—	—
126.	Shows jerky, irregular movements when asked to turn his hands over and back rapidly	—	—	—
127.	Is spacey; has head in the clouds; is absentminded or in "another world"; lacks common sense—has many accidents, trips and falls a lot	—	—	—
128.	Is bored by libraries, bookstores, museums, and the like	—	—	—
129.	Hates reading, word games, or crossword puzzles, but likes picture books or magazines	—	—	—
130.	Can't find a word in a dictionary or a specific fact in a paragraph	—	—	—
131.	Is demanding, never satisfied—doesn't give in or know when to quit	—	—	—
132.	Arranges things "his way"—changes around furniture, etc., without asking permission first	—	—	—
133.	Has wild, fantastic ideas such as decorating schemes or trips	—	—	—
134.	Feels greater attachment to parents and other familiar adults than to peers	—	—	—
135.	Always wants to be entertained or to be going somewhere	—	—	—
136.	Is irritable and touchy	—	—	—
137.	Changes in mood seem unrelated to happenings around him	—	—	—

		0	1	2
138.	Feels sorry for himself	—	—	—
139.	Seems self-absorbed—daydreaming and reveries are excessive	—	—	—
140.	Feels misjudged	—	—	—
141.	Mistrusts others and their intentions	—	—	—
142.	Has good vocabulary but tends to respond simply and with little elaboration	—	—	—
143.	Makes multiple errors in oral reading, but can answer questions about the meaning of a passage	—	—	—
144.	Mixes capital and small letters	—	—	—
145.	Gets into trouble during free time—recess, lunch, after school, etc.	—	—	—
146.	Displays supernormal emotions—throws things, threatens, or breaks windows or objects	—	—	—
147.	Sneaks out of doing fair share of chores	—	—	—
148.	Home adjustment is satisfactory and difficulties emerge only in school—or vice versa	—	—	—
149.	Takes no responsibility for own work	—	—	—
150.	Makes careless, impulsive errors in schoolwork—oversights, omissions, insertions, misinterpretations of easy items, etc.	—	—	—
151.	Demands constant attention—can't share you with others, accuses you of favoritism or not loving him	—	—	—
152.	Does bad things, then cries or says "sorry" but does same thing again the next day	—	—	—
153.	Doesn't speak respectfully to elders	—	—	—
154.	Is oblivious to weather or changes in temperature	—	—	—
155.	Is excessively concerned with physical skills and strength—brags, overasserts	—	—	—

		0	1	2
156.	Asks personal questions of others he doesn't know well	—	—	—
157.	Has sharp business sense, seems materialistically oriented	—	—	—
158.	Is very bright in some ways, foolhardy in others	—	—	—
159.	Always wants to run things, can't work or play well with others	—	—	—
160.	Moves about excessively during sleep, tears up bed	—	—	—
161.	Nightmares, night terrors, bed-wetting, sleepwalking, or encopresis (BM in underwear)	—	—	—
162.	Talks about things in public that he shouldn't	—	—	—
163.	Has difficulty awaiting turn in games or groups, is extremely frustrated by delays	—	—	—
164.	Has trouble sitting still with hands relaxed	—	—	—
165.	Doesn't understand cause-effect relationships—e.g., that teasing others gets him disliked	—	—	—
166.	Loves horror movies and/or violence	—	—	—
167.	Makes inappropriate comments, doesn't sense the mood of a conversation	—	—	—
168.	Shifts excessively from one activity to another	—	—	—
169.	Forgets names, telephone numbers, conversations, or directions	—	—	—
170.	Leaves lights on, water running in sink; forgets to return to a task after an interruption	—	—	—
171.	Puts up provocative opposition to authority figures	—	—	—
172.	Longs to do age-inappropriate activities such as drive a car	—	—	—

		0	1	2
173.	When reprimanded, claims "irresistible impulse," temptation too great	—	—	—
174.	Dominant, pushy, persistent	—	—	—
175.	Laughs and cries easily	—	—	—
176.	Draws complaints from other adults and peers	—	—	—
177.	Becomes calmer and more organized with antihistamines (e.g., Contac), cough medicine, or anti-motion sickness medications (Dramamine, etc.)	—	—	—
178.	Talks about morbid or off-color topics that make others uncomfortable	—	—	—
179.	Has unusual sense of humor or is humorless	—	—	—
180.	Is rigid and inflexible—hangs onto early ways of thinking or doing things	—	—	—
181.	Has difficulty shifting point of view or focusing on more than one aspect of a problem at a time	—	—	—
182.	Constantly tries to get away with things— is devious or delinquent but gets caught	—	—	—
183.	Clumsy, maladroit	—	—	—
184.	Messy—never puts things away; room and closet are impossible	—	—	—
185.	Slams doors, knocks things over, runs into things	—	—	—
186.	Never forgives or forgets a hurt or slight	—	—	—
187.	Frequently gets bored—complains of "nothing to do"	—	—	—
188.	Argumentative; picks fights	—	—	—
189.	Seems to have good manual dexterity and aptitude, but does poorly on performance tests	—	—	—
190.	Manipulative, a "con artist"	—	—	—

		0	1	2
191.	Waits eagerly for favorite TV show, then wanders away during it	—	—	—
192.	Embarrasses adults by disagreeing with them in public	—	—	—
193.	Objects if asked to do something; is usually against any and all suggestions	—	—	—
194.	"Sees" vivid images at night (may cry out in fright, misinterpret shadows in room, hear name called, etc.)	—	—	—
195.	Draws horizontal lines from right to left	—	—	—
196.	Exhibits peculiar motor sequencing when forming letters or numbers	—	—	—
197.	Uses exaggerated extension of arms when walking on tiptoe	—	—	—
198.	Waves arms or postures them oddly when extended	—	—	—
199.	Can't extend both arms and spread his fingers, eyes closed, without tremor or jerkiness	—	—	—
200.	With eyes closed, has difficulty touching his nose (may be unable to find it)	—	—	—
201.	Can't flap his hands over on his lap, palms up and then down, rapidly and in alternating movements by 9 years	—	—	—
202.	Noticeable difference between muscle action or tone on one side of his body and then on the other—lacks symmetry, holds one shoulder lower, neck tense, etc.	—	—	—
203.	Disturbs, pushes, fights; touches objects or others when he shouldn't	—	—	—
204.	Has to open presents immediately	—	—	—
205.	Unable to keep a secret	—	—	—
206.	Has difficulty touching each finger to the thumb on the same hand, both hands at once, at 9 years	—	—	—

		0	1	2
207.	Has trouble clenching one fist while keeping the fingers of the other hand extended, and then switching hands rapidly	—	—	—
208.	In word attack, decodes the initial sounds but then makes errors of substitution or omission within the word	—	—	—
209.	Becomes belligerent, irritable, or anxious when demands for performance are made	—	—	—
210.	Reversals— ƨ (2), Ɛ (3), ♭ (4), ɘ (e), И(N), ꟼ(P)—and rotations—10$, etc.	—	—	—
211.	Switches from subject to subject, or brings bizarre ideas into conversation and has off-the-topic ideas	—	—	—
212.	Is withdrawn or apathetic, or projects an image of "toughness" at older ages	—	—	—
213.	Homesick—refuses to sleep at friend's house, attend camp, etc.	—	—	—
214.	Overeats (especially sweets), shows sudden weight gain at adolescence	—	—	—
215.	Pursues solitary interests	—	—	—
216.	Unrealistic after 10 years—wants to go on "Family Feud" or the "Gong Show," take moped trip around the world, etc.	—	—	—
217.	Unable to function independently after 10—needs constant supervision	—	—	—
218.	Aloof, guarded, seclusive, excessively moody at older ages—may spend most of time in room watching TV or listening to records	—	—	—
219.	Expresses self-doubt, doubt about the future, or hopelessness	—	—	—
220.	Impractical or vague about goals	—	—	—
221.	Has had school suspensions and/or legal difficulties—e.g., thefts, vandalism	—	—	—

	0	1	2
222. Experiments with cigarettes, alcohol, or drugs	—	—	—
223. Shows desire for friendship but shrinks from contact with peers	—	—	—
224. Avoids situations in which others might become aware of his difference	—	—	—
225. Becomes moralistic, phobic, obsessive-compulsive, hypercritical, or suddenly religious at adolescence	—	—	—
226. Angry and self-pitying if required to take vitamins or medicine or if on a special diet	—	—	—
227. Feels his home, clothes, bicycle, etc., are not as good as others'	—	—	—
228. Fails to form attachments outside the family	—	—	—
229. You've lost friends over him	—	—	—
230. You worry excessively about his future and/or try to hide his failures from others	—	—	—
231. Professionals are now more interested in his emotional problems than his learning difficulties	—	—	—
232. You engage in a lot of self-defense, reviewing the past, wondering where you went wrong	—	—	—
233. Grandparents and older adults think he is mismanaged or misunderstood	—	—	—

120–180   points: "mild" category
181–340   points: "moderate"
Over 340   points: "severe"

Doubtless, by now, from your youngster's persistent symptoms and many dismal failures you suspect he may be destined for serious future difficulty in his encounters with the environment. Pediatricians or mental health workers may have already attached one or more labels to his undesirable behavior and attitudes, and his maddening inability or unwillingness to improve—attention deficit dysfunction, learning disability, behavior or conduct disorder—or value judgments, such as neurotic, emotionally disturbed, schizotypical, manic-depressive, or in a "borderline" condition of childhood, or, in extreme cases, psychotic.

Even if you don't agree deep down with the particular pejorative label, which may sometimes amount to professional name-calling, you know you need to do something right now about your child's behavior and learning problems.

In some cases, the clinical picture and diagnosis of biochemical stress behavior may be confusing even for the skilled practitioner. Certain children with neurophysiological dysfunctions may alternate between periods of calm and orderliness in which they seem to improve spontaneously and cycles of distractible, frenzied behavior when their symptoms worsen and launch into orbit just as mysteriously. A bewildered parent, too, as well as the experts, may end up wondering which is the "real" child.

This puzzle begins to fall into place when we realize that brain function is influenced from day to day, and even hour to hour, by many diverse factors—strong emotion, nutrition, motivation, health (such as an oncoming cold, a stomachache, or overtiredness), and even self-esteem. While the new scientific research offers an optimistic view of the possibility of improving behavior disturbance in children, it also points to the necessity of considering the functioning of the total child in repairing attempts. Remember that the common denominator of all—including the labile, on-again, off-again, Jekyll-Hyde child; the withdrawn and phobic child; or the impulsive and unmanageable disrupter—is the same.

All these youngsters are living with the special pain of a permanent variation from normal brain operation—the pain of a body which is exquisitely susceptible to stress, is "unsure" inside, has no feeling of "rightness," and cannot conform to what others expect of it, try as they may.

From the wild, disobedient child, class clown, or sullen outcast who looks at others only out of the corner of his eye to the cheerful honor student or the introspective grade schooler who writes a letter on disarmament to the president and gets his picture in the newspaper, all are in this together . . . and we, the parents, are in it with them. The important point is that there is *no* child, whatever his biochemical, genetic, or native endowment, who cannot gain from early understanding, appreciation, and acceptance of his uniqueness and individuality.

Despite the familiar moments of exasperation and waves of desperation, it would probably be difficult to love or want your child more than you already do. The problem resolves into helping him become a more acceptable person so that those around him—adults and other children—can see his good points, like him as you do, and want to treat him in positive ways.

Or else, if the goal of your superparenting isn't to provide him with the skills necessary to interrupt his odd growth, help him achieve a little control, and allow him the option of leading a happy, comfortable, and useful life, there is little point to all the psychological tests, the medical consultations, or the perplexity, heartache, and strain you have endured, along with him, except suffering for suffering's sake.

Trust that the greatest overture of love and hope you can give your child is to be found in the exercises, techniques, and basics of survival on the next pages.

PART
TWO

4

A Program of Home Therapy

Early Nurturant Methods

An abundance of research with laboratory animals and young human "subjects" in foundling homes—where the opportunity for detached observation once tragically presented itself—underscores the importance of touch, affection, and physical contact in early life not only for emotional health, but, even more basically, for normal physical and perceptual growth. From dogs raised in isolation to infant laboratory monkeys supplied with "mothers" of wire mesh or terry cloth, and from non-stimulated (versus "gentled") rats to infants reared in institutions who suffer the debilitating symptoms of anaclitic depression, the effects of a deprivation of touch are lasting fearfulness, withdrawal, and impairment in all species.

Other research has indicated a timetable of need in infancy, or critical periods beyond which the need for touch, skin contact and caress cannot be adequately fulfilled or made up for. The physical basis for these temporal boundaries lies in the fact that in the first year of life, the infant's brain grows more rapidly than it ever will again afterwards—reaching almost 60 percent of its adult weight by one year. By the age of three, it has reached 80 percent.

Physical Therapies

Up to now, the benefits of systematic programs of physical handling have been most striking in childhood illnesses such as polio. The methods pioneered during World War II by Elizabeth Kenny, the Australian nurse and physiotherapist, led to considerable success once her small band of followers was able to overcome the resistance of the medical establishment, which fought vigorously to keep on encasing the functionless limbs of child patients in plaster casts.

Sister Kenny's physical techniques bear a strong similarity to a number of recent treatments for brain-damaged and retarded children, such as "*patterning*," in which a good deal of time is spent moving parts of brain-injured babies' bodies on the theory that a damaged brain can search out new "circuits" to the spinal cord and thereby relearn various functions. While the claims of this practice have sometimes been overstated, the fact remains that in some cases, the results of the program have been impressive.

Sense-stimulation methodology, which uses olfactory, gustatory, tactile, auditory, and visual treatment, is also being developed in some modern hospitals to revive child coma victims. Pungent odors such as garlic, onions, and horseradish may be held under the child's nose, and peppermint, bacon, spices, and other sharp tastes placed on the tongue to promote brain recovery and rehabilitation. Tape recordings of familiar sounds—telephones, pets, music, people talking, and so on—play in the background, bright lights are directed in the eyes, and there may be feathers, brushes, hot and cold bottles, and sandpaper for touching the skin. The techniques are typically deployed along with massage and exercise.

In successful cases, the critical element may well be not so much the specific physical or sensory strategy as the devotion, love, and kindness of the various therapy specialists. A new theory of what may cause SIDS (Sudden Infant Death Syndrome) or crib death offered by a southern California anthropology professor nicely captures and summarizes the vital relationship between physical closeness, infant development in general, and infant malady in particular in a stunningly vivid way. James McKenna of Pomona College has pointed out that since the beginning of time, babies slept with their parents or sibling caretakers, were nursed frequently, and were carried everywhere by the adults. They slept for short rather than long periods, all the while stimulated by the sleep movements of the parents, and their breathing patterns were constantly stimulated by the breathing of others. In SIDS, the infant almost always dies while he is sleeping alone in a basinette, often in a separate room, removed from close physical contact.

Societies may change with time, McKenna notes, but the basic physical systems and physiological needs of infants have not correspondingly "evolved." Our present-day neurotic drive and anxiety to push our infants into a premature independence and separation—and not a medical malady or physical defect, as has been commonly presumed—may account for this leading cause of nonaccidental death of infants between the ages of one month and one year. It may be that infants who die of SIDS actually die from bodily loneliness and a deficit of physical love.

The biochemistry of early touch and physical handling can even show up visually, in x rays of the bones of infants. Anthropologist and social scientist Ashley Montagu has reported on the difference in the ossification of the baby's bones at the end of just one month of postnatal life, that is directly related to the variable of emotional health in the mother during her pregnancy. In Montagu's report, mothers who were emotionally healthy were easily able to fill their infant's need for sensitivity and physical warmth and love, while mentally disturbed mothers related to their babies only perfunctorily and distantly. This difference in maternal responsiveness correlated with the enhancement or retardation, respectively, of the baby's biological process of calcification of soft tissue into bone.

At the other end of the life spectrum, psychologist James Lynch of the University of Maryland Medical School has pointed out how the fulfillment of need and intimacy with an essential person or life partner can result in prolonged mental alertness, greater freedom from anxiety, reduced susceptibility to the diseases of old age, and even increased longevity. He attributes these desirable outcomes to the calming psychophysiological influence one person can have on another, which his associates have called the "effect of person."

Now gerontologists are finding that beneficial biological effects can be produced even when the other "person" is an animal. Stroking and talking to a pet not only reduces loneliness and depression in elderly patients and helps them cope with day-to-day frustrations, but also lowers blood pressure. It has even been reported that victims of heart disease who have pets survive longer than those without.

Hints from Animal Research

Close parallels to the development of behavior disturbance in human infants have long been observed among captive and wild animals who suffer the strain of childhood trauma. Jane Lawick-Goodall, whose book *In the Shadow of Man* contains a moving portrayal of mother-offspring relations in a chimpanzee colony, has recounted in some detail the social fate of several orphaned infants. The behavioral deterioration in these chimpanzee babies is so similar to the anomalies in many learning impaired children that the comparison is striking.

The deprived young monkeys fail to appreciate or "read" the signals of impending aggression in their elders; are extra aggressive or submissive toward other juveniles; and show declining playful behavior, strange posturings and rocking from side to side, excessive dependency, depression, lethargy, exhaustion, staring into the far distance, perseverative behaviors and excess self-grooming, immaturity, retarded manual dexterity, and clumsy and incompetent manipulation of twigs, grasses, pieces of straw, and other tiny "tools" for poking into termite holes.

Lack of adequate social security—which for young chimps means close physical contact with a large chimpanzee, a constant companion who knows what to do in times of trouble or social excitement, and who can rush the youngster up a tree during an aggressive encounter, running fast and carrying the two of them to safety—created abnormalities in the infants which interfered with their mastery of both the physical environment and the complex social structure of chimpanzee society. And later, the orphan infants who survived into adolescence struggled endlessly to find the protection and strength they still needed, and would always need, from another.

Lawick-Goodall concluded that the orphans' pain was mainly psychological, and that their pathetic physical condition resulted more from a profound depression and impoverishment than from any nutritional deficiencies or disease. This impression was supported by the observation that when the physical condition of one orphan named Merlyn was at its most wretched, shortly before he died, he seemed to brighten mentally, as though, gradually, his mind might have been recuperating. But by then it was too late.

Prebirth, Delivery, and Touch

Because of the special vulnerability of biochemically stressed infants, early touch and caress may well be even more critical as a mediating or tempering influence between their well-known extreme reactions and stimulation from the environment. More than just for reasons of future mental health, then—though this is also an essential goal in child rearing—early "physical therapy" by the parents may be paramount if the neurologically immature child is one day to maximize his potential and rise above the underlying personality disorganization which is based on his biochemical makeup. Simply stated, touch may be, ultimately, humanizing for these infants.

One has only to think of the many stories of abandoned domestic or wild animals who may become dependent on kindly human providers for food but, because of their lack of contact and touch during a critical early period, never become really affectionate or dependable pets. When pain or deprivation is extreme, the defenses become very strong in order for the individual to survive.

Even earlier on, it would seem important to give the excitable baby the best and most relaxed possible start via the new, "nonviolent" birthing methods such as Leboyer's technique of delivery, which seeks to ease the birth trauma and help the newborn start life with a minimum of pain, confusion, and fear. Leboyer has described how he participated in the births of approximately 7,000 babies before he recognized that their first cries were really screams of terror. The people around them are so alienated from feelings—their own and those of others—that they smile and are pleased that the baby appears physically healthy. Hell does not come at the end of life, Leboyer remarked, but actually comes at the very beginning.

Innovative, farsighted physicians who are receptive to natural obstetrical methods are still the minority despite an impressive and growing body of data, but the controversy over these techniques has stirred a sensitive response everywhere. More and more doctors seem willing to shift the focus of attention from efficient hospital administration, apparatus, and schedule—including lunches, coffee breaks, vacations, and staff meetings—to the infant just born, and to consider the momentous impact of birth on all the subsequent days of life.

If we were to catalog the hospital experience as it is typically—a blaze of blinding lamps and floodlights; loud noises; exposure to rough textures; abrupt separation; unnecessary harshnesses such as ensuring the child's first breath will be a fiery ordeal, jerking the spine straight, and squeezing drops of burning liquids into the eyes—we would have produced a list of environmental horrors which could not be more inimical to the touchy infant than if we had set out deliberately to imprint an everlasting nightmare upon his first moments. All these traumas, not the least of which is an atmosphere permeated by distractibility and anxiety in the adults, create a biological and sensory overload which is just what this infant emphatically does *not* need.

Many believe that the Leboyer method provides the kind of strength to master later adversity and stress that can be acquired in no other way. But even if an absolutely natural birth is not an option in your community, there are new birthing centers and remodeled labor and delivery rooms at many local hospitals that provide a warm and homelike atmosphere in which women with low-risk pregnancies can give birth as well as receive pre- and postnatal care.

Stirrups and awkward, unnatural delivery positions are eliminated, a mother's arms are not strapped down to a cold metal table, family and friends can be present, and the mother can hold her baby immediately. Dim lighting, whispers and muted sounds, comfortable furniture, sound-proofing, bath water which has been warmed to body temperature, and an attitude of patient and respectful waiting all contribute to making the infant's birth a happy and relaxed awakening.

The new methods—which are largely a concession to the women's movement in which women are granted a say in their bodily processes hitherto orchestrated by men—are designed to be supportive of the mother, but by extension, they also benefit the infant. It's axiomatic that anything which contributes to the naturalness and simplicity of birth and makes the experience less agonizing for the adults will also be good for the newborn. Most important of all, the child isn't treated as an object, but is recognized as a person from the first moment.

"Reading" the Body

Some of the implications of the research in social deprivation and the new delivery methods are that the infant should sleep with its parents as soon as it comes home from the hospital and later be carried around Indian-style in a harness or baby carrier close to the parent's body. Although the baby's environment may often shift, his contact with his parents will remain dependable and will provide a constant sensory vantage point to serve as his window on the world.

Giving your baby a full measure of physical assurance and handling also means that he should be fed on demand for at least a year and not be left to cry alone in his crib. Much later, any verbal correctional or disciplinary method should be accompanied by the simultaneous comfort of physical affection—a touch, a chuck under the chin, or an embrace.

Our instinct and desire to do right by the child should also tell us that the stages of infancy should be prolonged for the infant with a developmental difficulty. For instance, he should be allowed to give up his tactile-kinesthetic and oral dependencies—breast or bottle, back and body rubs, pacifiers, sleeping with the parent—at his own pace rather than be tied to an artificial calendar of "normal" development.

A satisfactory quota of sleep and rest, which does not come easily to these infants, is also essential. Most neurologically stressed babies arrive with a full repertoire of responses with which to signal when they are hungry or tired, but they usually have poorly organized controls over their reactions to sensory stimuli.

Signs such as changes in skin color, "gaze aversion," peculiar body postures, body stiffening or floppiness, frantic movement, screaming, and increased heartbeat are reactions to distress which are often misunderstood or "misread" by the parent. *In the first few weeks, they are a warning to respect the child's level of physical energy and reduce the stimulation in his immediate environment by removing him to quieter surroundings.* The blood oxygen level may be too low even for extended "pleasurable" stimulation.

Because their nervous systems are immature, the environmentally hypersensitive infants may experience several different states between sleep and wakefulness, ranging from deep sleep to light. Parents should pay sensitive attention to changes in breathing or movement, which can also indicate their child's nervous system has had an overdose of stimulation for now and needs a rest.

Skin sensitivity—showing up as irritations, outbreaks, or allergic reactions—should be offset by soft sheets and blankets and loose-fitting clothes which do not restrict the baby's movement or "swaddle" him. Baby lotion, powder, or premoistened diaper wipes, which may contain artificial colors and fragrances, should be avoided. (Ordinary cornstarch, which has no artificial ingredients or irritants, can be substituted to help absorb excess moisture.) Later, the child should be allowed to go barefoot and wear soft Orlon sweaters and other smooth-textured, lightweight fabrics. The parent should be alert to digestive problems or constipation, which can show up in sudden flushing of the skin (reddening or purpling), excessive crying, or skin rashes. Often, these reactions indicate a formula change is needed.

"Reading" the body also means that your infant's extreme reaction to hunger, fatigue, and other internal states—which is the global definition of "neurological" babies—should be countered by protecting him from his excessive responsivity. Not making him wait overlong for feedings or delaying his quiet sleep time will make his first weeks far more relaxed and comfortable. Show sensitivity to just those two things alone—and your baby will have a favorable start.

It will also be an advantage if a parent can discover as early as possible what calms the excitable child best—whether rocking, holding, a certain body position, sucking, quiet, or darkness. Reliable and consistent physiological patterns of response to stress (physiological "stereotyping") that persist into adulthood have been found in very young babies, so it makes sense that self-selected or "natural pacifiers" can serve as a support in times of infantile discomfort and can sometimes be used to quiet stress even at much older ages.

It's still a long way from being a useful tool, but in the last few years scientists have begun to develop computer profiles of the cries of normal infants for comparison with the cries of sick or neurologically handicapped infants. In several studies, computers have identified jaundiced babies and those who were ill with respiratory problems with a level of accuracy exceeding chance.

It may be a truism that biomedical engineers may merely be confirming what parents have recognized for thousands of years—that different states of distress produce distinctive cries in infants. Yet no computer program or "cookbook" will ever be able to tell us what to *do* with all the diagnostic data being spewed out. Only our feeling and compassion for a child can ever tell us that.

Tolerance Training

Sudden and startling movements, abrupt changes in temperature, and noises with high decibel ratings—lawn mowers, radios, telephones and doorbells, singing birds, screeching tires, and subway trains—are all around us in the real world. After several miscarriages left her fearful of any risk, the Italian actress Sophia Loren lived out her two successful pregnancies by retiring to a secluded chalet in the Swiss Alps which provided food delivery and all the material comforts, and ensured an atmosphere of unbroken tranquillity. But unless you are planning for your child to live his life without ever descending from a rarefied mountaintop, painstaking avoidance of stimulation after the first few quiet postpartum weeks would not be a wise idea.

Even were you to devote your whole being and energy to this one cause, the cost of such overprotection would be excessive for everyone. *Rather than contrivance or flight from the world, the solution to an overexcitable nervous system lies in gradually raising your baby's threshold for stress and frustration by creating opportunities for safe exposure.*

Myelinization

The physical parallel to this psychological process of tolerance is *myelinization*, the slow development of a fatty sheath over nerve axons (stems) in the vertebrate nervous system which acts as an insulator and mediator of nerve conduction—much like the outside insulation around an electric wire. The development of the myelin covering in humans is a protracted process which may last beyond the first decade of life in some cortical locations; in many lower animals such as the rat, whose brain development has been the most extensively studied, the process is completed in a matter of weeks.

A spate of experiments in the early 1950s drew on the discovery of myelinization to investigate the effects of early environmental experimentation in laboratory animals. Most of the studies showed that rats reared in special "enriched" environments were superior to rats reared in the usual small, drab, and uninspired laboratory cages on adult tests of problem solving, mazes, and form discrimination. The experimental animals which had been provided with platforms, swings, blocks, marbles, and other toys appeared to develop more efficient brains as a result of their complex, "free" environment.

To the extent that the results of the rodent research could be generalized to human development and behavior, they obviously had important implications. The degree to which such extrapolation may be justified, though, is still a matter of controversy. Even so, over the last three decades parents have been bombarded with advice on nurturing intelligence by providing a stimulating early environment, paralleling the experimental cages.

Within a few weeks after a child's birth, we are all made to feel guilty and neglectful if we aren't always showing our baby oversized flash cards with the names of different objects, playing classical music all the time, placing colored shapes on a white background to accelerate the development of eye convergence—allowing a "quality" child to recognize words that much sooner—and applying other techniques to "multiply" a toddler's intelligence.

It starts as a way to improve the child's beginning, but soon spills over into compulsion and enslavement. In all of this, we lose sight of the important thing—which is not whether children can read or perform arithmetical operations before they enter school—but rather what they have learned in later life that can contribute to a gentler, more compassionate and rational world.

At the inglorious end of the temperamental continuum, parents of active, difficult-to-rear children are doled out just the opposite advice. At all costs, they are cautioned to avoid frustrating encounters, confrontations, and stressful situations that are said to do the impulsive youngster no good.

About the only clear victory we parents seem to have won is the recent acknowledgment by the professional community that there *are* in fact difficult children who exist from the first breath of life. Researchers have suddenly "discovered" newborns who exhibit a constellation of irregularity in biological functions, muscular tension, sensory threshold, and general activity; negative withdrawal responses to new stimuli; non-adaptability or poor adaptability to change; and intense mood expressions which are frequently negative.

The various contemporary theories of child development, *all of which hold some truth*, desperately need reconciliation and, in particular, useful application to the vast population of physically stressed babies. A middle road between the extreme views of deluging the child with complexity and avoiding most stimulation is needed that takes into account a child's biological difference and provides him with the missing mediational responses.

The Gate Theory

The middle path lies in the method of progressive increments of stimulation that the child under stress is likely to find aversive. These practical suggestions take their cues from the neurological theory of "gating."

According to the gate control theory of pain perception, a valvelike mechanism exists in the brain's signaling system. Depending on circumstances, the neural passageway or "gate" leading from the body to the brain may be open, partly open, or, so that certain messages from an injured site on the body never reach the brain, closed.

Pain impulses are believed to be carried by small-diameter fibers with little or no myelin covering in the sensory nerves traveling from the body's surface to the central nervous system (brain). When these tiny fibers are stimulated, they transmit signals to the brain that "open the gate" and produce an increase in pain sensation. Large (myelinated or sheathed) fibers in the same peripheral nerves have an antagonistic action—when stimulated at supposedly critical points, they reduce or eliminate the sensitivity to pain by instructing the brain to "ignore" unpleasant signals from the nervous tissue—thereby closing the gate.

Psychologists believe that acupuncture, an ancient oriental art for alleviating pain and anxiety, may work by stimulating the large fibers with twirling needles, much like such folk medicines as ice packs or mustard plasters, which have a direct physiological effect. An alternative explanation links its effectiveness to such psychologically mediated influences as hypnosis, placebos, and cultural conditioning. But whichever turns out to be closest to the truth, legend has it that this mysterious medical treatment was discovered 5,000 years ago by Chinese soldiers who realized that their previous aches and pains disappeared when they were slightly wounded by arrows. This is consistent with the observation that people tend to rub a spot on their body that has been recently injured or bruised.

Counterconditioning

Several useful implications follow from the gate theory. Specific stress or stimulation-overload reducers for the sensitive baby which mimic the action of large sensory nerves include:

The presence of a familiar adult

Removing extraneous stimulation from the home

Making your child's daily activities as predictable as possible

Holding, touching, and cuddling when in stimulating situations

Spending short periods of time in arousing circumstances, gradually building up to longer periods of 15 or more minutes

All of the counterconditioning or "counterstimulation" techniques for sensory inundations work on the premise that environmental desensitization can be brought about by slowly increasing the exposure to a noxious stimulus ("fading in"). In the case of noises, which may make your tense infant fairly frantic, you should use a sharp sound such as an alarm clock, kitchen timer, or radio, but at such a low initial level (muffled, if need be) that your child does not become excessively anxious.

Associate the sound with a pleasant activity—physical affection, rocking, a well-liked nutritious food, or a social game. If your child cries or appears extremely apprehensive, discontinue the sound on this occasion and try again at another time. What you *don't* want to do is directly acknowledge his fear or provide too much sympathy, which will only aggravate the problem.

Conditioning or "shaping" methods build on successive approximations to a desired response, which should always be rewarded. Your main auditory conditioning technique is to start with a faint sound level and increase it over a number of days gradually enough that your child can always cope with it. Begin with no more than five seconds of sound, and work up to a reasonable time such as two or three minutes.

Another technique is to start by using a high-noise appliance such as a vacuum cleaner, food blender, or stereo behind a closed door—or one or two rooms away—and slowly move the sound closer as your infant's tolerance increases. You can also stand on the subway steps or at a comfortable distance from a road until your child is able to manage close proximity to trains or passing cars. *Light sensitivity* can be adapted out by gradually adjusting window blinds, shades, or drapes so that the stimulation is kept just below a painful level.

A similar stratagem can help reduce anxiety in social situations, which the vulnerable child often finds aversive as much for the increased physical stimulation associated with socializing as anything else. The section of Chapter V on social remedies describes the techniques in more detail, but the general formula is that very short periods of time should be spent in social situations at first, and the parallel or interactive social behavior should always be tied to an enjoyable, positive outcome like playing, singing, or eating together. When a situation deteriorates, your child should be removed immediately.

So long as a young child has a strong sense of security and organization in his home life, it is to his enduring advantage to learn these basic lessons in screening out or modifying environmental messages (which amounts to normal reality testing) as soon in life as possible.

Increasing Concentration and Attention Span

There is a wise saying among the teaching community in Jerusalem that "the mother is the first school of the child." While this is generally true throughout the world for informal, everyday kinds of learning, there is a more definite way a parent (of either sex) can prepare a distractible child for the transition from home to school, which often comes as a "body shock." A "minischool" which simulates the structure and expectations of a regular classroom and serves as a "psychological warm-up" can be set up easily in a corner of any room.

Only a few materials will be needed for this enterprise: a clean work space (table or desk top), paper, crayons, and picture books—and perhaps buttons, coins, or other props which accompany a daily lesson. In working toward the goal of a daily half-hour of "school time," you should actually begin with no more than four or five minutes, and increase the time a few minutes each day, up to the maximum of thirty minutes.

Structuring to Increase Concentration

Structuring the learning environment to eliminate distractions and hyperactivity necessitates, first of all, providing your child with a place to work which is free of interruptions and as quiet as possible. This can involve seating your child with his back to the room, separating him from visual stimuli with a folding screen or other partition, and/or placing his table close to a wall, bookcase, or large piece of furniture so he can't jump up and down or thrash about easily.

Everything except the immediate task should be cleared from the work surface, and the number of objects your child is working with at one time should be reduced to a minimum. Playthings and other distractions should be out of sight, and a routine should be established wherein trips to the bathroom or refrigerator are taken care of before the learning session proper begins.

An Attention Deficit "Curriculum"

Playing together with buttons and looking at storybooks might seem like an amateurish way to head off such profound problems as school failure, but each part of the "home curriculum" plays a key role in your child's development as a way to help him build confidence and acquire skills in a supportive way.

The basic idea is to set a definite assignment or "challenge" each day, which should be kept brief and should lengthen only as your child's control improves. The possibilities are limited only by your imagination, ingenuity, time, and interest.

One day, you could work on familiarizing your child with the names of different animals, modes of transportation (boats, airplanes, automobiles, trains, buses), or delivery services (postman, milkman, paperboy, etc.); trace alphabet letters and numbers in sand or shaving cream on a cookie sheet; or help him name the parts of his body. Another day might be reserved for more sustained subject matter such as working on an art project involving cutting and pasting; learning what sounds each animal makes; or exploring a question from the "how-things-work" children's literature: what snow is, where all the leaves go that fall from trees, how an elevator works, and so on.

The large selection of *activity and game books* for young children can be invaluable aids. You might plan to do one or two pages a day from one of these workbooks that seems appropriate to your youngster's ability and span of concentration. Because there is no positive reinforcement more effective than success itself, your child should naturally be given only work at which he can succeed. *If he fails at a task, give him a second chance to succeed quickly.*

Gentle quizzing should be included each day to stimulate his concentration ("Is this picture/shape, etc., similar to that one, or different?" "Where are there circles/squares, etc., on this page?"). Buttons can be used for counting and matching and sorting into piles according to size or color. You can work with your child on selecting coins from the collection on the table, introducing concepts of *larger, smaller, more,* and *less* as he drops them into a cup; teach conservation by pouring water from a tall jar into a flat pan and asking him which is more; or acquaint him with the uses of a magnet, a compass, or a magnifying glass. *Communication skills* as well as attention span can also be promoted by simply talking with your child across the table about a TV show, the seasons, or the weather.

You might even be able to enlist the help of a friend or relative who will visit with you occasionally in the guise of a "master teacher" in order to check on your youngster's progress. Praising him in front of another person, by the way, is a very special way to light up your child's self-esteem.

The essential aim is not the curriculum or content of learning per se, which can be just about anything, but, rather, the gradual, gentle, and consistent introduction into the routine of school—including training in remaining seated, building tolerance for concentrating, and deriving a sense of accomplishment and interest.

Appendix II contains more ideas for a home curriculum which relates to most kindergarten programs.

Concentration Enhancers

Improving your child's ability to concentrate on the work at hand should be your main aim in all this effort. Helpful interventions are pointing out when his attention seems to be wandering, and using timers to help him attend to a task quickly and efficiently. Make sure your child faces you directly when you are talking to him—you might need to isolate a very anxious and hyperactive youngster from other visual stimuli by placing your hands lightly on either side of his face or holding his chin while you are speaking to him.

Begin each session by telling your child clearly what you and he will be working on that day, and let him know that you expect the task will be completed. Reduce the number of words you use in instructions or explanations to the fewest possible to convey your meaning. If your child still seems confused, ask him to repeat the directions with you simultaneously. A tape recorder with earphones can be used for giving directions to an older child, who can in turn dictate written work into the recorder.

Verbalizing their actions or talking a project through while they work can help some children to concentrate by putting a "brake" on their runaway thought processes. And while your child is working, try not to interrupt him with comments or questions, which should be saved until he has finished his task.

Away from the learning situation, let him experience how certain conditions, like looking at a book while a noisy activity is going on in the same room, can make concentration harder. You can also help him to grow aware of the things that cause him to become distracted—such as sounds or movement outside the window. Then show him how retreating to a quiet spot such as your "learning center" can make it easier for him to work or play. When he is playing alone, you can encourage his attention span by showing interest and talking with him about the project.

Work pages for your schoolchild should have words or pictures spaced far enough apart that he can discriminate easily between items.

Your older child's concentration can also be improved by providing him with plain white paper or a "window card" to eliminate distractions on the page while he works on one item at a time. If necessary, a hyperactive young child can be given a scribble pad to channel his activity and avoid defacing books and papers.

You can also try linking ideas to images in order to increase your child's memory and attention span. The point is to connect what you want him to remember to a strong visual image. For instance, most people easily remember the shape of Italy because they have been told that Italy resembles a boot. Another technique is to repeat new pieces of information, like the name of an unfamiliar animal, at least three times to ensure that it becomes locked into his "memory bank."

It's also helpful to organize new information since most things are remembered more readily if they are incorporated into categories. For example, you can paste pictures of different animal groups (farm, aquatic, and domestic) on separate collages and hang them in his room or near your learning center. It's also a good idea to provide your child with a notebook to serve as a record and help him organize and review previous material.

Motivating Your Distractible Child

Motivation is a well-known and powerful reinforcer of attention span in children. One wise way to promote your youngster's concentration is to save up a new toy or a special treat, which can be as simple as spending extra time with you, and introduce it *after* the learning period. But the best way of all to choose a reward which will wedge the "have-to-dos" in between the "love-to-dos"—the heart of motivation—is to ask your child what *he* wants most. Anything he enjoys can become a reinforcement.

Every couple of weeks, introduce a break in routine and a change of scenery by presenting a "class outing" to strengthen his learning motivation. Visits to nature and science centers, planetariums, zoos, train stations, pet stores, airports, sporting events, county fairs, and so on will broaden your child's experience and encourage an appreciation of what the world has to offer. This will turn out to be especially true if you tie the trip to what you are working on at home so the continuity of life and learning is underscored. Or a recreational activity can be as simple as watching a children's television show together, and talking later about the important parts so it becomes a learning experience.

If your child isn't enjoying the program, there is a risk that both of you may grow tense, angry, and impatient, destroying the learning atmosphere. To avoid this sort of deterioration and drop in morale, you should try, as much as possible, to follow your youngster's interests and build your attentional program around them. On a day when your child seems particularly restless, permit him to move around for a minute or two and then resume his seat and his task. And as you expand the daily learning time to half an hour, it may help both of you to alternate quiet periods with brief active breaks of exercise or stretching.

Your child's response will be gradual—it may take up to three months to see an increase in his concentration abilities. You should be prepared to wait out this "incubation period" tolerantly, tranquilly, and optimistically.

Stress and a "Laying On of Hands"

Most fundamental of all, when you sit close to your child and become involved in his learning, you are shaping his physiological responses and lowering his threshold for worry and anxiety. The process is similar to the recent biofeedback therapies that can actually modify a person's autonomic reactions in beneficial ways. Researchers now believe that the stress of academic settings not only produces neurotic behavior in some children as their biological "fight-flight" response to enclosure, but also releases chemicals in the young brain which can actually *arrest* the development of intelligence. In extreme cases, the effect of too much school stress can be permanent, and a child may be left with reduced intelligence for life.

It is no accident that children often become ill on Monday mornings—catch colds or suffer from nervousness, insomnia, and diarrhea—and show a sharp drop in their IQ scores as a result of stress, sometimes to levels so low that they cannot be expected to succeed in school. A body of medical literature has documented how tension and strain can actually promote the disease process.

Studies on the physical and mental effects of stress have shown, for instance, that simply discussing a "life change event" such as moving, divorce, the death of a relative, sickness, unemployment—or even an impending visit by a disliked mother-in-law—can cause physiological changes indicative of a diseased state. The tissues in a subject's nasal membranes would react by becoming wet, red, and swollen. The symptoms were identical to those found in the course of developing a cold.

And observations of captive animals show that they develop many behavioral abnormalities that we often associate with children who suffer from a chronic, painful kind of "body pressure" when cooped up in classrooms. Facial and bodily tics, masturbation, stereotyped activity, rocking, pacing, tooth-grinding, and phobias are some of the behavior disturbances that distractible children share with other mammals. Overstressing may also explain why many wild animals in zoos such as cheetahs, otters, and mink die suddenly when construction work is being carried on near their cages or they are moved to a different cage. These animals exhibit a hyperactive response to stress, which, presumably, depletes the normal supply of adrenaline that is necessary for their adaptation. The effects of the stresses of captivity and restricted mobility have long been known to be particularly devastating for young zoo animals whose nervous systems are simply not suited to their environment.

A calming and reassuring "laying on of hands" is exactly what the minischool technique is meant to convey to the child who is at risk for school problems. Medical science doesn't know how the physical techniques which are offshoots of the ancient art of laying on of hands work, but nurses practicing this method of touch—passing their hands a few inches over patients from head to toe, or touching them lightly while concentrating on healing their pain—have been able to reduce the anxiety levels of heart and cancer patients, women in labor, and backache and migraine sufferers. Now that the therapeutic effects of touch and closeness have been revalidated all over again in our skeptical Western world, the technique is being taught at a growing number of universities and hospitals.

In any learning situation, the student is required at some point to take a potential risk by allowing another person to judge his work. For neurologically imperfect children, more than just ordinary courage in involved. Almost all learning for these children takes place in an atmosphere fraught with so much anxiety and peril that it may be a disorganizing and ego-shattering seascape of reefs and shoals. At a deep level, every moment in school, the different child is risking his very self-concept.

Our humanity and tolerance for differences among individuals should tell us that anything we can do as parents to ease our child's adjustment into nursery or public school—though it places a great initial burden on us—will have far-reaching and enduring benefits. What this special help comes down to in the case of overactive children is the need to improve their ability to concentrate by lengthening their attention span.

Improving Sensory and Perceptual Learning

An effective home program for your different youngster includes helping him to orient himself in the world by exposing him to a wide range of sensory and perceptual experiences—along with interpretations and explanations of what he notices around him. The expenditure of time in this basic area of learning need not exceed more than a few minutes a day, and can be integrated into many ordinary activities.

As early as possible, you need to discover what *kind* of learner your child is—whether he learns best through the visual, auditory, or tactile-kinesthetic channel. Awareness of your child's perceptual style is important not only as a recognition of his uniqueness—which helps you to be more committed to his reality—but also for practical reasons since pairing a weak sense with a strong one can often facilitate learning in a difficult subject area during the school years.

Identifying Your Child's Sensory Style

The simplest way to detect your child's sensory pattern is to observe his everyday behavior. Does he notice details and objects others often overlook, and appear to learn best by watching? This is evidence he has *visual* strength. Does he talk and sing to himself, tell stories, know his address and telephone number, and enjoy nursery rhymes, music, and other rhythmical activity? Then he shows strength in the *auditory* area. A sensuous child who loves the feel of different textures (fur, soft quilts, and rugs under his bare feet), takes appliances apart and puts them back together, and touches everything he walks past leans toward the *tactile* mode of learning. Along with talent in one distance receptor (vision or hearing), the developmentally different child is usually also a physical "mover" or *kinesthetic-motor* learner.

A game which can help discover your child's strong point is to arrange several "sensory arrays" in separate places on a table. Old film cylinders filled with fine rice or sand, dried beans, small macaroni, and paper clips can create the auditory grouping. Have him shake each closed container in turn and guess the contents. A plastic lawn bag in which you have placed a stuffed toy, a sponge, a metal mold, and a piece of corrugated cardboard can serve as the tactile presentation. Ask your child to feel each object without looking into the bag. For the visual display, you might use a cup filled with salt or sugar, a ceramic statue, a keychain or showerhead spray, and a corkscrew. Now ask him to guess the names (or uses) of as many objects as he can, and compare where he is strong and weak. The most efficient learner of all is gifted in every sensory area, but the neurological child is most likely to be either a visual or tactile learner, or both.

If you are open to the sensory world around you, just about any household task, errand, or excursion outdoors can become an opportunity to provide your child with experience in the different sensory categories.

Visual Learning

Activities that nourish visual skills are wrapping gifts; finding circles, squares, and other shapes in the home or outdoor scenes; identifying colors in sunsets and dawns; mixing colors with poster paints; picking out images in the clouds; looking at long-distance views such as from a tall building or a hillside; examining aerial photographs; writing with colored chalks; using flashlights at night; watching fireworks; taking nature walks (especially in autumn) and going through collections of natural objects (shells, leaves, insects, rocks); reading charts, graphs, and maps; viewing filmstrips or kaleidoscopes; learning about magnifying glasses, prisms, and optical illusions; collecting stamps; making collages; looking at neon signs or pictures of beachscapes and boardwalks; collecting plants grown from seeds and cuttings; making floral arrangements; visiting greenhouses, flower beds, and Japanese rock gardens; and studying the solar system.

Point out as many *details and visual subtleties* as you can in casual sensory experiences—for instance, the three leaves on most clover plants, the wide wingspan of a hawk in flight, moss growing on the north (shady) side of trees, the different phases of the moon, the gradual darkening in a solar or lunar eclipse, how birds are attracted to certain plants, or the way the bands of violet, blue, green, yellow, orange, and red curve across the sky in a rainbow.

You can ask your child to describe what he sees out the window or around him on a walk, and improve his visual memory by having him recall the visual characteristics of a familiar place—such as a room, playground, or street—with as much detail as possible. He can also practice *visual concentration exercises* like staring at a store window or a landscape, noting the colors and textures, and then looking away and seeing how many fine points he can remember.

Over time, these techniques can train a child with a poor visual memory to transfer the outside world inside his "mind's eye."

Hearing Games

Hearing games for your child include closing his eyes and listening and reporting what he hears (indoors and outside); recording his own voice on a tape recorder (or the sound of ocean waves, crickets, a busy city street, a train, or a jet engine); identifying and imitating animal sounds and bird calls; modulating his voice in the high and low registers; working to a beat or a timing pattern; chewing crunchy foods such as cold cereals and tacos; listening for echoes; playing rhyming games; learning about foreign accents; paying attention to natural sounds like the wind, rustling trees, and thunder; identifying the sounds of water and fountains and sirens; and studying sonar hearing in bats and dolphins.

Touch Reinforcers

To develop your child's sense of touch, you can provide him with opportunities to trace pictures and patterns with his fingers or through transparent paper; feel different grades of sandpaper and sponges; run fine sand and rough gravel through his fingers; compare hot and cold objects; practice touch typing; place his hands on a radio to "feel" the music; fold paper into airplanes and fans; become acquainted with sign language; touch with the "wrong" hand; knead dough; shape long rolls of clay into alphabet letters and numbers; create sandpaper and/or raised, clear glue letters; feel textures in clothing and fabrics; fingerpaint; and go barefoot indoors and out.

Visual Coordination Techniques

A frequent problem of learning impaired youngsters is the combination of a strong sense with a weak one that causes the child's strength to spiral into a frustration. *Visual-motor or eye-hand difficulties* are particularly common. Since most reading retardation is related to visual perception problems, this trouble requires a special remedial effort on your part.

A number of techniques, based largely on suggestions from the American Optometric Association, can help improve your child's visual coordination while he is still an infant.

During the first few weeks, a bright, light-reflecting mobile attached to the outside of his crib provides visual stimulation. When your infant is about *six or seven weeks old*, hang the mobile over his crib. Array interesting "reach-and-touch" objects such as a small framed mirror, photographs of faces, Christmas decorations, and other visually catching three-dimensional objects—which should be large enough to prevent swallowing—within his focus, about 9-inches away. (Interestingly, when the infant first opens his eyes on the world, his visual focus is fixed at approximately 9-inches from the cornea, which corresponds to the visual distance from his mother's face during nursing.)

In the first three months, keeping a small light on in your baby's room day and night, and rotating the location of the crib and his position in the crib frequently, will give him new scenery to gaze at and condition him to respond to light from different sources. Alternately holding him in your left and right arms during feeding, and varying where you sit at mealtimes, will also expose him to a range of stimulation and movement—as will propping him up with pillows or carrying him in an upright position against your shoulder or in a baby harness.

Singing or talking as you are walking around his room will give your infant a target to track and help him link sounds and sights. You can also help your *two- or three-month-old* to hold and shake a rattle (have him switch hands), and play peekaboo holding his hands in front of his eyes. When he's lying on his stomach, patterned sheets and blankets serve up visual variety.

Between 3 and 6 months, a sturdy crib gym or various objects hung across the crib for your child to grab, pull, and kick will develop eye, hand, and foot coordination. For auditory stimulation, you can attach a few gentle noisemakers, like small bells, rattles, or keys, to the crib toys. And a sorting and stacking board with doughnut-shaped pieces in several sizes and colors is also ideal for this age.

Handing your baby small, smooth objects and helping him to grasp them, then removing the object and offering it again, also fosters eye-hand coordination. To reinforce visual memory as well as coordination skills, you can play hide-and-seek games using toys or your face, and make a game of picking up objects your baby drops on the floor. Permit him to repeat the process of grasping and releasing. *Around six or seven months*, you should introduce building blocks, balls of various sizes, zippers, and books made of heavy cardboard to help with his small-muscle development and manipulatory skills.

The best coordination exercises *between one and two years* are rolling a ball back and forth to your baby, and providing him with one or two four-wheeled toys, such as a wagon, and a rocking horse or a riding toy that he can straddle and push with his feet.

Visual-motor practice for your older uncoordinated child includes throwing at a target (darts, beanbags, horseshoes, and so on), pitching a ball back and forth between you, and having him aim a ball up in the air so that it just misses the ceiling. Make sure your child knows how to track a ball with his eyes as well as his body as it curves toward him in an arc.

Creating hand pantomimes or "shadow pictures" (birds, snakes, faces, and the like) on a dark wall with a lamp, "finger spelling" (forming letters with his fingers), and a variety of games and activities—bowling, badminton, golf, croquet, deck tennis, fencing, "shooting" galleries, laying out and nailing down miniature railroad tracks, and playing with remote-control racers—are more easy ideas to improve your older youngster's visual perception skills.

Stimulus Accentuation

Highlighting a stimulus or a key element of a problem by the use of magnifying, outlining, spacing, spotlighting, coloring, or shading can be helpful for the learning imperceptive child of any age. Framing an important feature of a learning situation in a bright color, paring down to only a few items or sentences on a page, enlarging with capital letters and "headlines," and borrowing large-print books for the visually handicapped from the public library are some simple ways to sharpen the perceptual contrast between a stimulus and its background "noise."

With your help, your child can make a "window frame" out of Balsawood or cardboard to narrow his attention onto selected items and help him move from point to point with a minimum of confusion. And surrounding distractions can be screened out permanently by designing a homework "cubicle" for your schoolchild.

Promoting Sensory Integration

Some educators relate the difficulty developmentally disabled children have in processing the information they receive simultaneously from different sensory channels to a lack of "internal language" or verbal mediation skills. The synthesizing functions of children of all ages can be improved if you break up tasks and skills into smaller, more manageable steps. First do the project along with your child, saying aloud what you are doing during each stage, and then have him repeat the sequence with his own verbalization. You can also ask your child to close his eyes after each part and "picture" what the next step will be.

A severely "neurological" child may need to use language and imagery in this deliberate way, in all schoolwork and play, until he is able to mediate automatically.

Whether or not you choose to do any of the specific exercises in perceptual learning, a receptive approach to your child's expression of his sensory perceptions will enrich all of his early experiences, and should help bridge the seeming ravine of difference between you. Time and patience—and, especially, catching onto his idiosyncratic and special ways of taking in the world—are what bonds you.

Balancing the Right and Left Brain

Fascination with the brain and controversy over its proper "discipline" has persisted for thousands of years. Philosophers in ancient Greece heralded the brain as "the divinest part of us all"; the famous English physiologist Sir Charles Sherrington described the brain as "the great ravelled knot." Recent researchers Diane Desimone and Jo Durden-Smith have compared the human brainscape to "a forest of a hundred billion nerve cells . . . the branches of which, if laid end to end, would stretch to the moon and back." And many primitive peoples have always felt that intelligence resides in the heart.

Most modern educators envision the brain as two separate minds or "selves" side by side. This notion, popularized as the "left brain, right brain" theory, grew out of various observations following the "split-brain" surgeries that were performed on epileptic patients during the 1960s to provide relief from violent seizures by severing the connecting nervous tissue between the two brain halves.

According to the concept, the left hemisphere deals with language and abstract reasoning and is analytical, logical, rational, unemotional, and well organized; it solves problems by figuring things out step by step and taking them apart. The right hemisphere, which processes information in an intuitive, emotionally expressive, and impulsive manner, is imaginative and insightful; it specializes in spatial analysis, the perception of geometric patterns, and the gestalt image of entire patterns or whole problems.

In the last few years, the theory has been applied to the physiological and chemical differences between the male and female brain that may go deeper than culture, reaching back into the meanderings and bends of our evolutionary past. Many scientists believe that the right hemisphere, the seat of visual-spatial skills, is better developed in males than in females, who are "prewired" to excel in verbal communication. Consequently, they conclude, boys are generally better at math and girls at reading.

Since our educational system clearly places greater value on left-brain learning, children who are experiencing difficulty with reading, writing, and spelling might be thought to be suffering from a loss of function in the left hemisphere. A "right-brain dominant" child who processes input from the environment in a global, nonverbal way would be at a serious disadvantage in most classrooms—not because he is inherently slow or inferior, but because his learning style is biochemically different.

A rush of expensive diagnostic and learning centers, aiming to remediate academic weaknesses through right-brain approaches, sprang up around the theory of two different sets of hemispheric functions.

The newest and most precise research uses brain scans, by which scientists can actually observe which parts of the brain are being activated in different learning situations. Measurement of the brain's blood flow has generally contradicted the theory of independent functions in learning, which turns out to have been overdramatized. While it does seem to hold true that some areas of the brain are more specialized for certain functions than others, the new information shows instead that most learning takes place with *both* hemispheres of the brain acting as a coordinated, integrated whole.

At the same time as the recent discoveries have largely dispelled the theory of right- and left-brain differences in the processing of new input, they have led to instructional methods that encourage a pooling of the various styles of learning. More balanced curricula are being developed in some school systems which emphasize educational strategies that are "brain compatible"—i.e., in accord with what we now know about the nature of the brain in relation to the acquisition of learning and memory.

The "new" methods, which are intersensory, involve techniques that have actually long been part of good teaching practice. A major advantage is that they enhance the responsivity of all children—not just the atypical learner—allowing learning to take place with less effort and more success.

Multisensory Methods

Multisensory techniques which challenge the "whole brain" are based on *visualization and visual imagery*, which are often found to be deficient in neurological children. Most such children have serious difficulty in short-term memory and sequencing ability, which interferes with the translation of what they see or hear into speech or writing.

Even for normal learners, the prepotence of visual imagery as opposed to what is heard can be demonstrated easily. A recent Canadian study showed people remember pictures (and faces) better than words (or names). They also tend to recall concrete words that evoke mental images—such as "chair," "bird," "car," or "tree"—better than abstract words like "energy," "ego," "justice," or "theory."

If you have attended multimodal presentations (listening to lectures or explanations while looking at filmstrips, slides, pictures, or maps), you may still be able to remember coming away from the talk with a solid sense of learning. In a similar way, you are doubtless more self-assured when driving to a new place if you are given both a map *and* verbal directions.

This is just the theory underlying multisensory methods—a child will be more confident, and hence learn more efficiently, the more sensory dimensions he can fall back on.

In adapting some of the new instructional methods for home use with your schoolchild, it's basic that the learning environment be free from threat and criticism of his effort and generate a positive trust. You can promote *bodily relaxation* in your child by offering him positive suggestions such as telling him that today he'll succeed. His fear of failure can also be reduced by dimming the lights and practicing relaxation techniques like deep breathing.

An overview of the lesson is important for his sense of gestalt or wholeness—so that he can grasp "the big picture," you need to let him know at the outset where you and he will be journeying together that day.

Easy techniques such as picture writing, charting, pictographs, mapping, and cartooning are based on the old wisdom that a picture is worth a thousand words. All of these methods capitalize on the power of visualization to build in long-term memory and enhance the language arts.

Picture Writing As you read a short story or a few pages from a children's book, have your child close his eyes and consciously visualize what he is hearing. Before you begin the story, tell him to form mental pictures of "who," "what," "when," "where," and "why." Then read the same story aloud again—perhaps while playing restful music in the background. (While music is usually highly distracting for younger impulsive children, it can often be used effectively in learning situations with older youngsters, where it may actually *enhance* concentration by reducing body tension and "expanding" the brain's receptivity.)

During the second reading, have your child take "picture notes" in which he attempts to capture on paper the essential elements of the story. If he is like many learning disabled youngsters, he will be able to recall the story from his pictorial representations at a later time in amazingly accurate detail.

Fantasy Flows A similar stratagem is to have your child look at a close-up photograph, of a flower, bird, airplane, or landscape, for example. Then go through your relaxation techniques—perhaps lying on the floor with soothing music, or tensing and then relaxing each part of the body. Afterwards, have him scan the picture again and ask him to imagine that he is "becoming" that flower or other object.

Depending on his age, he can reproduce the photograph either by drawing pictures both before and after the relaxation exercises, or by writing descriptions of it both before and after. Following the relaxation, drawings are likely to stream freely and contain many more and sharper details. Handwriting will usually become more flowing, rounder, larger, and more "natural," and language more fluent, descriptive, and colorful.

Mind-Mapping In "mind-mapping" or clustering, another technique of teaching with few words, a new concept or key word, such as an animal, a mode of transportation, or something seen on a field trip, or a feeling like joy or sadness, is introduced as the center of a circle. As you "brainstorm" together, your child develops "radials" which are additional ideas, thoughts, or concepts branching off from the center. Either of you can jot down these related ideas. The purpose of this exercise is to improve your child's sense of organization and associational and applicational skills.

An example of a mind map one child developed around the emotion of anger looked something like the diagram shown in Figure 1.

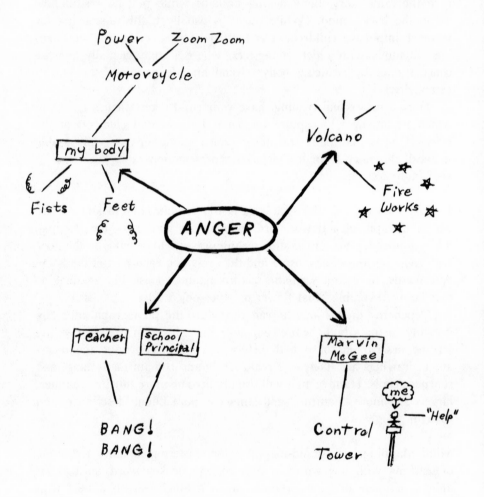

Fig. 1

All of this training is designed to give your youngster the means to become *self-monitored* in his learning—preferably before he ever reaches the school system. In mind-mapping, for instance, he is learning to extract the essential elements of ideas and schematize information in a variety of ways. The nucleus is the main percept, concept, or paragraph from which his brain spurs off and makes associations, out of his experience, that are pertinent to him. It's also a good method, by the way, of centering your child's learning in the context of his "real" life.

Since the technique promotes divergent or creative thinking—at which learning handicapped children are often surprisingly good—it's especially helpful for the youngster who learns in a *random* or *inclusive* way rather than the step-by-step, rote manner stressed in most classrooms.

Depending on your child's age and abilities, the finished product of his mind map can be a story, a drawing, an actual outing, a retelling of a trip or an event, or just the map itself.

Mnemonics, Emphasis, and Exaggeration   Age-old memory tricks that provide mental "hooks" via vivid images and techniques involving the use of association, color, size, rhymes, acronyms, humor (riddles, jokes, puns, absurdities), and rebus representations such as

are all useful aids for improving your child's memory for facts, vocabulary, names, concepts, and the like. School children have long been aided in remembering by narrative chaining (making up a story containing the items to be remembered) and coding numbers to letters. For many years, children have also remembered the notes corresponding to the lines and spaces of the musical staff by recalling that the lines are the first letters of "*every good boy does f*ine" and that the spaces spell "face."

You can present letters or numbers to your child on cards as large, white figures against a black background. With this method, he can actually close his eyes and see an afterimage. (You can ask him to draw his lingering impression.) Different colors can be used to block off critical words for emphasis in sentences, and trouble spots in spelling words can be exaggerated like this:

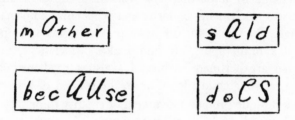

And word recognition can be increased by configurational methods in which you draw lines or "build houses" around the contours of words and/or structural word elements:

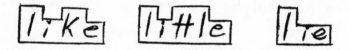

Cognitive applications abound, but the most valuable potential of multisensory techniques may lie in their deployment for *affective education*—the root of all other learning. By encouraging an exploration of emotion, mind maps created around such centers as "My feelings today," "I feel up (or down) when . . .," "I can," or "I am" can expand the personal meaning of learning and your child's wish to learn and ameliorate his poverty of response.

Just as your youngster's senses are a filter, allowing him to select out of the environmental panorama those sensory impressions most relevant to his survival as a person, so are his philosophies and emotions a "screen," allowing only certain impressions to become part of his self-perspective and influencing his idea of his place in the world. While the perceptual range of human beings will probably always be smaller as output than as input, intersensory and holistic techniques have taught us that, through proper training, almost all people can learn to perceive much more than they do ordinarily.

If your child can discover through these methods the real motivation behind his own behavior and the actions of others—if he can learn just this one skill—he will have an enormous, lifelong advantage in being able to see straight through the illusory complexity of the behavioral surface to the psychological core. Trust that this gift of crystalline insight can know no price.

Managing Anger and Violence

When I recall the tidal wave of group psychotherapy programs in the prisons a few years back, when "rehabilitation" was the magic word of the day—the endless, flat discussions and droning postmortems of violent behavior which led in circles—I am more convinced than ever that the achievement of control must begin very early, on a subliminal, limbic-system level. Later on may be too late for reclamation, once impulsivity and hostile expression have become a way of life.

Change becomes a monumental task for the thousands of men and women, some of them beyond middle age, whose nervous system "short circuits" have been operative for a lifetime. The great tragedy is that a high percentage of prisoners who commit violent crimes and are diagnosed as "explosive personalities" were once children, like yours and mine, with slight organic dysfunctions.

School Anger

The prevalent view since the 1950s has been that a violent youngster is almost always a child who has been brought up in a violent home. By being aggressive, the child is giving some release to his pain. And because he has been hurt, the angry youngster appears to be always on the defensive, waiting for somebody to hurt him or even *seem* like they may be thinking of insulting or slighting him so he can rush in to hurt them first.

All of this background may often be true, but what is not given sufficient recognition and due in the case of the child who is hyperactive or has an obvious developmental difficulty is that *not only his home but also the regular classroom environment may be a source of painful dissonance and emotional violence, violating him in his very act of being by discounting all the things he does well which don't seem to matter.*

Beside the alien, anxiety-producing requirements of the school setting, which may be truly impossible for him, all he has achieved and felt proud of in his young life may come to nothing: how he can push a couch across the room, run fast, fly a kite, pump a swing, climb a tree. His need to feel safe, protected, and good about himself shatters in the face of the school onslaught, which quickly destroys his confidence in himself and often leads to vengeful thoughts.

To sit in the schoolroom or blunder about on the playground with the feeling inside them that they aren't normal—that they are not even *persons* like everybody else—is too much for many children. Their hurt over the exposure of their weakness and inadequacy may be on such a monstrous level that getting angry is all they can do.

And there is no incentive to try to succeed where they know they cannot or get along with others who are ever sources of pain and rejection. No matter what one of these children does, it seems he is forever at the bottom of the pecking order—except, perhaps, in outangering everybody else and being the "bad guy," which becomes his form of competition and winning.

When a child feels deep down that he is unworthy of love and respect, he will often act out or "be bad" in order to be punished. An inner conflict swells up in which, on the one hand, he feels his parents and teachers are *supposed* to protect him, take care of him, and help him feel safe—and, on the other hand, he harbors a gnawing fear that he is being treated badly because he deserves no better than to be the brunt of everyone's disapproval and criticism. At heart he blames himself for his failure (and even for being born), but just the same, being angry can amount to an assertion of his will, a surge of his right to live as a person among all others.

For the opposite of being angry, as every prisoner, prizefighter, and abused child knows, is being meek, vulnerable, and powerless, and it may seem to the child who feels mistreated that if he doesn't get angry about his fate, he will be wiped out—actually erased from the face of the earth as he is annihilated by the regimentation, indifference, and psychological violence of his school. The fear that others will downgrade him, shame him, laugh at him, bully him, tease him, walk all over him, and strip him of his dignity because he is different is too painful to withstand for long.

This core of oppressive feelings about themselves is what is meant by the smashing blow that many learning handicapped children who have actually grown up in benign and caring homes experience when they enter the school system. The reason that discipline and punishment don't seem to work is that there is no consequence a teacher or principal can impose that will hurt as much as the hurt that is already inside this child. It comes down to: *I have to get them before they get me.*

Anger which is chronic and menacing becomes a way for the child to build a wall around his sensitivity and keep others at bay. At times when he is feeling most helpless and impotent, he may pretend to be angry for the sense of power and control it gives him. Soon, anger and retaliation become his leitmotiv: Better watch out because here comes tough Timothy with that look in his eye. The most fearful and withdrawn children can become masters at saving face—disguising their vulnerability and their inner sense of themselves as targets behind a mask of bravura and aggression which puzzles even many experts.

Even if a child's resentment is linked mainly to his experience at school, he may still turn against the parents who in the first place sent him there, then have insisted he show up for his daily dose of hurt and humiliation, and still apparently see nothing much wrong with the arrangement. His Mommy and Daddy may seem like conspirators in his terrible feeling of violation, which becomes overgeneralized to just about everybody. His parents are there to take care of him and make the world a safe place, but they are not doing their job.

Because the stress feels like a life sentence with no possibility of parole, a child who is miscast in school will react with the full vigor of his temperament and poorly controlled emotions. Sooner or later, he will perceive himself to be a marked man and embark upon his own private "war path."

A Tale of School Woe

Here is the way one single mother who didn't catch onto her son's attentional difficulties soon enough described the shared torment of their first school experience:

"Billy lasted approximately ten days in the first grade class at Westside Elementary School. And even those few days were far from easy. I had to take time off from work because his teacher kept calling me in to talk about Billy's 'badness,' and his non-existent school skills. Each night he'd receive volumes of homework to 'catch him up' which he couldn't do at all, but which I was supposed to 'supervise.'

"Something, somewhere, just wasn't connecting. The daily recitation of my child's crimes and dumbness struck deep chords of sadness in me. I could only imagine the damage it was doing to Billy. Not yet seven years old, he was being labeled one of life's losers.

"After two weeks, he was abruptly demoted back to the kindergarten class, which also warehoused about forty children. His teacher tried to insist the move was due to overcrowding, but of course Billy saw straight through this lie. 'Overcrowding,' and only *one* kid is removed, and the problem kid at that? Billy wasn't quite as dumb as the school had counted on. He took his revenge in the new classroom where the pencils and erasers went flying. He acted exactly how everybody expected him to, and not one person was able to see his desperation.

"When he couldn't be managed in the kindergarten class, the principal ruled he'd have to stay home until an assessment could be done to 'certify' him for a special class. All well and good, except the problem with this was that the school psychologist lived out in Malibu and her home, which was supposed to be a showcase and her pride and joy, had been damaged recently by fire. Nobody seemed to have any clear idea when this woman would pull herself together enough to return to work. After being turned down for a leave of absence, I ended up having to quit my job and go on unemployment so there would be someone to stay with Billy. He was too old for his day care center to take him back even if they had wanted to, which they didn't. That night, Billy cried about how no teacher wanted him and the other kids didn't like him because he wasn't as smart as them.

"Thinking back on that time, I believe the most painful moments of all were before Billy got expelled, the afternoons I was called in, when I'd watch him come down the corridor with his new Lassie lunch pail dangling at his knees. I know the look on his face will always haunt me—a mixture of anger, hurt and defiance—like a small, trapped animal. When he would first see me, it was as though he were asking with his eyes why all this was suddenly happening to him. And I couldn't answer because there was no real answer that made any sense.

"About this time, Billy started to avoid eye contact and to have nightmares and episodes of sleepwalking.

"In the evenings I used to walk the dog past the darkened school and stare up at the windows. That innocuous-looking brick building was supposed to have been a happy place, releasing a child's potential for learning and capacity for a fulfilling life—all that good hype—but it had quickly become the embodiment of incredible (and needless) pain and suffering. I had to turn away to preserve the part of myself which was still sane, but whenever I'm in the neighborhood now I still drive by that school and remember.

"Waiting for the psychologist to begin the evaluation, Billy and I sat idly through the days. Twice each day, we watched from the window of our second-story apartment as the other kids went to school and returned. At precisely 8:30 a.m., a yellow school van stopped across the street to pick up a physically handicapped little girl and transport her to a special class. Around three in the afternoon, the van dropped her off.

"As the season deepened into autumn, we were wrapped in a stark gray emptiness. Depression on my part and boredom on Billy's set in, till I knew we were just barely holding on. I simply wasn't in a financial position where I could have afforded a private school or a full-day babysitter. And so, more and more, we were locked into the tiny space left us, which consisted of the walls of our fortress two-room apartment.

"During all this time, no one from the school called or tried to reach out to us in any way (most likely our compliant disappearance came as a relief to everyone), but I would call the School District office many times a day. At this level, the staff were usually either tied up in meetings, or away at some conference, or the person I finally got through to couldn't do anything about the situation. The chief psychologist for the district bemoaned her own situation for a good twenty minutes over the phone one day, letting me know just how hard the absenteeism among her staff was making *her* life. The latest word was that it would be six weeks, more or less, before the evaluation for an appropriate placement could begin.

"This next part is excruciating to write. Now Billy had always been 'different,' kind of an oddball loner who had trouble fitting in with the other kids despite his very normal looks—that had been apparent from the start. Even so, there had always been a lot of positive interaction and good times between us, and a bond in the evenings and on the weekends, which I believe had balanced out Billy's life and sustained in him some measure of enthusiasm for life. Suddenly all this changed.

"Suddenly, as though his rejection at school triggered a world of rage, he was running out in front of cars, stealing from the neighborhood stores, smashing the colored floodlights in the building next door, grinding his teeth in his sleep, and beating Beanbag, the dog and companion whom he had always loved. The bottom line quickly became his physical survival—his right to live to grow up despite his damage—and I started to live in terror each moment he was out of my sight.

"Later, I blamed myself for not being able to hold together, emotionally and financially, through those six weeks, which loomed as endless, until the evaluation would (maybe) begin. If Billy couldn't be in school—if I couldn't work—then I had no way to feed either of us for much longer. As it was, we no longer had a phone. Had my mistake been in counting on the fact that when my child was six years old, he would go to school for certain hours of the day like all other kids? I had depended on his being in public school for our survival as a family.

"On November 15, 1981, Billy was placed in a home for emotionally disturbed children on an emergency, short-term placement which was to last for over a year and become a lifelong hurt for both of us. At six years old, my child, for whom I had wished so happy a life, had become a ward of the state. In his eyes, the one person who had ever loved and wanted him had turned against him. He still cries over that time and is still angry with me for 'giving up on him.'

"A big part of both of us—the living part—was torn out of us the day I left him screaming in the lobby with his suitcase and his poor box of toys and keepsakes from home. And I just couldn't explain why he couldn't come home and live with me like we always had. That terrible time of helplessness to save my child, or even soften his suffering, is locked forever in my body.

"A year later, the very same day Billy was released from placement, an answer to one of my letters written before he ever left home arrived from the Office of the Superintendent of the Los Angeles Unified School District. In her crisp, optimistic reply, an administrative assistant apologized for the situation at Westside School and promised an immediate investigation and follow-up.

"Four years later, I've worked my way up in the banking business and am making some real money at long last. I have Billy in private school and in treatment with a psychologist. But because that first ordeal turned out to be a grim foreboding of his whole career in the regular schools, it's been a long, hard and expensive fight to try to get him to feel better about himself—that he's worthwhile and people will like him. As of this writing, he still has no friends but he's doing well for being Billy. Only looking back on the panorama of the last few years, I start to shake when I realize how close he came to some sort of permanent institutionalization because of the school problems which have seemed intractable.

"And while I can say we are both doing okay just now, there's an undercurrent of pain flowing just below the surface, as well as scars inside us from wounds that won't ever heal completely. I think that the sadness is an ache for all that might have been different and all we might have been spared in a more enlightened and humane system. Like a distant ray of light or hope that's almost, but not quite ever, tangible. We have the technology—medical, educational, biological and psychological—and yet we're still producing Billies because our priorities are always elsewhere.

"Long ago, I began a scrapbook for Billy which is filled with such pathetic memories of the false starts of his school life that I sometimes cannot bear to look at it. I can only hope that in the end, my voice will join with the voices of the parents, relatives and friends of other Billies, and one day prevail over all the ignorance and mismanagement."

Retribution and Revenge

An eye is owed him for an eye, your child feels with his primitive, simplistic logic—and some retaliation and a chance to even the score for what he is suffering. And if, in addition to school trauma, his home is truly a violent, hostile, or dangerous place, he will feel doubly wronged and unforgiving.

At older ages, despondency and depressive emotions which derive from diminished self-worth may be a little-recognized cause of physical and verbal assaults. The angry expressions are a reflection of your youngster's essential feelings of hopelessness and helplessness, which become his defensive coping strategy. As such, like a good deal of seemingly random destructive behavior, the aggressive acts are his cry for help.

Holding Actions

The achievement of control in a susceptible child is easiest if begun in infancy with the *tolerance training* which provides progressive increments of stimulation and frustration that his chaotic body can handle. The *exercises for movement control* described in the next section are also helpful in the area of inhibition of negative emotion. But at any stage along the way to adulthood, it is never too late to interrupt and remediate your youngster's pattern of impulsivity and violent expression. This is because most of his hostility is merely counterphobic to his feeling of anxiety and failure.

No method which bypasses your child's deep hurt can be curative, but there are a number of palliative techniques which allow children to discharge some of their hurt and violence safely. All of the early interventions described under social remedies, such as holding your immature child back from school, and ensuring that his first experience is positive by arranging a gradual introduction and a small, stable group of peers, will definitely help if your youngster has not yet been traumatized by school.

An older child who is enraged and beginning to generalize his anger may need *a two-part remediation* in which the first phase is a holding action until his nervous system matures and he has gained a backlog of experiences and enough ego strength to tolerate the second phase, which is the kind of professional therapy which attempts to get at the roots of his rage and buried need. (As to when, or if, your child will need professional help, the answer is when all the corrective methods you have tried, such as providing him with therapeutic friendships, school help, and especially, a good deal of positive attention from you, have failed to bring about any noticeable improvement in his self-esteem.)

It can be a serious mistake to try to force your child into feelings he cannot really handle or push him into revelations which can arouse great anxiety and guilt. This can only be felt as a deeper invasion of his privacy. And if, besides school humiliation and failure, he is harboring other great hurts—such as abandonment or rejection by a parent—psychotherapy will almost certainly have to wait on his biochemical and emotional growth. No therapy is going to work for anyone of any age who isn't convinced he really needs the treatment.

Holding actions for the child with impulsive reactions consist first of all of *encouraging mastery of the environment in which he feels out of control by fostering his skills and abilities.* Inborn talents can become enduring sources of richness in a lonely, frustrated life. For instance, your child may have a gift for carpentry, mechanics, or drawing which, encouraged, can hold him together through some difficult times by providing him with a sense of achievement and self-respect.

Most of us believe instinctively the celebrities who reveal in intimate, tell-all interviews how they have overcome deep-seated feelings of shyness, worthlessness, or ugliness, or speech defects and the like, but for some reason we lack the same faith in our children. Yet some of the specific talents and compensations of learning disabled children can be nothing short of remarkable.

One enterprising boy with mechanical skills who was otherwise an abject failure started a bicycle repair shop in his backyard. The business not only thrived, but led to the begrudging respect—if not the friendship—of the neighborhood children. The boy reminded his amazed father, a veterinarian, of the many domestic animals with amputated limbs or sightless eyes who spring and leap everywhere, and appear to enjoy life as three-legged or blind creatures fully as much as they enjoyed it before their trauma. Compensational psychology, as a separate division of the psychology of loss and grieving, is a virtually unexplored area which could teach us all a good deal.

Other ameliorative methods to keep the tension level down include being aware of *timing*, especially when your child is under special stress, such as during the mid-morning or late afternoon "peak" times when his blood sugar level drops sharply between meals, or before a test or a sports competition at school. None of these times would be right for pressuring your child to finish the yard work or clean out the garage.

Physical expressions like sports if he is comfortable with them, hurling a tennis ball against an outside wall, yelling about his problem, pounding a punching bag with boxing gloves, or using battacas (foam-rubber paddles) and Hula Hoops are all useful in helping break up the masonry of inner feelings. Velcro dart boards can introduce a welcome, restorative note of humor if your child draws cartoons or caricatures of hated or hurtful persons to throw at.

When your growing child is angry, he needs room to resolve his feeling, so don't crowd him at these moments. To diffuse your own anger and frustration, try to stop and look at the conflictual situation from your youngster's point of view. Power struggles can be never-ending as well as destructive to your relationship. *The best way to handle disputes is by offering your child a choice.* If, for example, he refuses to do his homework, tell him he can either stay at the table and do his assignment or leave and take the consequences the next day.

Another holding approach that can eventually become a self-screening technique for your child is to ask him to tell you the three or four things he can think of that make him angriest of all. Sentence-completion worksheets with blanks to fill in like those used by elementary school teachers to help children explore their emotions—e.g., "I feel upset when——"; "One of the things I feel angry about is——"; "It bothers me when——," can be borrowed for home use. Another technique is to get your child to describe in a direct, two-part sentence situations that make him furious. In the first section, he should say just what the problem situation is. In the second, he should tell the other person(s) how the situation makes him feel.

For example, your child might say to his friend (on paper), "When you go off to play with the other kids and leave me alone, I feel like smashing you." "Because that makes you feel how?" you prod ever so gently. "Like you don't want Peter for your friend? Like you're nobody at all?" Such sore spots and sensitivities are likely to be sources of recurrent resentment that crop up time and again, so save all your child's worksheets for continuing conversations about the situations that trigger his rage and indignation.

Deep and calming breaths, "sighing" exercises, and other relaxation techniques are quick ways of reducing tension by changing the physiology of the body. *Breathing exercises* like those taught in yoga class (or yoga books) can be especially useful in dissipating angry energy. Tell your child to inhale deeply through his nose, hold his breath for a slow count of five, then exhale forcefully so he makes a sharp sound and can feel his body go limp. He can repeat this exercise at one-minute intervals until he feels the tension ease.

With his eyes closed and his hands on his diaphragm, your child can practice counting to five as he breathes in, holding his breath for one count, then exhaling in five counts. The time-honored stopgap of counting to ten when he feels rage starting to build up inside can also buy some time which will allow him to think about the consequences of a temper outburst. And, in a calm moment, you can ask your child to list two or three adults in his school he can turn to for help at those shaky times when he is about to spell out his anger. Your child can also be aided in remembering to think before he acts if you tell him to visualize your face as he feels his anger about to overflow. Or perhaps his visualization can be a mental image of you pointing a finger and warning him to "think, think."

"Flooding" techniques consist of having your child release his anger about a particular situation over and over again in imaginary ways beyond the point where it has an emotional impact, so that it "neutralizes" or becomes boring. It's also helpful to try to get him to express some of his angry feeling *before* he becomes overloaded.

Most therapeutic of all is if your child can learn to tell you when he's losing his temper so you can intervene to help him with his fragile control. At early ages, you can devise a *signal system* such as eye contact, winking, or a certain hand movement by which either of you can indicate that removal from a stressful situation should be imminent.

Moving your older child from a physical to a verbal or talking-things-through level of anger expression is easier and more effective if you first help him to become aware of the *cognitive and/or emotional precursors* or precipitants of his anger. Fatigue, hunger, frustration, impending illness, and certain "dangerous" children, situations, or times of the day are some of the common influences or "cues" you can help your child identify which increase his vulnerability to provocation.

For neurological children, the fear of showing weakness and lack of skill is an extra source of touchiness and emotional lability. The reassurance that you are on his side as a partner in helping him control his outbursts will help your child to feel better about himself at any age.

It can sometimes help immensely if you promote self-assertion in small things such as encouraging your child to speak up to his teacher about a minor injustice which may otherwise build with other grievances into a major blowup or declaration of war. Similarly, helping your child to recognize the *shades and variants* of his angry feeling—whether annoyance, disappointment, discouragement, loss, or deep rage over a humiliation or rejection—can give him more cognitive control, as can helping him formulate *alternatives to violence*. Writing a letter to a senator or the president of a company about a defective product (and receiving a replacement), returning a toy or other object for a refund, or simply suggesting "Let's try this and this and this before we give up" are simple examples which can teach your child to make up for a disappointment or relieve a frustration.

Malevolent Transformation

Occasional expressions of unfairness and revenge, specific sensitivities, sporadic argumentativeness, and physical fights, up to the age of ten, are not necessarily causes for concern. It's when anger and resentment become chronic, and irritability, sullenness, and discontent a way of life, that there is reason for worry. This sort of corkscrew twist in a child's development proclaims louder than any words how cheated he feels. Through his rage, he is trying, though doomfully, to make things the way they *ought* to be—rather than the way they really are. And if your child's home life is as unrewarding, random, and empty as his school life, there is just no respite for his anger over why any of this has to be.

All children—even learning retarded ones, who are never likewise handicapped in their capacity to feel—recognize with a deep instinctive wisdom that nobody's life ever *has* to be so all-out hard and miserable. But for reasons which do not add up to sense, living in a painful, hurting way seems the conscious choice of the adults who rule him. While waiting for your child to grow strong enough to confront the sources of his store of wrath directly, you need all the anger-management techniques at your disposal to promote reasonableness and a more controlled and conforming emotional approach. The time when he is ready for therapy, you have to accept, may not come until late in adolescence.

During psychological treatment, your youngster is likely to experience long plateaus of barely suppressed anger, black moods, and magnified outbursts before there is any permanent improvement. But with each cycle of rising and subsiding rage—provided he stays with the therapy—his reactions will even out and "mellow" more and more.

Remediating Anger in Your Preadolescent

·   Preadolescence is one of those critical times in development when children are wide open to change—for the better or the worse. If you are faced with the knotty problem of tempering anger in a preadolescent, the guiding principle you need to trust is that *no child can hold out for long if all the adults around him remain firm, consistent, and unswerving in their attitudes, behavior, and expectations.* Despite how your youngster's violence and storminess might have caused you to distort his "powers," you need to remind yourself he is only a child after all, unable to provide the necessities of life or fend for himself without your support.

And because your preadolescent may well be poised on the brink of a full-scale rebellion, it's all the more crucial that the significant adults in his life do not give him any ammunition for his "cause," such as taking his side against a teacher, school, or legal requirement. If everyone insists that he behave appropriately, he must give in to this solid barrier which acts like a dam for the pounding waves of his emotions, *simply because he has to.*

Standing your ground may be especially difficult if you have allowed your child to count on the soft, hesitant part of you that always relents and changes sides in the end. Above all else, as your youngster grows into independence, he needs the sense that you are still bigger and stronger in an emotional way, and in control of things—or else he has no real stability but only a sidewalk of perilous cracks under him. If your guilt over his difference has crippled him even more than the neurological condition itself, then he cannot truly put his trust in you.

At some strategic point, the responsibility for his negative behavior will have to shift to him. At that time, as the occasions arise, you will have to give him the credit for being able to rescue himself from the problematic situations he has created (up to and sometimes including legal difficulties). One twelve-year-old whose exhausted parents finally made the decision to have separate lives—a brand new attitude they needed to reinforce repeatedly over a number of months—asked to see *Return of the Jedi* five times. It turned out to be part of the working out of his inner conflict between "good" and "evil" impulses which he identified with Luke Skywalker's dramatic technicolored moral battle in outer space.

What is sad, but so often true, is that by puberty your child's nervous system may have "caught up" so his physiological control over his impulses has increased but his feelings have not kept pace with his body. Lowered self-regard and habit—and perhaps also the violent example of those around him—outstrip his improved judgment time and again. But even if this seems the case with your youngster, at some point before adolescence, which you can judge best, you are going to have to trust all the survival skills you have helped him learn in his early years.

What you will be giving him in this momentous passage—though it may frighten both of you since it conflicts with the longing to remain attached—is the gift of control over his own destiny, which is tantamount to the dawning of maturity in him and the liberation from too much intensity in you.

The Wellsprings of Rage

In a few cases, a violent child who shows learning difficulties, unpredictability, and blowups which do not improve over time may be suffering from a mild form of a seizure-related disorder such as epilepsy. A youngster over the age of ten who still hits, pushes, bites, or kicks when he gets angry, and appears genuinely amnesic for what occurred immediately before an act of aggression or consistently distorts the cause-effect sequence, should be scheduled for a neurological examination including an EEG (electroencephalogram or brain-wave test).

All neurological children have problems in communication to a greater or lesser degree, and may not understand why a physical way of reacting is worse than a verbal way. The "obvious" often escapes them, which is why you need to spell out right and wrong over and over again. But if you have made a sincere effort to improve your child's life and he is still responding with inappropriate rage reactions in which he is the aggressor, the possibility that he is suffering from psychomotor or temporal lobe seizures needs to be explored at a special clinic or children's hospital.

Far more frequently, a child's chronic disagreeableness, negativity, and grossly inconsistent behavior, which can mystify even the best therapists, comes from his feeling that no one seems to be responsibly involved with him. All the adults in his world—parents, teachers, counselors, and grandparents—may appear overworked, harried, exhausted, and barely making it through the hard days themselves.

Your child's behavior can escalate into almost total impulsivity as an expression of his desperate attempt to force someone to find the time and energy to direct and control him, and organize his life, so he can behave better and doesn't have to feel so bad about himself. He may feel great scary urges to get even or hurt others back, but what frightens him more than anything is the dangerous beast inside him (bear, lion, or tiger) howling out his hurt—which is the reverse side of his need to be liked and treated well. *For the child who is feeling murderous is really trying to kill the pain inside himself—the feeling that no one cares.* What he needs to silence his hurt is simply a person who cares enough about him to help him tame his violent response.

An older youngster who can't get the recognition, appreciation, and acceptance he craves from adults may discover that he can easily earn the respect of his peer group by violent episodes directed against others or their property. When a conduct-disordered child acts as though he has a *need* or a compulsion to get into fights, constantly harass and tease, and watch the scariest TV shows and sexiest movies, it's because he knows he will gain status in the eyes of his peers.

Sometimes your impulsive child may be angriest at himself, and needs help in self-forgiveness. The pain of failure, which amounts in his mind to the loss of parental love, is just too unbearable, and he may project or "give" the blame for his shortcomings and lack of success to others.

Often, of all the deterrents which may be straws in a windstorm of primal forces, the most effective of all when your child is walled off in his angry, living hell is if you make the first offer of friendship. Tell him firmly that you disapprove of his misbehavior, but then speak straight to your good little boy or girl of bygone days: "No matter what happens, you won't ever lose me. *I will still be here.*"

Movement Therapy

Traditionally, remediation of academic difficulties has focused on the smallest, most molecular elements of a child's performance, such as painstaking drill in the slants, lines, and curves of penmanship. The movement therapy approach through large-muscle activity and behavioral "wholes" has become a way to break with this restrictive educational practice—as well as a way to introduce a little fun and success into a problem youngster's life.

The theory behind exercise, dance, and movement principles is that these subject areas can be powerful tools for promoting the integrative processes of the young brain. By incorporating the simultaneous experience of time, space, and energy, and reinforcing concentration, "muscle memory," and sequencing ability, they reach beyond specific skills to enhance a child's *general* learning potential—for even the most academic discipline. And a bonus is that many educators believe that movement therapy curbs violent outbursts and antisocial behavior in impulsive children by improving their bodily control and redirecting their enormous physical energy into more positive channels.

At-Home Baby Dynamics

"Baby dynamics" classes, which are exercise programs for infants to two years, have become popular offerings in neighborhood recreational centers in the last few years. The training is especially helpful for "high-risk" babies who have shown some neurological maladaptation or sensorimotor retardation. Because the child must be accompanied by an adult, the experience involves touching and stroking your baby, and in some cases may even have the added benefit of helping you tone your own body.

A home analogue of the infantile programs would involve helping the child who seems slow or inept to achieve certain behaviors, all of which can be observed easily in everyday contact, at approximately the usual ages. Special help consists of guiding your infant's face, hands, and legs with your hands. Most activities will have to be repeated over and over again until a sense of self-awareness develops and the behavior becomes a fixed part of your child's repertoire.

The following chart of developmental "milestones" can be used as a guide in creating your own program of early "adaptive" physical education for your infant's specific needs and hiatuses. When a deliberate attempt is made to increase the infant's motility and coordination, to expand his experiences of kinesthetic and tactile feedback, and to integrate his sensory impressions from different modalities (including visually directed reaching and grasping), the rewards will always outweigh the parent's effort.

> *1 month*—lifts head slightly to clear chin while lying on stomach; focuses on faces about a yard away; attends to sounds; regards rattle placed in line of vision; looks at objects overhead; tracks a

dangling ring to the midline of body; grasps fingers placed inside
his own; turns head from side to side; follows a moving object a
few degrees

2 months—holds head erect without sagging when held in sitting
position; tracks objects past midline; stops movements and listens
to voices; follows a moving object 180 degrees; smiles spontaneously

2¹/₂ months—brings hands together in front of chest

3 months—elevates head and chest on outstretched arms while lying
on stomach; rolls over partially either way; holds objects placed in
hand; babbles; swings or "bats" at toys; smiles, laughs, coos

4 months—rolls over on both sides; holds head steady when propped
up; reaches arms toward object on a table; notices voices and
recognizes parent; looks at objects placed in hand; plays with
hands in front of chest; struggles when face is covered with a cloth

5 months—rolls over onto stomach from back; participates in playful,
simple games; removes a cloth placed over face

6–6¹/₂ months—sits alone leaning on hands; reaches and grasps
with one hand; turns head to sounds; grabs large objects; repeats
self-produced sounds; distinguishes between familiar people and
strangers; cries on separation

7–7¹/₂ months—takes weight on feet; sits without support; reaches
and grasps with two hands; transfers objects between hands; holds
onto two objects briefly; reaches for toys placed out of range;
plays with feet; turns toward a voice from behind; imitates speech
sounds

8 months—sits well with back straight; plays with two objects at a
time; pulls to a standing position

9 months—creeps on hands and knees; pokes with forefinger; picks
up small objects such as raisins, crumbs, or threads with thumb
and fingers in opposition; vocalizes demands; waves bye-bye; walks
holding onto furniture (you can line up a path for him); responds
to name; rolls, kicks, arches back; shows pleasure at familiar voices
and faces; persists in interest in one toy or object

10 months—says "dada" or "mama" to mean parent; sits steady for
long periods; stands briefly

11 months—walks with hands held; shakes rattle; bangs two objects
together; plays pat-a-cake

12 months—walks without help; holds up arms to be picked up; retrieves hidden objects; rolls ball back; holds still for dressing and feeding; gives objects on request; recognizes objects by name; understands "no-no"

14 months—uses spoon crudely to get food to mouth; plays taking things out of a container (not dumping)

15 months—piles objects; says three words besides "mama" and "dada"

18 months—walks toddler gait and seldom falls; climbs up stairs; pushes and pulls toys; seats self in small chair; builds tower of three blocks; names or points to several common objects; takes off coat, shoes, socks, or pants; scribbles spontaneously with pencil; imitates vertical strokes with crayon; turns pages of a book singly

21 months—kicks a ball with demonstration; squats in play; builds a tower of five to six blocks

24 months—runs well; kicks a ball on command; walks up and down stairs alone; opens doors; builds a tower of six to seven blocks; listens to stories with pictures; imitates circular scribbling and horizontal strokes in drawing; combines two or three different words to make a meaningful phrase (e.g., "allgone milk," "mama go store"); points to own body parts; uses "I," "me," "you," "mine"

Body Awareness, Balance, and Agility

Infant swimming classes help develop body awareness and sensation, and also provide an opportunity for holding, cradling, and reassuring your child as he bobs up and down in the water. *Modern dance, gymnastic, mime, or martial arts classes* are all excellent choices for an organized exposure to movement for your preschool child. Aikido or T'ai-Chi, gentle and subdued forms of the defensive arts which are really more like dances in slow motion and self-control, are especially recommended.

If your time is limited, arranging to have your youngster's school or babysitter transport him to one of these special movement groups several times a week is well worth the effort and any additional expense it may entail.

At home, your child can bounce on a trampoline to improve his body alignment and increase perception of his body boundaries, practice walking on a straight chalk line (indoors or outdoors), use hoops or safety stilts, pump a swing, play waiter with trays containing paper cups of water, and imitate the Balinese islanders who gracefully bear baskets or calabashes filled with food on their heads or the Kaleri tribesmen who skillfully stride erect under heavy loads by balancing baskets or books on his head to improve his balance. You can make a *balance beam* for your child by placing a smooth 3-inch board between stacks of phone books a few inches from the floor. Have him walk on this surface without shoes.

Activities in slow motion such as having your child imitate the mechanical qualities of a robot or a machine, or the slow, lumbering, heavy movements of a polar bear on all fours, can teach muscular control. So can exercises alternating between sharp, angular, primitive movements (imitating a storm, a tornado, a jackhammer, or a forest in rainy season) and smooth, gentle, and restrained motions (mimicking the fragile, tinselly fall of rain or snow with the arms and body, or inching along on the ground earthworm style).

A simple exercise in controlled movement is to have your child practice alternating between running, skipping, and galloping, and making right and left turns sharply and smoothly while running. Avoiding the ball in a game of dodgeball can promote agility by teaching him to adjust his position speedily.

Often, your learning impaired child has to *feel* the subject matter before he can grasp it. Children can actually "become" letters, numbers, and shapes by bending and stretching their bodies, writing letters in the sky, and feeling numbers, letters, and words traced on their back or arms. And all these physical movements are closely associated with verbal experiences, making them that much more valuable as learning situations.

Exercises to expand your child's awareness of *position in space* include locating and identifying body parts ("finding" the parts of the body when told to touch his neck, ankle, and knee, etc.), knowing right and left on his own body, and learning to go *under* a table, *over* a chair, *around* or *behind* a desk, and so on. Judgment of spatial relations can also be strengthened by copying patterns with pegs, beads, or marbles, and by assembling large, simple puzzles.

Coordination and Manual Dexterity

Fine motor coordination can be increased in your child by providing him with small tools or objects which he has to manipulate in a given way in relation to his body. Interlocking cubes and blocks that can be clipped together and taken apart only by using both hands are especially helpful for the youngest children. Everyday exercises include pouring liquids, dialing a telephone, screwing on bottle caps, washing fingerprints off walls, spraying and misting plants, stirring batters and mixes in small bowls, and sorting pictures and pasting them in an album.

Play activities which foster coordination, finger dexterity, and arm-hand steadiness are cutting, coloring, pasting, "shooting" in a game of marbles, knitting, stringing beads, and playing with blocks, Legos, yo-yos, jacks, stencils, weaving looms, pop beads, cookie cutters, Ping-Pong sets, and Velcro dart boards. Coordination in large-muscle activities can be bolstered by bicycle riding, swings, minimotorbikes, scooters, skateboards, and bowling games. Simple outdoor activities in which young children can use the muscles in their hands, fingers, and arms are pouring, mixing, and experimenting with sand and water.

More creative activities are telling your child to pretend his fingers are raindrops ("It's raining hard and now it's sprinkling") and having him pretend to be "typing" a letter. If you have your child simulate the whole sequence—first typing, then folding the page, licking the stamp, and mailing the finished product—this exercise can also advance his *sequencing ability* (and verbal skills, too, if you ask him to talk about the steps as he moves through them). Other simple game sequences which have a definite beginning, middle, and end are tennis strokes, which necessitate follow-through, and reaching for an imaginary apple you "place" in front of him, bringing it slowly to his mouth, biting into it, chewing, and swallowing.

Since it's especially important to emphasize slow movements with excitable youngsters, you can ask your child to wait before reaching for the "apple" or other object until you count leisurely to five (or beat five times on a small drum), and then to take five more counts to bring it to his mouth and another five counts to chew the bites.

Another strategy for using his body in space is to have your child maneuver from one corner of a room to another while lying prone on the floor. Meanwhile you can plant an *"obstacle course"* so he has to crawl under a table, step over a box, and so on, to get back across the room.

Specific exercises to promote *body coordination and flexibility* include bouncing, rotating stretches, sit-ups, and touching the floor while keeping the knees straight. There are a number of well-illustrated paperback children's exercise books which can be important home aids—especially if your child practices in an uncarpeted room, in front of a full-length mirror. Another option is taking an exercise, aerobics, or yoga class together.

In all of this effort, the goal of slowing down your child's activities and helping him gain a range of movement from light to heavy should be foremost. Starting with large-muscle activity, you can introduce a pattern of brisk walking or jogging alternating with slow, deliberate movements like body bends or catlike stretches.

On fine motor work, you need to make your child aware when he is using too great pressure on a crayon, pencil, toothbrush, or hairbrush, and to point out or demonstrate the varying degrees of force actually needed for different tasks. You may have to place your hands over his to help him become aware of when he should stiffen or relax his grip. Handicrafts; lacing kits; sewing; cooking; polishing furniture; washing and drying dishes; shampooing; massaging; staining wood; using pliers, tweezers, and screwdrivers; and scraping insulation off electrical wires—these are among the simple activities which promote flexibility in increasing and decreasing hand pressure.

Steady, sustained movements requiring greater effort which teach your child to *focus and prolong his attention span* include hiking (especially uphill), backpacking, sledding, climbing trees, weight training, skiing, skating, surfing, pushing a manual lawn mower, and shoveling snow. Any game with a ball can provide practice in controlled movement and coordination—*if* your child can be eased into competitive situations without excessive anxiety. Or you can try him on individual, "fail-safe" sports such as acrobatics, tumbling, or horseback riding.

Outdoor tasks which teach control of physical energy include gardening chores such as raking leaves, clipping hedges, watering lawns, and sweeping pathways with a broom. Indoors, your young child can learn to make a bed, fold sheets and towels, and dust the furniture, baseboards, and walls.

Some heavy, concentrated work activities for older children are building pet houses, chicken coops, rabbit hutches, sheds, or brick walls, and painting, hammering, sawing, and repairing furniture. Physical boisterousness can also be channeled into vigorous household chores like scrubbing the floors and woodwork, beating out pillows and rugs, vacuuming, and kneading bread dough.

Rhythm and Music

Many academic and play activities carried out to music can enhance your slightly older child's coordination and awareness of his body
rhythm. Some Little Golden Books now have music in the records
which accompany the texts, and several department stores are marketing
Multiplication Rock records, which introduce a "learning beat" into
rote memory tasks. For the youngster who shows an interest in music,
banjo, drum, trumpet, piano, or guitar lessons can become his ticket of
acceptability into a social group in lieu of verbal-social skills.

Over the last few years, music lessons for children have changed
dramatically into a child-centered activity. The contemporary emphasis
is on presenting musical patterns in a variety of different ways so that
youngsters hear, sing, and otherwise *experience* the music before they
ever learn to read the notes.

Often, music becomes an enduring balm for the lonely, different
child, just as reading develops so frequently into the supreme comfort of
the neurologically normal but solitary and alienated youngster.

Tailoring an Exercise Program

Just observing your child as he goes about his daily activities can
give you important clues to specific exercises he could benefit from. For
example, you may notice that he lacks leg strength and needs practice
with movements requiring *leg muscle effort* such as knee bends, skipping,
jumping, stair-climbing, and broad jumping. Doorway chinning bars,
sit-ups and throwing objects improve body integration in a child who
lacks *upper body strength*, as does swimming—which has the attractive
potential as well of becoming a family activity, involving his brothers
and sisters.

Learning *directions in space* such as right, left, north, and south can
help if your child always seems slightly disoriented and confused in a
crowd. When you are out, you can teach him to look for landmarks like
tall buildings, large rocks, or odd-shaped trees. Helping him to draw
floor plans of his room, home, and school can also sharpen his ability to
recognize spatial relationships.

An extremely scattered child with only a patchy sense of geography
can gain a degree of independence and pride by carrying a *notebook* with
detailed directions or photographs of the path he is to follow to the store,
the routes he must take to school or the playground, and so on.

Your child's *physical posture* can speak more plainly than anything else of his emotions. Tense or sagging shoulders, neck, or head usually mean he's feeling down. He may protect certain parts of his body with his hands, appear withdrawn or too "wide open," or avoid eye contact. His eyes may tell of his anger, hurt, disappointment, or self-shame.

Getting your child to express his emotion physically won't solve all of life's problems, but a healthy confidence in one's own body is an important part of self-esteem at any age. An increasing number of psychotherapies for adults are including "body work" to break down somatic defenses and resistances—the bodily "armor" an individual has hammered up around himself over the years. For normal adults who have lost the connection with their bodies and retracted like turtles into their heads, this physical rehabilitation is a helpful way to get to know their bodies all over again.

Movement-Socialization Techniques

Sensory living room games which involve teamwork include having two partners "move" an imaginary table (with a glass on it) across a room; letting them "become" concepts such as hot and cold, objects like can openers, or emotions like anger, fear, and happiness; and assigning one child to play a sculptor while another acts as the clay. Two or more children can be given hats, scarves, makeup, and shoes with which to role-play somebody else (the "new" person can then be interviewed by the other child), or they can guess what a pantomimist is doing, whether combing his hair, drinking from a cup, driving a car, or walking a tightrope.

Children can practice hand clapping and finger snapping to music and "pass along" a rhythmic activity, beat, or movement from one child to the next. Social activities which make use of *keyed instructions* such as square or folk dancing combine physical exuberance with a large number of mental operations. And it also helps immensely to further your child's socialization if you take another movement-oriented child along on hikes, nature walks, and excursions to playgrounds and amusement parks.

Expensive educational toys like "creative activity centers," toddlers' gyms, climbing equipment, rocking boats, special learning steps, crawl-through tunnels, and puzzles with knobs are all nice but totally unnecessary. Most public parks have swings and jungle gyms—and hillsides, mountain trails, and snow for sledding on cardboard are free to anyone who might want to enjoy them.

Playground apparatus can be used to teach prepositional, adjective, and adverb concepts (on, under, near, toward, over, and so on) as well as synonyms and antonyms (up/down, fast/slow, etc.). Presenting activities in which your child and a companion walk, hopscotch, or skip the shapes of letters and numbers—or feel each other's facial and neck muscles as sounds are being made—are more simple ways of strengthening kinesthetic-motor perception along with social skills.

One last physical technique that links your child's body response with a wide range of learning is to train him to *consciously relax* the muscles of his body while he is trying to acquire or assimilate new material. This method works really well for youngsters (and adults) of all ages.

By focusing on the spatial and temporal dimensions of movement which cause the neurological child special difficulty, all of the exercises described in this section support the academic curriculum. And because almost every child responds enthusiastically to physical activity, movement and exercise therapies are about the easiest, most enjoyable way to ready your child's unruly body for learning.

5

Helpful at Any Age

Diet

The passionate controversy in the last few years over the role diet and sensitivity to foods and food additives play in hyperactivity has served mainly to confuse and discourage parents. This regrettable situation has come about because all too often the claims of proponents of the various special diets and vitamin regimes have been exaggerated, global, and overly optimistic.

Books on cooking for behaviorally troubled children almost always start out by citing case histories of the class disrupter or "cut-up" normalized overnight into a solid citizen who cleans the blackboard erasers and empties the trash, merely as the result of removing a few foods or additives—such as milk, chocolate, wheat, and food colors—from his diet. Any person who eats properly, the new evangelists maintain, balances the proportion of zinc, potassium, and certain vital trace minerals in his body, and eliminates the need for tranquilizers, sedatives, stimulants, antidepressants, and other medication.

Nutritional theories are especially seductive because they are nicely linear, involving a behavioral response or output that is directly proportional to the input. The only problem with the theory is that human development and behavior are not so correspondingly simple.

Sadly, all the undocumented and hearsay accounts have obscured the solid information about nutrition that *does* exist and does indicate that paying careful attention to your child's diet can definitely help in controlling aggressive, violent behavior. While poor diets or specific food intolerances are rarely the whole cause or solution in behavior deviance, enough facts have been gathered to suggest that improving children's diets is well worth the effort.

Most of the evidence comes from studies done in juvenile detention facilities which have shown decreases in assaults, fighting, disobedience, violent episodes, suicide attempts, and verbal threats when high-sugar food, candy, and soft drinks were removed from meal lines. And since, paradoxically, our era of increased nutritional knowledge coexists with a decrease in quality (though not quantity) of diet in a large proportion of the American population, you may well find that *all* family members, including yourself—not just the target child—will function better and increase their coping ability with an improved diet.

Switching Your Child's Eating Habits

One precaution: Any change in food patterns needs to be an enterprise in which the whole family pulls together. To head off a revolt on your hands, it's best to begin your nutritional effort with a gradual elimination of certain foods, along with the introduction of others in small quantities, rather than to attempt a sweeping, New Year's changeover.

Some easy substitutions you can put into effect immediately are:

White cheese for yellow

Whole-grain breads, rolls, and crackers for white

Unrefined honey in gradually reduced amounts, or vanilla, carob, mashed banana, sorghum, natural fruit flavorings, or fruit concentrates such as date sugar or syrup, all as replacements for refined sugar

More natural sweeteners are the so-called sweet spices like cinnamon, ginger, cloves, nutmeg, and allspice. Combined with fruits such as baked or stewed apples and pears, these spices can create desserts that fill your child's craving for cakes and cookies.

Any project that involves nutrition must begin in the supermarket or health food store with *a careful reading of labels*, which will permit you to recognize offending foods. Sugar, for instance, masquerades under several different names; dextrose, sucrose, lactose, glucose, corn syrup, maltose, sorbitol, mannitol, and molasses are the most common disguises or "hoaxes." Any products which include one of these ingredients in the first five items on the label should be left on the shelf. You should also be aware that the word "natural" on food products has no official definition, and doesn't automatically exclude harmful substances.

Some suggestions for books on diet and recipes are given in Appendix IV, but generally speaking, any diet that eliminates or reduces the intake of salt, refined white sugar and flour, artificial flavorings and colorings, and "junk food" will ameliorate behavioral and physical difficulties—especially irritability and depression—and increase energy, staying-power, and stamina to withstand frustration. Other foods which have been implicated in children's behavior problems are concentrated fruit juices and grapes, oranges, and other fruits which contain excessive amounts of the fruit sugar fructose.

Changing a child's (or parent's) eating patterns won't work an instant cure if he has been physically hooked on sugar. It may be as long as two or three months before you notice any appreciable easing off of your child's frantic chasing, racing, and chaotic behavior. For the first few weeks, as his body undergoes physical withdrawal from certain foods to which he may have been "addicted," his symptoms may actually worsen into escalated touchiness, moodiness, sadness, and susceptibility to outbursts. Just in case, you should be prepared to counter these temporary setback behaviors with self-assurance, forgiveness, and optimism for the future.

Sweets-Craving

Pinpointing the reasons why so many hyperactive children turn out to be sweets cravers has been a matter or sterile debate in some medical circles. Many physicians are convinced that overactive children begin life with an enzyme-chemical dysfunction that produces a fluctuating blood sugar response, which, in turn, leads to erratic behavior. Others argue that it is just the other way around—that the dangerous foods themselves bring about the physiological changes that result in impulsivity and loss of control. But this futile "cart-horse" argument aside, the primary reason why your child's behavior falls apart with concentrated sweets is that these foods stimulate the release of adrenaline, an anxiety-accompanying hormone which acts on the body the way flooring the gas pedal "acts" on a car. "Normally" keyed-up and thrill-seeking children surely don't need more of this substance.

From the parental perspective, it doesn't really matter whether your youngster's hunger for sweets is part and parcel of the biochemical imbalance basic to his organic pattern, or whether he has simply stumbled on his "drug of choice" precociously earlier than the rest of us. (The greatest trouble with this is that, like most drugs, sugar impairs, coarsens, and disorganizes behavior.) All we truly need to know is the basic fact that *reducing sugar and increasing protein and selected carbohydrates in a child's diet acts like a nervous system sedative.*

The staples which should form the bulk of your child's diet are high-protein foods like meat, fish, poultry, eggs, cheese, wheat germ, and soybeans, and carbohydrates such as dark-grain breads and cereals. All of these "core foods" increase the supply of three essential brain chemicals—norepinephrine, acetylcholine, and serotonin—which researchers believe are responsible for feelings of well-being, "time-released energy," and the ability to learn and remember new information.

A multi-vitamin and mineral tablet given after breakfast, with the addition of C and B-complex vitamins during the day, and the availability of high-protein snacks (peanuts, peanut or almond butter on half a slice of whole-wheat toast, hard-boiled egg, a cup of bean or lentil soup, cheese or meat) will also help ease your child's bodily transition. And your older youngster can help you menu-plan by selecting balanced meals from the free pictorial charts and booklets published by the National Dairy Council (see Appendix IV).

Early Nutritional Strategies

The facts on diet, behavior, crime and delinquency may not yet be all in, but the specialized branch of medicine known as nutritional counseling is growing by almost daily leaps and bounds. At this very minute, some far-seeing parents are trying a nutrition "experiment" in which they are rearing their children in the first two years on a diet of limited salt intake and no sugar on the theory that a youngster whose metabolism has not been "deranged" or thrown off kilter by a diet of nonfoods won't miss what he has never known.

Only time and a good deal of effort, patience, and caring will tell whether such early "food conditioning" methods, which involve preparing all baby foods yourself, will be helpful in reducing behavior difficulties. But if you are inclined to give this worthwhile project a try, you will find it reassuring that making your own baby food isn't that hard. A bonus is that homemade food costs far less than the commercial product.

Until a few years ago, there was a valid concern that the prepared foods had too much salt in them. Since then, most of the baby food manufacturers—ever willing to defer to changes in parental attitude when huge sums of money are involved—have eliminated the salt problem. The ongoing problem is that many commercial baby foods still contain fillers such as water (used to thin the product to a desired consistency), corn starch, and/or sugar. And some of the enzyme systems that metabolize various substances are not fully developed in young children, which is why foods like sugar and alcohol have a much greater effect on them.

Parents making meals from scratch like pureed vegetables can choose to add more nutritious thinners such as vegetable cooking water, plain yogurt, fruit or vegetable juices, a sprinkling of brewer's yeast, milk, or meat broth. After the first ten months, when your baby is ready for a thicker consistency, you can add uncooked wheat germ, hard-cooked egg yolk, cooked brown rice or buckwheat, a variety of cereals, or nonfat dry milk powder before pureeing. Many excellent paperbacks on preparing and storing baby food are in the bookstores.

Mid-Afternoon and Evening Relief

As your child grows, it's helpful to always keep protein snacks handy for nibbling, and also to feed him half of his dinner about two hours before the regular family meal. This stratagem is a stopgap which helps to combat the terrible mid-afternoon behavior that is intensified by a sharp drop in the blood sugar level late in the day. For the same reason, a protein snack is mandatory in the late morning—another "peak" period for the obstreperous child.

Some youngsters can be lured into eating their vegetables by growing a garden—which is also a constructive way to work off their excessive energy. You can also substitute acceptable "junk food" treats such as popcorn or potato chips at a sports event or a movie.

Wild activity and insomnia at bedtime can be relieved by eating foods rich in the amino acid tryptophan, which produces a substance called serotonin in the brain. The richest known sources of tryptophan are cashew nuts, sunflower and pumpkin seeds, meats, poultry, cheese, and milk. As with most other foods, nutritionists aren't sure that eating more of the amino acid influences behavior directly, but they *do* know that a low level of serotonin in the brain can affect our moods, causing wakefulness and depression.

Protein for supper, with no dessert or sugar, is also helpful. And two or three dolomite (calcium plus magnesium), bone meal, or calcium lactate tablets taken an hour or an hour and a half before bedtime have long been known to promote relaxation and ease the transition into sleep (for parents, too).

Any nutritional supplement is that much more effective if offered in an atmosphere of evening calmness. To go with that wholesome snack, a warm soapy bath, a quiet bedtime story, or just sitting on your child's bed talking to him in a reassuring, accepting manner makes a warm and fuzzy sendoff likely to last into the next morning.

Reducing Fears and Insecurities

Just as neurological youngsters are more susceptible than their normally developing age-mates to the confusing and disorganizing effects of family strife, so are they also more likely to experience fears in intensified physiological and emotional ways. The sources of this special vulnerability lie in their "chemical chaos," lagging independence, and poverty of inner resources. Such physical and behavioral immaturities make it enormously difficult for them to build a separate world, apart from their caretakers, where they can feel comfortable, safe, and befriended. What it comes down to, once more, is a lack of psychological "cushioning" in times of stress or fear.

Where the physiological amplification enters in is that the response of fear, like any strong emotion, increases the level of the adrenal hormones, especially epinephrine (adrenaline), surging through the body—and research points to the fundamental fact that the developmentally disabled child already has a "normal" oversupply of this chemical charging and revving up his system. It's the same reason why high-sugar foods, which also stimulate an outpouring of adrenaline, are so strongly contraindicated in your child's diet.

Early Scares

The young learning disabled child has his basic troubles with various tricks of mind—misperceiving messages from the environment, social situations, and the feelings and intentions of others. Because of his kaleidoscope of misplays and misunderstandings, many common childhood fears—thunder, lightning, darkness, witches, monsters, animals, the toilet, drains, burglars, kidnappers, doctors, and scary movies and stories—strike with added force and disorganization. Given his pittance of internal stability, which renders him "biochemically defenseless," they can become prolonged traumas.

Besides a whole wagonload of general fears, which he does not outgrow easily, the neurological child often has a desperate fear of separation from his parent—a terror of aloneness and abandonment which begins in a very early fear of separation and strangers, is kept alive and replenished regularly by a lack of confidence in himself and by a school and social life ridden with failure, and persists into late childhood in the threat that punishment and disapproval rouse.

He may hide his fear behind a cocky insouciance—an apparent belle indifférence—act it out in reckless ways, or bury it in embers of resentment which are counterphobic to his dread of loss of love. But considering that his parent, as a *mediator* of long standing between his extreme reactions and any environmental threat, has always been an even sinewier-than-usual lifeline, his fear makes a good deal of instinctive sense. Early on, an overbonding has often come about out of necessity, for the sake of his very physical survival. At later ages, then, a parent's anger may be the most fearsome and panicky situation of all, an emotional tornado he may need to flee from as fast as his wings of fear can carry him.

Preschool Fear Ameliorators

One extremely important way to reduce your child's general level of fearfulness is to take care that you do not direct the peaks of your anger, disappointment, or discouragement his way, cutting into the core of his being and violating him as a person. Sharp criticisms and belittling words will reverberate hurtfully through his body and become lodged in his feelings lastingly. And if the adults around him show that they cannot control their strong emotion, there is just no way that your child can trust the world as a safe place in which to feel the things that well up in him—including expansive positive feelings like happiness, joy, and hope.

Mastery of many popular early fears can be promoted by training your child in simple ways to switch from a passive, "recipient" role to an active one. For instance, teaching him to adjust the sound on a loud radio or telephone, helping him learn to operate the vacuum cleaner and blender, and offering direct explanations of natural phenomena like thunderbolts (which you can find easily in the children's literature) will give him a sense of control. So will providing him with symbols of safety like nightlights and allowing him to clutch onto favorite objects or toys such as small cars—which connect him with his home—when he ventures out into the world.

Keep a shoebox filled with creative "emotional outlet materials" such as clay, poster paints, and a jump rope, and as your child grows, add such adult "essentials" as a watch, a magnifying glass, binoculars, and a temperature gauge to increase his active dominance over the environment.

The child who gets scared at night should be allowed to sleep with a pet or get out of bed, several times if need be, to reassure himself that he is safe. And it won't hurt during a stressful time if you take him into your bed or let him fall asleep in a quiet corner of the living room. If you permit your child an occasional late night in special circumstances—which should not of course turn into a familiar routine—you would do well to remember that his sense of fearfulness and uneasiness will be enhanced, despite your company, by horror movies and violent TV shows, including the nightly news.

With some children, it helps immensely in combating fears, from both within and without, if they practice a series of vocal exercises (singing or yelling) geared toward developing the higher and lower registers of the voice. Producing a big sound of their own, more powerful and dynamic than anything they have imagined, can give some fearful children the vital feeling that they can assert themselves in a positive way—thereby making a mark in the world.

Extreme Measures

Allowing your child to prolong the stages of development, and not pushing him away from you or driving him bulldozingly to grow up—even though it places a great short-term burden on you—will reach a long arm into the future. Because he is simultaneously clinging, overdaring, and painfully open to his surroundings, your sensitive child may have to be given permission *not* to be ready for certain usual experiences such as preschool. A home care situation where he feels secure and shielded, and where he can bring along his own toys, bedding, and snacks, may have to substitute temporarily for a more socially threatening nursery school.

Other ways to protect him from his excessive separation anxiety are finding a small school with a high staff-to-child ratio, and/or curtailing his school program to no more than an hour or two a day. If he stays at home with a sitter, you can reserve a special toy for the hours you are away or ask another lonely child in as a playmate.

In severe cases where your child is unable to function independently in a variety of areas, you may have to consider, as a temporary expedient, hiring a tutor who will come into your home for an hour or two several times a week—or even educate your child yourself. And if you are at such a tortured juncture, you should know that home tutoring is one of the educational alternatives provided for in U.S. Public Law 94-142, which mandates a free, appropriate education for all handicapped children.

You need not worry that you will cripple your child by these extra measures of attention. Few things are more strengthening to a young child than his parent's acceptance that he isn't prepared to move on to the next stage at the expected time. Tendered without signs of worry, disparagement, or blame, special ministerings, compromises, and rearrangements of your child's developmental timetable can be instead signs of confidence in his future—a looking ahead positively to the time when he *will*, in fact, be able to make the transition from home to community. They can be gestures of respect which will one day make him whole. And in an age in which childhood as a time of long and leisurely flowering is all but lost, they help create the island of safety and protection a parent is meant to be.

Separation-Fear Fighters

When your child is ready for school, remember that a classroom might look scary to him if he doesn't know what to expect: the bright lights, big teacher's desk, blackboard, and chairs and tables crowding the room. It's wise to plan brief, introductory jaunts to the school he will be attending, both when it's unoccupied and when it's in full session.

On the way, try to be sensitive to his reactions—especially what his body language and various expressions of "littleness" may be telling you. Most fearsome of all may be his terror of getting lost at school and never being reunited with you. Temporarily, behavioral regressions such as staying close to you and "shadowing" you around the house may increase. But his shrinking from contact with other adults and children almost always coexists with a hidden desire for affection and acceptance—so try to keep his healthy and positive urges for friendship in the foreground.

Show your child the bathroom he can use, and let him know that school isn't a place like the doctor's office where he will have to undress, and that no one will know what he is thinking or feeling if he doesn't want them to. If you know of other children in the neighborhood who will be going to the same school, you might plan with the other parents for the children to meet beforehand.

A technique of sports psychology known as "imagery rehearsal" can prove useful in separation fear as it has in sports anxieties like stage fright and fan pressure. A home version tailored to fit school avoidance would involve taking snapshots of your child's school and classroom or having him construct a mental replica of them in order to "rehearse his performance." As he visualizes the schoolroom or looks at a picture of it, help him to people it with the teacher, other children, and various activities going on. When he stumbles on a snag or comes up against a potential anxiety, you can suggest strategies to head off the specific predicament—perhaps reminding him of the similar problems he has already conquered on the playground or in his playgroup.

Ask him to picture himself in the room in various situations and activities, then ease gently into how he would feel if the teacher asked him a question he couldn't answer, if another child called him a name or harassed him, and the like. Your role is to give him insight into things he might do that are positive and constructive in handling a new and difficult situation, then stand back while he improvises a solution or problem-solves on his own—all before he ever goes to school.

Schoolphobia

During the primary-school years, changes like moving, a new school, or having to make friends in a new neighborhood are stressful events for your easily shaken child which, if not recognized and ameliorated, can lead to long-term problems in adjustment. It's important to hearten your child during a time of flux about the things that *won't* be changing—for example, tell him he will still have a place to live, three meals a day, his pets, and parents who will stand by him.

School panic, a rampant problem for children with slight developmental dysfunctions, may be a reaction of "learned helplessness" that masquerades as a stomachache, headache, nausea, vomiting, or general feeling of sickness which strikes suddenly on school mornings, especially Monday or after a vacation. It tends to hit hardest the sort of reticent, nonverbal youngster who holds his feelings in and won't talk about what is troubling him, whether that is a bully in the playground or schoolwork that is really beyond him. He may feel there is nothing he can do to escape from this pain except to avoid school.

Either he acts out his anxiety in rebellious, aggressive displays, or he buries his fear that others won't like him and will find him wanting—and actually feels sick. From one day to the next, your child may alternate unpredictably between these self-defeating maladaptations, but at the heart of both his acting-out and acting-in (becoming sick) behavior lie fears of failure, ridicule, exposure, and weakness.

The best preventive medicine for school fear is to make a real effort to draw your child out about his day at school and the next day's worries. When frustrations arise, offer him your time and interest to brainstorm ways in which he might handle the academic and social expectations that are throwing him. There may be demands for performance which he can't realistically meet such as sports and reading aloud, or just a general susceptibility to embarrassment and humiliation that needs to be aired.

If the problem is an academic one, take the practical step of arranging for tutoring, which could be with an older student in the neighborhood. You could also request that his teacher "individualize" his program. Just make sure he sees your ground-plan approach of defining the problem and setting up the steps to overcome it. Emotional difficulties which are school-related may need to be solved in a "group therapy" threesome of you, your child, and his teacher. Later, one or two of his classmates may also have to become involved. If you remember some similar hardships when you were in school that you were able to master, talk openly with your child about them.

And as part of bringing his fears out into the open and accepting them, rather than minimizing or ignoring them, let him know from time to time in a relaxed, supportive way that you, too, have fears and apprehensions, rather than pretending to be fearless. Of course, you want to avoid burdening your youngster with emotional confidences and painful details of your adult problems he can do nothing about. But sometimes an appropriate reassurance can be letting him know that everyone has occasional worries, tensions, and uncertain or "mixed" feelings. Lots of times, tell him with a conspiratorial hug, backward steps come just before big strides forward. It really is true for all of us.

The master goal of child rearing is to help your child develop the confidence to deal with fears and frustrations by himself. By teaching him to take positive action in which both of you draw on your own resources, a threat or temporary black cloud can pull you together so each of you emerges as a stronger, more assertive individual in a more united family.

Combating Social Fears

As they weather a torrent of humiliations, rebuffs, and failure at school, many youngsters who were outgoing, well adjusted, and once developing normally in at least some areas as young children may suddenly become quite dependent. What happens generally during the school years is that children transfer their primary fears of getting hurt physically onto social hurts and slights. No longer afraid that the washing machine or a fire engine will eat them up, their new fears revolve around the *people* in their lives—the children who may bully them, the friends who may turn cold and cruel, parents and teachers who may humble and shame them in front of others. To add insult to injury, the learning disabled child has a special dread of having his inadequacies and transgressions exposed to others, and a deep fear of having no friends and nobody who will want to play with him.

Concrete reassurances of your existence and the continuity of his home can comfort your child while he is making his way in the world, in school or playing outdoors. You can slip a snapshot, a note, a high-protein cookie or fruit bar you baked together, or some similar memento into his lunch pail or jacket pocket, and allow him to bring a souvenir from a weekend trip to school on Monday.

An older child who knows how to tell time can be soothed by letting him know that every time the classroom clock reads half-past the hour will be "our private moment when we'll think of each other and reach out with a silent 'hello.'" And when he is away from home, your child can maintain telephone contact every couple of hours in order to touch base.

As he gains in confidence, his need for such token supports will dwindle until one day you are likely to find you're alone in your thoughts of him at 10:30 A.M.

Home Atmosphere

The experts have taken a couple of generations to discover that the child who is allowed the reign and run of the house feels just as guilty about his terrible behavior as the overdominated youngster whose adult problems tend to revolve around the inhibition of emotional expression. Since the undercontrolled child feels, deep down, that no adult has cared enough about him to formulate a plan for his young life and then follow it through, he turns out to have as many psychological "complexes" as, or even more of them than, his emotionally annihilated counterpart. Specifically, there is a long-recognized relationship between aggressive, impulsive behavior and children who come from homes without order.

And so the paramount rule to minimize behavior problems in the home of the overreactive youngster is to reduce the stimulation to a Spartan minimum while maximizing the predictability of his everyday activities. The behavior modification psychologist would say that the wise parent is the one who arranges an optimal environment for the child in order to eliminate undesirable responses and acquire healthier behaviors.

Lately, "structure" has become an overused word in the field of child-rearing, much the way the equally vague catchall "communication" has soared to become a supposed panacea for just about every marriage ill—when the sad but true fact may be that the marital partners are actually "overcommunicating" with each other. These days, no one seems really sure just what is meant by structuring a child's environment, and no two authors ever quite agree on its meaning. But because structure, or order, is the key element in the life of the disorganized child, it becomes necessary to spell out its substance.

Structuring for Your Child's Life

The concept includes *a core schedule* of up at the same time each day; all meals, homework, and household chores at a fixed hour; and all these followed by a regular bath time and bedtime. Free time for pursuing indoor and outdoor recreational activities should also be restricted to the same time blocks each day—usually the late afternoon or early evening. The sample weekday schedule in Appendix III spells out the details of just such a master plan. The purpose of all this regulation is simply that daily rhythms and "everydayness" settle children. By "streamlining" their biological processes for them, a routine simplifies everyone's life.

The superstructure needed by the youngster at loose ends also encompasses *organization*, which ranges from the mundane—neatness, frequent cleanups, removing extraneous objects and distractions, and ensuring that your home is as well run and appealing as possible—to more creative challenges like blueprinting a place for each category of objects (writing materials, toys, tools, hardware, camping gear, exercise equipment, etc.) so that your child's inner impermanence, and perhaps your own, will be counterbalanced to some degree.

Reducing stimulation involves keeping lighting and noise at a subexciting level. Carpeting, insulated drapes, storm windows, acoustic tiles, and quilted wall coverings are some helpful sound-absorbers. Sound transmissions from outdoors can be reduced by using more than one pane of window glass, or by using panes of different thicknesses. Fluorescent lighting should be avoided, since many children become more hyperactive with this kind of illumination—probably because the subliminal vibration that is created by using only a selected band of wavelengths from the full spectrum of electromagnetic radiation, such as is found in sunlight, sparks an irritable, stressful throbbing in the cerebral cortex of some susceptible children. And at night, it will definitely aid sleep if stories, puzzles and games are substituted for television and other commotions.

The structuring concept also includes a foundation of *affirmative discipline*, which means that definite, meaningful outcomes for wanton violations of house rules that your child is well aware of, such as disrespecting the furniture or the belongings of others, are present *in advance of any misbehavior*. The credo of domestic responsibilities can either be repeated congenially each morning or, for an older child, posted in an obvious place.

While it doesn't really hurt to be flexible in unimportant matters, you need to be firm about not allowing certain negative behaviors like throwing objects around the room, striking small siblings or friends, or mistreating pets. Your child also needs clear-cut *outdoor ground rules*, like staying within a certain radius, not crossing streets, and looking both ways in alleys and driveways.

Early on, you don't have to explain or reason with a wayward, disobedient child. Just insist that he observe the skeletal framework of home rules in a firm, friendly way. Later is soon enough to start talking about values such as respect for self and others, and explaining why stormy, overwrought behavior like attacking others or their property won't be successful. Share your feelings with him—and especially, let him know how much you care about him and worry that he may be hurt or injured foolishly or unnecessarily so he will understand the logic of the rules.

If your child has to spend half an hour in his room or miss a favorite television show because of a behavioral transgression, *remember to employ some physical means of closeness and body contact, like leading him off with your arm around him, to reassure him of his worth as a person.* (Withholding food from neurological children as a disciplinary measure, by the way, might be a next-to-fatal mistake because of their fluctuating blood-sugar–behavior problem.)

When he comes out of segregation, your child has another chance to reenter the family group which will be more than just a spin of the wheel of fortune if you welcome him back in an accepting, cheerful manner.

Floor Plans and Furniture

The physical layout most conducive to a sense of order is characterized by a flexible floor design and room arrangement which allows children to move around freely and ply their individual interests with a wide variety of materials. Space should be carefully mapped out in terms of traffic management so that young children can move smoothly from one activity to another.

Lightweight, movable furniture, such as beanbag chairs, large floor pillows, cotton-duck director's chairs, inexpensive upholstered chairs, or "bedsits," which flip into beds, and room dividers like bookshelves and plants are all ideal for a versatile environment adapted to your child's strenuous physical needs.

Large rooms can be divided into comfortable areas or *centers* such as a "silent space" or corner "learning area," which should contain books, crayons, paper, art and hobby materials, and equipment for listening to music with earphones—and perhaps a globe and maps—within easy reach. Low bookcases can be used to define the perimeters, and examples of your child's best work can be displayed attractively in this quiet section.

Organization can be furthered by frequent weeding out of closets, drawers, garages, and other easily cluttered spaces so storage is always reduced to the essentials. *Organizational aids* include toy chests on wheels, stacking cubes, magazine racks, see-through containers for shoes and sweaters, bathroom organizers such as poles, children's clothes bags, coat and garment racks, hooks on doors, mail and key trays, underbed chests and storage boxes, and slotted or partitioned drawers. Apartment dwellers can make use of basement storage bins or, in a pinch, rent commercial warehouse space.

Here are some other ideas. In the kitchen, hang cooking utensils like pots and pans on Pegboard, or on ceiling or wall hooks, and use multipurpose turntables and pullout shelves. Creative carpentry may have to be deployed to enclose sinks and shelves with cabinets underneath for secreting things away.

If your child's room is small and overcrowded, building a loft or platform bed for him, or storage blocks, a bookcase, or shelf space, could become a special Christmas or birthday treat.

When your child is young, supreme *safety measures* such as keeping pills, household cleaners, and poisons in locked cabinets and always using childproof caps on medicines are essential. Even for fast-moving older impulsive children, cabinet safety latches, poison warning caps marked with a scowling face, safety goggles for hammering and woodworking, and decorative decals to make sliding doors and large glass panels visually apparent are still musts. And not buying toys that are fragile or too advanced will avoid a lot of unnecessary frustration at any age, as will investing in the sturdiest tools, toys, and bicycle affordable and then keeping them in good working order.

Forgetfulness and short-term memory problems in a child do not necessarily need to mean incompetence. You can install an "orientation center" in a convenient spot with a calendar, clock, and blackboard or magic slate publicizing relevant communications: "Today is Wednesday, June 5. Eric has dentist's appointment at 3. Mom home late today." *Labeling* with bold printed signs, hallway directions, and arrows also helps jog a spotty or reluctant memory. "Dad's Cabinet," "Eric's Play Area," "Mom's Things," "Letters," "Off Limits," "Keys," and so on, can become pointed reminders.

Somewhere in his home, a child who doesn't have his own room should have *a special place* all his own, which can simply be a large box such as a stereo or refrigerator carton furnished with wallpaper, or a small light and a few personal treasures, like a stuffed animal, a pillow or a quilt, and a sign on the "door": "Bobby's Box." Or a hideaway for private moments could be a canvas tent, a window seat, or a corner penned off from the rest of the room by a folding screen or throw pillows. Just a cranny where your child can shut out the world and read; draw; nurse a hidden sadness, a transient unhappiness, or a quiet feeling; or let his mind become a magic carpet transporting him away from the prosaic activities of daily life—a "great escape."

During a seismic day, your distractible child may have an actual bodily need to get off by himself in order to attend to one thing at a time. While he is in his little corner of the world, let him twirl his hair, suck his fingers, rock, and leech onto a blanket for as long as he needs to. Let him eat in there by himself.

And any way in which your child's individuality can be reinforced—like buying something in his favorite color, printing his name on lunch sacks, cutting out an article or cartoon that you know will appeal to him, or giving him a cup, dish, or bicycle license tag with his name on it—will strengthen his positive image of who he is as a person.

"Chemical Alert" Measures

The use of all-natural materials in insulation, fabrics, and clothing can work wonders in the case of the "hidden" (undiagnosed) allergies which sometimes plague erratic children.

The increasingly common "environmental illnesses" are the subject matter of a new branch of medicine called clinical ecology. They are believed to be brought about in sensitive persons by exposure to large doses of one chemical or another such as formaldehyde. After the initial exposure, which may not even be recognized by the person, the body's general immune system seems to "go berserk" and becomes damaged so that overreactivity to most other chemicals, including the "normal" pollutants in our air and water supply, is triggered in a bitter, unending cycle.

A wide range of symptoms can follow: hyperactivity or excessive fatigue, headaches, skin rashes, puffy eyes, memory loss, irritability, confusion, dizziness, aching joints, bloating, easy bruising, shortness of breath, or cardiac and vascular problems. Adult victims, dubbed "universal reactors," often have extensive and frustrating histories of off-target medical diagnoses, since many of them appear to be drunk.

The home environment, too, may contain irritants which can trigger allergies. House dust, pets, insects, woolen clothing, and carpets are some common, unidentified causes for a youngster's living a "toxic life."

The main diagnostic clue is that most signs disappear when the affected child leaves the house and reappear when he returns—just as some adults react with selective sensitivity around cigarette smoke or gases from a stove or furnace.

Even though you of course can't rebuild your house to rid it of offending contaminants like asbestos, lead, and formaldehyde, which are everywhere—in insulation, flooring, paneling, cabinets, particle board, and plywood—there are a number of combative steps you can take.

Improving the ventilation in your home or apartment is the first expedient. Summer and winter, windows should be partially open to introduce fresh air. And a regular and focused dust-control effort—especially on windowsills and on floors near windows, where lead dust has been found to be thickest—can cut down on lead-tainted house dust.

Other tips are choosing unprocessed rather than synthetic foods and diversifying your family's diet to avoid the progressive development of allergies to certain foods; using unscented paper products, household cleaners, cosmetics, and laundry detergents; never spraying insecticides indoors; and keeping up a program of frequent exercise in the open air and pilgrimages to the (relatively) rarefied air in the mountains or beside the ocean.

Behavior-Color Effects

One behavioral influence revealed in the burgeoning new psychology of color that you should be aware of when choosing wall paint, fabrics, and accessories is that of high-arousal colors such as *reds* and *oranges*, which increase energy and mental alertness but can also be disinhibitory over time and even bring up repressed rage. Most shades of *yellow* are also energizing. *Greens* and *blues*, on the other hand, which are among the low-arousal colors, have been shown experimentally to slow down heart rate, respiration, and brain activity. One study of burn patients exposed to a constant green light found that they suffered less pain and recovered more rapidly than expected—as though the green light had healing narcotic and hypnotic qualities.

Thus along with relaxing neutral tones—browns, beiges, grays, and sands—blues and greens would be wise choices for your overstressed youngster's room since they radiate a biologically soothing effect that can aid concentration. And solid colors rather than prints or plaids should generally be used to avoid a busy look, even for the lining in his drawers, cabinets, and desk.

A certain shade of bubble gum pink—known in scientific circles as Baker-Miller pink, after the two researchers who first discovered it—has been much in the recent news. This hue has been demonstrated to reduce aggressiveness and neutralize physical strength in violent children and adults—who usually stop fighting and resisting, settle down, and sometimes fall asleep within fifteen or twenty minutes after being confined in small cells painted bright pink.

Currently, the somewhat controversial shade is being used in more than 1,200 psychiatric hospitals and correctional institutions in the United States. But despite the favorable results, it does not seem appropriate for use in major areas in the home. Besides the aesthetic dissonance of flaming pink, the effects have been shown, paradoxically, to be stimulating and irritating over long periods.

Muted colors and sparse furnishings don't mean your home must be a gloomy place. Pillows, posters, and plants can add bright, inexpensive splashes and accents of color to toned-down surroundings. *The marrow of domestic wisdom is simply to flow with your child's nervous system, not against it.* (And to know and be able to sort out the things that can and should be changed in your child from the parts of him that you need to accept and be glad for.)

The Lonely Hunter in Your Home

The best antidote for life's ubiquitous hurdles (bruised feelings, school difficulties, being the new kid on the block, alcohol and drug temptations in adolescence—everything up to and including adult love relationships) is a good life in which your child perceives his individuality and feels a certain power that he can influence his destiny and be the captain of his fate.

It begins with a sense of acceptance that is governed by the general mood and the feeling tone of his home—which should be a place where others are not sources of pain, rejection, and disapproval and where your child can feel, if nowhere else in his life, like Linus hugging his blanket: "This is where I belong." The way to promote this good feeling is to focus on what is unique, special, positive, and promising about your child.

"Who had an interesting dream last night?" you can ask at breakfast as a way of helping your youngster express who he is. And two or three times a day, regularly as prescription medicine, when he least expects it, "catch" something to compliment him on that is *inside* him, rather than always focusing on his appearance, achievements, or productions. You can also ask him to do at least one rewarding or healthy fun thing for himself each day and report it to you in the evening.

When your child is down, get him to create with clay or crayons what it *feels like* to be lonely or left out. Give him a *hand mirror* when he's small for looking into and finding positive things to say about himself ("I look nice today," "Blue is my color," "This is me"); so the whole person can be viewed approvingly, a *full-length mirror* should be provided for your older child. Other lonely times, he can sculpt or draw the car he's going to get when he is sixteen, plan a camping trip or a vacation route, or do whatever keeps up his spirits and hope.

Because of his inexperience, your child can't know that hurts pass, that the pain of loneliness and failure he is feeling so sharply just now will ease. You have to let him know this directly. From an early age, talk about his "insides" should be given equal time and at least as much importance as his surface. And when you are feeling sad or apprehensive, don't always hide from your child the human way you feel. Withdrawing from him in your worried or depressive moods only widens the feeling of isolation for both of you.

Some researchers think the rash of "contagious suicides" among some well-off suburban teenagers is due, partly, to the fact that they are simply unprepared to deal with the pain every individual eventually faces, be it romantic troubles, the death of someone close, or the fitful competition for college entrance and jobs. Suddenly, as adolescents, they are hit by an unforeseen trauma and don't realize that the agony is temporary if they but endure the moment.

So as your child escapes into painting, molding, wood-carving, or ruminations, tell him frankly that though he is miserable right now, the pain will let up. Later, with the calm of distance, he will be able to approach the situation which set him off with more self-possession and a saving coolness.

Today, as never before, people of all ages and stations in life search for security in the world outside themselves, in the safety net of a weekly paycheck or a retirement fund, the routine of family and friends, the structure of the TV schedule, or a community of like-minded religious believers on all sides of them singing out their hearts and hopes. By the tens of thousands, Americans approach ministers, physicians, teachers, beauticians, lawyers, and bartenders for emotional support and guidance.

Your child may be different from others in many ways, but he is surely no exception in this increasingly frantic human quest. It becomes all the more important that in the privacy of his home, then, for this moment, you let all he has to know be how safe and warm he feels. And that whatever waits for him down the road—no matter how he may trip up and be tossed about on life's waves—his home will always be there and feel the same caring way.

Wisely remember that *traditions* take on a special meaning for the child locked out of so many other activities. Carving a pumpkin together on Halloween, coloring eggs at Easter time, and using favorite cookie-cutters or decorations year after year at Christmas become living experiences commemorating his lovability and worth. Without a sense of fun, after all, no one's life feels like much of anything.

Demonstrate sensitivity and protectiveness by paying attention to your child's *grooming and clothes*, which should be simple, comfortable, and chosen for both durability and suitability, and make sure that you correct any physical defects like unattractive, crowded teeth that detract from his appearance. This is especially important to increase his presentability and desirability in the eyes of others—so they will see him as a child with something to offer.

The old song may turn out to be literally true for your child, that little things will mean the most; little things like once having celebrated a birthday by breakfasting in the company of his family at the local pancake restaurant, a free-for-all water pistol "duel" with you in the yard one summer day, a bike ride together, or an overnight campout (even if the two of you slept in the car). They can be as rock-bottom simple as throwing a ball back and forth between you, flying a kite, working on a puzzle, shopping, or hoisting a flag as Dad's helper one Memorial Day on the front porch. Just the two of you.

It's the same sense of permanence your child feels when he observes the cycles of the seasons—knowing, for instance, that first the snow melts and then flowers bloom. Baby birds hatch in the spring, a heartbeat in a ball of feathers. In a few weeks, they learn to fly out of their nest, and wing away to the south when the cold sets in again. (They'll be back next year.) In shoeboxes, closets, and secret places under houses, kittens and puppies are born, a source of great joy, and they are licked into life by their mother, stalk strings for all they're worth, shred slippers and newspapers, and chase in circles.

All of these regular events give your child the feel of dependability and never-endingness—like landmarks in a constantly shifting expanse of sand—and the abiding sense that all is well in the world.

And not only because so many of his school days will be downers, but just because he is yours and you love him, always greet him cheerfully in the morning and when he returns from school, a weary and hassled scholar, or when you come home from your work—as though you are really glad he's here on this earth. The last thing at night before you turn off his light, smile an affirmation his way which he can carry within him, a locket imprinted in the backroads and recesses of his memory, to savor forever.

Visualization and Relaxation Techniques

Practiced together in the quiet of the home, relaxation and visualization methods induce a kind of "self-hypnosis" which can be used for ego-building, blues-shaking, or working a hurt out of your child's system. The techniques have proven extremely useful in cancer therapy and the treatment of vital (biologically caused) depression. A recent experiment at Ohio State University found that in a period of one month of relaxation training, which consisted of tensing and relaxing various muscles for forty-five minutes three times a week, elderly residents of retirement homes showed greater resistance and immunity to disease. The blood-sample measures used in this research actually revealed a 50 percent increase in certain types of white blood cells, called "natural killer cells"—granular leukocytes that attach and destroy disease—causing bacteria and viruses.

The theory is that the relaxation and mental imagery stimulate the immune system in some patients by sending positive, hopeful messages through the limbic structures of the brain. With a few modifications, these holistic techniques can be expanded to ward off and alleviate *psychological* states of unhappiness and strain, too.

In the olden days, we had a lot more time for loafing and daydreaming, and more hammocks and long, moonlit strolls after dinner. Now we are reduced to squeezing into our overscheduled days programmed approaches to relaxation like progressive techniques in which each part of the body, starting with the toes and working up to the neck and face, is systematically tensed in turn and then relaxed.

In a dark, quiet room, your upset child can search his mind to discover his favorite place in the world: perhaps drifting on a sailboat, feeling the sun and breeze on his face; exploring an island with wavy green trees, mazes of paths, patches of ferns, bird calls, and fish jumping in a pool; walking along a stretch of secluded beach smelling the fresh sea air; or journeying backward in time to a low-geared, slow-paced age he has read about. Perhaps he has a "friend" who is a condor or an eagle, and he can soar on high with him, over land and sea, as he lets the tension slide away, all away.

Visualization goes hand in hand with relaxation. After the tranquil mood is set, tell your child to imagine his present problem, insult, or fear as a body wound which is healing slowly and ever so slowly returning to its normal shape and color. If he visualizes his painful feeling as a color—for instance, an angry purple smear—try to get him to "see" it fading into a healthy, flesh-colored glow.

If he has the impression of a flaw, deficiency, or core of unlovability in himself, he can imagine this supposed fault as a mound of soft beeswax (or butter), and his bodily forces (the positive parts of him like the things he does well or the good feelings he has about himself) as an army of hot, white lights. When they meet, the bad beads of wax melt on contact and are carried out of his body. . . .

Self-massage is another effective method of dispersing or "breaking up" an accumulated deposit of painful emotion. First, have your child identify the body part that seems to especially signify his hurt. Then, using the palms of his two hands or the thumb and fingers of one hand, tell him to knead away the angry or hurtful pressure trapped in the muscles of his arms, legs, neck, back, or shoulders. He should use gentle, rhythmic motions and visualize the body part as if it were a lump of dough that he is going to knead and shape into bread. Using a circular motion, he can picture a wheel that goes around and around.

It will also help your child to get in touch with his inner healing potential if you appoint a solitary, regular spot—such as an old, cozy rocking chair—expressly for licking his everyday wounds and nursing himself back to a more optimistic outlook. Like all the techniques described in this chapter, this sort of self-nurturance removes him from a passive, "victim" role and puts him on the path toward becoming an active participant in his own recovery process—the road to wellness.

Recently, medical laboratories have been busily developing expensive new programs using "biofeedback toys" to help even normal children tame their stress and "hyperactivity." The field of stress-reduction has opened up enormously with the recognition that most people in our society, including young children, learn very early on how to accelerate into a feverish pace, but have very little practice in downshifting.

The biofeedback equipment is attached at its output to tiny racing cars which zoom along a winding plastic track, and at its input to the hands or foreheads of child "patients." If the child can relax and concentrate on the toy, the cars keep going; otherwise, his bodily tension, impatience, and worry will stop the cars. Older children hooked up to electrodes work on adjusting the patterns and displays on computer terminals and color televisions by relaxing the muscles of their body.

A home analogue for the elaborate laboratory techniques lies in the relaxation methods. The exercises given throughout this section are based on the biofeedback principle that soothing thoughts directly influence such physiological variables as muscle tension, skin temperature, blood pressure, respiration rate, and brain wave activity—not to mention their analgesic effects on emotional states.

For it is turning out that the constant advice doled out to parents to maintain a settled, low-stimulation atmosphere has a neurophysiological as well as a philosophical basis. Many researchers believe that the transfer of experience and learning from short- to long-term memory storage may be particularly vulnerable to the chemical changes set off in learning disabled children by strong emotion. Organization and a climate of calmness and optimism will definitely help in countering your child's inner turbulence, spotty memory, and too easy cortical "slippage"—and generally help to relieve the strong effect of his chemistry on his emotional life. In this case, environmental engineering becomes not only a therapeutic tool, but also the principle of the least possible pain for everyone.

Social Remedies

Neurological difference doesn't start out as a social handicap or a disease of delinquency, but a child who grows up untreated or neglected will often have these problems to look forward to in life, sooner or later. Observations of minimal-brain-dysfunction children as young as one year show that they tend to be "disrupters" in a group and don't keep up with the other babies. By the age of three or four, it's often the other children in a school or neighborhood who first diagnose a child's "oddness."

For all the potential for future difficulty inherent in your child's condition, you can take heart that there are proven methods to help protect children of all ages from the vicissitudes of their faulty (read "no-fault") neurology. Where a child is already into social troubles, recovery means the management of emotional difficulties—the biological causes won't vanish, but the symptoms can be diminished dramatically.

Positive Social Preconditioning

The methods of *progressive frustration tolerance* described earlier are also the basis of social adaptability and communication skills—only the stimuli here are not loud noises or bright lights, but other children. This is true because a child's early social deficit grows out of some of the same general physiological variables that hinder him in many other pursuits—a shortened attention span, impulsivity, low frustration limit, awkwardness, constant activity, lack of self-control, and perceptual and balance problems.

From the first few months of life, your child needs exposure to his peers for very short periods of time which should build up gradually to an hour several times a week. Lengthen the time dosages by five- or ten-minute increments only as your child shows he can play peacefully alongside other children.

Ideally, play experience or a "socialization group" of one or two other babies would take place in the security and familiarity of your child's home, but it will also work if you make a special effort to first acquaint him with a new setting such as a neighbor's house or a church basement.

The first social group should be kept deliberately small—a good rule is no more than two other children to start with. If you don't find appropriate infant friends on your doorstep, you can start your own group by placing an advertisement in a local newspaper or a notice on a supermarket bulletin board—a social adventure, by the way, which has an adult counterpart in the many singles and "lonely hearts" ads currently found in newspapers and magazines across the country.

Infants and very young children do not, of course, play together in an interactive way, or share toys or thoughts, but the physical curiosity and exploration of each other's faces and bodies is still the beginning of important learning. This mutual grooming behavior is a "pediatric preview" of the complex social structure in the world to come. And no child is ever too young for the early rules of positive social reinforcement.

Every effort should be made to keep the time together with other children positive with a variety of toys and activities. The infants should be monitored constantly so that an adult can intervene immediately to remove a child from a deteriorating or potentially negative interaction. The time spent with other children should not be so long at first that a child becomes overtired, excessively fussy, or bored or has an adverse social experience.

Thirty minutes of structured contact several times a week is ample, but if your group is longer for practical reasons, breaking up play periods by planning mealtimes, bath times, or nap times together on a regular schedule is also a wonderful way for babies to begin their social life.

Half an hour in a park or playground each day will also work to build up your child's tolerance and repertoire, but the fastest learning will accrue if his social group is dependable from day to day. The newest studies are finding that even very young children may become so attached to each other in nursery schools or day-care centers that they undergo physical and emotional upsets when they separate by changing to a new school. Both children who leave and those who stay behind show increases in crying, aggressiveness, fussiness, fantasy play, and night disturbances. They also suffer from more illnesses and regressions, such as toileting accidents, and display changes in eating and sleeping habits indicating anxious and depressive feelings.

Surrounded by consistent social partners, your infant will soon begin to surmise, in his embryonic fashion, what can be expected from (and tolerated by) the other faces, bodies, and psyches.

If your child seems unusually apprehensive or fearful around other children, you'll have to *decondition* him to their presence step by step. Start out by holding him on your lap while another child is present in the room. Cuddle him, give him a food treat, or let him hold a favorite toy or blanket. You can also remove a treasured object as much as possible during other times, and reserve it for special occasions so he'll look forward to "people" times and places. Or you can teach your child to associate other children with an enjoyable experience by taking out a special toy only when you are about to open the door to guests.

As he tolerates the presence of other children better, you should move physically closer to them, and gradually let him creep off your lap and onto the floor.

Even though the social time may seem very brief, you still need to structure and guide your child's initial learning. You can gently rub one baby's hand along another's cheek or arm, or have one infant "give" a cracker, a few raisins, or a toy to another. Speaking softly all the while, *actually go through the movements with their hands* as you help two children share a quilt or a sturdy touch-and-feel book, or pat or "exchange" a stuffed toy. A simple game of ball-rolling will also spark social interest and attention.

At young ages, *rechanneling* your child's energies by removing him for a few minutes of quiet activity works best if his behavior becomes disorganized at any time during a social "session" or park outing. Watch carefully for any undesirable behavior patterns such as biting or hitting another child, pulling hair, and the like. The first time you notice your child behaving destructively, quickly substitute a desirable behavior instead — stroking, pat-a-cake, or blanket sharing, for instance.

If your child persists, remove him while telling him no. The minute he stops on his own or makes any gesture that is not negative, reward him by smiling and giving him positive attention. Eventually, undesirable behaviors can be "programmed" out of your child's range of responses in this way.

Keep in mind that when your child is stressed by being tired or hungry or having a cold or illness, his resources for coping with new situations decline sharply. Since it's the prestressed child who is most apt to have a hostile exchange, you should make sure that your baby is physically up to par each day.

The most helpful part about early social conditioning is that large and long-term gains result from very short time blocks. Even if you are a working parent, you can still provide for half an hour of regular "group time" after you get home. This arrangement, in fact, would have the added advantage of presenting your baby with two or more simultaneous "social reinforcers" at dinnertime. And probably also endear you lastingly to a stay-at-home neighbor mother.

Just remember that the rewards of early intervention and parental structure are so great that any sacrifices or inconveniences are truly worth the effort. The biggest mistake our research parents said they made was in leaving evolving social behavior to chance or, wishfully as it turned out, to a "natural unfolding," as they had done with their normal children.

It may hurt to think about it, but in some ways our special children are like aliens on a new planet, and a parent has to approach their early interactions as though she were teaching a class in the basics of living in a strange country. Later, for example, your social program should include a lesson in "angry language" and gestures to familiarize your child with obscene and abusive words and expressions which should alert him that he is not in good company or even, possibly, that he is in physical danger.

But for now, you only want to make his induction into the social milieu as benign and positive as possible. In this endeavor, you would be wise to take absolutely nothing for granted.

Choosing a School

Because your child is neurologically immature and has primitive perceptions and interpretations of the things he sees and hears, he is going to be to a greater or lesser degree socially immature as well—no way out. One of the best ways in which you can promote positiveness in him and ease his transition into social activities is to pick a nursery school or day-care center that encourages a high degree of contact between staff and parents. Recall the evidence showing that a parent's presence may act like a soothing, acukinesthetic-type distractor—something that elicits a warm feeling, focuses a child's attention, and may actually have a blocking biological effect on traumatic emotions.

To locate the best care your community has to offer, you will have to visit several schools or day centers (preferably unannounced), and meet with the staff on all levels. Asking about the program of activities is important, but not nearly so important as your intuitive impressions—your overall "feel" for a facility.

Physically, is the outdoor play area all under the blinding sun, or are there shade trees that offer coolness and a retreat from group activity? Do the children seem happy and bright, or are they strangely quiet and dulled? Does the staff seem concerned and sympathetic, and to like and *respect* children?

Generally, does the school seem like a nice place for kids to be? How would you have felt there as a child? You should make a point of talking to the other parents—what complaints or feelings do they have?

(The most spontaneous way to talk with other parents is to wait outside the school around five or six in the evening.)

If you are aware of special difficulties such as intense separation anxiety, constant hyperactivity, or gross or fine motor limitations, now is the time to bring these situations out into the open and find out how the staff would handle them. Adults who seem friendly, feeling, and caring to you will probably come across that way to your child, too.

It can also help to smooth a frightened child's passage if you can arrange for him to develop a relationship with his teacher before he starts school, or hire a school aide as a babysitter on several occasions.

Be sure to ask on the first visit if parents are permitted to stay with their child in the first few weeks—or for as long as it takes for him to feel comfortable. If the answer is no, or you sense an edginess or hesitation on this question, steer clear of this facility by a wide margin. Any school which cares more about routines than individual programs is definitely *not* the place for your child.

A good school should immediately feel relaxed, peaceful, and well run. The ambience which best describes the ideal school is "friendly structure"—a middle-of-the-road balance between authority and permissiveness. Either a rigid and overstrict or a chaotic and constantly stimulating social landscape will only make it that much harder for your child.

Even after making an initial choice, you should think of any arrangement as merely *a trial placement* in which you are still looking the school over, and which you are free to terminate if it doesn't seem to be working out. Allow an adjustment period of at least three weeks before making a final decision, but if your child is growing noticeably *less*, rather than more, enthusiastic about going to school each day, be prepared to step in with an alternative plan before his failure becomes ingrained.

If a school doesn't work at first, you can always remove your child and try again in a few months. You can also try moving him to a younger class within the same school, or find a low-cost cooperative nursery school where the parents take turns as teachers or aides one or two days a week. Many child care central information services, listed in phone directories, have booklets describing how to set up your own parent-run center which they will happily send you free of charge.

Shared babysitting and an at-home play group are two more workable compromises.

All of these efforts are so effective because they provide a bridge between home and school. A distractible child who is "anchored" in the stimulating world of school will still feel that deep connection to you, and the reassurance of your support, rather than an abrupt and profound loss.

Sometimes it may be easier to find a private school which is more accepting of your presence or participation, but opportunities also exist in many of today's public schools. Underbudgeting and chronic staff shortages have driven some primary schools to welcome parents as volunteer classroom or playground assistants. Local schools may also be surprisingly flexible in arranging occasional lunches or special "recesses" for you and your child.

There are some Head Starts, private day cares, and church-affiliated nursery schools which have lounges where parents can interact informally with the staff and reassure an anxious child of their presence nearby. The "family concept" can be extended into the regular grades by asking to have weekly parent-teacher meetings where your child is present for at least part of the time.

At the beginning of your youngster's school career, it may be important to accompany him back and forth to school so that he knows you will always reappear at a certain hour. As he gains in confidence and acquires a grounding in time and space, you can substitute a "surrogate" older child with whom he is comfortable.

All of this careful preparation is geared toward preventing an early school trauma which will imprint great vulnerability into your child's system. So if you can't, or don't, choose to stay at home when he is young, the best countermeasures to touching off a chain of suffering are a slow and protective introduction into school, and prearranging an "overlap" between home and school which includes, initially, some physical contact between the two of you.

Social Tutorials

Besides a structured program of group activities, your child should have one-on-one "tutorials"—which are brief, relaxed social insight sessions—soon after the start of his school life. The primary purpose is to head off potential long-term problems in adjustment.

The young child who lacks confidence in social situations and is getting into negative interactions can often use his body to express his lonely, sad, or angry emotion through *masks or puppets*. Making puppets together from old stockings stuffed with cotton or polyester fill, secured with a simple running stitch, and topped with yarn hair can also improve his fine motor skills. A paper plate with cut-out eyes and a painted mouth can become a "social mask."

During tutorials, you can initiate social games which recreate your child's emotion by asking him, "What did you *feel* like today when Jason didn't want to play with you?" "How did you *feel* when (you got refused/you didn't get chosen for the team) at school?" Sit on the floor with your child and encourage him to practice the feelings and responses common in social rejection situations. Depending on the experience you are reenacting, he can be an angry, a happy, or a sad puppet.

Even the youngest child can begin to learn in this quiet time with you that all our social initiations are usually directed at wanting other people to like and accept us, but there are both good and bad ways to get the attention we hunger for. Some, like being disruptive, calling names, teasing, or hitting someone else, miss their mark badly.

A lot of trouble in the world occurs because so many people are trying to fulfill their needs for recognition and attention through aggressive, abusive, and violent behavior. Your child needs to discover as early as possible that there really are better ways to realize his human desires to be special and appreciated, and to have others choose him for a friend.

Friendship has the same meaning for adults as for young children, and so this lesson will last a lifetime. It makes us feel good inside—loved and cared for, like a hot bath, a snuggly feeling, nestling, or having a story read to us when we are children. If we don't get the physical and emotional nurturance we need to feel good, then we always feel hurt, empty, resentful, and unworthy.

Help your child to recognize his deepest social needs by having him visualize a circle of his classmates (or look at a class picture) and say slowly and deliberately to each child, "Please like me and pay attention to me. Please want me for a friend."

In talking with your older child, you should point out how certain behaviors in an "initiator" child may elicit rejecting responses in a "reactor" child. Use this time to discuss the wrong initiations you have noticed your child engaging in. It may seem self-evident that little Lisa didn't have a good time with your youngster's interrupting, lunging, and thrashing about while she was trying to color, and that she was reacting to those initiations when she called him a name and burst into tears, but it may not be obvious at all to your child.

Acknowledge your child's feeling of failure *while emphasizing what he must change in his own behavior if he wants to have friendships and fun.* Correct his perceptions of the actual truth of situations by helping him to figure out, in step-by-step looks at his social mistakes, what is and isn't appropriate behavior to get the favorable response he wants under his seemingly random superactivity. For example, sometimes an angry look, a frown, or a too-loud tone of voice can sabotage a situation.

At the same time as you are being sympathetic, help your child to understand the basic social rule that in any friendship, a personal commitment involving loyalty, fair play, and thoughtfulness will be required of *him* as well as his friend. Once he has made a friend, teach him to cherish the relationship through a constant respect for individual differences like religion, race, and ethnic or social group.

Tutorials are also a good opportunity to practice facial expressions, and nuances of inflection and emotional tone—the more subtle social clues learning impaired children often miss. Point out, for example, that frequently it's not *what* a person says so much as *how* he says it that can provoke a negative reaction. Have your child try saying neutral sentences like "Let's have pepperoni pizza for lunch" sadly, or with hatred, love, anger, enthusiasm, and so on, varying his voice, modulation, and emotion.

As to the difference between a smile and a frown—researchers are now finding that the act of smiling is not only a way of crossing social barriers, but it actually changes a person's mood by lowering blood pressure and steadying heart rate and pulse. In one study, professional actors asked to mimic expressions of anger, joy, disgust, fear, or sorrow showed physiological reactions typical of each of these emotions. They had "fooled" their bodies into really feeling happy, sad, fearful, and the like.

This is also the time when you can discuss with your child the importance of keeping within his own "space," and make lists of greeting words (nice ways to say hello to someone), complimenting words that make others feel happy, and cooperation words ("thank you," "please," "would you mind," " may I," and so on). *A "feelingful" vocabulary—expressive words and phrases that take the place of physical action—should be stressed from your child's first social encounters.*

You can use this individual time with your child to teach him some simple social skills, too—how to greet visitors, shake hands, set a table, pour milk or juice (it's easiest if you first put the liquid in an empty, clean ketchup bottle). He can play-act greeting guests until he feels confident, and then invite another child over. Even emptying trash baskets and dusting promote a nice-to-be-around atmosphere that reinforces social concepts.

An older child can be taught *individual games and hobbies* (e.g., solitaire, sewing, cooking, building, stamp collecting, handicrafts, woodworking, gardening) so his lonely time won't seem so burdensome. You can also promote positive self-esteem by teaching your child to dial a phone, take a message, shop with a list, write down phone numbers and addresses of special friends, and call the paramedics.

Other exercises in practical life which foster independence are making his bed, meal-planning, laundry, general grooming, cleaning, budgeting with a savings account or a "checkbook," reading a map, and using the phone directory (a magnifying glass makes it easier).

All of these activities can keep up your child's hope by boosting his confidence in his social future, regardless of his latest reading or spelling scores.

One situation which can lead to long-term and persistent problems occurs so commonly as to merit a special caution. Because parents may be overgrateful for any companionship offered their child, a parent may inadvertently expose a trusting youngster to inappropriate role models. Usually they will be other disruptive and aggression-prone children, but sometimes an adult like a delinquent young uncle or black-sheep-of-the-family neighbor son becomes the deprived child's hero at a sensitive stage of his development. The bond that springs up between your child and the miscreant is almost always instantaneous and can act as a disinhibitor or aggression-releaser, setting off a chain reaction of behavioral horrors and misdeeds, much like sparks leaping along an electrical wire. The moral is to keep in mind the importance of *positive role-modeling* throughout the stages of childhood.

As your child grows into preadolescence, he may need continuing help in managing his friendships. This is the age when he can join a rap session or a "grow group" at a school or neighborhood counseling center to build on the good start you have given him.

Cycles of Rejection

As parents (or professionals), we may find the social area to be the most difficult to deal with because it brings up the ghosts of our own rejections, slights, and failure. Now our offspring may remind us, painfully, of what once may have happened to ourselves.

Like them, we may have lacked companionship, closeness, and someone to care about us through long stretches of our lives. Out of a background of loneliness, our relationships, when they occur, may tend to be
too intense—all-consuming, perishable, and lacking in good judgment.
Given this history, breakups can be thoroughly devastating whether
we're adults or children.

The good news is that it's possible for parents to open up to their
own ongoing need for intimacy, and to resolve some of the trauma of
their past failures in relationships, while helping their child.

Probably the single most insidious social problem is the all-too-
common situation in which a child who anticipates that others won't
want him acts out his expectant feelings in such a way as to ensure
what he dreads most, and what hurts him most deeply.

Shane was just such an angry, sullen, and lonely ten-year-old. The
psychological interviewer described him as "guarded, aloof, and non-
communicative. Getting him to talk was a case of pulling teeth, and
even when the process was somewhat successful, he was evasive and
monosyllabic. A young James Dean in torn blue jeans and blue Levi
shirt, estranged, hostile, defiant, impassive. Occasionally he would deign
to respond with a sneer of contempt; the rest of the time he kept a
straight poker face. The way he had entered the room gave him away:
He hesitated at the threshold, his eyes darting and scared, then he walked
in tentatively and furtively as a cat burglar in his tennis shoes (or really
as if he couldn't believe anyone would want to have him there). He kept
glancing out the windows to the athletic field, where a group of boys
from his school was playing soccer, and to the trees beyond.

"Something in me told me to forego the standard props of diagnostic
interviews: the toy cars and trucks, and the word-association tests and
the ink blots, and the rest. Somehow I knew that although the school
had presented a history of both behavior and learning problems and
had suggested that this youngster might be mildly retarded, he would
be sharp enough to see through the disguises of the tests, discern their
true purpose, and hold out on his secret inner life all the more. Besides,
the real-life Rorschach slice of life occurring outside the window seemed
just too opportune not to take advantage of.

"Feeling inspired, I moved my chair closer to his and gestured
toward the window in a friendly fashion. 'What's so fascinating out
there?' I asked him. His answer, when it finally came, was derogatory
and devaluing of the other children, as I had known it would be. 'Who,

them? Who cares about a bunch of little whimp asses anyway?' he shot back at me, testing me out by venting his contempt for the other children. 'No one you'd care to know out there, huh?' In his longest speech of the afternoon, he treated me to a recitation of the behavioral atrocities that he, in contrast to those sissies, considered to be 'real' fun: He liked to set fires, he relished pulling weapons on kids who bothered him, he enjoyed destroying their property if they annoyed or teased him or tried to misuse him. He ended up by saying that he needed no one, see? When he said that, he kicked a toy train at his feet aggressively across the floor and met my eyes squarely for an instant. I caught a flash of the little longing child inside. His basic ability to trust others or have a close relationship was obviously impaired, but on the windward side of that was a gentle, pained soul with a tremendous desire to have a friend. He substituted the only thing he knew, the thing that had never deserted him and had become his constant companion, his anger."

"Conditioning" experiences of repeated rejection have plunged such children into a painful dilemma: getting close hurts too much, but so does loneliness. Because of their poor self-regard, they disparage and tear down others, especially other attractive children, in order to rationalize the hurt and dicomfort of always being on the periphery. This approach/avoidance kind of relatedness only leads in the end to still more loneliness.

At the heart of this tenacious problem are "expectancy effects." They may operate on many different levels—from the child who is provocatively reckless and oversensitive to perceived criticism or rejection and actively pushes others away, to the teacher who "sees" a child's schoolwork as better than it really is because she has been told (falsely) that his IQ is in the genius range. It's also been shown experimentally that if a host only pretends to pour gin in his guest's gin and tonic, that guest may get "high" just the same.

Your locked-out child is feeling ashamed, discarded, shy, and diseased because others don't seem to want him around. It's easy to see how, later on down the road, drugs take away his empty feeling and alcohol gives him the confidence to be close to other people. Fortunately, there are a number of successful interventions you can use to help your child grow out of his distancing behaviors long before things ever reach this serious stage.

When a young child is being shut out by his peers, you can use the principles and techniques of *play therapy* to increase his insight and get out some of his depressive feeling right in your home. The therapy is built on the premise that play is a child's most direct and expressive language—it's a safe "imitation of life."

All children use play to communicate their feelings and needs, but the troubled child often closes himself off in a make-believe world as a way of burying his hurt. Just as in adult therapies, traumatic experiences and fears become reversible only when they are expressed, instead of repressed.

Start to watch your child sensitively while he plays—he's telling you how he views the other people in his life, including other children, and how he feels about himself. A period of close observation can awaken you to many important clues to his feelings.

Then as you become more involved in his play, sit on the floor with him and translate into words, for example, his play actions with toy weapons, "stick characters," and imaginary assailants. Encourage him to give names to the dolls, figures, or objects, and guide him to "play out" significant situations such as school, playground, or neighborhood scenes. All the while, strive to see the experience he is struggling with through his eyes.

The best way to do this is to recall the last time when you felt little, naked, helpless, incompetent, and shamed—as if you were being destroyed. That's what your child is feeling when the other children don't include him. When you think you have captured his feeling in a certain play situation, some of the best words to use are "It's hard to always feel lonely, and like you have no friends on your side."

Relearning for a discouraged older child starts with letting him know that you understand his hurt, but even so, it's sometimes necessary to take risks in friendships like making the first overture. Together, you can plan small steps to help him over the hurdle of finding a friend. A realistic plan might be to say one nice thing to a different classmate each day, initiate a game with a child next door, or start to look other people in the eye.

Be sure to point out the times and occasions when people *have* liked him and found nice things to say about him. It's especially important to comment on his good points when your child is down, and to show your approval whenever he's friendly or helpful toward another child. And since he is plainly "hiding out" from his real needs when he withdraws or behaves aggressively, wildly, or belligerently, you will have to keep reminding him of his underlying feeling—he really wants to be liked, respected, valued, and treated well. When he isn't, he's hurt and angry.

It isn't "cheating," but survival, if you make use of little lures to enhance your youngster's social desirability—backyard wading pools and sprinklers, a supply of balloons and water pistols (or soap bubbles and wands), a special riding toy, a jungle gym, or a hutch of rabbits or chickens. All are "magnet" activities which will draw other children to your home, and make them want to visit with your child.

These attractions may not necessarily promote long-term friendships, but they can afford the solitary child an afternoon's release from the straitjacket of loneliness, and provide a "holding memory" when the going becomes lonely once more.

Pet Medicine

A deeply troubled child whose behavior creates a danger to himself or others, or involves his family in a high-risk, threatening situation in the neighborhood, will have to be restrained temporarily from contact with other children. He needs a period of concentration on the basics of give-and-take interaction, ranging from a few weeks to several months, which reaches back to a very early stage of bonding and attachment.

Modern therapists are finding that pets can be valuable aids in teaching relationship skills to withdrawn or antisocial patients, and remediating disturbances in social trust which may have had their onset as far back as the preverbal stage in development. The new pet therapy approaches draw on a number of studies in nursing homes, mental hospitals, and university laboratories which have shown that pets may have a beneficial effect on a person's physical and mental well-being.

For example, heart attack victims who are pet owners recover more quickly, and they also tend to live longer. Watching fish swim around in an aquarium lowers blood pressure in dental patients who are undergoing stressful surgery, and reduces anxiety and pain just as effectively as hypnosis. When people talk to a pet, their voices become softer, gentler, and slower than normal.

Some counselors are bringing pets right into their offices to treat children who cannot otherwise relate. Initially, therapist and child talk to each other through the pet, who is a nonthreatening, nonjudgmental, and always affectionate "intermediary." The goal is that once a relationship which is emotionally rewarding develops between the child and the animal, the child will transfer this positive bond first to the therapist, and eventually to other people.

When pets are credited with creating the initial "breakthrough" in therapy, they are seen as providing an avenue of access into a child's tender, nurturant emotion and filling some of his need for companionship. Many child and adult patients find it easier at first to give and receive love from their pets than from other people since pets are noncompetitive and unconditionally accepting—they don't have bad days or moods, argue, or make demands. Not only do they unlock a "secret" door into their owner's feelings, but they also seem to protect the person from stress in many other areas of his life.

Outside the doctor's office, pets can teach important general lessons in nonverbal communication and expressive-emotional language—"listening" without words, focusing attention, spontaneity, physical forms of closeness and caring, self-control, responsibility, and response to the needs of another. Researchers are even finding that pet fish use "body language" such as arching the back, changing color, or flipping a fin; they "communicate" that way.

While animal allergies can be a serious problem for some children, a recent professional meeting of the Asthma and Allergy Foundation of America proposed several alternatives to banishing the family dog or cat. They include washing and brushing pets more often, confining them to certain areas in the home, and restricting contact with the hair, skin particles, feathers, dandruff, and other parts of the animals that may trigger allergic reactions.

Other ideas to draw a socially isolated child out of his shell are to visit a hands-on pet farm on the weekends—perhaps you can even arrange for your child to become involved in the grooming and training of large, spirited animals (dogs, horses, cows)—and to begin over again with only one other child for short periods of play, even if it means you have to be a volunteer babysitter for the neighbors, temporarily. A younger foster child in your home is also a workable idea, especially for a socially imperceptive only child, provided he is not physically destructive and you have the time, energy, and desire to parent another child.

But no matter how you choose to help a youngster in serious difficulty, any home treatment should be a joint undertaking together with the guidance of a mental health professional. For at this point, as much as your child needs the assurance that you will stand by him come what may, he needs long-term supportive psychotherapy as well.

Plant and Nature Therapy

Another new rehabilitation activity that sometimes brings about marked changes in the lives of withdrawn patients is plant therapy—raising flowers from seeds and cuttings, cultivating flower beds, raising vegetables, and general gardening. Several prominent psychiatric hospitals now have special greenhouses on the grounds which have become an integral part of the daily therapy program.

Recreational therapists believe that the process of connecting with the natural world offers hope of restoring self-esteem and confidence in regressed or socially alienated patients. Like pets, plants are safe, living things which can provide a peaceful focus of attention and renew feelings of pleasure and hope. And ultimately, they may help to build a bridge back to ordinary life.

Along these same lines, a geography professor who is studying the influence of nature and outdoor environment on human behavior has found that patients who have a "tree-view" in their hospital room windows rather than a brick wall scene require less pain medication, recover more quickly, and have fewer complications after surgery.

Parents of stressed or overactive children can take a cue from these new approaches by arranging for frequent outings and trips to the mountains or beach, away from the turmoil and confusion of the city. Gardens or window boxes, shell collecting, rock gathering, and taking long, leisurely walks in the neighborhood may also provide a routine of tranquillity for a very hyperactive child.

School Therapy

Social Rules   The more your child understands what will be expected of him when he reaches school, the more he can prepare his mind and body to comply. Following is a list of some of the most common classroom rules which you should acquaint your youngster with *well in advance of the first day of school*. Although these guidelines, which will help him to avoid negative consequences, seem simple, you may find you need to reinforce them time and again.

1. Hands, feet, and objects should be kept to himself.
2. Never interfere with anyone else's activities—others should respect his work, too.

3. No fighting, teasing, name-calling, hurting others, or destructiveness—no one should touch or harass him, either.

4. Work quietly—no unnecessary noises, shouting, disruptiveness, interrupting, etc.

5. Follow all adult directions promptly.

6. Use a "classroom voice" and appropriate manners and language—no swearing, arguing with a teacher, or bossiness.

7. Stay in his assigned area—ask permission to leave.

8. Return all materials to their proper place after use—keep work areas neat and orderly.

9. Complete all assignments to the best of his ability—ask for help if he cannot do it by himself.

Home play groups should follow the same general system of management. A child who is being disruptive should be redirected by being given a puzzle or solitary task to work on until he has regained control, or by being asked to help another child.

All children should be expected to respond appropriately to signals from an adult. For instance, you can switch a light on and off or play a few bars of music to gain group attention.

Joint Parent-Teacher Ventures Some strategies for ego-building are truly worth the effort in enlisting help from your child's teacher. She will probably be glad to watch for the child who seems most attracted to your child, or has the most in common with him. This is the youngster you should invite to spend time with your child on family outings, movie matinees, skating parties, trips to amusement parks, and so on.

A sympathetic teacher can also give your child "nice" classroom jobs that integrate him into the group, like distributing art materials or juice and crackers; display his best work on the bulletin board; and assign tasks to be performed in small groups or by pairs of "buddies." Even academic work in which one child acts as the "tutor" can be arranged in a corner of the room. A friendly teacher or aide can be invited to visit with your child in his home.

More ways to encourage a tie between home and school are carpooling with other children to and from school, before- or after-school snacks and games at your house, inviting a classmate to lunch or dinner once a week, and in schools in which it is possible, joining the staff and children at meals occasionally to simulate a family atmosphere.

Easy ideas to amuse school friends indoors for short periods include storytelling, arts and crafts projects, music, guided exercise, and having them help you prepare such simple treats as health-food "cookies" or popcorn.

Now is the time for social card games like Old Maid and Go Fish, and board games like Backgammon, Monopoly, Checkers, or Battleship. You can even give your school group a colorful name (e.g., the Torpedoes, the Ten Speeds) to reinforce a sense of belonging. And if the other parents are supportive, children can take turns bringing snacks or creating a "phone chain."

Some other sure-to-succeed games are charades, tag, hide-and-seek, and acting out short skits or dressing up in costumes (Sam Spade, Detective; Lois Lane, Reporter; Peter Parker, Spiderman; etc.) and then being "interviewed" ("What kind of voice/job/problems do you have?"). A line of kitchen chairs can become a "train" for young passengers, and sharing "life stories" in a relaxed and homey atmosphere can draw older children closer together.

Overseeing these activities will also give you a unique opportunity to offer your child *specific* praise and approval for his efforts at social mastery—which is a lot more effective than general statements. Noticing the sensitive way in which he helped a classmate to stroke his pet hamster is more meaningful than vague remarks like "You did really well today, sweetie."

Options at older ages include activity groups such as Cub Scouts, Campfire Girls, and 4-H clubs. In response to clamorous demand from parents and educators, many of these organizations now have special chapters for learning disabled and/or socially immature youngsters. There is something almost magical about how wearing a uniform can diminish loneliness in an outsider child.

Solitary children often grow up oversusceptible to any kindness or act of acceptance. Later, their feeling of rootlessness will drive them to join organizations, religious cults, political parties, unions, fraternities, communes, and so on, in an effort to make up for the comradeship denied them as children. A simple "glad to have you here" by a scout leader or a drama coach in the here and now can go a long way in preventing such painful, prolonged searches for inclusion and identity in adulthood.

One of the most effective therapies for school problems is to help your child identify the people and situations which produce stress in him. Some severely learning disabled children may really *not* be able to understand the cause-effect connection between, for example, telling the teacher off and getting suspended from school, but with a little encouragement, most will be able to verbalize that their worry mounts when the other children tease them, or the teacher calls on them and they don't know the answer. A chaotic classroom or a workload which is beyond a child's grade level can also be a source of irritation and stress.

Knowing the *specific* elements at school that trigger his anxiety is a giant first step. With this preparation and the support of his teacher, he is then in a position to curb his response or avoid certain stressful situations outright. But without this awareness, he is constantly at the mercy of his impulses and peak emotional reactions.

It's also important for your child to understand how emotional pressures affect his body. Sudden tension in his muscles, frowning, clenching his teeth or fists, an accelerated heart rate, cold hands or feet, an upset stomach, a headache, or strong impulses to lash out are the physical signs of his stress.

At home, you can make posters of acceptable outlets for stress and display them in a hallway or play area. Some suggestions are verbalizing his emotion, simple breathing and relaxation exercises, and rechanneling his rising energy into physical tasks or playground games. Have your child carry a miniature version to school on an index card.

Your youngster should know that there are definite biological variations in the way different people (and different animals) respond to emotion, but this doesn't mean that a person of any age can't learn to control his inappropriate responses. He doesn't need a lecture on the chemical base in all of us that affects our brain and behavior—a visit to the zoo or a marine park in which you point out some of the diversity will get the point across nicely. (You may need to read up beforehand on some of the dissimilar ways in which various animals compete for food, defend their territory, rear their young, and so on.)

Many friendships (and even marriages) are killed off by angry words, impulsive deeds, constant bad moods, and other nonnurturant actions. The same goes for relationships with *authority figures*—another area which plagues children with poor expressive-social skills. It's critical for school success that your child know how to relate to authority in a positive way.

One of the most important things you can teach him is that when he feels himself about to lose control, he should back away from his teacher or friend at once (like the wise lioness or mother bear). When he is being demanding, bossy, argumentative, and "entitled," or is using verbal threats or obscene language in your presence, say to him firmly, "I understand what you meant, but this would have been a better way to say it."

Starting at an early age, you can use *social reinforcers* to enhance the valence of friendships. A reward for a very young child who completes a certain amount of work can be taking the small pet he loves to school (in a secure cage) to share with the other children. Later, when homework or chores are done, he can invite another child on a cookout or overnight campout in the backyard or for a hot dog lunch on Saturday. Point out how going out to a restaurant or park is even more fun when another child goes along, too.

On the cold and dark day when you believe you have exhausted all the possibilities for helping your child to find a friend in your immediate neighborhood, remember there are still phone mates and pen pals with whom he can establish a base of communication to keep his hope alive. A cousin in a distant city, a sponsored "foster" child in a developing nation, or a schoolchild in a foreign country may be happy to exchange ideas, snapshots, and even empathy.

There are deep human reasons why isolated adults such as prisoners and seminary novitiates often have long lists of correspondents on their approved mail lists. When all other avenues seemed closed off, keeping in touch with a long-distance friend can help your child to reach out of the prison of his loneliness.

A Network of Support

Even as they regard their living but odd and distractible youngster, many parents seem to be mourning for a "lost child" who comes closer to their ideal of normalcy. Their sense of ambivalence and loss may deepen when they notice other children happily at play or recognize in the bright, courteous, and coolheaded paper boy the normal youngster their child will never be.

If a mother believes that her child's difference resulted from some prenatal abnormality, she will have a great sense of failure adding to her strain in not being able to complete a normal pregnancy. Bouts of sadness and a silent aching for things to be different may follow her everywhere. A "macho" father who identifies his child's damage with a weakness or defect in himself, and feels threatened by the exposure of his helplessness, may end up denying the relationship with his child altogether.

A difficult situation is made worse by the fact that their child looks so deceptively normal; teachers, grandparents, and other adults may find no obvious reason to adjust their expectations and demands. Often, then, both parents will see their child's handicap as yet another criticism of themselves in a long line and will feel an intensified loss of control over their own lives. Several parents I interviewed expressed a mounting need for permission to voice the mixed feelings of pity and anger they were harboring toward their child.

At as early a point as possible, you need to admit and accept that you cannot do it all alone—all the emotional nurturance, special attention, educational advocacy, worrying, and mental disquiet—and come out whole.

Association for Children and Adults with Learning Disabilities

One of the most valuable things you can ever do for yourself is to join one of the local chapters of the Association for Children and Adults with Learning Disabilities (ACLD), which has branches in most states and many foreign countries. This organization will gladly put you in touch with parent advocates who can spare you the time-consuming, and sometimes exhaustive, job of making the rounds of the local schools to find a program suited to your child's needs, or who will accompany you if you want to check out the options firsthand. They can help you formulate relevant and cogent questions to ask the school staffs when you visit, can attend educational planning meetings at your child's school, and can refer you to children's mental health clinics, tutors, parent workshops and classes, juvenile lawyers, after-school programs, and weekend respite care.

Fully as important as any of the above will be the feeling of relief that you are not alone, one thin, hollow voice crying out in an emotional wilderness. Many lasting friendships spring up among the parents in the support groups as well as among the problematic youngsters. The cost is the best news of all: as of this writing, $15 for yearly membership covers an abundance of informational, educational, and instructional services.

Some of the "professional parents" in this association, who have reared two or more learning disabled children, may be able to help you with long-term planning, which takes on a special importance to shield your vulnerable child from too many changes. And the earlier you look at the problem in its entirety—as a whole system spanning the growing-up years—the better life will go for everyone.

Parents experienced in neurological difference can also give you an invaluable overview of neighborhoods and school districts through junior and senior high school, and fill you in on vocational and trade schools. Recently, some colleges have developed programs for learning impaired young adults who are motivated to continue their education—there may be post-high school possibilities in nearby communities that you are not aware of.

Some superparents may even be able to help you unlock some of the self-blame and guilt trapped inside you, possibly leading you to a positive perspective and outlook. They may point out to you objectively when your intense wanting of a normal school situation, and life, for your child and yourself is getting in the way of a more clearheaded decision.

Though it's a lot lonelier, it's also possible to create your own self-help program consisting of a pediatrician, private psychologist, speech or movement therapist, tutor, drug counselor, or whatever specific professional helper seems most urgent.

Taking Care of You

In the daily hassles of rearing their special child, it's all too easy for conscientious parents to forget that their own lives need relief, solace, and balance every bit as much as their child's. For precious moments out of a disorganized day, you need to let go of your special pain, sadness, and loss.

Everyday respites can be simple and time-limited. Calming activities during tense times include telephoning another parent, reading a magazine, singing in the shower, soaking in a hot tub, window shopping, walking the dog, taking a night class, playing the radio, and planning and doing the things you need to do for your own growth as a person.

One mother who is now a grandparent found that lying on her stomach for half-an-hour in the evening, listening to the songs from her youth, and letting the feelings overtake her restored a sense of continuity and intensified her awareness of who she was as a person in her own right—had always been and would always be, no matter the turmoil of her present life as the parent of an aggressive, acting-out teenager. She came to understand the child-rearing period of her life as but a passage, part of the "middle learning" of her span of years. And because this nightly activity promoted both a sense of rejuvenation and separateness from her child, she came to trust slowly, for the first time, that with or without her, her son would live—he would grow into a man.

A physician father would sneak off to science fiction movies and sports events, which helped him escape the daily pressures. A more child-centered mother managed to build in quiet times during frantic days by setting a kitchen timer for ten minutes before the hour every day that her children were at home. When it buzzed authoritatively, all noise and exuberance had to stop at once. For the next ten blessed minutes, each person was free to pursue what he or she wanted most to do, including interrupting ongoing chores, just so long as it was a quiet activity.

Relaxation is such a highly individual activity that all family members need to discover which ways work best to calm them and help regain their perspective. Crossword puzzles, knitting, and needlepoint are time-honored methods, but for some persons, reading the contemporary scandal sheets, cutting the grass, or jogging might be just the mind-freeing activity that can give them renewed energy and the determination to carry on. Quiet activities for children include coloring, reading or looking at picture books, woodworking, art projects, and model-making.

If you are into patterns of self-neglect or self-abuse, you can be certain that your neurological child will be deeply sensitive to your negative treatment of yourself, and his depressive feelings and resentment will increase. One eight-year-old boy whose home was on the verge of breaking up couldn't express directly his deep fear about who would take care of him, but became increasingly upset because his father—whom he felt he was losing—kept putting off buying floor mats to protect the carpet in his new pickup. This wordless anxiety went on between them until one day the father "accidentally" burned a large hole in the upholstery. Only at that point could this large, muscled "man of steel" break down and acknowledge his lack of caring about most things in the face of the impending dissolution of his family.

Like his son, the father had maintained a stoical, expressionless, frozen and "masculine" exterior, but his despondency showed in his neglect of his belongings—especially the new car he had looked forward to for so long. The message conveyed to the anxious boy, who saw himself as one of Daddy's possessions, was that he, too, would be passed over, slighted, and left out in the cold.

The Light at the End

Perhaps you may not realize it just now in the middle of your "learning years," except in occasional flashes or rare spells of peace, but there is indeed a reward—or a "purpose," if you will—in all your present suffering. Were I to dwell on it now, many parents would simply not believe the enormous inner strength, coping ability, and real-life "assertion training" they will gain over the years, no matter how withdrawn, fearful, and inclined to defer to the opinion of others they may have started out, or how cruel, unfair, and depleting of their resources their load sometimes seems.

As you stand by your errant child, becoming his advocate in school and his support and ally in the world at large, persevering in the fight for his chance in life, you will find yourself changing incredibly from within. Because it's almost inevitable in this protracted process that you will retrieve major parts of yourself that you were forced to give up (or were robbed of) years ago, when you were as young and vulnerable as your child, you will become more and more who you essentially are, a strong and competent adult able to stand up for your rights along with your child's. Through your child you will reclaim your own lost reality and discover a new faith in the healing power of feeling.

This growth experience, which is a way of getting yourself back, can only be lived, and live it you will through all the years while your child is growing. The day you are on top of things—the diagnosis finally agreed upon, the school program working out, your child blossoming into a more acceptable person and beginning to build a life apart from you—your feeling may be slightly heady and disorienting because it is so unfamiliar, one most of us seldom know in our quiet, conforming lives. That exhilaration, which feels like having scaled a mountain and standing at the top, is triumph.

Along the way, when times are hard, you should never, ever hesitate to seek as much outside support as you need to carry you through. This can mean a commitment to long-term, in-depth psychotherapy for yourself, or just an occasional session or two to ease your overload of feeling during a particularly stressful period. Nothing in the rule book says you can't go in and out of therapy, for as many sessions as you feel you need to sort things out.

Becoming more intensely involved in your own life, by the way, can often be the greatest boon and ego-booster of all for your child. For the dialectic is that the more attention and care you allow yourself, the more your child will feel the goodness and the possibilities in his own life.

Now at the outer limits of your endurance, if you are truly at a place where nothing you have tried has worked and the world seems to be crumbling around you, you may need to seek asylum in the literal sense of the word as a place where relief, protection, and care are given temporarily to life's emotional refugees. Some residential treatment centers for children now have experimental living units which can surround a troubled family with a strong community of support and structure. The goal is that one day soon, everyone in the family will be able to lead a more normal life.

County mental health offices can put you in touch with transitional family live-in programs, which may be an especially good choice for the single parent of an emotionally disturbed child to consider. Many more such programs are needed in a compassionate and caring world, but for now, the important thing to remember is that no matter how pain-ridden and tangled your lives may seem, there is always some option in life that can nurture you both back to an expanded hope.

Novel and Neglected Ways to Learn

The Hoax of Intellectuality

So often in middle-class families, a youngster's academic difference and "underachievement" become more significant sources of pain than they really need to be. Many parents who are well intended and committed to ensuring that their child's life will be successful have great difficulty in letting go of their Judeo-Christian upbringing that tells them it's important to be constantly working, and makes them guilty if they are not always "getting ahead." All too frequently, the tradition extols (and distorts) academic achievement and college into the only paths to material security and a comfortable life.

This hard-driving, high-pressured attitude serves only to tighten nerves and increase irritability. The fears associated with our American work ethic are not even based in reality, yet they have been responsible for generating more anxiety and stress in parents and children than just about any other attitude. Their legacy is to produce alienation and rebellion in a child who may simply not be able to achieve, and foster feelings of failure and estrangement all around.

Many *normal* youngsters succumb under the onus of a competitive lifestyle, with its nonstop emphasis on "excellence" and upward mobility. The child with a neurological dysfunction can be even more messed up by parents' ambitions and image of what he should look like, act like, and *be*.

Broken Dreams

The false strivings born of our social conditioning—coming as they do from our parents' sincere but misguided efforts and, in turn, their parents' falsifications—may be very difficult to combat when they surface in us, but we can begin to work our way through them to a saner reality by being aware of the roots of money hysteria in our past. Perhaps your parents drove you to produce and achieve lest you never "amount to anything," or become a bum, lazy, unmotivated, or worse. Depending on their own background of deprivation and impoverishment, they may have insisted a college education was the passport not only to a "nice clean job," but to your very survival in this world.

The strong statement that over half of all students who enter college each year make when they drop out before the end of two years should tell us all a compelling truth, yet it never seems to register in the psyches of many competition-oriented parents. Carried to an extreme as it is in some homes where the parents are highly successful workaholics, the philosophy that only intellectual or materialistic undertakings are worthwhile can engender depression and anger in a child who is not valued and respected for himself.

In striving for a more balanced view of the world of work, you need to keep in mind the national labor statistics that show that young persons who have a skilled trade (with or without a high school diploma) earn more average income than most college graduates.

It may also come as a relief to learn that a recent study which followed up the progress of 450 men who were seen for emotional problems in a child guidance clinic in the 1920s found that these previously troubled and troublesome boys turned out to be more financially successful and to have higher IQs and more full-time employment than a control group of their normal peers. The researcher, a psychology professor, plans more studies to probe other possible links between financial success and slightly offbeat behavior.

Frequently our mechanized and technological urban society, in which the ultimate symbol of the good life is yet another glittery new shopping mall, is invoked as a justification (rationalization) for pushing academic supremacy. But somewhere along the line it should occur to educators and parents that *someone* with less than three college degrees will be needed to service all those expensive high tech gadgets and equipment. And landscape and maintain the lush surrounds of our modern computer- and space rocket-producing castles.

Before it is too late, you need to ask yourself whether you honestly believe people are happier or better off because they join Mensa, read abstruse books, and work in offices which are often unhealthful sources of indoor pollution. Does it really signify a person is "inferior" if he relies on TV news, enjoys heavy metal music, and works outdoors? Nowhere has it ever been shown that intellectuality makes any essential difference as to how a person feels about himself, or how much trust he is able to place in himself, others, or life.

Perhaps someone needs to do a study to determine whether there are more erudite or wealthy animal lovers, foster parents, and antiwar protestors. But since the truth appears a lot simpler than any corroborating statistical analysis, the world can probably be spared still another study. Most of us react instinctively with more openness and friendliness to persons in business suits than to laborers and blue-collar workers, who may be no less compassionate, humanistic, or useful citizens. But because sexuality is intimately linked to "dirtiness" and "sweatiness" in our puritan-antiseptic society, the real barrier may well lie in our own denial and negative feelings about our bodies.

Methods for Natural Education

Any child's education must guarantee only that he knows how to obtain the means for subsistence and how to live in harmony with others. A parent's role is merely to ensure that a youngster does not end up living in a needlessly narrow and senselessly constricted world simply because he is different from many others. Once a child becomes a person on his own—once he knows who he really is and how to recognize and fill his deepest needs—neurological difference can become but one detail in his life, not the be-all and end-all.

The best way to promote freedom of choice in your child's future is to see to it that he does not grow up feeling he has disappointed you. If you can manage just this one thing—allow him his difference from you and readjust your expectations downward, without malice or blame, when that is called for—you will not have failed your perpetual underachiever. Nor will he feel he has failed himself.

Some little-used methods of learning are not inferior to traditional academics except insofar as our prejudice has made them so. It's also part of our cultural heritage and shared neurosis that the "hard way" is seen as superior, while things that come easily to a person are suspected of being frivolities, indulgences, or outright cheating.

Eons before the first schools, people managed to transfer the fund of acquired human knowledge smoothly from one generation to the next. They did so through a tradition of *oral history*, in which the elders in a clan, tribe, or social group passed on the insights and common memories they had learned in the same way, through exemplary teaching and hearing stories and legends.

Perhaps your child has a grandparent, great-grandparent, or elderly friend who can tell him stories of what it was like to grow up on the plains half a century ago, ride a horse to town, live through the Roaring Twenties, the Great Depression, or a World War—or talk to him about mountain folklore such as theories on medicine and healing.

As he sits at your feet, you can create your own curriculum of oral learning which can instill a world awareness by recounting mythology and special characteristics of his own race or ethnic group, and stories about other peoples who live differently from him—the Eskimos in the Arctic, the Indians of the Southwest, the Moors of the North African desert, the rice farmers of Asia, the aborigines of Australia. Evolution and prehistory can be taught with the aid of picture books from the library.

By acquainting your child with cultural differences which foster a sense of empathy, respect, and compassion, this effort can turn into the most humanistic of all learning. A child who is involved in such activities, even though they make no use of pencil or paper, will gain in knowledge, sensitivity, vision, and courage. He will feel that fullest of all surges, that he can forge a more idealistic and beneficent existence for himself and his fellow human beings in a world which is opening up its untold possibilities to him.

Recordings for the Blind have captured a wealth of knowledge in virtually every subject matter and area of interest. The tapes, which are available through application at most public libraries, can be a godsend for your older learning handicapped youngster. Since so much of his education will have been spent, out of necessity, on basic, molecular kinds of learning, he usually arrives at adolescence lacking a fund of *general* information in many areas of learning. This difference can set him apart and weaken his sense of identity even more.

Talking Books cover everything from the classics to popular magazines and best-sellers. The many magazine articles, especially, can catch your child up quickly on current events, social studies, history, and geography.

For the school-age neurological child, a good tape recorder and a set of headphones are one of the few pieces of "must" equipment.

Many frustrated children are strong *visual learners* whose powers of observation exceed the normal. Your child's visual strength can become the basis of a wide range of learning through trips and travel, and through providing him with opportunities to observe adults at work—construction workers, computer programmers, stockbrokers, engineers, welders, bankers, and so on. Depending on where you live, your child can explore a Vietnamese fishing boat, an Indian reservation, a Swedish dairy farm, or the architecture of an Ionic cathedral, or observe a vineyard, an oil field, a logging mill, an old gold or silver mine, a bridge or building under construction, the wildlife and vegetation of the desert, or sea lions and porpoises at play.

Matching your child's all-consuming interest with a real-life opportunity can also lead to amazing gains. For example, a trip in a hot-air balloon or a train ride might kindle a curiosity about aerodynamics, motion, or motors, which you can follow up with an inexpensive basic technological "learning kit."

Some educational outings need not reach further away than your front step. Watching an ant colony, or a spider spinning a web, can evoke the whole world of home-building including nesting, territoriality, and migration. Standing on a hillside at night, listening to the coyotes howl, can lead to a discussion of ecology, conservation, and the biological necessity for all creatures to live together peacefully.

For the young dyslexic child who gets the message with his ears, there are cassettes with lessons and stories on all subjects that he can even use while racing around the block. You might want to ask him to give you an oral report on what he has heard.

Your older child can become an apprentice to a friendly neighborhood carpenter, landscaper, electrician, plumber, or furniture mover. Or together you and he can create a vocational "workshop" or home work-study program in an area of engrossing interest.

The point is that any activity that gives your child a sense of achievement and satisfaction and reduces the tension level in the home must be considered a viable alternative in adjusting his learning to the realities of his body.

Even, from time to time, the lowly TV set, go-cart racing track, or video arcade.

PART
THREE

6

Losing and Being Lost: The Lorelei Link

Lana, a curly-topped, diminutive brunette in her mid-thirties, squinted through coils of smoke. "The worst moment for me?" She flicked her ash nervously in the general direction of the table between us. With no hesitation she winced, "The Halloween Todd was twelve."

"I had been hoping against hope—halfway praying even though I'm not a religious person—that that year he would consider himself a big boy, too big and sophisticated to go out masquerading with the little guys. But he was really a giant five-year-old, you know—he hadn't grown in any normal way except for men's shoe sizes and husky-size pants. Otherwise he hadn't kept pace with the others.

"I remember being in sheer agony for about a week, from the minute he announced he wanted to go out trick or treating and teepeeing and asked me to get a costume for him. E.T. if I could or failing that, a cowboy; the poor kid never did have much imagination. And one of those decorated shopping bags the kids all carry.

"I couldn't bear to tell him No, Todd, you're too old for this anymore because he was just so pathetic. It seemed the more he grew, the more pitiful he became. I didn't want to hold him back from growing up because I knew he had the same strong drive in him to grow up like all kids, but he just seemed so totally vulnerable to life—unprepared to survive the smashes I knew were in store for him.

"As a toddler and young child, Todd had had this great pull toward life like it was a bunch of balloons on a string, and this hearty cackle of a laugh, but that was before the Fall. As he got taller—and he was exceptionally big for his age—and then started to put on weight, he became almost stout.

"Before, he had been a bony, fragile kid with no hips and elongated legs like a heron, but all of a sudden waffles of fat were cascading down his belly and he even got breasts from all the inactivity. After a really hyper childhood, he became a big, gloomy artichoke overnight. Never any friends to play with or even telephone calls. Sitting around the house vegetating and hibernating, with no energy even to move, it seemed—I know now it was his depression—just sitting in the same spot on the couch in front of the cable TV.

"So many times I would see him sitting there out of the corner of my eye and ache to hold him in my arms and tell him not to worry, everything was going to be okay. Only as time passed I couldn't do this or say this anymore. Not without starting to cry myself because somewhere in those years I had truly begun to feel it would have been a fat lie and nothing but false hope I was giving him. I'd lost hope for both our lives, and how could I give my child hope when I didn't have any myself?

"He would look at me every so often with big sad doggy eyes, as though I could make everything all right if only I would. I couldn't tell him the terrible truth that his Mommie couldn't help him anymore—I couldn't change the world or the way the other kids or the teachers looked at him as a freak of nature. I couldn't make the wicked world go 'way like I could when he was a baby, cuddling there in my arms, when I would cradle him and shut out the bad parts of the world like they were so many skinned knees.

"And I couldn't tell him what was maybe even a worse truth, that I simply could not bear the pain of dragging door to door with him on another Halloween, with him the only kid trying to have fun alone, and a feeling that there was this secret pact between us not ever to speak of the fact that he was alone or even recognize it, except in our eyes.

"From many other solitary Halloweens—and birthdays with just the two of us sitting across the table with a big sugary, frosted cake between us—I knew that the searing, raw pain of it would close in on us from all sides of the dark Halloween night, and trap us there in the porch lights, immortalizing our loneliness for all time. Coward that I am, I couldn't stand to put out the little light of hope in my child's eyes in a direct or honest way.

"I believe that this was the most intense moment of all—the moment I split off from him and just went for my own survival. I ended up exploding at him the afternoon before Halloween. I hadn't gone out and gotten the costume or the bag so I found a phony excuse—some tools he had left out in the yard to rust—and then I hid behind the Effective Parenting Training logical consequences bullshit.

"What I did didn't seem the least bit logical, but for a minute there I even felt self-righteous. I said because he hadn't done his chore, then he couldn't go out trick or treating. I'm not proud of myself, but I felt at the time it was the only way I could spare myself more agony. And let me tell you I was at the point of bursting with all the pain, just not functioning myself.

"Isn't it funny how you go along day after day trusting that maybe there's been a little progress or things aren't so bad as you thought? Then a little nothing thing like Halloween comes along and blows the whole thing up in your face and lets you know how really flimsy your hold on reality has been—what really thin ice you've been skating on, and the load of god-awful feelings you're sitting on.

"I loathed Todd, this child of my body and my heart, for what he was doing to me—robbing *me* of the chance for a happy, carefree life. I despised myself even more for my weakness. And I hated my husband because he couldn't seem to make things better for any of us."

Because the self-images of persons close to each other tend to interact—expanding, shrinking, and reflecting off each other—a time will inevitably come when the parent, however supportive and steadfast he or she has been up to then, will begin knowingly or unknowingly to reject the normal-appearing but no less handicapped child.

Usually this cruel day will dawn when the child is beyond the early years of childhood, when the distance between him and other children has widened and become more visible. He has grown larger and stronger along with the rest, and has even painstakingly gained a little in other significant areas of growth such as academics and play. But he is still—inexplicably, damnably, and despite the various enrichment programs—a little falteringly out of step, out of synch, with his age-mates.

Even if nothing more sinister or alarming occurs, he is sure to cause cringing, frozen embarrassment for his family because he talks louder than anybody else, talks out of turn, and does not seem to grasp the subtle nuances in others' facial expressions or tones of voice. At what should be the advanced age of thirteen, he is still autistically playing a version of *Star Wars* in the supermarket, charging head on and jamming his shopping cart into a line of stationary carts. At the movies, in the midst of a deep surrounding silence, he snorts or laughs boisterously and inappropriately at all the wrong times and places.

Earlier on, the young child may have been protected within the pillowy bosom and relative anonymity of his family, in a home which has sometimes become out of necessity a fortress of defenses against the larger world: an oasis of milk and honey in an otherwise desolate landscape. At home, the tenderness of the parents, who have usually sensed his "difference" from the start, has often served to manipulate the immediate environment in order to avoid frustration for him—and the rest of the family.

And that is as it should be, up to a point. It is as though the other members have instinctively molded themselves to the individual peccadilloes and shortcomings of his behavior, which may have come to seem like normal everyday events to them. Just George and the way he is.

Until the ill-starred day they take George to a restaurant other than a fast-food emporium or pizza palace or to visit relatives or friends, and his supercharged emotionality reveals itself in public. The nagging, rankling doubts which have been suspended inside the lamplit rooms of the family sanctuary rear their ugly but no less truthful heads.

The real psychological damage and the behavior problems which soon follow, we have seen, begin not in the fact of neurological inequality itself, but in the child's gradual and distinct awareness of his inadequacy in relation to his peers, and his recognition of the world's hostile response to him. Theoretically, a carefully nurtured young child could weather even these storms of development without irreparable or long-term damage to his evolving ego.

But what he cannot withstand—what no sentient creature on earth could withstand—is the malevolent transformation of his loved ones. All too often, the withdrawal of his parents' support in middle child-hood—their defection to join the ranks of the other side, as he is likely to perceive it—is the finishing touch in a long and increasingly unbearable line of hurts and rebuffs.

There may be valid, realistic reasons for a parent's curtailment of customary support and encouragement—a new job, returning to school, a separation or divorce, a death in the family—but he will surely not see these changes from your parental perspective. Just as he once seemed biologically hungrier for food and drink than a normal baby, he will later seem more ravenous for your affection and acceptance. In fact, he truly is feeling unfilled even at home since he is likely to get so little positive recognition for who he is as a person elsewhere.

With each change or disharmony in the family, he becomes more threatened and voracious. Because of his great dependency, he is certain to sense you don't feel quite the same way about him at this older, less appealing age. The sad part is that it is probably true.

In a forlorn as well as foredoomed attempt to recapture your love (which he will generally equate with your attention, regardless of whether it is positive or negative), he may regress to early behaviors. "Caa caa shit, me go caa caa shit," you may be startled to hear your sixth-grader singing behind the bathroom door in imitation of the preschooler down the street whom he fantasizes to be a treasured and beloved object in his home. Because his repertoire of constructive, age-appropriate behaviors which may win you over is so limited, he may follow this musical impromptu by crawling furtively on all fours across the living room floor.

Let him. Only say to him gently, "It's sad, but you can't be the baby anymore, can you?" Or alternately, "It's hard to have to grow up, isn't it?"

Otherwise, feelings of persecution, self-pity over your lot in life, irritability, criticalness, and depression in you will transfer to your child through the invisible umbilical cord still between you, and engender in him feelings of low self-worth, alienation, loneliness, futility, humiliation, and even, when things have reached an abyss of despair, thoughts of suicide.

No matter if you have to write this message down and carry it on your person, it is essential at this crossroads that you do not lose sight of the fact that *your ascending anger and resentment are your defensive reaction to an overload of pain which seems without a clear end in sight.* Holding onto this thought may sometimes keep you from going a little crazy.

This overburden consists of the distress this child is undeniably causing you in the here and now—including the recurrent disruptions, frustrations, and postponements of your plans or pleasure (you may not be able immediately to work at a job outside the home or have a normal relationship with the opposite sex; your life may lack real satisfaction)—added atop the residual trauma deriving from your own past which is the psychological legacy of each of us. It is this double dose of pain that seems to be driving you beyond the limits of tolerance.

For the one thing you can be absolutely certain of is that this child, more than any other, will bring up your whole life as though it were passing, panoramically, before your eyes in a series of flickering mental pictures. All the ghosts and demons of your own unresolved but unforgotten feeling will be captured in the fragments of images and events from the past that he stirs in you: an undercurrent of needs, wants, and hurts beckoning to you with the sweetness and melodiousness of a siren's song from long ago and far away. The longing to connect with your own mother's body will be there; the need for your father to open his arms to you; the need for them to smile at you, gently touch your cheek or hair, read to you, look at you just once with eyes that know you are there. All you were denied and never got from your own parents.

There is more. Your child's monstrous behavior will actuate in you feelings of being a bad parent—and ultimately, a bad boy or girl yourself. Your own defenses against such painful feelings are likely to be formidable: a mixture of intense fear mingled with servile withdrawal in the face of the symbols of parental supremacy who surround you in your daily life—mothers-in-law, neighbors, teachers, friends, store clerks and managers—all those who judge your present life. After a while you are likely to feel trapped in the midst of a hundred smoking volcanoes, any one of which can erupt at any time with no warning. Or with more predictability, the next time your child rides his bike straight through the apartment manager's flower bed.

In fact, it *is* true, in a figurative sense, that you are surrounded by ever-ticking time bombs. What are you to do at this excruciating roadblock when your back is to the wall?

Rejecting your child is usually a gradual process which is apt to begin subtly and without much awareness on your part, in put-downs, criticisms, sarcasms, and belittlements which quickly become habit, or in unfavorable comparisons of him with others which seem almost irrepressible as the months pass and your intensity of feeling mounts.

The truth sinks slowly in that you will not soon have the release you had looked forward to from certain onerous tasks of parenting such as supervision of his play in the neighborhood or seeing that he gets safely to and from school. His special economic needs may even have trapped you in an unhappy marriage.

Since you are blocked and thwarted at what should be the threshold of your liberation from parenting a young child, impatience, exasperation, and resentment may seep poisonously into your daily interactions with your child, along with damaging and self-weakening feelings of inadequacy that, try as you may, you cannot seem to save him from his reckless course. As he grows older, you may no longer be able to maintain even the *surface* appearances of correct behavior when you take him along on shopping trips or family outings. There just do not seem to be any rewards with this kind of child, a situation which makes for feelings of desperation if the other parts of your life are equally unrewarding.

What can you do to keep your perspective and hold onto your humanity at this stage of nearly uncontrollable, body-trembling anger at him? For one thing, you can be keenly aware that this is the turning point of turning points in your relationship with your child—a stage of transition in which his self-image (and maybe your own) balances precariously between satisfactory adjustment and lifelong dysphoria, ready to tip over onto one side or the other. He is looking to you, with hope or fear, as the case may be, to tell him which way to go.

Most children have only one or two classic experiences of expulsion from paradise, such as at the time of weaning, which signals the end of infantile omnipotence, or, later, with their entry into school. This child has legion.

For another thing, you can keep in mind that much of your annoyance and impatience has really nothing at all to do with the peanut butter jar top he has left off again (you've *told* him a hundred times) or the shirt he has put on backwards for the third morning in a row, but is instead counterphobic to your great, underlying dread that this child cannot survive in the world after you have left it the way he was created—whether by divine design as a supreme test of your endurance and mental stability, on account of his father's genes, or as a result of your irrevocable Friday night mistake a decade ago—whichever fits your philosophy and current point of view.

The third thing to bear in mind is that just as it is perfectly okay for him to think about and fantasize about his rage and vengeance, but not okay to act these feelings out in real life (his *feelings* are right and true, let him know, just not his abusive and violent *behavior*), it is similarly all right for you to entertain fantasies of child abuse or otherwise doing him in, or conjure up visions of island paradises where he has never set his klutzy damn foot. As part of your program of self-nurturance, it sometimes helps to give yourself permission to indulge these extreme thoughts.

Once you have gotten things a little more balanced in your mind about where your own feelings and exasperations are coming from, what sorts of things can you do that are affirmative and effective to help both of you through this vulnerable time of middle childhood?

A number of things you can do require only a little time and effort but will benefit your child more holistically and lastingly than any special reading or mathematics technique or perhaps even an Ivy League college education.

The most important is teaching him from an early age to label or *name the feelings* he is experiencing. Two or three years old is not too soon to begin this process of making his feeling conscious. There is almost something magical about the way that saying out loud or putting a concept on a suppressed feeling defuses the urge to act it out in negative and destructive ways.

By bringing feelings *up and out* of the body in this way, channeling them safely onto the outside through the mouth, they become much less threatening to the child. The explosive energy behind them seems to become watered down in the process of struggling up through the body. It is as though by verbalizing a hitherto nameless fear or painful emotion, the "roots" are yanked out along with the psychic energy. And a trauma does not become permanently encoded in the nervous system as it would otherwise.

If your family is not used to acknowledging let alone talking about feelings, your own or those of others, you will have to lead your child into this naming process step by step, as a horse with failing eyesight to a trough of water. If he is feeling censured by his teacher, ask him what it *feels* like to be criticized. After a little thought and reassurance of your sympathetic attention, he is likely to answer, "It feels like I'm nothing but a little piece of brown shit. If you flushed me down the toilet, that would solve everybody's problem." Or he may say, "It feels like nobody likes me." Or simply, "Like I'm all wrong."

"Why didn't you and Dad have a big wedding?" he asks suddenly while you are driving by a wedding reception spread regally across several acres of lawn in the best section of town.

After absorbing the shock, you answer tentatively and casually. "Dad and I didn't have a big wedding, but we did have a nice wedding."

"Everything we do in this family is so *cheap!*" He kicks the glove compartment and bursts into tears.

With a little effort, probing, and encouragement on your part, together you will be able to link this seemingly out-of-the-blue outburst to the recent mood of worthlessness he has been experiencing—the I-don't-deserve-anything-good-or-nice-or-expensive feeling—due to a tightening up of the family finances. Despite your previous explanations ("Dad is only working part-time now, you know, and the rest of us have got to be on a strict budget"), he has plainly related this deprivation directly to himself.

"Where's the big knife?" Your child stomps into the house, his flushed, tear-dirtied face foreboding trouble.

"What do you mean, where's the knife?"

"I'm going to kill Alex and Becky."

"Just what happened out there?" Here you are trying to get him to open up and be as specific as possible about the stimulus for his extreme reaction.

"Those little fuckers said I couldn't play with them."

"I know what you mean. They left you out so you're feeling hurt." This is hardly the time to correct his unacceptable language.

"No, I'm not hurt. I'm angry and I'm gonna kill them." Because he senses he has your interest and empathy, it is becoming safe to express his feeling. Tears are welling up.

"You're hurt."

"I'm not."

"Say it, Joey. Just say you hurt." The important thing is always that he learns to recognize his fundamental feeling.

The tears are spilling over now. "I called them names."

"How come?"

"Because that means the bitches don't like me."

"Come over here and say it. Say 'I hurt.'"

To help your child in sorting *specific feelings* he can then master out of the many emotions which seem to swell up in him like so many derailed roller coaster cars, you should keep in mind the general hierarchy or *structural "arrangement" of feeling*.

The aimless overactivity, irritability, or anxiety he displays much of the time is but the topmost layer. Below these surface manifestations lie deeper and more painful currents of despondency, emptiness, insufficiency, and nothingness, which are his endemic and reflexive response to his life situation. You can generally assume that his excitability and annoyance are his defenses against these less bearable emotions.

Closer to the heart of your child's trauma is the third "level" of feeling, which can be likened to a storage bin of hurt. It consists of all the hurts and coldnesses he has felt in his lifetime: repudiations, rejections, suppressions, exclusions, and times of neglect and loneliness, each a big or little psychic wound which has clipped his wings in midflight. The most damaging and enduring of these hurts are the rebuffs he has felt from you.

At the core of this structure of feeling is the deepest stratum of *need* born of his basic human condition of prolonged helplessness and dependency, and his terror of being alone in the world. It is tantamount to his need to be alive.

As he grows up and you seem to turn away from him, your aloofness reactivates his primary fear of being separated from his loved ones and left vulnerable and alone. Several studies have shown that the number one fear in children is losing their parents or caretakers. They're keenly aware of their helpless, little state and that their parents are their only link to safety.

This break can only make things worse. If it goes on long enough, it becomes as irreparable as the chaotic brain cells which cannot be repaired surgically in his cortex. When you push your child away, you condemn him to an isolation wide and arid as a desert. Part of him will always be fixated back there at the age of his psychological abandonment. Some children have even been observed to stop growing physically and hormonally around the time of a significant trauma.

Remember that the *want* is the hurt. And your child longs desperately, at fever pitch, for the old life-giving bond with you which lets him feel he is okay in the world.

When internal speech has developed, around the age of three or three and a half, it also becomes possible to help your child inhibit the possible consequences of his feeling if he acts it out in behavior.

At this age, you can begin to train him to say to himself: "When I wave this crowbar in Becky's face, about to smash her head in, I am acting (crazy/wrong)." "I am starting to itch to throw the dog down the stairs (into the swimming pool, incinerator; poke out his eye; etc.) so I should *stop right now* and go into the house (where Mom or Aunt Suzy will take control of me for a little while)."

This way, your child will gradually learn inner control over his automatic responses and impulses to do harm and will become his own schoolyard monitor or peace officer in the neighborhood. The awareness of just what it is he is feeling is his "antenna," his internal "feeler" that radiates and receives the waves of energy behind his impulses. *As such, this sensitivity to his feeling must be taught to him first*—and *experienced* by him rather than short-circuited via his angry actions—*before self-initiated control over his spur-of-the-moment behavior can be expected to follow with any regularity.*

This is the reason why all the talk in the world—the endless appeals to his "reason" or sense of fair play; the exhaustive postmortems dissecting and analyzing his misbehavior, or brooding or mulling together over it; or long-winded lectures or preaching—simply cannot reach him. These things will do no good because they tap only the *cognitive* level of behavior (the "new brain" activity originating in the outer cortical layers), while his rash, hotheaded reactions actually stem from the *feeling*, limbic or "gut" level. These primitive responses have much more in common with the "old brain" functions initiated in the emotional centers of the limbic system, or "animal brain"; this is also why it is so critical as a first step to get *under* or "read" the behavior you are trying to modify.

He will already know from your earlier teaching that while it is okay to think about, fantasize, depict in drawings, or write stories revolving around such themes as mass murder and mayhem, thrashing Becky, or chopping the dog into kibbles and bits, it is *not* okay to act these urges out in his behavior.

The way will already have been paved to facilitate these practical lessons in feeling which can serve him for a lifetime if you have answered his questions about exactly what is wrong with him, in simple and concrete words, as soon as possible. (It may also be the first time you have gotten it clear in your own head just what the problem really is.)

Because by now, with all the trips to doctors and psychotherapists, appointments for educational testing, and so on, his anxiety about himself is enormous. Even if he pretends never to notice the special concern and worried glances directed his way by adults, he is sure to be wondering, Am I retarded? Am I crazy? Why am I so different? Will I ever be able to hold a job, get married, drive a car?

It's possible to talk to children about anything under the sun if you do it in a natural, open, and feeling way, using concepts that are within their reach of understanding. Avoiding such frank discussion may actively encourage maladaptive defense mechanisms in your child such as denial or projection (blaming others or inanimate objects), and create crippling confusion and fears of inadequacy in him.

Talking to your child about his difference, provided of course you are open to your own feelings about it, helps him to see it as one of life's normal discrepancies, and lets him feel you are with him in his otherwise lonely struggle and sadness. And it readies him gently for the painful situations he will no doubt encounter.

The fear of growing up flawed and defective is even greater than the usual terror of growing up that normal adolescents have. If you approach his difference matter-of-factly, you demystify it for him.

You can say something like this to him: "When you were born, there was a little something different about the way your body reacted to things. This means there will be some things you won't be able to do as well as the other kids, but some things you will do better.

"Look at Whiskers and Panther (two household cats). Panther is always racing around while Whiskers likes to sit in a sunny spot and cuddle. They were born with different natures, but we love them both dearly and could never decide between them."

(Sitting close to him and tousling his hair): "What kind of world would this be anyway if everyone in it were the same? Pretty boring, don't you think?"

What needs to be brought out is the fact that different means only *dissimilar*, not better or worse.

Another beneficial thing you can do during this stressful period of middle childhood is to recall the holding, physical closeness and touch reinforcement that were prescribed at early ages as an analgesic to calm his restless body. Often feeling and touching—relating contextually to people and objects through the fingers and other somatosensory activity—still preempts the more distant, intellectual, or "mature" ways of establishing intimate connections for this child at older ages.

Just as in his younger years, he needs to touch and be touched in order to feel you like him. In the midst of his hurt and bewilderment, he needs a quick squeeze or your arm encircled spontaneously around his shoulder—simple actions which impart more than volumes of words—as much as he ever did.

Along with and apart from touching your child, one of the most important things you can ever do as a parent is to keep alive in him the hope that some day things will be better. He will be able to do more of the things that frustrate him now—catch a ball, run fast, assemble model cars and airplanes, draw or sew with more dexterity. The day will even come when he will be more capable in friendships.

As you listen for the feeling or the fear behind his casual remarks, you may notice that your growing child wants to have a lot of abstract discussions about the latest freeway murderer or the guy who tried to kill the president. Where is he now? In jail? A mental hospital? Will he ever get out? Will he get the death penalty? Who will kill him?

Alarming though this may be, especially if it catches you off your guard, there is no mistaking it. He is telling you he is terrified that he will not be able to control his impulses even when he is an adult. He lives in dread something horrible like this may happen to him, too.

This is another of those red lights when you need to stop what you are doing and take the time to reassure him incidents like these are very rare in life. Most of his hyperactivity and impulsiveness will pass. He will be able to control his moods of revenge and rage more and more as time passes. Point out how he no longer plays with matches or starts fires (or strikes other children or breaks windows), and let him know it will be the same for the other impulses he may still harbor to do forbidden or dangerous things. The future will be different. It will treat him kindly. There will be another chapter to his life, other mornings.

Many of these children with strong conscience development may not be able to express their terrifying anxiety for the future on a verbal level, even obliquely, but may symbolize their fear of losing control of their hostile impulses only in night terrors or nightmares. Eight-year-old Eddie had just moved to a new house across the street from a line of railroad tracks. He was unable to verbalize the mounting fear of his urges to put objects and other children whom he wanted to destroy on the tracks and annihilate them, except through a series of recurrent nightmares in which he did something of this sort.

But his nocturnal schemes would backfire on him as the enraged Amtrak train would suddenly swerve off its track in retaliation and head straight for his house. He would wake up screaming just as its gigantic silvery maw was about to swallow up his family.

At such moments, tell him to hold on. The terror, the painful feelings, the despair and sense of utter hopelessness will lift. He will feel better and want to be alive tomorrow or maybe the day after tomorrow. But surely it is there for him.

The problem is intensified today, when our society promotes an early pseudosophistication in its children and the ever present threat of nuclear extinction looms larger than life. Even normal youngsters reach adolescence full of agitation and terror of what lies ahead. These modern-day fears are exacerbated for the neurologically different child who is having a hard enough time as it is coping with the inner churning that knows no calm or rest, even in sleep—let alone the external pressures over which he has no control, including sex, drugs, and rebellion, bombarding him from all directions. Little wonder this child seems in a perpetual state of fog—or a spacey zone.

The antidote to give him hope and counter his fears, whether emanating from his inner urges or the outside world, is still the same: Give him the security to stay close to you for as long as he needs to.

Along with the safety to feel little and protected, try to put some pleasurable moments in his life that he can hold onto during the storms. If you have an interest, say, in astronomy, take him along regularly on night walks when the two of you can star-gaze and draw close in your search for the Big Dipper and contemplation of the infinite. Think of this time together as part of your child's therapy—probably the most important experiential therapy he will ever know—and take these promised times with him as seriously as you would an appointment with your car mechanic or a business client. Never allow your schedule to become too crowded with other things.

From time to time, to maintain his hope in the future, you can refer to the happy times you shared—even if you begin to feel a little like you are building up a mythology around his past. While looking through picture albums together, point out to him the huge grin on his face in his baby pictures and early school photographs. (Try to ignore the scribbles and pencil punctures with which he has marred the album cover.) There he is with a big curvy smile holding hands with Fred Flintstone at Marineland. He'll feel that way once again, glad to be alive.

You can also let him look at scrapbooks and boxes of souvenirs and mementos so he can see for himself you are still treasuring the green bear and the other drawings he crayoned for your office wall or the Mother's or Father's Day card he made for you in first grade. (Never mind that the letters are reversed and scattered over the page along with the gold glitter.)

The point is to connect his cheerful early days to his future at this age when the world is already beginning to seem lost to him. Keep the record up to date by commemorating his ongoing successes—such as the time he trained his pet chicken to ride on the handlebars of his two-wheeler—with a snapshot.

And when you have been wrong about something, when you have accused him falsely, been unduly critical or made a wrong decision—or when you have acted improperly by raising your voice to a checkout clerk or a receptionist at the Phone Mart—make a special point of telling him openly you are sorry for your behavior.

Perhaps you chose the wrong school for him, one with open classrooms and an unstructured environment you would have liked to have gone to as a child, but one that has turned out to be a disaster for him. He will not love you less for your fallibility and will learn in this quiet way life holds not only second chances, but oceans of chances.

We all have a certain respository of madness within us; it only seems more visible or tangible in these children. The problem resolves into how many comforting or safe thoughts and memories we can evoke when we need them to lift us out of the quicksand of desperate feelings, terror, and bizarre ideas we all share—as though to glimpse an inner sun shining through.

There is a new sickness afoot in our land which as the parent of a deviant youngster you will have to take special precautions against because of your child's excessive impressionability, his basic misperceptions of reality, and his sense of self-pity. In bygone days, the fairy tale, idealistic view of life was confined chiefly to storybooks such as the classic Dick and Jane (and Puff and Spot) primers. Now it has crept silently, treacherously into our homes.

The scene on the boob tube: the Brady clan are gathered in their spacious family room for informal verbal exchange, witty but stingless teasing and banter, before dinner. Enter Dad Brady waving the nine airplane tickets to Hawaii he has just purchased. (Forget how he got the extra cash. And they always take their maid Alice along with them on trips, so that is why nine tickets.) Squeals of delight and spontaneous yet painstakingly nonsexual body contact all around. Cut to a shot of the smiling, gladiola-dripping Bradies rowing in smooth sequence in a canoe on Waikiki Beach, the whites of their teeth matching the glints of sunlight bouncing off the caps of the waves.

Substitute any scene from any episode of "Little House on the Prairie" or "The Waltons."

"My life is *never* any fun," your child sulks, picking up immediately on the sharp and comfortless contrast with his own emptiness.

This prevalent unreality assails us everywhere, in an unbroken stream of advertisements, commercials, and billboard posters that hold out their false promises to fill our void of love. You will have to be a bulwark of strength in impressing on your child how *real* life is a continuous series of problems to solve, but with time along the way for occasional fun and fulfillment of desires.

There is a more serious danger lurking in this than your child's disgruntled comparisons of his home life with the supercharged slices of sitcom life beamed by satellite into his living room. Because there are so few opportunities for rewards or success in his life, but ample occasions for failure, rejection, and discontent, such a child is more prone than the average child to fantasies.

There is considerable controversy among professionals over the role of fantasy in normal persons, with points of view ranging from lighthearted optimism—that this mental discursion is the precursor of artistic or creative production—to stern warnings of psychological deviation from an assumed normal state of "groundedness" in reality. The important question in all this is, At what point does "normal" fantasizing become disturbance instead?

Most experts believe this occurs when fantasies and daydreams begin to substitute for gratifying experiences of work, love, and play in the real world and to supplant realistic attempts to overcome our obstacles and frustrations—the normal "odds" that crop up against all of us each day. Pathological fantasies derive from a chronic state of inner impoverishment, a feeling of emotional meagerness, and rising urges toward self-assertion that the person cannot express in any other way. With a high-risk child, the increasingly unbearable reality of being a "reject" in a world of perfection may cause him to compensate or console himself for his failure in mental (and visual) "if-onlies." Unfortunately these days, he is also keenly aware of the great attention and celebrity status, which is a form of power he may hunger after, accorded our assassins, murderers, and other law offenders.

In your efforts to keep your child within the acceptable limits of reality, it becomes important to get across to him that sometimes you really *do* enjoy his lively company, and to seek out and maintain associations with people who welcome the companionship of feisty, active children—though the opportunities for these relationships may seem few and far between.

Usually they are hardy types, do-it-yourselfers and outdoorspersons who can be found watching transistor-powered televisions inside their campers on rainy summer nights or cooking on propane-fueled stoves in good weather. They are particularly concentrated along the coasts of our nation on holiday weekends.

But you may not have to pull up stakes and flee to the nearest shore. Sometimes, when you least expect it, these people turn up, proverbially, in your backyard—an athletic scoutmaster, an enthusiastic drama or music teacher, a friendly and compassionate neighbor—bringing with them a shower of mercy, goodwill, and hope.

I recall one such godsend person, an auburn-haired former Playmate-of-the-Month and current would-be starlet who lived a few apartment houses away from us in West Hollywood the summer my son was seven. The sparkly aquamarine pool in the courtyard of her terraced complex was a magnet for his inner "noise." Being only nineteen years old herself, this young woman felt an emotional kinship and closeness to rebellious young children who seemed lost and having a hard time of it. In addition to her other attractions, she was a high school dropout and thus an instant heroine in his eyes.

Since she worked only sporadically at modeling jobs, Claude and this young sex goddess drifted and dreamed away many idyllic summer afternoons. Wrapped in each other's arms, they would sunbathe on a beach towel on the concrete slab which encircled the pool.

I no longer remember this young woman's name, but I recall how glad I was she was there for him that lonely summer of the empty clubhouse. He had spent weeks building a boys' club—his pride and joy—out of a scrap heap of old two-by-fours. He furnished it with everything from dishtowels and foam "beds" to ashtrays.

Everything except other children. Though he hung a sign over the door and sent out invitations to join, nobody ever came. This structure leaned against the side of our duplex, a little misaligned with the perpendicular, until the rainy winter season, when it collapsed ignobly with all its miscellanea onto the grass.

When my child asked whether this young woman could replace me as his mother, I didn't even flinch. By law, there ought to be more beguiling, liberated young bunnies.

There are paradoxes at work here, at least at first glance. One is that the more you can manage to baby this child, the faster he will grow up. Another apparent paradox lies in the fact that because his bond with you has been stronger than the average from an early age, the more he will need to challenge you for his separateness as he grows into independence. Insofar as his opposition is part of his struggle to free himself from his difference, it is a positive sign of health.

Recall Mary, the impassioned letter writer of Chapter 2, who described the distress she felt when B. J. seemed at the peak of his despair to be not only raging against the rest of the world but turning harshly against her as well. The B. J.'s of the world do this chiefly for two reasons. First, as already mentioned, their prolonged and tenacious early ties with the parent may lead to a fierce rebellion as they strive to become persons on their own.

Second, and more difficult for a neurologically intact parent to comprehend is such a child's rampant and recurrent sense of life's unfairness—his sense of having been cheated out of the chance for a normal, happy life. This feeling is not confined to school, playground, or the other usual sites of his failure, but at some time or another spills over into all the other areas of his life, including his home.

At some point he is certain to direct his bitterness and discontent against those he holds most dear and needs the most. Then he will try savagely to make enemies of them.

"Did you put cheese in this omelete?" "Yes, I said I would." "How come it doesn't taste like it?"

"I'm going to put this hunk of shit on the porch and smash it." He heads outside with the remote-control Corvette Stingray racing car that has cost a fortune, or at least half a week's grocery money.

"Why don't we ever have anything to eat in this refrigerator like a normal family?"

"Guess what, Mom? My teacher took us to the beach today and my friend and I had to be pulled out by the lifeguard."

Your whole lifestyle will come under his microscopic scrutiny and disapproval.

"Why are you always the slowest driver on the road?"

"This house is so *ugly* I can't stand to be in it another minute!" He slams the door so the windows shake.

"Why is this the only house in town with *roaches* in it?"

Incessantly and unflaggingly, he will push to get the rejection he suspects you are feeling underneath if it is not readily apparent in your behavior. (After all, why *not* you along with everybody else he knows?) All persons seek verification of their reality through a process of consensual validation—try to confirm what they think, believe, and feel about themselves and their role in the world by measuring these ideas against the yardstick of another person. And his reality is that he is unwanted, unneeded, and superfluous in this world.

When he is testing you in his devious and often ingenious way (If I throw the cat off the table, will you still love me? Will you want to get rid of me?) and you are about to swoop down to his childish level and scream abusive and hurtful insults back at him, separate yourself from him on the spot. Order him outside for a while if he is old enough or else seal yourself off in a room. Physical distance is critical at this impasse when all the lights are flashing red.

Pound the stuffings out of an upholstered chair or burst into tears, phone a friend, read a magazine, smoke if you absolutely must. Do whatever you need to do for yourself, whatever works best in exorcising the anger from your system. When you have recovered your perspective and feel calmer, then return to the encounter with your vision cleared.

If you place this wall of distance between you and your child and give both of you the chance for a cooling-off period, you will emerge from the depths of your anger and pessimism with the knowledge that this moment is not the end of the world—and maybe a bit of hope for the future.

You may even be able to glimpse behind your child's pout and stony, defiant eyes the frightened animal whose rage and disappointment in himself are overwhelming. Like a longer reprieve of an afternoon or evening away from him, getting off by yourself for a few minutes may enable you to recall the moments when your child was more honest in his agony—usually after experiencing still another failure or rejection—when he was openly able to sob out he wished he had never been born, or his greatest wish to be "just a normal, good person."

You will not always be successful in warding off an imminent physical attack by removing yourself from your child's immediate vicinity and giving each of you the opportunity to regain your equilibrium, dignity, and calm. Because his indignation and sense of betrayal are so intense and unfathomable to him, he will sometimes fly at you with crippling kicks and punches. At these moments of supreme pain, he will seem prepared to fight to the finish lest anyone dare to interfere with his bodily stance—his sense of his physical inviolateness or *structure*—which he perceives as the last bastion he can call his own in a world which is forever trying to change him.

Although his resistance will inspire awe and wonder (he will lunge at you with strength astonishing in one so young, swing and kick out at you wildly), *physical holding, the safety of bodily contact, is his greatest need at this angriest moment.* It is just because reconnecting with the body and skin of someone who cares about him is his deepest need that he will fight against it all the harder.

There are several techniques that have been suggested for these sometimes unavoidable physical contests, such as restraining your child in a harness or "chairing" him (pulling him down into a chair and "handcuffing" his arms behind the rungs with your arms). But the simplest, safest, and most dignified method is to get behind him and grasp both of his arms firmly between elbow and wrist with your own so you effectively "crisscross" his arms over the front of his body and lock them there. He can still kick you. To prevent this, put one of your legs between both of his and fasten your foot over one of his.

Hold him there until his curses, obscenities, and banshee screams turn into little boy tears.

At less extreme moments when he is shutting off the people who are most important to him—when he is most in pain and seems to be withdrawing from you and building a wall to keep you at a distance—you can give him a personal pillow. The Steve-opening-the-door-to-his-insides-and-feeling pillow. Let him pound on it till his arms ache, let him hug it, boot it around the room, spit on it, pee on it, cry into it, tear it apart with his teeth. Little by little his feelings will come pouring out.

The harder problem may be to get the other important people in his life—grandparents, aunts, uncles, and even other immediate family members who may be hiding from their own feelings—more involved and connected with him. Even if you have got things fairly straight in your own mind, it may seem next to impossible to impress upon these other significant persons that Steve is an invisibly handicapped boy struggling with loneliness, hurt, and failure.

As much as you, they need to understand that his foul language and angry and abusive behavior are not in most instances directed against them, but have the more general meaning of fury against a world which has cheated him. And therefore they are the expression of his feelings of helplessness and powerlessness.

Perhaps some simple analogies may help get your point across. We can all readily recall the caustic and insensitive remarks that have popped out of us, uncensored, when we were tired and dinner was long delayed, or when someone prematurely awakened us out of a cocoon of sleep which seemed vital to our sense of bodily integrity. Therefore you can tell these other people in your child's life to imagine this is his "normal" everyday state, a condition of mild biochemical imbalance in which his perceptions, verbalizations, and behavior may sometimes be slightly deranged. No doubt they will be familiar from a personal experience or two with the upsets in perceptual motor function, concentration, and mood associated with "jet lag" or alcoholic hangover.

It may also help to explain to them that one of the reasons why children misbehave, or lie, steal or set fires, is to get a peculiar kind of attention—to generate almost *any* kind of interaction with the other person—because they feel so impoverished. Anger directed at them at least sparks some activity with another person, and the smart of negative caring may be less painful than their feeling of neglect and nothingness.

Sometimes, you can also bring up, your child's antagonistic behavior may even be a kind of offbeat compliment. For when a child is sure a person really loves and cares about him, that person becomes a safe target for all the awful feelings he's having.

It is also worth the effort to try to get the other people in his life to keep the handicap separate from the child, and to see him as a child who has more in common with all human children than not.

If all else fails, ask them to mentally picture that your child, when he is in their presence, is wearing a football helmet of braces on his head.

The trauma of battered, abused, and/or sexually molested children has recently received a good deal of media attention, but up to now we have lacked the specific background studies which I have no doubt will one day link this epidemic to the increasing numbers of difficult-to-rear or "different" children among us. Only after many years of casual observations by juvenile probation officers, social workers, judges, and officials in the youth correctional centers and detention camps across the country did we undertake the cost-effective studies that conclusively connected conditions of minimal brain dysfunction to delinquency and childhood crime. And when those results were finally in, the evidence was fairly overwhelming.[1]

[1] Several studies conducted in the various facilities of the California Youth Authority in the late 1970s found this correlation between learning disability and juvenile delinquency to be shockingly high. Nearly 80 percent of the wards under the age of eighteen

An informal calculation I once made among the incarcerated child abusers at the California Institution for Women, which is the largest women's prison in the nation, revealed the rather stark statistic that as many as three out of four of the children who were mistreated and sometimes killed were mildly neurologically impaired or behaviorally "difficult" children. The women were virtually all first-time offenders who had been convicted of child-related crimes such as inflicting traumatic injury on a child, willful cruelty, neglect, or endangerment. They spanned the spectrum of age, ethnic group, and educational and social class.

Often, as in the case of Diane, the abused child turned out to be the only one in a large family of children who had been consistently singled out for punishment.

Diane had received even more than the usual share of publicity in the local newspapers because her full name is ironically, Diane Beastly. The reporters, the deputy district attorney, the judge, and even the public defender could not seem to let go of this rather remarkable semantic coincidence.

A soft-spoken and introverted woman of forty-two who wore a blue bandanna over her white-blonde hair, Diane immediately reached into the pocket of the splashy print duster that served her as a dress in the county jail and took out the packet of snapshots of her eight children she carried with her at all times. She offered them shyly, as a small girl would hold out a Girl Scout badge or a good report card.

Diane is so fearful that over the last twenty years she has peopled her own small world in order to feel secure. The only times she has strayed outside that world have been to take an early morning newspaper delivery route, and to attend the local Pentecostal church on Sundays.

This voluptuous and full-breasted woman, who had been jailed only a few days when I met her, broke down completely when she talked about her parting from her children and how they had asked, "Mommie, are they going to give you bread and water?" As she talked about her own parents, her husband, and her children, they seemed to expand until they filled all the spaces in the cell, leaving no room for her. Her brood included a ten-year-old girl, Quinn, who had been diagnosed hyperkinetic at an early age and was the victim in the crime for which her mother had been incarcerated.

were identified as having problems with reading (dyslexia) and difficulties with symbolization serious enough to qualify them for county-funded educationally handicapped school programs.

One spring day Diane, who had always been nervous about driving, had gone on one of her infrequent trips to the grocery store. Quinn, who had been left at home with instructions not to leave the house, had crawled through a hole in the fence into a neighbor's yard. The police officers who were summoned by this neighbor a short time later observed Quinn cowering beside the woman who had called them. They noted a blackened left eye and numerous bruises, sores, and open cuts down her body. She was holding her right arm in a suspiciously stiff, bent position and appeared frightened and malnourished. Her clothes and body were so dirty they gave off a pungent odor.

Quinn allegedly was clinging to the neighbor lady and asked if she could live with her. In a small, thin voice she related that her mother beat her many times a day with her hands and a black leather strap. She did not go to school and her mother had once thrown her against a wall.

The detectives took out their notebooks and began writing. When Diane arrived home an hour later, she was taken into custody on charges of child abuse and endangerment.

At the police station, she described herself as "overwhelmed by everything." She readily admitted her life was a "mess" and revealed tearfully that she had been having serious marital difficulties for several months. Her third husband's threats to leave her had totally unhinged her so she couldn't pull herself together enough to clean her house or send the children to school; she mostly relied on fast foods to feed them. Only two weeks ago she had delivered her eighth child, and though she had been hemorrhaging ever since, her extreme fear of doctors had kept her from getting the proper medical care.

Not only had her children suffered, but Diane had clearly not taken very good care of herself either. Passive and deprived, the only way in which she has ever managed to get a little of the tenderness and care she has always needed so desperately has been through the kind attention of the nurses at the local prenatal clinic. And even as she has measured her sense of worth in life by her ability to produce children, she has had only a dim sense of herself as a person with needs separate from those of her husband or children, who overshadow her.

A long, empty stretch of time flowed uneasily between us before Diane was willing to talk about Quinn. Then she began slowly and tentatively, making the connection between her husband and her father by herself.

"I felt my husband blamed me for everything that went wrong like my father would act like it was the end of the world if I made noise and woke my mother up or I wanted to go somewhere after school with another girl. He never hit me or even yelled but he'd punish me with these bone-chilling silences that were massive and scarier than any screaming, just a big emptiness which told me I'd ruined his life.

"Sometimes those silences went on for days and scared me so much I felt driven to fill them with the craziness that would well up inside me, and the terror. And I'd be shaking, though I tried not to let it show on the outside. I was terrified because I was losing him right there in front of my eyes and then there would be no strength outside myself. I was on my own, a small girl, and I had to be strong enough to survive alone but I couldn't—I just couldn't. Like with my husband, I'd try and try but I couldn't force him to give me anything out of those silences, something personal or just something that would connect me to life—pull me back from a scary ocean I was floating off to.

"It felt just like that after my husband went out and bought himself a new pickup we couldn't afford. It felt like it was all my fault. Everything went downhill with inflation and that truck until there was no stopping it. And I knew he blamed me for Quinn, who wasn't his child. He'd say, If I weren't married to you and didn't have to support other people's kids, I could have a bigger truck. Idiot that I was, I just kept thinking if I could control Quinn and if I stuck with him everything would work out okay. I guess I was like a kid who wants so badly to believe in happy endings."

Gathering up my satchel and writing materials, I was suddenly afraid for Diane and reluctant to leave her alone in her cell. I remembered the ominous warning in one of the psychiatric reports about the consequences of further punishment on her precarious mental condition. In addition to the guilt and chastisement she already felt keenly by being separated from her children, the very real possibility existed that she might be attacked by the other inmates in a custodial setting because of the child-related nature of her crime. With one stress piled on another, Diane might well develop stronger and more urgent suicidal impulses than she already had.

The psychiatrist had concluded his report: "I am honestly relieved that the question of detention or punishment for this unfortunate woman is outside the boundary of my expertise."

I think there is a good possibility that when we talk about behaviorally troubled youngsters or when we discuss the children most frequently targeted for physical abuse or psychological scapegoating by parents, stepparents, and other adults, or most prone to depression, we are talking—with some minor variations in conceptualization and scientific language—essentially about this same group of "difficult" or "different" children. Can our terror of nonconformity, the stigma of standing out a little from the crowd, be the common thread underlying many of these diverse misfortunes of childhood? I believe when all the evidence is finally in, the answer will be a resounding yes.

Many of us seem never to have grown beyond the painful self-consciousness of high school with its code of mass-produced homogeneity and rigid obedience to social norms. More to the point, the strong urges to get rid of our troublesome children in all of us—even, from time to time, in the most devoted, enlightened, and educated among us—connect with the internalized admonishments from our own past not to be disruptive, noisy, demanding, or *needy* children.

We go through life hurt children in parents' clothing who are forever lured by the old, sweet, hollow song of the Lorelei, the promise of our own parents' approval and "love" if we are quiet, mannerly, or subservient, deny our feelings, never complain or ask for anything, not even admit we're afraid when we're afraid—in short, take care of ourselves. I think it is this ancient tug in all of us that causes us the most distress in rearing our unconventional offspring.

Instead of admitting our painful feelings and attempting to come to terms with them, we try relentlessly to force our children into some more acceptable, cookie-cutter mold which will lessen our own load of pain. We seduce, bribe, cajole, scream at, or beat them or do anything we can think of, ignoring the old wisdom that the elbow bends only one way.

Sometimes, in this "shaping" process, we destroy them.

The story of Yvette is horrifying because it tells of the ultimate tragedy, the most incredible loss, the death of a child. It also speaks volumes about our economic and sociological policies in that it is as much a depiction of what it is like to be young, poor, black, and depressed and have no family or qualified and caring professional persons to help with advice and pragmatic treatment in coping with the additional stress of rearing a neurologically impaired child.

Yvette's story begins in the recesses of a southern state prison for women on a serene and sun-drenched morning during the last week in December. An unpublicized uprising which had as its slogan "Kill the baby killers" occurred in this facility on the morning of Christmas Eve.

These words are still painted in bold capital letters on the walls of the inmate dining hall, known euphemistically as Walgreen's Cafeteria.

I have written this account in the present tense to maintain its intensity and immediacy.

From a distance, from any vantage point along the country road that skirts the prison, everything looks ordinary. The parking lot that fronts the administration building is emblazoned by multicolored state flags undulating in the breeze. Tractor lawn mowers driven by blue-jeaned inmates move choppily over the lawn, a tan-uniformed correctional officer supervisor trailing slowly alongside each machine.

Just as on any other day, the air is alive with the buzzing of horseflies and carries steaming drifts of manure to the visitor's nostrils from all directions.

An incongruous border of nature and serenity, complete with grazing cows, encloses a brick fortress of man-made misery.

Inside Hastings-East, the maximum security unit named for a stern and venerable parole board member of long ago, all is far from normal on this luminous morning. The cells along both sides of the corridor bulge in the aftermath of yesterday's riot.

Chanting and the rhythmic beating of plastic cups and plates against the table edges had started up in the cafeteria during breakfast, in the cool of morning. By two o'clock in the afternoon the rifles had been brought out of their storage sheds, loaded, and positioned strategically on the roof of the administration building. Manned by a supplementary army of officers borrowed from a neighboring sheriff's department, they pointed straight into the mob of approximately three hundred shouting women.

Many of the women were wearing bright print bandannas on their heads against the hot sun and some were brandishing crudely fashioned knives and clubs, called "shanks" in prison idiom.

Fights broke out here and there throughout the facility all morning long. A male counselor trapped in his cottage office was battered by a dozen or so biting, scratching, hair-pulling women. Several officers and a vocational instructor were injured seriously enough in the skirmishes to be driven to a nearby community hospital. Three child abusers who had had pots of boiling water thrown at them were sheltered in the prison infirmary.

By four o'clock most of the women had lain down on their stomachs in the grass and allowed the officers to pull them back to their cottages by their arms. The doors of their single rooms were locked quickly behind them by means of a centrally located electronic control switch. As soon as night fell, the officers had swept from cottage to cottage unlocking approximately forty of the rooms and spiriting away the denizens—women with child abuse cases who were the objects of the seething hatred of the other women.

They had secured the child abusers in the maximum security lockup of Hastings-East. The other women also remained locked in their rooms, but with their personal televisions, books, clothes, writing paper, and other belongings as solace. Sometime during the night, the entire contents of the child abusers' rooms had been tossed hastily into cardboard cartons, which disappeared into the dank, cavernous basement beneath the prison hospital.

Today, all that these 6-foot-by-9-foot cells in maximum security contain, besides a cot, toilet, and sink, is a lone offering from the outside world: a package consisting of a Bible or other inspirational book along with a religious-motif calendar and bookmark.

Every woman at the prison has received this same yuletide gift, which is the yearly contribution of a minister from one of the local beach cities. Each Christmas week he drives to the prison gate with a station wagon load of identical beribboned boxes.

Some of the calendars and bookmarks are propped up decoratively on the window ledges in Hastings-East, but most still lie in their tissue on the floor. A slim blue box of tampons is also displayed prominently in every room. Three times each day, the slots in the heavy cell doors rattle as a sack meal is passed through to the other side.

Clothed in bathrobes or pajamas, the women inside the cells sit or lie on their cots turning over the pages of the devotional literature listlessly, chain-smoking or staring off into space. Along with the anxiety for their lives, the cancellation of holiday visitors just announced by the deputy superintendent has strained some of them to the breaking point.

A few casement windows outside the bars have been cranked partly open. Strident cat calls from the other cottages, obscenities daring the baby killers to come out of their protective custody, drift through these openings along with a cooling breeze. As I enter one of the cells and sit beside Yvette on the rim of her bed, I can hear the tail end of one particularly terrifying curse.

Yvette, a pretty young woman in blue jeans with luminous eyes and cornrowed hair, has been waiting for my visit. She is glad to have someone there and eager to talk about what has happened to bring her to this strait.

"Check this out, Miz. There's things going through my head 'bout my case that keep coming back. Different stuff like when I was growing up runs through my mind, and the way everything came down and when it all started. I was nine months pregnant when I went to jail, plus my patience was running short. And then her father would come over on and off and he was high off that PCP stuff.

"So I asked, Who is it? and he said, James. So I said, So what you want? And he said, I want to see my baby. That's Robin. I mean he was pulling on my clothes and saying, Gimme some. So then up jumps the devil and I was backing out the door and he was coming after me. Hey, I'm not no fool. I took my two kids and I moved to my own apartment.

"So then that's where everything started. When I was little I'd get accused of everything like James accused me of running around on him when I wasn't. It was his own guilt for doing it himself to me. Once I set the bed on fire 'cause my big sister told me to, but not two of us got a whooping, jess me. I was close to my mother in a way, but all the time I was coming up she had this drug problem.

"The big difference between me and my brother and sister was I was the darkest child. Robin was dark. It meant being the black sheep as far as my Daddy went. I said I would never treat my own kids that way, 'cause one was dark. Then I told my mother when I got a little older and got pregnant, I really want this baby 'cause I want something that belongs to me.

"Robin was a preemie baby. I gave her more attention with her not walking real well. She was a year and a half before I'd sit out on the steps and watch her play ball. And James sitting beside me, he'd say, I'm trying to figure on if I should claim her or not.

"Okay, I'm gonna bust out crying, but if she were alive today I'd tell her how much I loved her. We'd probably be gone somewhere to the park like we always did. Robin and Lakeshia and me. Or over to my grandmother's . . ." (Here Yvette is crying for several minutes and wiping her face with the end of the bedsheet.)

"Once James was sitting up on the bed and he said, Yeah that's my baby, that's my baby. And I seen the love that was denied. I seen she needed more love than Keshia. She was more so like me. I stayed under my mother, she stayed under her mother. She'd run over and you could see he didn't want to pick her up. So I said, Come here, Robin, and held her on my lap and jess looked at him like he was crazy. All this time my grandmother kept saying, You better stop arguing over that baby 'cause something's gonna happen to her sure as I'm sitting here. 'Cause God don't like that.

"Due to the circumstances of my case I really don't know how or why I did that to my baby, but I never meant to harm her. I jess snapped. I'm only eighteen and I was pregnant with Calvin my youngest and things didn't go as planned. I didn't receive what I was supposed to from the county and I was trying to potty train Robin 'cause she went back to acting like a baby again when I started showing. I thought of taking the kids to my grandmother's but she was sick, and my sister worked, and my mother was in the drug program. Truth is, I couldn't take them nowheres. But I thought about it 'cause I felt myself losing patience and starting to get real depressed.

" 'Specially when James came over to see 'his baby' a couple of days before the incident and he was holding her. But that didn't stop the hassle we had and then he was down on the floor wrestling me. She started looking like her Daddy and his conscience was eating him plus I had a lot of bitter feelings toward him and what he did to my babies. I felt like he rejected my babies, Robin and the one that was coming too, and I felt like I should never have had no babies by him but I never did once regret my kids.

"Robin messed on herself so I put her on the toilet and washed her, and then she peed on herself. When everything started coming back I knew I had a lot to do with my baby being slow 'cause of the PCP I smoked with James.[2] I felt it last week in my room 'cause I smoked that with her when I was pregnant. I thought about that, where she was slow and wouldn't catch on, and I wanted to rush her into doing it and by whooping her. It didn't dawn on me then but every time I come around now that girl is on the potty. It flashes on me that I knew I did that and that's why she wasn't doing it fast enough for me. I

---

[2] One of the saddest facts about PCP is that, just as with heroin, LSD, marijuana, and other drugs, the sins of a parent's habit can be visited upon the child. While only a few cases of "PCP babies" have been studied longitudinally as yet, the data that are already in support the notion that these children are generally neurologically and behaviorally abnormal. A number of these babies have been born blind, deaf, or severely retarded. Some are born having seizures. (PCP appears to concentrate in the fat cells of the body and is easily transmitted into the baby through breast milk, which is largely fat.) Others, like Robin, survive into childhood with more subtle but typical signs of neurological irregularity.

know it reflects on me and it was my fault 'cause I smoked with James. Any time something happened between me and him I'd run over to my friend's house and get me some dust and smoke. So then that's where everything started. I loved him, but I jess couldn't stand no more.

"I talk to her picture. I tell her I wish she was still here, and I do love you from the bottom of my heart so very much. I wouldn't be able to change what happened but I didn't never stop loving her. This last week I told her I know it was my fault she was slow and I didn't try to hurt her on purpose. But it still eats me up 'cause I did love her so much but at the time—I think that was only the first time when she was at the hospital, that I cried. Then at the county jail I couldn't cry so the judge felt like I didn't feel sorry for her, like I had no remorse, 'cause I couldn't cry in the courtroom in front of all those people.

"But back in the holding tank, that's when I'd cry. And when I came up here and had to show my face around all these hostile women, I really couldn't cry. Only for the first time yesterday, right after the riot, I did cry when I was talking to Robin. Everything that's been bottled up inside me has been coming out. Now why would you think that is?

"Like how I always wanted three kids. Two of them jess a year apart and one to come later. I didn't want no only child. And when Robin died, Keshia went to the hospital with me, and every day I was in jail they'd tell me she'd be playing by herself and she'd be talking to Robin in the corner. 'Cause they was so close she felt like Robin belonged to her. She'd treat her like she was her own baby so when the babysitter came, she'd say, Don't let her take my baby. Then I know Keshia will always miss Robin, same as me, and she'll always know Robin was here.

"I tried to explain to her, but when my baby came along, wasn't till he was a couple of months old, then Keshia started gradual to want to hold him.[3] Then sometimes when I'd get on the phone, she'd suddenly say, Momma, where's Robin? I'd say, With God, but it was like something stabbed me everytime she said it.

"I've wanted to say, Keshia, I'm not in no school like they told you, I'm in prison. I did say it, last time she was up here on a visit. She said, With the police? Yes. Then she said, Momma, when you

---

[3] During the time period Yvette is referring to here, she was out in the community on bail while awaiting trial on charges of involuntary manslaughter. It was in this ten-week interval that she gave birth to her third child, a boy.

coming home? Tomorrow? Two days? No. Fourteen more months. A year and two months. When you come home, Momma, you gonna live with us? Yes. You sure, Momma? Then she'll be looking at me like she's puzzled.

"All the time we were at the hospital and they was trying to save Robin, I can feel where she felt it and it's not a pretty situation 'cause it hurts a lot. Keshia slipped back. Then when my brother got murdered last year she slipped back more and so did I. I went back to the time I was home and the way Robin died. All that hurt stirred up again where I thought I was handling it, and it got even deeper. That's when I knew for sure I hadn't realized it and I had to deal with the past instead of trying to block it out like I was doing. I know they're both gone but I'm not facing that fact. On campus, you know how you sit up there in your room? Every now and then I'd get this real soft hurt and pain, and it would stay there, and then it would go away, and I knew it was Robin.

"Then sometimes I think that happened to teach me a lesson. 'Cause me and my kids would go everywhere together, wherever we went we went together. So long as I had them I was uppity and didn't need no one, but I was backsliding from church.

"Other times I wonder if it would ever happen again and I get scared of my mind jess snapping again. After I hit Robin and then I was jess hitting her, something wouldn't let me stop, and I jess kept on hitting her. Then that night her eyes was dilated more and she wouldn't eat. She was barely breathing and she had stopped breathing on me. As I drove her, I was holding her up here next to my heart and driving with my left hand, and I was shaking her so she'd be warm. I felt her stomach and she wasn't breathing. Then when we got there this car was parked in the way and I told the woman to let me park in there in the emergency, but she wouldn't and I called her a bitch. I screamed my baby isn't breathing and she told me to go out there and park in the parking lot but jess then the security guard came out.

"Robin was stubborn, that she got from me. I knew she was jess like me, stubborn and headstrong. I was telling her to say potty and she wouldn't. That's when I hit her, when she wouldn't say it. I kept on telling her to say potty and she jess kept on looking at me so I hit her again. Then I was whooping her with a switch off a tree. I'd stop and say, Say potty, and she still didn't say anything. Then I fed her and put her in the bed. I said, Until you learn how to say potty.

"I went and laid on my bed 'cause the whole time I had one of my migraines that the pills don't help where I was seeing white. She was over in my bed like she'd do and I reached for her and was hugging her and telling her I was sorry. After that it was around six o'clock and I was looking at the TV. The light went out as I was laying up there holding her. She kept moving around so I said, Robin, what's wrong with you? But she'd jess shake her head so I told Keshia to put the light on and I looked at her.

"Her eyes was going back in her head. She had her pajamas on and I told Keshia 'Come on, we're going in the car. I stopped at my sister's and run in and asked her boyfriend to ride with me to the hospital and keep my baby warm but he said he was going fishing. I ran right back and kept on going. I was running red lights and didn't care. Once I stopped in the middle of the street and gave her mouth-to-mouth breathing like on the TV.

"She lived till then. I got to the hospital at nine, till 10:17. I called my grandmother and she called the church and the whole church came up there, the minister and all the choir people. They heard me in there being hostile toward the doctors. 'Cause I don't know how many people came in there that night and asked me the same question. What happened? What happened?

"My grandfather went in and looked at Robin in her Snoopy pajamas." (Yvette is crying again.) "First I said that James did it 'cause I didn't want to go to jail right then so I told them that. But later on at my grandmother's something said, Don't lie, jess go on and tell the truth. Then I called James's house but he wasn't there so I put on a dress and went with the police. My grandmother was telling them, Don't put no handcuffs on her.

"By the time I got ready and came out in the living room James was there. He was staring at me and I felt in my heart it was as much his fault and I wanted to hit him. But I jess looked at him and kept on walking 'cause the police kept telling me to come on. He hadn't helped me and I couldn't pay the rent and I couldn't pay the food. Only one time since I moved away from him he gave me $25 to buy her an Easter dress and that was it. So in my heart I still feel like it was as much that nigger's fault.

"I feel like I'm paying for what I did. There's two ways I'm paying. The hurt will always be there and I think about her often and I dream about her like she wasn't gone away. In my dreams the three of us are walking over to the park with the stroller. Plus I'm locked up in the jail house. She'll always be part of my life, a part that's missing. All I have to do is look at Keshia and I can see her. And I can't change what I did but I can better myself. On campus before this thing happened I didn't get no help 'cause I didn't want to sit in no group with all those angry women. But no one can blame me for that, and I've thought if they do come at me I'll get me one of those metal things. . . .

"Yeah, I flash back a lot these days. I remember how I didn't want nobody close to my Mom so when she got a boyfriend, well, I had a fit. 'Cause I felt like the closeness we had would never be there again. You know, my Daddy and her separated 'cause of how he was treating me. Plus he was another one like James, he liked to play the field. I'd fall out in the middle of the floor and the dudes would try to buy me. I'd jess tell my mother, I want something, everytime a dude got close to her. So sometimes I can see why I took up with James 'cause fighting's all the family stuff I knew.

"Like once I watched my Daddy try to hit my mother in the head with a table. They'd fight 'cause he didn't come home and she was home with us. He'd end up fighting my mother and he'd have me so I'd be shaking 'cause I didn't want him to hit my mother. My youngest sister, Lakeshia Bernice, God took her when she was only two weeks old and my Daddy was going around saying she wasn't his jess like James. They was fussing over her and the next day my mother went to change her diaper and she wasn't moving. They called the ambulance and my baby sister died. My mother, she blamed my Daddy for that too, but then after a while my grandmother talked to her and told her why. Because God don't like no fussing over babies.

"I really had no doubt that James loved me, but he wasn't ready to settle down. Long as he goes out and plays, everything's cool, but jess let me go out somewhere. Thinking 'bout James I flashed back on how my Daddy hit my mother with an ironing cord. I thought, You ain't my Daddy, when he went out and stayed all night. That night my mother jumped under the cover with me and then I seen my Daddy with the ironing cord and I got a knife 'bout this long and I told him if he hit her again I was gonna kill him. My mother got in between us and that's the onliest reason my Daddy's still breathing.

"And in my unconscious like the psychiatrist told me, I knew James was no good for me. My mother said, I can read between the lines and I know that nigger ain't no good. Twice we went through the motions of getting married, but he didn't want me no smarter than him. He came to the county jail and said he was gonna kill me. My brother told me they had gone to the funeral home to view the body and James whispered in his ear, I'm gonna kill her. That's his guilty conscience 'cause he couldn't deal with his part of it. Then in jail my sister said with this gleam in her eye, Do you want to talk to James? 'Cause he's right here. I said No, 'cause he wasn't no Daddy and I don't want to talk to him, but she handed him the phone anyway. He kept saying, Why did you do it? But I could only cry and then it was twenty minutes and the time was up.

"During that time they was getting Robin's dress and all her things and he was paying for the funeral and the baby doll she was buried with. I said, he ought to, he ain't paid for nothing else. He came over and gave my grandmother the money for Robin's casket and dress. But none of them knew it till he was in the back seat at the funeral and lit up. They told me James parked up on the grass at my grandmother's and he was out in the back yard screaming and hollering.

"It was all of a sudden hard for me to believe 'cause when I was growing up and running with these older women, they told me, Don't take no shit. I was very mature and went to clubs and if anyone came up to me and tried to joke I'd snap off their head. Now here they heard something screaming and it was him out in the yard stone face and white eyes screaming he was gonna kill that nigger witch, me. I tried to laugh and said, That sounds like that sick sucker, but I was real scared jess hearing that.

"Then my grandmother said, That PCP do it, and then she had a gun in his face—I call it her Big Brother. Next she was the one screaming. My sister Miz Mouthpiece said the last thing before they all got in the car to go to the cemetery and James had claimed Robin too late, my grandmother was still hollering, Whoa, James, over and over, Whoa, James, till I believe like my mother came between me and my Daddy, that's the sole reason I'm here today to converse with you."

Another psychological truth we have only now awakened to, even more recently than the evils of child abuse and neglect, is the syndrome of childhood depression. A contemporary spate of newspaper and magazine articles has estimated conservatively that approximately 500,000 American youngsters suffer from these "killer blues." (My own belief is that the correct figure is much higher.) Childhood depression differs from the transient, occasional kind of sadness most children pass through during times of hardship or change, or as a reaction to a specific loss. It refers to a deep-seated, protracted despondency and negative self-feelings that interfere with and cripple a child's social-emotional, and even intellectual and physical, growth.

One reason we have only lately become alerted to this syndrome, and the related problem of childhood and teenage suicide (which claims an average of eighteen young Americans every day and has become the second biggest killer among the fifteen- to twenty-four-year-old group, second only to accidents) has to do with our stereotyped picture of childhood as blissful, sunshiny, and innocent of death wishes. The denial of this problem that has existed until now actually was sanctioned in the psychiatric literature in the official classificatory system of mental disorders. Except for the group of affective maladies which are disturbances of mood and self-image believed to have their onset in adulthood, serious depression has been relegated to a place of insignificance as an almost inevitable disease of the elderly. Involutional melancholia has long been considered an incurable but "natural" reaction of the older person to his loss of power, prowess, and capacity to enjoy life.

Once again it is too soon for the necessary research to have been carried out. Government and privately funded grants to explore this fledgling area are still too few. But my own observations give the strong impression we are again covering basically the same well-trodden ground—only using slight modifications in our theory and terminology.

From my personal experience and hundreds of talks I have had with other parents, I firmly believe we are describing in depressive disturbance a syndrome that includes among its victims a large percentage of this same group of children whose heightened sensitivity derives from their underlying biochemical difference. Their slight irregularity not only gets them into behavioral difficulties, including crime and delinquency if they are neglected, but renders them unusually vulnerable to every type of emotional difficulty known to befall the human race. Throughout their childhoods, they are the proverbial sitting ducks of mental illness.

If this overlap were not the reality—the "norm" for these youngsters as they grow into adolescence—how else account for the withdrawal, sullenness, moodiness, and alienation which most often supplants their former supercharged activity and gross motor difficulties around the middle years of childhood (ages 7 to 13)?

Depression is the "different" child's intrinsic (and predictable) response to his lowered self-esteem and his feeling of inadequacy. Like the antisocial activity such as petty theft, joyriding, or vandalism by which the lonely child affirms he belongs to a group in which others like and accept him, depression and withdrawal can as easily—and with about equal probability of occurrence—become this child's protective coloration.

Surely if childhood depression is defined in its broad sense as a state of chronic unhappiness including irritability, negativity, hypersensitivity to criticism, inability to have fun or sustain friendships, touchiness, physical complaints and pains, a persistent sense of loss and worthlessness, and excessive guilt or contrition, then it is safe to say the evidence for a correlation between minimal neurological dysfunction and childhood depression has been staring us in the face all along. It is confirmed just about every time we talk with the parent of a behaviorally disturbed youngster who has reached the threshold of adolescence.

Yet even in the most troubled cases, those that seem to hold no resolution in spite of everything that has been tried, I believe so long as there is life in you and your child, there is reason for hope. There are many stories like Lana's with the theme of pushing the child away in an attempt to spare yourself more pain when you feel already overloaded and then this strange child's behavior threatens to overturn your balance. There are narratives of searches to find neighborhoods where the child's peculiarities will not stand out in sharp, sore-thumb relief or schools where he will not be ostracized, kill or be killed. Often parents succeed in these endeavors.

An intriguing finding emerged from the collection of these odysseys which can perhaps offer some relief. A number of parents I interviewed found their child seemed to fit in with the least amount of environmental "resistance" in an urban environment, which absorbs its deviant children under a camouflaging umbrella of indifference as mercifully as its bag ladies, winos, and other schizoid adults.

Alternately, some of these children appeared to thrive in the country, with its unobstructed space and privacy, which gives free reign to open-air activities such as woodworking, horseback riding, or go-cart building at which these children frequently excel. (You can, of course, simulate this free environment in a corner of your garage or backyard.)

Often the other children in rural areas appeared not yet so sophisticated or mature in a worldly sense as their suburban counterparts—who are generally known to poke fun at any and all variations on the theme of uniformity, whether racial, ethnic, economic, or behavioral differences. Schools are usually smaller and more intimate in these districts and the pitfalls that trap behaviorally handicapped adolescents such as alcohol or drugs on campus are relatively rare. It is certainly not a place for everyone, but for those parents who like this kind of life, it may be a compassionate option.

The sense of peace some parents have found in these out-of-the-way settings is similar to the feeling of relief Suzanne Massie, the co-author of *Journey*, found in the womb of Europe with its greater tolerance for suffering and imperfections. Massie wrote about the devastating effects of hemophilia, which was her son's illness, but her account of her fifteen-year ordeal with this sickness relates movingly to all handicaps of childhood.

In France, where she lived with her family for a year, she discovered a healthy acceptance, unlike the youthful American castle-building, that in life one cannot always expect perfection or success. She described her amazement at how much pressure this simple shift in attitude lifted from her shoulders:

> Actually, in many ways it was easier to cope with Bobby's illness in France—psychologically, much easier. The French are an earthy, practical people. They sentimentalize less over children than we do in the United States. When it comes to the problems of chronic illness, they are quite matter-of-fact and unemotional. This attitude may seem cold to some, but it actually relieved me. Everywhere, in the schools, among doctors, I met the same reaction: Well, all right. It's difficult, you have a hard life . . .but then, *c'est la vie.* There is suffering in this world. People have problems. Chronic disease is one of them. No reason to stop living. Fight. *Life* is hard.

For Massie, it was like finding a huge family that belonged to her, but that she had never known existed.

More than likely, you do not have the prospect of changing your physical surroundings at will. In this day of unreasonable inflation and a constricted job market, you probably do not even have the choice of moving to the next town where the school system seems better and the yards more spacious. At this point, you have consulted interminably with educational and psychological specialists about your child's learning and behavior difficulties. You have tried family counseling and although it has helped somewhat to structure your child's life more lovingly, your day-to-day tension and his problems still seem to be ascending.

Some days you can barely control your hostility toward him and your desire to retaliate. The difficulties in your marriage and your relationship with your other children appear too many and complex, the solutions draining or only stop-gap measures. You spend a lot of time crying or screaming about absolutely nothing at all and sometimes feel as though you may be falling apart.

The bottom-line reality will have to be faced at this time that both you and your child may be better off temporarily separated from each other.

Supportive, caring relatives or friends with whom your child could live for a time would be the ideal, but unless you are more fortunate than most, such people are no more available to you than geographical utopias.

Even at this razor's edge, you do have at least one last option. You have the choice of placing your child in a residential treatment center which offers both special education and programs of intensive individual and family psychotherapy.

Several things hold us back from seeking this kind of relief even when we need it so desperately: a false hope that the child will "grow out of" his trouble; a dogged belief that determination, gritting our teeth, piety, or the good old-fashioned discipline our friends and family may be urging on us will pay off if we but persevere; and the fact that the hysteria sometimes lets up on its own.

All three are illusion.

Of all the human trauma written and rewritten about in the national magazines and the advice columns in the popular press, nowhere could I locate a recent piece on temporarily relinquishing custody of a child whose behavior is out of control or deteriorating into serious disturbance. Perhaps this is not so surprising in view of the great shame and disgrace, and the extreme sense of failure, which still shrouds this increasingly common parental experience in the middle and upper-middle classes of America. Possibly, too, this action is regarded as contemptible in the case of a child who looks—and often acts—so normal.

Karl's story—a narrative of reclamation—is one of initial turbulence but ultimate triumph over what seemed a confusion of insurmountable problems. Because Karl was recently separated and did not have the finances to pay for a special residential school, he had temporarily to give up custody of his boy in order to get the kind of help—twenty-four-hours-a-day, seven-days-a-week structuring and supervision—Aaron needed so glaringly. This case also illustrates how the problem is aggravated for the single parent struggling alone to rear a behaviorally nonconforming child.

His first wife had abandoned the family when Aaron, who was not Karl's natural son, had been a little over a year old. Rather reluctantly but with strong pangs of conscience that would not allow him to do otherwise, Karl had assumed the responsibility for Aaron and the two had moved in with Karl's parents. Three years later, he had tried marriage a second time, to a quite immature but well-meaning young woman, Cindy, who worked in the office at the fiberglass plant where he was a quality control inspector.

One of the main attractions had been that Cindy appeared unbothered by her sudden motherhood. For the first six months of the marriage, she had stayed at home with Aaron, who was then four, and the two of them seemed to have some good times together. Later Aaron said with downcast eyes of his stepmother, "The first year I had fun, but then she didn't seem to like me as much."

Serious difficulties between Karl and Cindy soon set in and led to over six years of conflict, arguments, and discord, with some verbal and physical violence on Karl's part as the marriage disintegrated. During these stormy years, Aaron was shunted aside more and more by both adults. Since he was a socially handicapped child with few companions, this parental rejection made his situation even more painful.

Around the age of five, he could no longer hold in his lonely and angry feelings and began to act out in the typical ways: at school he displayed aggressiveness and teased the other children; in the neighborhood he threw rocks, committed malicious mischief against the property of others, and provoked the older children, who would then gang up on him.

Throughout these years there had been a number of separations—especially stark times when the family just abruptly dissolved for a few weeks or months. These periods were followed by precarious reconciliations that were more truces than anything and resolved none of the underlying problems in the marriage.

When Aaron was eleven, Karl and Cindy separated for the final time. They divorced a few months later. Both had agreed that Aaron should remain with his stepfather, who was financially more capable of supporting him. But by then Karl realized it was too late for him and Aaron—whom he wanted neither to love nor to give up for adoption—to work out a life together without a good deal of outside help.

Aaron's inability to attend even a seriously emotionally disturbed class in a neighboring school district was threatening Karl's very survival.[4] He felt in danger of losing his job because of the urgent phone calls that would reach him at work several times a week from Aaron's teacher, the school principal, or even the classroom aide. There were many hastily arranged, last-minute meetings at the school office to determine Aaron's immediate fate, and week-long suspensions when there was no one at home to supervise him.

Left to his own devices, he would get into still more trouble. The local police all knew Aaron's address and phone number by heart. They complained that troublesome kids like him were not the reason they had gone into police work.

Here Karl is describing the first of his several court appearances when he surrendered physical (but not legal) custody of Aaron to the Los Angeles County Department of Public Social Services (DPSS) through the Juvenile Court system.[5]

"Driving groggily into L.A. at seven in the morning. Sitting beside me, Aaron seems subdued and scared and little, not the usual thing for him. Christ, why do they have to have the goddam Juvenile Court in the same building as the Criminal Court? Could it be part of a master conspiracy to make a parent feel even worse? Except how could you feel any worse, or any more of a failure? This has to be the rock bottom of parenting—an experience I can't even tell my relatives about. Not yet anyway. Not till this whole thing is over and there isn't a fucking thing they can do to stop me.

---

[4] Aaron had been identified in kindergarten as an attention deficit disordered child and placed in a special program. As his behavior became more unruly and difficult to control, he had gone from straight learning disabled classes at the local school to a county-funded seriously emotionally disturbed (SED) class outside the district, to which he was bused.

[5] Recent changes in law in many states including California have had far-reaching and deleterious effects on child care agencies such as residential treatment centers. In the past, parents who were going through a period of conflict, instability, or unhappiness which increased the behavior problems in their child could seek temporary "voluntary placement" in a protective and therapeutic environment. At this time, the courts in most states no longer make voluntary placements, and children who may simply need a period of intensive supervision are not referred to the courts by the department of social service. About the only way left for a child to be referred to the courts is if the parent can show that his life has actually been endangered by the home situation. The youngster is then made a ward of the court, the parent must relinquish custody, and placement outside the home becomes mandatory. This regrettable turn of events—which has come about because of cutbacks in government funding—has yet to be challenged in any state superior court.

"The cars on the freeway look like hundreds of ants scattered every which way by a giant footstep. Does Aaron see them that way too, I wonder? How did we get to this point anyway? What went so haywire? I guess I'll have plenty of time to figure that out after today.

"I was a little reckless when I changed lanes just now. I'm tensing up and going numb as the car plummets downhill into the narrow main street of Chinatown, the scant L.A. skyline off to the right.

"One part of my mind is cool and collected as I note the underground parking in the Civic Center has jumped from $3 to $7. The bastards know they have you. This is the part that knows I'm doing the right thing by placing Aaron at the special school. I'm doing the best—no, the only—thing I can do for both of us right now. His grandparents would never understand or see it that way, though.

"Another part of my mind is crazy. This part is telling me everyone on the street *knows* what's happening here, what a scumsack whimp I am. When I take Aaron's hand to cross over to the big gray flagstone Criminal Court building (which looks like something out of a Perry Mason rerun), I'm avoiding people's eyes. Inside, when my lawyer asks how I'm feeling, I joke. About midway between a criminal and a victim, I say and he smiles. But my heart is racing and I know Aaron's is too inside his small body. He is strangely quiet and sullen and stands very close to me.

"The wait with about fifty other families camped in the dim, stuffy corridor seems forever, but later, the morning has disappeared too quickly. Very little happened there in the courtroom. I didn't even get to say 'Here' when the bailiff called my name when everybody first crammed into the benches for roll call after the judge finally arrived at ten. Right away my lawyer jumped up and said it for me: 'Stepfather present this morning along with counsel, your Honor.'

"The face of the blonde lady bailiff was a blur, and the court referee who read the petitions out loud at a rapid fire pace. It reminded me of those old cigarette commercials on the radio years back, where an actor who was supposed to be a tobacco auctioneer mumbled a long string of incomprehensible words and ended up loud and clear with the name of the product: 'Sold to Pheeeleeeep Moreeeees. . . .'

"She was the one who led Aaron out of the court after no one objected to any of the terms of the petition (everybody *knew* there would be no protest raised) and after eleven years and seven months he was all of a sudden removed from my physical custody and not mine anymore. She took him into the emergency shelter for kids which was a sad imitation of a playroom off the main courtroom. It looked so normal, only this one was designed to protect the kids from further damage by parents like me. I could smell her perfume as she passed near the front bench where Aaron was sitting still between the lawyer and the referee.

"He didn't even look back at me as he went off with her, just forged ahead grimly with his left shoulder raised almost to his ear in the stiff, lopsided, self-conscious way he has of walking. Seeing him go, a slender boy with tufts of sandy hair, I kept thinking: I've lost him and he isn't mine anymore.

"Hard as it was to stomach, I guess I was luckier than a lot of the other parents because I already knew where Aaron would be spending the next year or so. I'd called in the DPSS people myself when I realized I couldn't handle the situation alone, not with things having progressed as far as they had. So there were no suprises that morning.

"I'd had a couple of meetings on my lunch hour with the children's worker from the emergency service who was the first one who told me about the school for kids like Aaron. By the second meeting we had decided definitely on this school. Only then, immediately after I had signed the papers for the placement, she told me visiting 'privileges' would be at the discretion of the school staff. Since I had just assumed I'd be picking Aaron up on the weekends—no reason why not—that part came as a jolt. The old terror of the system, of things being out of my control—my kid taken out of my hands and turned over to unseen and maybe unreasonable forces with the power to judge me as a fit human being or not—came back.

"I went into therapy myself right away, and not just because it was one of the stipulations ordered by the judge for eventually getting Aaron back. In fact, you could say I threw myself into it. I went to a group twice a week and saw the shrink who ran the group for private sessions whenever I could afford it, which was usually every second week.

"I was lucky here, too, because this shrink was into a feeling kind of thing, not the usual head trip that makes you sound smart but doesn't really change anything inside you. Still, it took this guy several months of chipping away at my defenses, week by week, in the group and the individual hours, till we managed together to dredge up some of the stuff that was keeping me from loving Aaron or wanting to take proper care of him—or even *liking* him—though I couldn't let go of him completely.[6]

---

[6] The worst feeling of all for a child, which in some cases is the reality, is that a

"What I learned was mostly it was my relationship with my own father that was holding me back from being able to give to Aaron or want him even though I had accepted the financial responsibility for him after Jeannie took off. Money turned out to be the least of it. I had seen him as a young bird alone in a nest, out in the cold. I'd related to him that way and kept him at a distance the way I would have a stray animal I felt sorry for but didn't really want to let inside my house. He sensed that from the beginning, that he really didn't belong to me because I wouldn't let him.

"Then a short time after I got married again he began to act out—I know now he did that because of his fear of losing the little sense of his place he had with me. Let me tell you it was a pretty thin reed, but it was all the kid had. All the time Cindy and I were struggling with each other to get what neither of us could possibly give, a kind of mature love and caring, this kid was getting sicker and sicker.

"With the shrink's help I had to relive the times I'd never gotten what I wanted or needed from my own father, and I had to deal with the fury and rage it would bring up in me if I saw Cindy or my best friend Bob (who used to ride Aaron around the block on his motorcycle when he came over) *giving* anything to Aaron. I'd actually think: Who the fuck does this little fucker think he is to get the things I never could? Those were the times I'd really punish him, if not with sarcasms and put-downs, then with my silence and withholding what I knew deep down this kid was dying for. Me to show him how to swing a bat or drive a nail, all the things a little boy needs from his Daddy.

"He'd get so frustrated trying to build a model or do some project from an electronics kit that was way too advanced for him. I'd just sit there reading my newspaper or watching TV. And I'd wait—I would be crouched there like a hunter in hiding—for the explosion to happen, the moment when he would throw the thing he was working on across the table or against the wall, so I could slap him or yell at him and feel justified in shutting myself off from him even more.

"Long winter nights when Cindy would be at her speed-writing class I'd be in my study with the door locked and Aaron would be on the

parent does not really like him and only feeds, clothes, and physically shelters him out of a sense of duty or legal obligation. For this child—no matter what else he is given, no matter how expensive the private school or the visits to the doctor for injections of megavitamins or to renew his prescriptions for pediatric stimulants—the world is truly lost. If a parent is beginning persistently not to like the child, or is unable to sympathize with him, this is a strong indication that he needs temporary foster placement.

other side of the door doing I didn't know or care what so long as he wasn't interfering with me or wanting anything from me. I wouldn't be doing a damn thing in that room, maybe half-assedly looking through the books I was supposed to be studying for my contractor's license or more likely leafing through muscle or hot rod magazines or masturbating over porno pictures, but having the grim satisfaction of knowing I wasn't giving in to him since no one had ever done this for me. No one had given me one goddam minute of their time or caring, and I wasn't about to give anything I didn't have to to a stray who wasn't even my own kid and gave me less pleasure than a well-trained dog would have.

"In the therapy all the pain of denial by my own father, and of realizing I couldn't love Aaron, started to come up, and how I hated to see anyone give anything to him, even so much as a smile, because I wanted everything for myself. I had to feel how my Dad would make me so mad because I knew so much less and he had all the power. And I had to realize that I saw my brothers and sisters in Aaron, the way I saw them back then when they were little and I hated every one of them with a passion—hated myself in them, really. A bunch of dirty, unloved, snotty-nosed kids wearing torn clothes who weren't getting what they needed and never would.

"He'd give me straight advice about Aaron, too. How I couldn't change any of the pain I'd caused him in the past, I couldn't ever make up for it, but the only thing I *could* do was give him a loving home in the present and that would bring up the hurt of the past, when he wasn't getting anything from me, just naturally, and then when it did we could start to deal with it. It would come up by itself and the worst thing I could do would be to hammer away at it and try to get it out of him artificially or probe too much when he wasn't ready for this.

"All during this time I kept having lots of new insights—like how I could no more have made a nest for Cindy and this child although in fairness to Cindy I have to say that at the beginning she seemed willing to try. But that set me back even more that she seemed to like Aaron—that took even more away from me because I saw myself as the really deprived one. Each time a bit of this would come out in therapy, I started to act a little softer and a little more giving around Aaron. At first he resisted my advances.

"He'd pretend he was too grown up for hugging or holding and it was embarrassing for him to be around that baby stuff anymore. He would act like he didn't care when underneath he cared more than life itself. But he didn't yet trust me or my feeling for him. Anyway, little by little I came on doing those things more each time I'd see him, and I started to look directly at him when I talked to him which was something I'd never done.

"Every Sunday when I saw him I'd realize a little more how hurt he was, how much his Mommie and Daddy had hurt him. I would be waiting at the reception desk in the school lobby to take him to Bob's Big Boy for lunch and I'd see him in the distance, out the big back windows with a view of the grounds, coming slowly across the lawn.

"He'd look so small and alone, and he would be wearing his best clothes, his long-sleeved yellow chamois shirt in the heat of summer, and his dark slacks. When he would get to the desk and first look at me there would be this flash of fear—this wondering if he was going to get anything from me that visit—that would cross his face. Then he'd say offhand 'Hi, Dad,' but he would avoid my eyes. (Before this he had called Cindy Mom, but mostly called me Karl as though to underscore the cold, distant relationship we had.)

"At these moments there was a confusion in his eyes (steady blue eyes like mine, I suddenly noticed)—and caution, too. He was stopping himself from feeling too much or hoping for too much before he got hurt again.

"What happened was that after a couple of months of learning to give to myself and feeling selfish about myself for the first time—including cutting myself off for a time from my parents and relatives—I found I wanted to give more and more to Aaron. I started to want him to stay with me a little longer each visit, first for overnights and then the whole weekend, whereas at the beginning I resented spending time with him even every other Sunday.

"And what I wanted to give him was different than the material things—the digital watches, motorized model cars, mini stereos, and all the other things he was always wanting to fill the void inside him and feel as good as the other kids. From time to time I would break down and buy those things out of my guilt for not loving him. I started to call him Spiky again, which had been his nickname as a baby, though God knows why. I put my arm around him as I showed him the room I had set aside for him in my new apartment. I no longer tensed up or got angry when he became frustrated, complained that things were unfair, or cried.

"All this led me to the amazing discovery that Aaron was going to get well as soon as I got well enough to be able to let him have his feelings, especially his anger, without trying to take them away from him. Meanwhile, if I could just manage to give him even a little and didn't add any more pain to his life, he would begin to cure himself instinctively with the almost irrepressible optimism, bounce and resilience that exist in all children, even handicapped kids. You see it in their faces as they race and pole-vault in the Special Olympics on TV.

"All the time I was learning that Aaron was just like me—he needed what I had needed as a small boy, no more, no less—I was also making these last-ditch efforts to contact Cindy and get her to come over to the apartment to talk. I knew it was no good, though, and she was never coming back. This was something I had to deal with on my own, apart from Aaron. I had to let go of my struggle with Cindy and the fix we had become for each other for all those years when between us we nearly destroyed a little boy.

"Things were starting to clear up for me—the reason why I had never turned this kid over for adoption in eleven years or handed him over to my parents to bring up even during the peak of my not liking him or wanting to be bothered with him. I even realized why I was willing to let go of my other love, my adult love, without much of a fight. It was just because Aaron was a castaway like me—unloved by his father, needy, broken inside, sucky. It was my own suckiness, my need to be dependent and taken care of, I couldn't stand when I recognized it so nakedly in Aaron. I'd push him to toughen up—to be a 'man' rather than a child—just so I wouldn't have to feel that need in myself.

"But I'm a Viking and stubborn as hell. Aaron, too, is a scrapper although the reason he never gave up on me completely was because he couldn't, because he would have been totally lost without me as his only lifeline. But I won't give up on him because I just won't, not because I can't. It will take a while longer—we'll have our ups and downs till we really understand each other and how we fit into each other's life—but we're going to make it.

"We tell each other that in our different ways. We'll be riding somewhere in the car and I'll look over at him and say, 'You know, Chief, you and I are gonna make it.' He'll look away and pretend to be staring out the window, but last weekend when I brought him back to school the old man-to-man handshake which is usually all he's comfortable with didn't seem enough to satisfy him. He's very rigid and self-conscious around people and embarrasses easily, but right there in front of the receptionist and the night supervisor, he reached up and put his arms around my neck and clung to me.

"When we finally separated, both our faces were wet and it wasn't possible to tell which one of us said it first. The words came out of us separately but simultaneously and mingled into one meaning.

" 'I love you, Dad.'

" 'You and me, Spiky old fellow, we're gonna be okay.' "

7

The Parental Underground: A Saturday "Buddy" Group

The littered suburb scallops for miles along the ocean, huddles of fast food chains, discount stores, and oriental massage parlors on the Pacific Coast Highway. A far cry from the beach cities with palm trees and marinas travelers envision as the California promise. Even the margin of sea is gray and rough and cold.

Improbably, two of the country's leading psychiatric hospitals for children nestle in this working-class community. Four parents in the group we are to meet have had children hospitalized there.

Late-afternoon sunlight slants through the venetian slats of the Hospital Medical Building. The spacious group room, which sports a temporary border of iced tea and cookies, has been lent by a social worker who practices here during the week.

At the far end, a circle of metal folding chairs has been stridently assembled.

Totaled up, fourteen parents of diverse backgrounds and income, banded together by an announcement in a neighborhood newspaper a year ago, make up the group. Of the eight who are present today, four are divorced and two have adopted children; five are college graduates, one is a high school drop-out. A teacher, a construction worker, and a hairdresser are among them; religious believers alongside atheists.

Several have been stable in their residence and a few have moved frequently.

A spectrum of identifications and lifestyles—but despite the surface heterogeneity, all are partners in a common problem: children who are more alike in their aggressive and impulsive traits than can be accounted for by chance alone: kids who pull knives when asked to take out the trash. The children share a similar biological inheritance—and thus a similar behavioral "fate"—which has leveled the variations among their parents in child-rearing practices and philosophies.

Five or six minutes into the session . . .

Lupe (*nervously, smoking, on the edge of her chair*):   Have I met all of you? If I haven't, I'm Lupe and my son is seven.

(*A new member, Lupe has been referred to the group by a local psychiatrist as a support to her individual therapy.*)

Georgia: Naturally a boy.

Dean: Is he left-handed? (*Group laughter*)

Lupe (*surprised*):   How did you know that?

Katie: Did everyone see the interview Barbara Walters did with the Hinckley parents the other night?

(*Katie, who is working on a degree in psychology, is the leader. Since she has had the idea to write a booklet about parent self-help groups such as this for her master's thesis, the meeting today is a special one. It will sum up some of the parenting experience and skills acquired since the group began.*)

Dean: Hey, a long time ago when he was being led off by the Secret Service guys, I knew right off. I said it to Sheryl. "He's one of them, he's one of our kids. How much you wanna bet?"

Georgia: You get this sixth sense so you can usually spot them a block away.

Janet: The thing that struck me was it was a case where they couldn't fall back on the usual kinds of, you know, professional criticisms. "They failed to set limits for their kids," or, "The home isn't well-run." Not that home anyway.

Liz: When his mother said a look into his closet was like a look into his mind—meaning the disorganization in his thinking, too—I saw Brandon's life going down the drain.

Janet (*shuddering slightly*):   There was an even sadder program a few weeks ago it reminds me of. Did anyone see the interview with Kevin Cooper's mother in Pennsylvania? (*Kevin Cooper is a black California prison escapee convicted of the mass murder of a family.*) I couldn't even watch at the end when she looked in the camera and said, "Honey, whatever you've done, Mama still loves you."

Dean: Right, it sums it up. The thing that scares us the most. Our kids aren't gonna make it—they're gonna kill or get killed.

Katie: I was just thinking, one of the things JoAnn Hinckley said was different about her son was that it was always difficult for him to express his feelings. And that's exactly how they are. They're very physical kids for a much longer time than normal.

Janet: It's been the worst problem I've had with both my kids, that the self-control just isn't there, and how do you build it in?

Katie: He came right out and said that, didn't he? He did that to let Jody know how he felt? Of all the things we've learned in here so far, I'd say it's the single most important. To get our kids to the place where they're verbalizing their feelings so they're not coming out in a dangerous or bizarre way.

Liz: Which I learned the hard way means that first of all, before that can ever happen, you have to be open to your own feelings, and able to say the feelings you're holding inside.

Lupe: But what if your kid doesn't know what he's feeling? He's acting crazy and out of control and has no idea? What do you do then?

Dean: Yeah, he's screaming and grabbing your clothes like Eric the other night when we were leaving him with a sitter. Just out of the blue he started up. Do you stay home at that point with him crying and clutching onto you, or coolly go on about your business?

Lupe: Jason screams and carries on when I drop him off at his school; it's an everyday thing we go through.

Liz: Well, that could be one of those times when *he* doesn't know what he's feeling, but *you* do, or you can make a pretty good guess as to what's really bothering him, so you do. You tell him. Like you come right out and say something direct that gets under the crummy behavior like, "You're afraid because you think I'm not coming back." Because there really was a time when you left him when he was a baby, Dean, that he's probably remembering.

Katie (*to Liz*):   You've been using that technique for some time now to pull Brandon back.

Liz: He'd have this look on his face I can't describe. Like a maniac or something subhuman. His eyes would roll around in his head and he'd have this stagey grin that was painful to see.

Katie: Did you ever find out what that look was saying?

Liz: When his eyes were rolling? See me. Here I am. I think he was saying something sort of like that.

Georgia: Look at me, I'm hurting. I don't like what's going on here. *Stop.*

Liz: It really was an awful time right before my separation when my husband and I were always arguing and fighting and having screaming matches. As I remember, it was mostly at those times when Brandon would look that way and then run all over the house tearing things up like a crazy person. And as far at least as I could tell, those were the times when he was the most hyped up and just, sort of crazy.

Janet: When he was in a lot of pain.

Katie: What do you do with that as a parent when your kid is out of control? What have any of us done?

Liz: What I did that usually worked was I'd just stop whatever it was I was doing, and hold out my arms and ask, "Brandon, do you need some attention?" I'd say, "Why don't you come here and I'll give you some attention."

Katie: Right. Exactly. Or you could be even more direct if you're at a place where you're comfortable with it. You could go right into the unconscious need and say, "Are you sad because your Daddy's leaving?"

Liz (*tentatively*):   The progress I feel I'm making lately has more to do with what Brandon's anger does to me, why I'm having so much trouble dealing with him when he's angry.

Katie: We can get into that. Anything you want to say about it.

Liz (*slowly*):   I've been seeing how it goes back to when I was a little girl, and there was a lot of anger and violence in my family. I've been recognizing how I'm still afraid people are going to be furious at me and blame me for everything. And I'm scared I can't control Brandon at those times like my Dad would be in these drunken rages when he'd come home.

Dean: But can you say it simply, Liz, the thing you're most afraid of when Brandon's angry?

Liz (*starting to cry*):   He won't like me if I'm a mean Mommy. He'll end up hating me like everybody I've ever been close to. It's my feeling like the fear. Nobody really likes me, nobody wants to be my friend (*crying a little, then recovering*). The feeling is still there sometimes though it comes up less and less lately that I could never have anything good in my life, like a nice dad who wasn't mad at me all the time, or a pet like the other kids.

Janet: And now a nice straight kid like everybody else.

Liz: Yeah, I guess that's pretty much where it's at for me.

Lupe: Everywhere Jason goes, if it's only down the street, he keeps getting rejected because of the way he acts, and I get frantic because there's this god-awful *something* I can't seem to get through, like some stone wall between us. I can't ever reach him to get him to stop acting whacky, and I get panicky. I say to myself, "He's going to die in the electric chair one day. I just know it." He's repeating the same violent behavior, and just won't stop.

Janet (*softly*):   If you're feeling hopeless, he's got to be picking up on that.

Lupe: I'm just so tense all the time. I go to work and then I come home to the laundry and the cleaning and the cooking, and there are always notes or phone calls from his teacher or the principal to greet me. She calls me almost every night after *she* gets home, and I'm always exhausted and irritable waiting for her to call.

And if I don't hear anything for a couple of days, I'll have my fingers crossed maybe things have been going okay, but then it always comes — Jason had a violent episode that day. And I lose it, I totally lose it and take out my frustration on him. I yell and scream and later I cry and tell him I'm sorry.

Janet (*sympathetically*):   When Heather was little and refusing to go to school, I found one way I could take some of the pressure off both of us was if I let her stay home for a day. I was under a lot of pressure myself because she wasn't fitting in, so it was a healing thing for both of us that every couple of weeks we'd take a day off, you know, sort of a mental health day, and bake cookies or just do something together.

Katie: The extra time with you probably made the difference.

Janet: Oh, but I never let her off the hook completely. I'd always say, "You know, when you have a good day at school, that makes me happy."

Georgia: We found most of the time when Mitch behaved horribly, he was really saying underneath the behavior he couldn't do it. Like he couldn't take the next step like school without some more help from us first. He just wasn't strong enough.

Dean: That's my gut reaction when Eric starts to get far-out.

Katie: He isn't feeling ready to be thrust out into the cold, cruel world. Is that what you mean?

Dean: Yeah, sorta, and if he doesn't get what he really needs from Sheryl and me, he's gonna keep on making those dramatic statements that are guaranteed to get our attention, whether it's in school or somewhere else. And even if he only gets my negative side, he still gets my time. I sit down with him, and so it's got to be better than his getting nothing.

Lupe: But I don't understand why Jason doesn't feel that from me? I give him a lot of attention. I honestly feel I do.

Georgia: Well, it doesn't matter why, we found that out. "Why" can be a waste of everyone's time, but a couple of specific things we did with Mitch, if you can arrange your work hours, might help. Like one of us used to walk him to school every day, and I was a volunteer at his school whenever I could take the time off from work.

Janet: I did a lot of those kinds of special things with Heather, too, and it's like being a port in a storm. I remember one Halloween years ago they had a costume parade at her school, and I was the only parent who showed up at lunchtime. She didn't want the other kids to see me so I stayed in the background. She was ashamed of needing me in their eyes, but she could feel my presence there and that gave her the confidence to participate in a social thing. She'd been dying to do it but felt she couldn't quite manage it on her own.

Katie: But while you're doing all these extra little somethings, and they do seem to help, you still have to help her to recognize her deep feeling. You still have to say, "You feel safe when Mommy's here," that kind of thing, to make the connection for her.

Liz: When Brandon was small, I had the instinct that he needed me to be stronger and protect him more than I was doing, but I just couldn't stand up to all those other people, like my relatives and his teachers, when they'd accuse me of overprotecting him.

Janet: I heard that a lot, too. I was overprotecting Heather.

Georgia (*exasperated*):   But it's commonsense. There *are* special dangers for our kids, like physical dangers.

Katie: Does anyone think there's a valid criticism somewhere in this that you can shield your child a bit too much because you feel bad about his limitations and, you know, want to spare him any more hurt?

Janet: During the peak of my divorce guilt, Heather would ask me why her dad wasn't getting in touch. I'd always have some cheery excuse—"Maybe he's busy," "He'll probably call us next week." Then one day in a rotten mood, I just came out and told her the truth. "Nobody's stopping him, I guess he doesn't really want to see us." And it hurt her, but I know that giving her that honesty made her life a whole lot saner than always walking around in a fog like she was, not knowing what the truth was, and always wondering whether she was going to get something from her dad that day or not.

Georgia: During that awful period when Mitch was screwing up in school day in and day out, and I was drowning in his problems, he was fourteen then and it was a sort of "reality therapy" that finally took over. Where suddenly I understood that what I'd been doing for years—trying to spare him by taking on all the blame myself—wasn't working, so I just stopped cold. I backed off from the school problems, and let him know he'd simply have to start watching his step if he wanted to stay in the regular school and not be bused to the school for problem kids. And I know in my heart it was the reason why his behavior improved so quickly. The feeling he'd never had when I was always pulling him out of the line of fire—running out and finding another school, or fighting with the teacher, or what have you. Now he was free of me, it would be his victory or his failure, and not mine.

Dean: But Mitch was fourteen at the time. It has to be a lot different when a kid is just seven, half that age.

(*Group agreement*)

Precious: I don't know if it'll help you out any with Jason, but when DeShaun was in the hospital, the best therapy they had was a group where the parents would just have fun with the kids, and it didn't have anything to do with anybody's problems. One time we colored Easter eggs, and another week we played baseball, and one time we had a pizza party. And before this I was always real serious, always so busy trying to make a living and make ends meet, feed my kids and put clothes on their backs. So having good times together was a big thing DeShaun had missed out on, and one of the reasons why he was always so full of fire and I didn't even know about it.

Katie: To get more into the things we feel our kids missed out on, somewhere along the line, we touched on that a minute ago with Lupe and Jason. Those are the therapy kinds of things we can do as parents, and in my experience they really mean the most. I remember one thing that helped me was a class I took while my daughter was in the hospital for anorexia on the stages of development. Even though Melissa was fifteen at the time and she was the real problem, David was eight and Teddy was just three.

Dean: That's like things were getting so outta hand when Eric was ten that Sheryl and I had to do something like that—go back and try to identify the gaps he had along the way, and plug them up if we could.

Lupe: It worked when your kid was ten?

Dean: I didn't do it on purpose, but I held my other kids a lot more. Eric was this strange baby. I mean, I *sensed* he was odd, and I didn't know how to react except to back off and let Sheryl take over. The dogs would run away and hide in their boxes when they heard him coming. So I started staying up half an hour later with Eric at night. Just we two buddies would watch TV on the couch and I'd have my arm around him, and during the day I'd tousle his hair and hug him so he could feel it on his whole body.

To answer your question, it opened him up. He dropped his toughie facade. He started to want things from me and ask for them, and

I started to feel more for him. I could give him more without it being a hassle I hated. But it was very hard for me to give to him in the beginning, especially the touching, and at first I had to force myself.

Katie: That's what we learned from Melissa's anorexia, that in a way it was like a security blanket and forcing us to start over again because soon after she started starving herself she became like a child again. Her body stopped developing and became a little girl's body again. It was a great comfort to her to feel that people were taking care of her, and coaxing her to eat. It took us a long time, but we finally figured out that starving herself was her way of asking us to go back and give her the things she hadn't gotten from us, and was too scared to grow up without.

(*After a silence*) For me that brings up something that links many of these symptoms, which I've been thinking about lately. It's this child's sensitivity. She has shaky self-esteem to begin with and is easily hurt, and then she has problems in not being able to handle the other kids. Can we talk about some of the things some of us have found to help with this extreme sensitivity? By this I mean, the protective kinds of things we can do as supports for our kids, and the earlier, the better.

Janet: I was at a lecture at the hospital last month where the subject was good or bad outcomes when a kid is emotionally disturbed. They came right out and said if he has a learning disability, that's a bad sign.

Dean: I don't buy that cop-out.

Georgia: It makes it harder, but it's still not the end of the world like some professionals would have us think. They as much as write the kid off. "Well, if he was born with one birth defect, he's probably got others."

Katie: But did they mention any "safeguard" kinds of things? You know, that parents could do at early ages which would help them through some of the rough times ahead?

Janet: Well, being attached to a parent. They talked a lot about how that early closeness was even more important for kids who were going to have it hard later on.

Precious: A couple of times when things hit rock bottom between DeShaun and me, I had these two friends who'd come to my rescue. I didn't want to ask them too often, but sometimes it'd save me if DeShaun could spend a couple of hours over at their place. When I was feeling I simply couldn't take no more.

Liz: You know, I've been thinking about this, too, and if I could pick any one thing, I'd have to say what helped me the most was learning to express my own anger. It was an eye-opener when I was first in therapy and my therapist had me hold out my arm and then showed me how easily she could push it down. I had no resistance at all. Brandon was feeling that from me, that weakness and how I didn't feel I had any authority at all. I didn't even feel the reality that *I* was the adult myself now, and it drove Brandon to an extreme to try to force me to take charge of him.

Then she had me do these karate exercises where I'd focus on an imaginary table and hold my hand out at an angle like this (*demonstrating*), and chop down hard through the "table" while giving my best Tarzan yell. "Aaaayh!" Or something that sounded like that. And she had me pretend I was a mountain. I had to practice standing with both feet planted solidly on the ground.

Valerie: That's all well and good, the exercises and all the other things in therapy, but I discovered in my own situation it's a different matter to take it out of the doctor's office where it's safe to do and you have the support right there.

Liz: Oh, I wouldn't disagree with you on that. Don't I know it, to try it out in the real world, that was by far the harder thing. About that time, Brandon's grandparents were laying these cruel trips on him when he'd do the least little thing wrong. They were always expecting it to blow up into something major, and I was still too afraid to stand up to them, so I'd put off calling them. I finally ended up having to write down what I wanted to say beforehand, and read it off on the phone. Even though I was shaking, they backed right off when they realized I wasn't going to let my son be a target.

And I had to cry about it. I had to cry when I looked in his grandfather's eyes because that's the reflection I saw. Being the big authority person for me in the present, he brought up all the ghosts of my father's anger. And all that time I was dragged down by feeling like such a failure. I felt I was a monster who had ruined my child. I had to visualize his grandfather's face and say that to him over and over again. "I'm not a monster. Damn it, *I'm not.*"

Lupe: I can't help thinking about the criminal tendencies. I'm so scared Jason's going to end up as one behind bars. What I want to know, what confuses me, is when a kid does something wrong, how do you let him know it was wrong but you still love him? Do you punish him, or what?

Janet: Oh, the power struggles. We could go on—

Dean: We finally came up with a way where we recognize Eric's feeling, but then we point out there's this other part of life called reality. Example? Okay, last weekend he came home pissed off and crying and acting generally shitty because he got kicked out of his Cub Scout meeting. As it turned out, he was walking all over the furniture in the scoutmaster's house. Now we've got this old furniture with the stuffing hanging out to where it doesn't matter, but he has to be able to make these kinds of distinctions. You act different when you're somewhere else. I *said* his feeling—"You're hurt because they made you leave"—but then I brought in the hard old facts. "If you wanna play over there, I guess you're gonna hafta obey their rules."

Lupe: Did anyone here see the article in Sunday's paper on young criminals? It said criminals are born that way. They consider that life exciting and deliberately choose it. They can pick out kids who are going to be delinquents in preschool, and there's not much anybody can do.

Dean: A lot of people are going to disagree with that article. Me, for one.

Lupe: And it talked about the iron will these kids have. The parents try to understand and guide them, but it's no use. They resist no matter what you try to do.

Katie: Is there a problem you want to talk about in this connection with Jason?

Lupe: Yeah, there is, lots of them, but I still don't know how you deal with it. He's being disobedient and crappy all the time, and isn't going to do what you want.

Katie: Well, what have some of us learned in here?

Dean: It's in your eyes. Sorta the old evil eye. Eric has to see my eyes to know I mean business. Then he might swear or throw some stuff around the house, but he won't cross the line.

Lupe: Do you just stand there smiling while he's doing that, or what?

Dean: The cursing doesn't bother me. It's harmless, and he's entitled to his opinion. And if he's only throwing pillows and small junk—you know, the grand gesture—or if he's acting immature and slamming doors, that doesn't bother me either. I don't deal with it at all.

Georgia: And you deliver a clear message with your voice. We found with Mitch that that was about the most important thing. Don't shout, but let him know it's a closed case.

Katie: What's the best way to handle an argument? Say he's threatening to run away from home because you won't let him saw the dog in half?

Dean: That's when we give Eric a choice, and in a way it's like calling his bluff, but we always give him a way to save face, some "out." The arbitrary control where you come on like Hitler can be the worst possible mistake with our kids.

Katie: Well, we've been talking about older kids, and that's where the problems get very sensitive. But when she's little, remember how you use physical techniques to restrain her? Like you simply pick her up and remove her from the situation that's gotten her out of control and hold her while she has her anger, while she yells it or says it or punches some inanimate object, and when it's over, you're still holding her.

Lupe: I don't know, but I think it's already too late for that in Jason's case. I didn't do the kind of body thing where you actually control his body sooner. And he's such a big kid for his age, so I don't think I could do it with him now.

Liz: So what you do now is switch to verbal methods, like an example is I said to Brandon—he's thirteen—the other night, "I know you want to stay out late and drink beer because you want to feel grown up." And he admitted that's what it really was, and then he cried a little about how he was really scared to grow up and lose me like he had lost his dad when he was eight years old. And afterward he decided on his own not to go out with the other kids, and we had a great evening just talking and straightening out his closet and watching television.

Katie: Another thing is to be very direct in opening up the issues. Don't try to hide from them. "Are you thinking of getting yourself kicked out of school?" "Do you ever think of killing yourself?" Hard as it might be to begin to break into your kid's pain, you have to let him know you're not frightened by the problem, whatever it is.

Lupe: Aren't rewards supposed to work better, if you keep rewarding him? Because I keep hearing that and it confuses me.

Janet: From my own experience, I'd say, yes and no. The problem is they're artificial, too, and every bit as temporary as the punishment. But if you decide to use rewards, give her a big hug or say something nice to her. They're the real rewards, and she really doesn't need the toy or the candy at all.

Dean: For a while there, I couldn't handle Eric's power plays worth a damn. I'd see myself if I tried to stop him from acting out his anger on his sister or brother as breaking his will. You know, his "spirit." That's what my dad would be yelling while he was beating on me with his fists. "I'm gonna break your will if it's the last goddam thing I do. You little shit."

So what it was, was I had to feel the things with my father through to the bottom, all that rage and hatred I'd stored up against him at those times and still had in me, before I could get it together enough to deal with Eric. The times he'd deliberately do something wrong to test me out, and I knew I had to be firm in not allowing his shitty behavior to go on right then and there, or all the progress we'd made up to then would be as good as lost.

Georgia: Without all your past feelings about your Dad entering in and undermining what you knew had to happen with Eric.

Liz: When Brandon was older and defying me, I had to find a way to cut through what he was saying he wanted to do, and get him to feel instead what he was really wanting from me. It was the only hope I had as a single parent when he was a foot taller than me, and it wasn't permission to kill himself or be in some dangerous situation that he wanted. So now if he's being persistent in some unreasonable demand, like wanting a big powerful dirt bike or quitting school, I have to make that old connection for him. I just put it as simply as I can. "Brandon, you really want me to love you and take care of you, but if you do such and such, I won't be able to anymore. And then we'll both be sad."

Valerie: I'd like to say something here about the testing-out behavior which is that we got into a lot of trouble on that one that we never had to. It was a situation where our son Craig, who was nine at the time, was being as difficult as he could be to test us, and we had brought it on ourselves. We found out too late that even if we only *said* certain things—if we threatened him with certain punishments—it had the same effect. We'd tell Craig, "If you do this or that again, we'll have to send you to live someplace else," or, "You're going to wind up in Juvenile Hall." Back at the time we were ignorant and didn't know how else to handle the sorts of scary behavior that were going on. But then one day it sank in when he misbehaved why he didn't smarten up. His desperate behavior connected to those threats, and was his way of asking us if we still loved him.

Janet: "Did you really mean what you said? You'd really send me away?"

Katie: The sad thing is, you didn't know any other way.

Georgia: Now that Mitch's older we also do the verbal, you know, "feeling-discipline" things with him, and he's finally beginning to be more verbal himself. We listen to what he's saying and accept it, but then we act very wise. Whatever he's going on about he says he wants, we always manage to bring it down to cat and dog, to those deep little boy needs like Liz was mentioning.

But I can sympathize with you being a single mother, Liz, because in his younger years there were lots of times when I just couldn't deal with Mitch, but his father could. Like when he was eight, he was picking up a lot of negative influences from his friend. He was disobeying his father and me, and smoking and stealing from the stores. But the thing about it I couldn't handle was his loneliness. Both of them were such lonely, misfit kids. Luckily my husband is a very different person than me. He could be respectful of what Mitch saw in his friend. Instead of kicking him out, he wouldn't let them go off alone on their bikes anymore because they were getting into trouble, but he said Danny was welcome in our home anytime we were there.

Lupe: And that solved your problem?

Georgia: Well, not for Danny because shortly afterward his mother packed him off to his father in Nevada, but at least while it lasted

Mitch wasn't so lonely. Danny was the first real companion he had.

Janet: After my divorce, I had to sit down and ask myself, "What do my kids need the most now?" Heather was so angry she wouldn't talk to me, and Jeff, my oldest, was hiding behind long hair and dark glasses and trying to be cool. I was hoping they'd get the message that even with their stepdad, who they had been very attached to, gone, they were still whole people, only I wasn't sure of that myself. I was feeling weak and scared and, you know, like my arms or legs were missing without Fred. A lot of my own depression and emptiness was coming out, but the strong part of me knew I had to find a way to make my kids feel safe and okay about themselves again.

Katie: You're right, but I wonder how you do this when you're not feeling safe yourself?

Janet: The worst thing was having to move, having to leave our home. At that point you could have blindfolded me and had me put a pin on a map. I was feeling, you know, rootless. What difference did it make?

And after a few weeks of not being able to make up my mind, somehow I just drifted back to our old neighborhood, the last place we lived before my marriage. And before I even knew what I was doing, I'd rented an apartment, just on instinct, and it happened to be a few blocks from the beach where we had lived before. I was drawn back there even though the rentals had gotten very expensive, really out of sight, and it was so small and cramped I had to sleep out on the living room floor with Heather. I figured it out only much later. Going back there was my way of trying to get back that closeness I'd once had with my kids.

Heather came out of her anger at me first. She responded to being back in her old neighborhood, but Jeff was failing in school and playing hookey, and would put up a book and refuse to talk if I got too close to the nitty gritty and he would feel a threat. I tried to bring out his feelings about his dad, but he just kept saying, "I don't care." And then one early evening he walked out on me in the middle of a conversation and I went after him. I was chasing him down the street and calling his name. This big burly taxi driver stuck his head out the window and yelled at me to leave the kid alone—"Lady, quit making a sissy outta him"—but I kept running after him and caught up with him on the beach.

It was starting to get dark, I remember, and rainy, and Jeff was standing in the mud accusing me of embarrassing him in public and being a certifiable nut, but I had him and I wasn't about to let him get away from me. I held his shoulders and said it to his face. "You do care, you care very much about Dad." And when I said that, he started to cry for the first time and collapsed on me.

Katie (*smiling*): That taxi driver was really saying, "Hold me, Mama."

Katie: Well, they're hurt and angry, both. I've always said there should be a word to describe the mixture. In a way it's the same feeling, like two sides of a coin, but with the extreme sorts of behavior that are going on, it isn't always easy to see that underneath our kids have got to be feeling very depressed. But you mentioned that a while ago, Precious. DeShaun was really depressed. But how did you know this? Because his feeling was coming out mainly as anger.

Precious: Well, now he had a dad only it wasn't what he thought it was gonna be. He'd lost out again. And I knew he was feeling cheated, but at seven and eight years old, he couldn't say he was feeling sad or lonesome.

Dean: One thing we did to get Eric more in touch with the emptiness he was feeling under the manicky behavior was to stop all the presents. Just cut off those expensive guilt trips for us and that phony escape for him. There was always some new toy he wanted, something big and special to make him feel special, and first it was a watch and then a CB radio and a stereo, and like a remote control helicopter was the most recent thing. We'd break down and buy him the thing he said he couldn't live without, and in a couple of days it would be broken or lost. He'd leave it out in the rain or over at somebody's house. After a while we caught on to how he was doing it on purpose. He was saying, "Fuck you, Jack."

Liz: "That's not what I really want. I really want my Mommy and Daddy to like me for myself."

Dean: And speaking of going back and giving your kid the security kinds of things he isn't feeling from you and are worse for him than for other kids, there's something else I want to say in this regard, which is that our German shepherd used to have this strange habit of collecting the family socks. Every night about nine he'd go from room to room picking up our socks, and then he'd drag them down to his bed in the cellar and sleep on them. My hunch is that it comforted him to feel that the people he loved were with him through the night.

After Eric started his new school, we took a cue from Big Mac and slipped reminders from us under his pillow. In a couple of weeks, when he saw he was going to make it, he came to us and said he didn't want to be a baby anymore. "I don't want a collection of junk under my pillow anymore, because if the other kids find out about it, they'll tease me."

Georgia: It's natural, and it proves absolutely our kids are normal in their feelings. You want to be with people you love most, most of the time, and then one day you want to be a separate person. Spread your wings and fly away.

Katie: Can some of you stay a little longer today, or does everyone have to leave right away? Because I've brought along some of my notes for the parent self-help booklet, and I'm needing a couple of listeners. You can? That's just great. Can we move our chairs in closer?

Katie's Premise

The idea I'm working on started with the discovery of acute post-stress syndrome in children, which is a reaction like traumatic anxiety in soldiers, a state of prolonged shock. The children in this research have all been very extreme cases—they had witnessed a parent get murdered, beaten up or commit suicide. Related to this, there's been a lot of recent attention on child abuse and physical violence in families, which is an American epidemic, but what's been missing all along is any mention of emotional maltreatment and neglect, which are even more common.

When you think about it, it's incredible because the norm for most of us is that our childhood is one long stress where we learn to be dead and constricted. It happened to us, and despite our best intentions, it's going to happen to our children, too—it's going to be more or less true for them. That's the emotional connection between the generations, and it's even more formative than the genetic link.

It's most people's darkest secret shame—and the thing they imagine others will blame them for all their lives—that they were never nourished inside and feel worthless. It's time to bring this more subtle abuse out of the closet. I see neglect as the newest frontier.

The most harmful result is what I want to focus on. The most damaging aftermath is that the way most of us grow up robs us of our reality—our essential "intactness," which is our deepest core. It involves every facet of our being—physical, emotional, intellectual and spiritual. We grow up doubting ourselves—never being able to trust our instincts, make decisions or assert ourselves because that's too dangerous.

Many of us even have to inhibit our spontaneous thoughts and appear less intelligent than we really are. We can't afford to be too smart or see too much because then we might also see that central truth of our lives—the people who are supposed to love us are treating us badly. We're little and alone and no one is giving us the attention we need. No one is reaching out a hand.

If the child tries to complain or tell someone about the pain he's feeling, it only ends up taking away more of the reality. "Look," the adults say, "you've got nice clothes and your own room and parents who don't beat you—that's more than I ever had. You eat three meals a day—what's the problem?" They don't take it seriously.

But no matter how tough and above-it-all they pretend to be, children are passive and weak and helpless. That's what being a child is all about. They can't stand up to the adults so they're swept along in the dishonesty and denial all around them, which is a form of shared craziness, and as a result they're mentally polluted. They grow up in a kind of mental smog where everybody is pretending the illusion, the appearance, is real.

In time, the child finds ways to bury his knowledge that he's slowly being destroyed in his designer's jeans or cute little dresses and hair ribbons. He has to survive somehow—he has to survive cognitively as well as merely physically—and he can't possibly survive with his mind split in two.

Most children choose the side of the adults because they seem strong and protective, which is another illusion, but I'm finding that there's often a particular moment in childhood we recall all our lives when we made the deliberate choice to surrender, to go along with everybody else and repress the knowledge that those tokens—the skateboard and the new clothes and the braces on our teeth—don't mean what everybody is telling us they mean—somebody loves and cares about us. The fact that we're walking the earth and haven't been actually murdered doesn't mean somebody really loves us.

The cost of burying our reality is tremendous. We never feel like ourselves or rarely feel like ourselves or sustain a period of feeling good. Our *real* selves get forgotten along with the knowledge that our bodies are crying out for the touching and physical closeness we need, and nothing is coming back to us. I sometimes feel the world is divided into two main types of people—those who *know* they've been mistreated and fight to get themselves back, and the majority who go under completely and are never heard from again.

If there's one thing I've learned in my practice counseling, it's that most of us live in a twilight space which is a kind of suspension in time, a state of perpetual mourning for the childhood we missed out on. The compensations we sell out to—getting high grades or being good in sports and making dad proud—numb us but never take away our pain completely. Our bodies still remember that we weren't held or cuddled or made to feel wanted so that later we would want to be nice to ourselves, but our senses, instincts, and feelings are blunted, shock-proofed, and deadened to a point where we can no longer even tell we're suffering.

Later, we don't whine or cry or throw temper tantrums or engage openly in auto-erotic behavior, but we drink, smoke and use drugs or develop psychosomatic illnesses to keep our bodies unconscious. We party till we're exhausted and imagine we're going to find somebody to care about us.

Young children who are showing a disturbance don't have these escapes, these false wings. They feel their emptiness, that void which should have been filled with love, very keenly. They're close to their pain, and often have vivid fantasy lives. They're great comics or ballerinas, and the whole world loves them. So somehow our bodies grow up around this core of pain—the bodies we starve or overfeed or deck out in the latest fashions "guaranteed" to get us liked and admired. Then we have children out of our untouched, unloved bodies.

The point is that children don't have to be physically or dramatically abused—just to be lonely, criticized or dominated, and have no one who is sensitive to them—to grow up in a constant state of arousal, always steeled against tomorrow. Emotional hurt is the invisible enemy of most of us, and we have to defend against the painful feeling of never being good enough, never having measured up and having anything to offer to others, for the rest of our lives—and sometimes even after. Now we buy our own cemetery plot and death insurance and pay for all the funeral arrangements beforehand.

Another thing I've been finding that fits in with this is that we usually remember the moments of supreme pain—the times that told us the truth that we were never going to get what we needed—with special detailing. The pattern on the wallpaper or the color of mother's dress when she left us, how her hair curled or the snow that was falling that day. And we remember *where* we felt awful—our heart hurt, it was beating so loud. But the emotional meaning of the memories doesn't penetrate—we can't make the step from those perceptual details to the primal pain and feel how alone and afraid we were. I'm starting to look at this phenomenon, and use it as a focus in therapy—a tract into the person.

And sometimes the most painful moments we remember years later in therapy, that make us open up and start to cry, are the most empathic moments. It's a paradox that one or two tender memories can bring up more of the pain of the past than actual mistreatment—being scolded or told to shut up or go away, or that a problem wasn't important. A parent called us by our nickname or played with us, a father once said "I'm sorry."

But since we didn't get enough of these kindnesses we carry the past around like luggage we can never leave behind. Boys especially have a lot of help in denying their feelings—"Show what a big man you are"—but so do girls. They get pushed very early into the mothering role where they have to take care of somebody with a lot of needs. I think it's true that most boys will identify with the aggressor and become tyrants themselves while most girls will identify with the victim or the protector, but both have to put up an invisible shield and live in an emotional fortress just to survive.

As adults, we may have occasional flashes of insight. We may wonder why our lives seem so hard, why we always appear to be doing "hard time" rather than "easy time." The fact is that we'll do anything and everything, including turning ourselves completely "inside out" and becoming insane or homosexual, to repress our feelings, to keep ourselves blind, dumb and mute. It happens very early. Right now I'm seeing a five-year-old child in the clinic who decided to become a clown after his father's sudden death. The old denial dies hard when it begins that young.

Now for the remedial work we have to do with our particular kinds of kids. Because they're different, they've had even more failures that have convinced them they're worthless. Failures in school, neighborhoods and friendships take their toll, even though the most painful of all is failing to make a parent love them. They may be manic and hyperactive, but they're joyless, burdened, constricted, and nothing in their lives is ever any fun—they can't play or laugh normally. As they get older, they simply put on a better and better "survivalist" front.

Our parent/therapist role consists mainly of providing a "holding environment" for our damaged children while waiting for the right moment when we can identify a traumatic reference for them. When a child is sad or solemn, that's the opportune time to bring up those painful moments from his past that shut him down and caused his passive, detached stance or his behavioral outrage.

You have to watch carefully for those moments, and then help him to reconstruct his experience—for example, "I bet you wish I'd been there (or your dad had been there) to protect you when . . ." And because it feels very dangerous for a child to give up his secrets, you have to support him at that very minute when you're eliciting his recall. Touch his arm to encourage him while you say, "Remember the dog we had at that time? The Big Wheel you used to ride down the street?"

The reason you always say "I bet you wish . . ." is because his wish is his hurt. He doesn't know how to touch his sadness with words, but he wishes above all else he didn't feel like a chaotic, unweeded garden inside. So slowly begin to tend that garden, pay attention to it for a few minutes out of every day, and put it back in working order.

These techniques also work when a child is reducing his insecure, painful feelings by behaving unacceptably. I'm finding that sad, lonely, angry or rejected feelings usually come right before a child's misbehavior—hitting someone or throwing his schoolwork across the room. Maybe he was feeling left out or stupid because his teacher had been very angry and disapproving of him, but unless he learns to recognize those trigger emotions, he'll go on dealing with them in the only way he knows, by acting them out on others.

Those awful feelings are a warning that urges to do destructive things are on the way. That's why you have to sit down with him and actually *resurrect* those initial emotions, painful as that might be. He has to learn to identify the physical precursors of those feelings in his body so he can "catch himself" before he acts out his great urge to let others know just how bad he feels.

There's also a handy technique some counselors are using with kids who set fires—young arsonists. After you've talked about his feeling, you ask your child, "What would make you feel good this very minute?" Some children want a sweet, others a hug or to play outside, some just want to go off and hide, but whatever he says, tell him that he should ask for that the next time he feels as miserable as he does right now—*before* he acts on his "irresistible" impulse.

Another thing we tend to forget is the tremendous courage it takes to live in continuous fear of disapproval and anger like almost all children do. I'm discovering that can also be a way out of the child's denial—the recognition of how brave he or she has been. Even being strong and silent is a defense, but it takes a certain courage. You want to let your child know he doesn't have to cover up his feelings anymore—it's safe to let them show—and one way you do this is by taking note of his courage: "Talking about this today was a brave thing to do."

Exposing psychological maltreatment won't be easy. There will always be resistance to the idea because our world is saturated with neurosis after all—cover-ups, punishments, repressions and false "macho" demonstrations—on every level from our sterile hospital births to our joyless schools, treadmill jobs and lonely relationships, up to our highest rank of government with its rock-pile and vengeance mentality against other peoples.

But when it finally comes, it won't be a passing fad. You know, like the talk show hosts are famous for unearthing those trivial minorities—physically attractive people with special problems, mistresses or cross-dressers who are living out a prolonged adolescent dream, people who feel guilty for not having participated in wars—but it's going to shake up the nation.

Abuse is *not* just physical. The child maltreatment which isn't reported, or even acknowledged, is just as harmful. Parents don't provide the security and love children need, and verbal abuse and neglect from a parent can be as damaging as physical abuse.

That's the rampant family violence in America, and the reason why most of us are still needy kids inside. Then we try to pressure our children into a premature, false adulthood because we can't stand to take care of them, but it doesn't work—it always misfires. Parents and children alike, we're all stuck at an early stage asking for another chance to be the beloved and valued child—longing for good old days that never really were. Years pass. We go to our high school class reunions and wonder why all we feel is a strange discomfort, a numbness and a sense that everything around us is unreal. It *is* when we're not fully alive ourselves.

Most of us accept our childhood doom quietly and obediently, as good little children, but occasionally someone comes along and kills half a dozen or so people to let everyone know how much he's hurting. Thousands more, I'm convinced, are prevented from going to that extreme only because they earn livings that allow them to have some material comforts and compensations, but they're still violent in their intimate relationships, behind closed doors.

It's perpetuated because our society doesn't discriminate against this sort of person. He can beat and malign his wife and kids and shoot, maim and abuse all the animals he wants to and still get his union benefits, send-off party and gold watch at retirement.

But there are solutions that can and should be tried. The Swedish system that provides attractive apartment projects where young families and/or single parents share the responsibilities of child-rearing is one idea. Government-funded home nursing programs could be expanded so that every expectant mother would have a professional friend to visit with her regularly and offer her a block of support. Once the baby is born, she could be introduced into a "family" group of other new mothers, nurses and child specialists who would meet frequently to talk about the issues and problems she is facing, and provide a source of emergency support and crisis intervention. A mother (and/or father) would join this temporary family freely, stay as long as she wanted, and leave only when she felt confident. And it should be an enforceable law that security, love and encouragement aren't luxuries but essentials to prevent long-term damage and untold, needless suffering.

Or else we can start right now to plant rows and fields of forget-me-nots where our children should have played, made noise and been allowed to be children.

8

Reclamation: Two Lives

As we have seen throughout these pages, the many faces of odd growth have had, and still have, as many names. The labels and the psychiatric reports are, of course, always negative and imply a *deficit* in functioning; they effectively "pigeonhole" or "straitjacket" the child (or adult) and obscure or minimize his specific capabilities and his positive attributes, such as his independence of judgment, his uniqueness of ideas, and, especially, his courage in making his way in the world handicapped by his difference. And the diagnostic terms and evaluations conspicuously omit the recognition that we can *all* be anxious, crazy, or stupid at times (perhaps because this truth is too threatening or too close to home for so many of our professionals).

Historically, the labels date back to the first recorded case of "congenital word-blindness" in 1896. The author, W. P. Morgan, a British physician, believed this perplexing affliction in a fourteen-year-old boy named Percy (who spelled it "Precy") derived from a structural dysfunction of the parietal region in the brain; for that reason, it could only be the result of family or genetic influences.

The modern-day diagnostic jungle not only reflects the continuing confusion in the fields of pediatrics, psychiatry, and neurology, but all too often leads to the sorry situation where the particular category and treatment a child ends up with depend solely on the bias of an individual practitioner.[1] Only in education has there seemed a consensus on at least the label (learning disability), if not yet the programs of treatment or the specific remedial techniques.

The syndrome, which I call "Winter's Child," has at its core what has long been thought of as minimal brain dysfunction or attentional disorder, but expands in my mind to encompass all those related behavior and learning problems linked in recent years to an ever-lengthening list of environmental causes.

Among the new contributors are prevalent parental drug involvement, our depleted and impoverished foods and natural resources, overabundance of food additives and preservatives, aerial spraying with insecticides such as malathion over vast expanses of our farmland, and clouds of herbicides like paraquat darkening the hills and mountains of our national forests.

Other sources include the very technological advances which permit us to save severely handicapped newborns of two or three pounds, or even one pound, in a blaze of medical and congratulatory glory for the physician, who would not have wished on his worst enemy the lifetime of pain, sickness, and institutionalization to which we often condemn our "Baby Does." And the burgeoning disturbances of childhood may relate in more circuitous, but no less intimate, ways to the cancerous fish, grotesquely deformed by tumors, discovered in our oceans as a result of the tons of chemical wastes dumped in their once sacrosanct watery paradises—and the sulfur emissions of "acid rain" that come from the industrial heartland and are killing off our lakes, rivers, and trees.

The wholesale poisoning of our children by neurotoxic metals is pertinent, too: mercury (found in water-based paints, pesticides, cosmetics, floor waxes, paper, newsprint, wall plaster, plastics, dental fillings, and camera film); cadmium (present in vinyl plastics, canned and dried fish, processed meats, automobile exhaust, batteries, fungicides, cola drinks, and tin cans); lead (gasoline additives, pipes, varnishes, paint pigments, pottery glazes, enamel, newsprint, and hair colorings); and copper or aluminum (cooking utensils, piping, buffered and children's aspirins,

---

[1] Even in strict medical diagnosis of major illnesses such as cancer or heart disease, involving much less subtle symptoms but more immediate danger to the patient, doctors make the wrong diagnosis in at least 11 percent of all cases. A recent survey in the *New England Journal of Medicine* described how despite major advances in diagnostic apparatus and techniques, physicians' track records have not improved in the last 30 years.

most toothpastes, drinking water, salt, processed foods, kitchen foil, baking powder, carbonated beverages, some cheeses, and many skin and burn preparations, and as a bleaching agent to whiten flour).

And we are seeing in infants an increase in herpes, hepatitis, and other social diseases whose viruses, once they infect, never leave the body. Even prenatal abnormalities, which may be caused by inflammatory diseases, are increasing dramatically: ectopic pregnancies, which occur outside the uterus, have nearly tripled in the last fifteen years, until they now make up one of every 45 live births in this country. Fluorescent lighting, digital watches, smoke alarm detectors, microwave ovens, video games, and garage door openers—all of these seemingly innocent contemporary conveniences have been shown to have a weakening, deenergizing effect on the muscles of the body, including the heart. (The reasons for this consistently demonstrated effect are largely unknown, but some scientists suspect that since the low-voltage levels of electrical current given off by these devices are similar to the low-frequency levels of the central nervous system, which is basically an electrical input-output system, they therefore interfere with or impede electrical conductivity in the central nervous system.)

Learning disabilities and growth disorders have also been traced to cancer-linked pesticides and other blunders in the manufacture of baby foods and formulas; and disabilities associated with fetal alcohol syndrome—including brain damage, growth deficiency, and abnormalities of the heart, joints, and kidneys—are known to be on the rise. As are pollution-related asthma and allergic and respiratory afflictions.

Then there is the wave of cesarean sections requiring anesthesia as a routine way of delivering babies. And birth defects and deformities have been attributed to dermatologic drugs that are prescribed to treat mild forms of acne and other skin eruptions in pregnant women. At the other end of the life story, we are finding that the dreaded Alzheimer's disease or premature senility may be linked to the inability of the human body to process and eliminate the large amounts of aluminum in our environment.

Last but perhaps not least is the use of potentially dangerous chemicals in cover fabrics and filling materials to protect our more prized material possessions such as upholstered furniture. Add the "normal" background levels of dioxin and other suspected carcinogens found in the bodies of many persons. Children's flame-retardant pajamas. The dolphins dead of pollution contaminants that wash ashore on our beaches . . .

Any and all of these modern curses can have deleterious effects on the delicate nervous system tissue, hormonal balance, and body chemistry of the developing embryo. Then in postnatal life, the same children are subjected to artificial diets which create a widespread, "invisible" malnutrition (deficiencies of the overconsumptive but "undernutrition" type). They are also being exposed daily to polluted air or smog, which they breathe along with the rest of us. Murky rivers of contaminants seep through the soil of their backyards and deposits of neurotoxins fall silently into their city sandboxes.

Perhaps the most frightening of all the recent reports are those describing the poisonous pesticides contaminating our groundwater supply. They terrify because they tell us outright that our bodies are being invaded and violated against our wills. At the same time, they render us passive and unprotected victims of the modern social callousness and old-fashioned greed among some of us.

We know next to nothing about the chronic health effects of the toxic chemicals found in high concentrations in our drinking water, food, factories, homes, and offices, but a report by the congressional Office of Technology Assessment released in March 1983 tells us plainly that one metric ton of hazardous waste is added to the environment each year for every American.

If professionals, teachers, juvenile correctional counselors, and parents have merely guessed the extent of the problem up to now, and have had only a dim, but persistent, sense of the rapidly multiplying numbers of oddly behaving children among us—befalling some doctors in their private practices like an avalanche—their suspicions have just now received long-overdue confirmation.

While this book was in progress, a study appeared which revealed that the number of American babies born with mental or physical defects has *doubled* over the last 25 years. During the same month, U.S. Department of Education statistics reported 4 million children were enrolled in special education programs during the 1982 school year, an increase of over half a million from the last survey in 1977—and this while overall enrollment was dropping.

A third study reported on chronic debilitating health problems in children like asthma, bronchitis, brittle bones, and bone degeneration, which have all increased in the past quarter-century as sharply as the incidence of mental defects. What all this appears to translate directly into is that we have begun to run into the limits of industrialization, and may be approaching a danger point where we will all just evolutionarily—helplessly—self-destruct.

When we put all these facts together—and add to them the progressive extinction of many species of birds, animals, insects, and plants which is destroying the precious bioecological balance of our planet—we may end up wondering whether this touch of doom, this shadow of winter, is inevitable in all our children. Our legacy to them is increasingly a world blighted, tarnished, and bent by the activities of men.

Nor are we in America alone, for there is evidence in the parallel reports from England, and as far away as Sweden and Japan, that the various handicapping conditions of childhood are spreading throughout our earth, creeping up on us like a modern-day ice age.

The situation is reminiscent of the toxic doses of lead in the wine and food of the aristocracy of ancient Rome, including most of the emperors. Historians have connected the widespread lead poisoning to the many obvious manifestations of neurological and reproductive damage—to erratic behavior, cruel pleasure-seeking, high incidence of mental retardation and infertility, and a variety of personality changes—and, ultimately, the fall of the Roman Empire. But by according our business giants and industrial conglomerates huge profits and public dumping grounds as their "entitlement," we seem to have chosen unwisely, and perhaps fatally, to ignore such clear warnings from the past.

As it turns out, the designation "Winter's Child" for all these related conditions of neurological, medical, and psychological impairment is not arbitrary. A new survey at the Maryland Psychiatric Research Center shows that people born in winter and early spring are 35 percent more likely to suffer from several kinds of mental instability including at least one type of schizophrenia. Teachers who work in special education have long noticed the disproportionately large number of winter birthdays among their maladapting students. And my own study found, interestingly, more deviant youngsters had been born in mid-winter—with December emerging as the "cruelest month."

Somewhere in all of this lies a common key.

Travelers to the People's Republic of China have returned with some intriguing information on the treatment of biochemical irregularities such as schizophrenia in this fascinating and labyrinthine country. (The basic statistical incidence of mental illness is reported not to differ significantly from that in Western nations.) What is so impressive is that there is no "treatment" per se for aberrations from the normal other than simple ordinary life—no prescriptions for tranquilizing drugs or provisions for psychological counseling or shut-away psychiatric hospitals.

But what apparently works very effectively in many cases is the total "milieu therapy" in the close-knit social structure of the communal farms. Interdependent members "carry" their nonconforming persons through the day—lead them out into the fields, where they remain beside their comrades as they toil away the day, make sure they eat their meals in the dining halls at the appointed times, and sweep them along to community meetings in the evenings. In this crude way, the deviant persons "participate" in the decisions which affect their lives according to their ability, share the workload as they are able, and, perhaps most important, are spared the extremely painful and damaging experience of exclusion.

In the coveted single-family residences and isolated psychiatric lock-ups of our Western culture, which speak of our technological advancement and social refinement, our mental misfits are prevented from experiencing the healing effects and comfort of this natural kind of "group therapy." It's as though after we damage our children by our overindustrialization, we then deny them their human right to be members of a group.

Though it's fallen into disfavor in today's more sophisticated (some would say, trivialized) psychological zeitgeist, there was a time in America not so long ago, in the 1940s and 1950s, when the "social isolation hypothesis" proposed by R. E. L Faris and H. W. Dunbar back in 1939 flourished as an important explanation of why things go so wrong for many young persons among us.

These investigators noted the high incidence of mental illness among urban dwellers who lived alone in apartments or rooms cut off from their family, neighbors, and other meaningful social contacts. Many of these lonely, schizoid people lived a withdrawn kind of inner-city "groundhog" existence in which they hid out in small rooms during the day and ventured out to all-night markets only under the cover of darkness.

They related the process of mental deterioration in these displaced individuals to descriptions of "feral" children, hermits, railroad hoboes, and other isolates, all of whom were reported to show a similar distorted relationship to the external world.

Scientific interest in this hypothesis has continued sporadically in the sensory and perceptual "deprivation" experiments still conducted, from time to time, in university laboratories. The important finding over the last decade has been that the experimentally induced effects of simple *social* isolation are just as profound and bizarre as the outcomes of *sensory* deprivation, including immersion in a tank of water or the wearing of special distorting eyeglasses or goggles, sound-muffling earplugs, and desensitizing cuffs and gloves.

Generally, however, interest in isolation phenomena has dwindled into random survival stories such as a recent account of an eight-year-old boy who vanished for seven terrifying days in a mountain wilderness in northern Georgia. Rescuers who had given up hope of finding anything but the boy's lifeless body stumbled on him as they headed back to their outpost for the last time. Having lived for a week on muddy water and unripe berries, he was covered with mosquito and chigger bites, dazed and hallucinating. The interesting thing is that when such reports come to popular attention, nobody seems at all surprised or questions *why* the person should be delusional—as well no one who has ever awakened in stark aloneness from a nightmare or night terror should.

Artists and writers have long described a similar process of cortical "slippage" after a prolonged and unbroken stretch of three or four days of concentrated creative effort during which they lose their usual contact with others and "become a little crazy." Solitary explorers, religious hermits, prisoners of war, and castaways who have returned to the land of the living have all given similar accounts of the depressive effects of isolation. It seems, then, there is a maximum amount of time away from ordinary people and events, or a preset quota of loneliness, that most of us can tolerate before strange ideas and disturbing thoughts begin to intrude on our senses.

Almost anyone who spends excessive amounts of time in his or her own company—from swing or "graveyard" shift workers to "survivalist" food and ammunition hoarders with their gas masks, grenades, and radiation-resistant suits—is soon subject to bizarre thoughts and irrational and illogical ideas. Often, the results of sensory or social isolation experiments are left in doubt because a number of student "volunteers," driven to the verge of desperation, walk out on the project.

But neurologically handicapped children cannot quit the "life experiment" so easily. The point is that the chronic experience of loneliness suffered by many "different" youngsters who are ostracized can, and often does, lead to psychiatric symptoms above and beyond the basic fact of biochemical inadequacy.

Loneliness—the driving force or enduring need to connect physically and emotionally with another person—is an additional neurochemical stressor, and in a touchy, sensitive, and frequently suspicious child this intensely painful experience can lead to a restless and difficult life.

Owing to their God-given or man-made physical imbalance, these children are born with a predisposition to misinterpret the environment. And at bottom, what else are symptoms such as delusions or hallucinations but *dysperceptions* of—or false messages from—the physical or social environment?

If the transmission of electrical impulses in the nervous tissue of the brain is altered, a misperception of reality occurs. The panic that overwhelms users of psychedelic drugs on bad trips is the result of a chemical overload—colors swirl terrifyingly; familiar objects are distorted in size, take on savage qualities, and emit odd odors; and the senses fuse. Thinking he can fly, the person may leap out of a window.

Another way to say this is that the same environmental upset which may elicit only a mild or moderate response in a normal youngster may produce a large and violent biological reaction in the child who is already stressed by a constant state of inner "noise." Because of the preexisting or prewired stress in impulsive children, then, much *less* stress from the environment may be required for a full-blown and inappropriate emotional reaction.

The really sad part is that emotional symptoms that are triggered by underlying physical causes are likely to be misdiagnosed as a sure sign of madness. But even if our contemporary experts are fixated on psychological explanations of stress and emotional problems, it behooves us all the more as parents that we do not let psychiatric symptoms (even striking ones) in our children blind us to the signs of "body" difficulties.

One key in ferreting out cause from effect is that mental illness rarely begins abruptly. If, despite some minor difficulties in coordination and keeping up with the others, a child has seemed emotionally sound and hearty in his early years, has appeared to have a natural enthusiasm for life, and has laughed and smiled more than cried, *any dramatic change in personality is probably the result of an underlying body problem that has been there, dormant, from his birth*. A child's life gets "tougher" with advancing age when school and environmental demands multiply all at once; it's then that his body problems, which cripple his response to stress, may first show up.

Some related research with mentally disturbed adults has indicated that in some cases, the source could simply be too much or too little of an essential body substance such as water, salt, blood sugar, calcium, thyroid hormone, vitamin B-12, folic acid, or adrenaline. For instance, simple dehydration and disturbances of salt balance have long been known to cause psychiatric symptoms indistinguishable from senility. And techniques of "chemical fingerprinting" that identify levels of trace metals in the hair have also linked certain chemical imbalances—especially deficiencies of copper, sodium, and zinc—to violent or criminally psychotic behavior in adults.

It's rather astonishing to think about it, but because our priorities are ever elsewhere, we have even neglected such simple tallies or "head counts" as would tell us how many of the approximately three million American children (15 percent of the child population) labeled "emotionally disturbed," "borderline," or "psychotic" were identified as having learning or attentional problems at early ages.

The observant visitor to any neuropsychiatric ward, state hospital, residential treatment center, or group home for disturbed children (most such children's institutions have special clinical classrooms attached to them) cannot help being struck by the numbers of obviously neurologically impaired youngsters housed in these maximum-security facilities. They sprawl across the floor of the schoolrooms, clutching pencils and scribbling violently, or are isolated in cubicles, bent over their work with strange postures and peculiar facial grimaces, tapping their feet, sweating, looking wildly around.

Often by the late primary-school years, the educational shortcomings that were so glaring at young ages will have receded or become "compensated," showing up only on close scrutiny as slight or "soft" learning disabilities. The subtle residual clues will usually not be noticed by most professionals, who seem to have a morbid bent for the more spectacular and bizarre symptoms such as the "voices" they suspect but cannot prove the child is hearing—cannot prove because such youngsters are inevitably reluctant to reveal themselves to another person. (If they were able and willing to do so, they would have long ago fulfilled their need for an intimate, gratifying relationship with an essential person and wouldn't be there in the first place.)

Once a child is past a certain age, no one seems to want to hear about or be reminded of his more mundane early foundation of overactivity and difficulties in concentration and learning. It says something disquieting about our "helping" professions that this quality of sensationalism, which is almost voyeuristic in its intensity—along with a conditioned reflex of readiness to blame the parent—should be so common rather than a balanced and scientific interest in the child and his family.

Yet over and over, this is the painful, punitive, and terminal experience of well-intended parents who seek help for their child. Perhaps the television producers and writers who argue that most people really *want* all the violence and bad news they keep churning out are not so far off. Never once have I come across a parent whose doctor or psychologist mentioned the things that she was doing *right* for her child.

What is repeatedly ignored or denied in the monomaniacal concern with unresolved psychosexual complexes, possible mistakes in weaning or toilet training—and all the rest of the psychological attitude ushered in around the close of World War II and still the most familiar orientation of mental health workers—is the fact that *perceptual mistakes, misjudgments, and miscalculations have dogged these children insidiously in all areas of their development—from learning to walk and talk, to bike riding or roller-skating, to school adjustment—not just the social.*

But so many professionals continue to cross up their orthodoxy and theoretical concerns with the reality of the psychological facts. In doing so, they disregard the harsh but basic truths of their young patients' lives.

Eons ago in the dawn of prehistory, the young Cro-Magnon child may have had to worry a good deal about large predators and other annoying reminders of a savage but real world looming outside the range of his cave fire—especially at times when he was alone. How much more marked the effects of aloneness might have been for our young, beetle-browed hunter if he had also been subjected to vivid imaginations other than his own, like the diabolical genius of a Steven Spielberg or a George Lucas, we can only surmise.

The lonely, friendless, different child in anno Domini nineteen eighty-six may well suffer the additional fate or stress of being a "latchkey kid." In the middle of the afternoon, he comes home from the peculiar hassles of his special education class to an empty house, mills around for a while inspecting the silent rooms, then maybe pours a glass of milk or juice or concocts a peanut butter and marshmallow creme sandwich, but almost for certain, in time, turns on the TV.

At three in the afternoon an independent affiliate station is rerunning a block of "The Twilight Zone," a cable station out of an eastern city is showing the thriller *Cat People*, and the local channel is airing an aerobic exercise program. He switches back and forth between channels for a minute, then settles on *Cat People* and sits down to watch.

Soon, little noises in the other rooms start to magnify, creaks convert into prowlers, and shadows become menacing. Darkness falls, and he discovers a burnt-out light in the living room but is unable to find a new bulb. His worry mounts into wild imaginings.

His parent returns home at supper time and for the next few hours he forgets his macabre fears, doubts, and suspicions. But later that night, falling asleep in his bed, he thinks he hears moans coming from the closet or thinks he sees mythical, technicolor animals at the window or hovering over his bed.

Now he is too grown up and ashamed to tell his parent about the groans in the closet or the voices under the doorway, but he suspects they may be real. Even if his rational mind tells him this cannot be so, his *need* born of his recurrent experience of loneliness may override his reason. Each night upon going to bed, he may begin to fall into a narcoleptic pattern in which he sees strange images in the folds of his blanket or hears someone or something calling his name.

Then one afternoon when he is alone in the house, the spooky, sound-track voices are suddenly there when the TV is silent. If they aren't real, he reasons, and if they don't have a special meaning or "message" for him, why should he be hearing them?

Repeated often enough, this process can lead to what is known in clinical circles as a thought disturbance—a state of social deterioration which may include idiosyncratic thinking, hyperalertness, feelings of persecution, loss of touch with reality, fragmented thinking (intrusive thoughts or frequent shifting between subjects), and sensory and perceptual disturbances such as "voices" the person perceives as coming from outside his head. Especially common are "hidden" or personal meanings in ordinary voices or sounds and derogatory comments on his ongoing behavior.

Somatic hallucinations such as unpleasant or scary stirrings inside bodily cavities, or tactile hallucinations involving tingling, burning, or electrical sensations, are sometimes experienced as well. Other perceptual derangements include sensations of bodily shifts and hypersensitivity to sight, sound, and smell. The sense of self-awareness and self-identity that pilots most people and gives them a direction in their everyday lives may be lost.

The most optimal and fertile breeding ground for the development of these disordered patterns of thinking is a psychological state of isolation or "corneredness" in which the person feels both overwhelming fear and the lack of a periphery of surrounding safety (which to most of us means the presence of other people).

And because the inept child usually also misses out on the normal experience of consensual validation of what he is seeing, hearing, or feeling, in those spontaneous conversations with chums or classmates in which children confirm the truth or falseness of everything from guardian angels to the special effects of *Star Wars*—"There are *so* boogeymen, my uncle told me so," "Your uncle is a crock," "Only babies believe in the tooth fairy," etc.—the line between reality and fantasy may be blurred even more.

If the marginal child has any mentors, they are likely to be other solitary youngsters struggling with the same deficits in reality testing, such as perceptual errors and failures of judgment. Since he never has the normal opportunity to dispel the myths and ghosts of childhood, his belief in their credibility remains suspended.[2]

In a similar misfiring of experience which is hardly uncommon, the young child with only one companion, a companion who happens to be a little older and more worldly but confused about his or her sexual identity (suffering "gender discomfort," in the psychological parlance), may be drawn into homosexual play or experimentation *not* because it is his hormonal fate or the fault of an overly dominant mother who has instilled castration dread in him, but simply because he lacks the ordinary experiences which would allow him to share his secret thoughts and provide him with the knowledge that what he is experiencing in a body bursting with growth is not unique. Because the "hovering" child doesn't sense or participate in the mutuality of social experiences, he may not even be aware that same-sex play is not the usual avenue of expression for his burgeoning feelings of affection and rising physical awareness.

"Didn't you *know* it was wrong?" yells his irate father whose sense of his own masculinity has just been shaken to the core after the school principal or a scoutmaster has brought a sexual indiscretion to his attention after the fact.

"My God, what next? Are we to be spared *nothing* with this kid?" writhes his equally frightened and anguished mother.

---

[2] I found some evidence in my research that isolated children tend to believe longer, and more tenaciously, than their normally developing peers in certain cultural falsehoods such as Santa Claus. While this may be part of their general social immaturity, it may also indicate a degree of eccentric thinking.

Many also seem prone, perhaps owing to their pervasive sense of failure and powerlessness, to believe in magic, witchcraft, voodoo, ESP, and other supernatural means of control, which further cloud the distinction between fact and fiction and set them apart even more.

Though he isn't believed, the child's downcast answer of "No" is no doubt honest.

There is really no way this child could have "known better." Whom after all does he have to confide his "grow-up blues" to, or compare notes with about his awakening and expanding feeling? The instructional talks we have with our children about the birds and the bees (or the ova and the spermatozoa), when we have them at all, do not usually include variations on the sexual theme such as homosexuality, bisexuality, fetishism, and other supposedly pathological displacements of erotic urges.

It may help to tell the lonely latchkey youngster to go out of doors at scary times and wait for you in the yard, take a walk, turn on the radio, or call you at your work. Or he could go next door and stay at a neighbor's house, provided you have checked with an adult in advance.

Contact with the real world is a critical safety net for all of us at terrifying moments, but in the end the question comes back again to, How many benign thoughts and memories do we have stored up inside us, as a foundation of security, to keep us from falling over a black edge into disturbance? Experiences of people simply liking us and smiling when we approach, when all is said and done. If our reserve is adequate, we will return to earth, and to what we know is the truth, each time we near this abyss.

But withdrawing into oneself, believing the world is a hostile and frightening place, and disordered thinking all go hand in hand. If his family life has been traumatic—violent, lonely, stark, and full of cruelty, hypocrisy, and humiliation, or detrimental in other ways—a child may not *want* to return to his earthly home which is synonymous with reality. In certain unfortunate cases, he may make the deliberate *choice* to run for his life in a figurative sense, by fleeing into his head—especially if the other-worldly attention he seems to be receiving comes to him as a comfort or a balm, entertainment or even simple creature comfort.

Jo Beth was one of the horde of vulnerable, impoverished, and emotionally malnourished children.

She grew up in the 1950s among the blue meadows and fertile farmland of the San Joaquin Valley in central California. Her family's small, dingy-white house was flanked by hills that turned to blankets of brown folds in summer.

From her bedroom window, Jo Beth would stare at the distant hills and imagine they were boxcars in a train, moving somewhere by degrees but taking a long time to get there. Grownups thought of her as a sensitive and poetic, if pipe-cleaner-skinny, child with hazel eyes hinting of glinting depths, long tapering fingers, and titian braids down her back.

But while her teacher recognized her "artistic" qualities and her surface serenity, she also knew that the small girl had great difficulty with learning, was extremely clumsy, withdrawn from the other children, fearful, and painfully shy. She always seemed a little sickly, even in good weather, paler than normal, and to have a "frozen" expression.

An examination by the school district physician when Jo Beth was seven revealed no physical illness but, rather, a neurological or "developmental lag," which translated that she was immature for her age, had problems with spatial ability and motor coordination, and showed "mixed dominance" in her eye and hand preference, but would probably be a "late bloomer," spurting or catching up with the rest by her teens.[3]

Probably the signs of late development were a family trait, for all this doctor knew, since he remembered an older brother had had some of the same early problems. A few years before, at the age of thirteen, he had been packed off to live with relatives in Canada on account of incorrigible, disruptive kinds of behavior in school and frequent run-ins with the law.

Never having lived in any other body but her own so she could tell the difference, Jo Beth believed it must be normal to feel the way she did—closed in, extremely self-conscious to the point of panic, timid around other people, and convinced others were staring or laughing at her. She held these feelings inside, which only made the problems worse, but there was no one sympathetic to whom she could reveal her greatest

---

[3] Not all children with disturbances in the cortex-environmental-feedback loop solve their body problems by becoming "approachers" who respond actively and physically to any and all incoming stimuli. *Hypoactive youngsters* are bombarded with too many environmental messages just as hyperactives—as if the world were too close and thereby menacing—but they overreact by withdrawal and isolation. They appear slow, frightened, apathetic, spacey, or paranoid, and respond with narrowed interest, dawdling, and excessive concentration on a single object or idea.

The common sensitivity of all is that ordinary events and stimulation are noticed more acutely, but the aggressive child who senses a threat fights back as a reflex. "Scared rabbits," turtles-in-a-shell, or immature ball-and-chains who need constant reassurance attempt to control their unbearable stress by clinging, hair pulling, bed rocking, thumb sucking, bottom clutching, and other tension-reducing, rhythmical activities.

There is a small amount of evidence that more girls than boys tend to become hypoactive withdrawers, and later may become either phobics such as housewives who are terrified to leave their residences, or hyperactive talkers.

torment, which occurred regularly as clockwork twice each day. On her way to and from school, the other children would follow her, surround her, and tease her about the peculiar way she dressed and acted, and about her wild brother, who had been the scourge of the school.

These avenging angels called her cruel names like witch, and sometimes pounded her arms with a rain of rabbit punches. It didn't help that her mother dressed her in long, straight, old-fashioned thrift store dresses, or that the family yard was an embarrassing junk heap of overgrown weeds and dismantled, rusted-out cars that her mother's boyfriend stored there.

The woodshed behind the house, on the rim of the property, became her refuge. Once her ordeal was over in the afternoons—and whenever there was discord in the house, which was often, since her mother's lover had come to live with them—she would sneak there. (On the slightest provocation, or even no grounds at all, this man would beat Jo Beth or her mother, sometimes knocking them against a wall or a piece of furniture.)

Her mother had several missing teeth and a torn mouth from her lover's drunken assaults, and Jo Beth bore a scar on her leg from the time he had struck her with a metal pipe. She wanted desperately to please her mother and this boyfriend, but given who she was, a dull and untalented child, there just did not seem to be any way to do this. So instead, she fell silent and submissive, hoping to become invisible or disappear into the background of the old, peeling wallpaper. She pictured the man's big white shark's teeth when he smiled, and though she wanted him to like her, she never wanted him to smile at her.

In the sixth grade, at age twelve, she got her first period. Not knowing what it was, she believed herself cursed with a mysterious punishment of blood and withdrew even more. With old rags and shredded-up sheets pinned inside the crotch of her panties even when she wasn't menstruating, she spent most of her time in the woodshed looking out at the world through a crack between the boards.

Through the long afternoons, she would daydream about the beautiful lady acrobats in the circus she had seen one winter in Fresno. They had swung back and forth in their luminous, spangled costumes, overhead, from ropes fastened to the ceiling of the tent structure. One day she, too, would be a radiant trapeze performer, and old enough to leave her family. Her secret hatred for her mother—who couldn't or wouldn't save her from her violent boyfriend—was as deep as her longing for her father, who had abandoned her two months after her birth.

One day in the shed, unexpectedly and with no forewarning, the "others" had come to fill her void of need. Once they arrived in her life, rising up from the smoky dust bowl floor, she was never again to feel like a vulnerable, frightened, and helpless little girl full of hate and pain. Years later, she still remembered what she had been doing at the exact moment when the dust motes and shadows first sprang into life.

Quickly making friends out of her need, she was able to identify three of the "presences" or disembodied voices. One, an old woman, reminded her immediately of her Grandmother Dawson, who had been a sane and grounding influence in her otherwise chaotic life and had died recently. She recalled cuddling with this woman in a rocking chair before an old wood-burning stove, and hiding behind her heavy woolen skirts, clutching them for dear life, when her mother or her boyfriend came at her with eyes filled with fury. Her grandmother would make the swollen hurt in her throat disappear after she cried and give her a cotton handkerchief for her plugged up nose.

This good, solid person who had been her rescuer on so many occasions had smelled like bad fruit or summer garbage. Though she was usually very squeamish, Jo Beth had never been put off by the foul odor emanating from the elderly woman. When the voices first descended on her, and whenever they came to her afterwards, they seemed to be ushered in by a faint reek of overripe fruits and vegetables like what she had smelled around the collection of trash cans and flies in her grandmother's dirt driveway.

The other presence was an elephant she could barely make out—big, strong, gray, wrinkled, and invincible, with a glittery harness and a world of patience, understanding and caring in his tiny bead eyes. She had seen several like this at the circus, but one in particular had caught her eye—the largest and strongest of all the animals. From his great height he looked down on her with unabashed kindness, kept other people away when she wanted him to, and, though unable to speak, communicated with her by shadowy gestures and signals that warned her of impending danger or harm.

The third voice, which belonged to a man, was less easily identified. It mostly echoed and backed up what the woman had to say. Jo Beth believed it might have been—yes, most likely it was her Grandfather Dawson, who had died after a long illness when she was four years old. Her memories of this elderly but handsome man with shocky white hair were of pleasant Sunday and holiday visits. He had lain in a big white bed in the middle of the living room all day and night. The relatives were always scolding the children to be quiet because of his sickness, which was never named, but he never seemed to mind the noise she made when she played close by his bed. A few times, he had smiled at her.

After she became acquainted with her guardian spirits—whom she did not see as a figment of her imagination evolving out of her constant hunger for companionship—the trips back and forth to school, and the rest of her life, became easier. The other children still tracked her like a wounded animal, threw tin cans at her, and called her a witch, and her body still went limp with fear and wobbly-kneed when they approached, but at least now she was not alone. She had "others" who shared her feeling, mitigated it, and believed it was wrong for her to be so persecuted.

She could not summon them at will when she needed them with her, which was something that always distressed her, but most of the time they would sense her predicament or "know" of her fear or danger in an esoteric way, and appear. They had never really frightened her—only startled her slightly at the very beginning and given her a momentary feeling of unreality as though bugs were crawling inside her abdomen, or a sense there might be something wrong with her because she saw and heard people and animals from a different world. But in time they came to seem as natural as breathing.

Her doubts were dispelled, once and for all, when the proof of their "genuineness" was revealed the day the sequined elephant stepped in between her and her stepfather and prevented him from striking her.

She was enormously grateful for their company when she made the difficult transition to a new school at the age of thirteen. They went through junior high school together uneventfully—a motley, straggly, unlikely "family" of secret helpers. She began to include them in the casts of the musical plays she wrote in the solitary afternoons in the shed and staged on a platform of old planks in a corner.

As she grew into adolescence, the presences would sometimes accompany her on Saturday trips into town. It was a small country town with one main street of stores paralleling the highway. A McDonald's, the first fast-food establishment in the town, loomed up prominently at the edge of the business district.

Jo Beth was always too shy to enter this outpost hub of teenage activity, but would stand across the road and watch as the pretty young girls on horseback trotted up to the hitching posts in the parking lot of the restaurant. She longed to be like them—free-spirited, laughing, their hair cut in contemporary styles, living in homes without mounds of rubbish in the yards, beloved. She also wished for a real-life horse friend.

There was an antique, tarnished hobby horse in the woodshed she had dragged out and polished and sometimes talked to, but he couldn't talk back to her. Not even the voices could do that in spite of their strong bond with her. The broken, discarded, and forgotten horse which had once been resplendent seemed to symbolize her own wounds and all her plight.

Somewhere in these years, her stepfather disappeared from the house. Though sudden, his departure was explicable in a rational way—the trucking company he worked for had moved to another part of the state, taking him along—but Jo Beth believed she had finally succeeded in willing him away with the "powers" lent her by her special entourage. It was her first psychical triumph as well as the first instance where she had been able to exert any control over her life, and she did not soon forget it.

Stuck on an immature social level for want of normal friendships, she was nevertheless maturing in all the physical ways and shortly became aware that others were staring at her for new and very different reasons. Her torment of name-calling and punches had mostly ceased, but was replaced by something that was in some ways even more sinister because it was unknown, sudden, faintly unsavory, and hinting of sin.

For a long while she didn't understand the magnetic attraction the young men of the town were developing toward her. If she did not exactly become a flashy beauty like the circus ladies and bore the traces of severe acne on her cheeks, she did grow out of her gangly frame into a well-proportioned and heavy-breasted, though still slender, young woman. Now she dimly but correctly perceived that the leers and laughter as she passed by were due not so much to her familial eccentricity as to her developing body.

One boy in particular haunted her. She had known Donny Graham since elementary school, when he had been one of her worst oppressors. He belonged to a gang of local hoodlums, some of whom had motorcycles and police records. Jo Beth was always careful to steer clear of these young toughs and kept her eyes on the ground when they zoomed past her in clouds of road dust, making obscene gestures and loud, disparaging, but intriguing remarks.

When first Donny and then his friends approached her for sexual favors, she was too timid, beaten, and submissive to protest or attempt to assert her wishes over theirs. Dependent and wanting male approval, she quickly earned a reputation for being accommodating in the back seats of old, souped-up Studebakers and Chevrolets. For a few moments in the half-dark she could fool herself into thinking she was loved and accepted, which was a new, and rather electrifying, experience for her.

She did not go to high school along with the rest, but stopped her education at the end of the ninth grade. On her mother's orders, she had gone to work at the food counter in the Woolworth's store in the small shopping mall in the town.

She failed at even this menial job when the manager noticed she spent excessive amounts of time daydreaming behind the counter, was infuriatingly slow and obsessively painstaking about her work, and couldn't keep up with the demands of impatient customers for giant slush drinks and submarine sandwiches. The latter were malodorous towers of bologna, tomato, and strings of lettuce between cut loaves of white bread that filled her with waves of nausea.

The five-and-ten job was just the beginning. By the time she was fifteen, Jo Beth had had a series of low-skill jobs including a stint as a short-order cook and one as an electronics assembler, but none of them lasted more than a few weeks.

At sixteen she was married for the first time, to an arrogant, hot-headed, and ultimately violent young roofer of eighteen who resembled her stepfather down to his muddy boots and scrawny tuft of a beard. The marriage, which by some miracle or oversight of nature produced no children, lasted for two-and-a-half months. The only noteworthy event she remembered from the weeks of this marriage was having her long hair cut for the first time into a pixie shape that was supposed to have been glamorous but made her look more than ever like a lost, large-eyed urchin.

Having survived her first marriage, but having become even more guarded and less able to trust anyone, Jo Beth returned to live at her mother's house. Over the next ten years, she was to leave home again three more times, for three more ill-starred marriages, each constituting only a short interruption in her life. The longest was one year.

In her chronically unwise and hapless choice of husbands, she showed the poor judgment and impulsivity that were the residuals of her child-hood problems. The second of these men was an abusive alcoholic, a tow truck driver; the third, a homosexual who was desperate to deny his perversion to the world; and the fourth, a heroin addict, small-time drug dealer, and local drifter. Jo Beth married this last one in the county jail.

He had just been sentenced to serve seven years in the state prison for armed robbery, and the marriage would provide him with the privilege and legal delights of conjugal weekends, or "bone visits," as they were vulgarly known.

During the years of young adulthood, when she had a good deal of free time between jobs and marriages, Jo Beth was becoming intensely involved in her flirtation with the occult, which increasingly absorbed her. People who had felt she was strange since childhood suddenly began to attribute exotic powers to her, and started to stop by to ask for advice or "readings" of their personal fortunes. A few of her mother's church friends were the first ones to "discover" Jo Beth, and their enthusiastic reports spread quickly through the countryside. By the time she turned thirty, a following of regular visitors had become dependent on her for tantalizing peeks into the unknown dimension of the future.

In her desire not to be disliked, hated, ridiculed, or possibly beaten, she tried her best to accommodate these seekers after truth and wisdom. And with this quiet, word-of-mouth beginning, Jo Beth the "psychic" was born. Certainly she looked the part as she made her way along the streets in her long, rustling skirts, sandals, a scarf over her hair, and a navy pea jacket in summer or winter, balancing large shopping bags on either side like a scale, and displaying a slightly cross-eyed, straight-ahead stare. First her mother and then Jo Beth herself began to think she did indeed possess a special gift of clairvoyance.

In the evenings the two women would prepare for their mystical excursions. They would clear and scour the dining room table, polish the furniture, sweep, then at the last minute draw the drapes. The dilapidated old house, with its small musty rooms, orange-fringed lampshades, and omnipresent curios and bric-a-brac, turned out to have the perfect professional ambience. Jo Beth never charged for the readings, but at the end her mother would pass around a collection plate for donations so her daughter could continue her all-consuming study without the necessity of having to work at a mundane job.

The surprising thing was that people were willing to pay rather generously, perhaps out of superstition or fear of reprisals from the dead if they tried to get away with being niggardly. Contributions of $20 were common. Most people seldom left less than $10, especially when urged to leave only what they felt the reading had been "worth." The sessions were never advertised in any way, which kept them within the letter of the law—something her mother, who was the businesswoman of the venture, kept a sharp eye on.

In an urban setting, Jo Beth might have passed through life as a garden-variety eccentric, or been considered just another bag lady, but in the rural community of gospel-wielding fundamentalists, she became a seer and slightly famous. One elderly woman whose long-deceased husband had been "contacted" during a ghostly soiree even began to speak of "Saint Josephine."

The prophecy of the school physician twenty-three years before that Jo Beth would be a late blossomer seems to have come true. For she has found not only her life's work, but also, at long last, a way of relating to people which is not hurtful. She has no more need to live in seclusion. She no longer prays every day to be normal.

Most people would probably not agree that Jo Beth's life is an American success story, though the ingredients are all there: financial security, a certain amount of esteem or respect in her community, time for hobbies and leisure pursuits, and a feeling of being important, worthwhile, and needed. Her career brings up the thorny question, Just what do we mean by "success" in our Western culture?

Do we have in mind mainly wealth and material possessions? If so, we would have to concede that in a good week, she earns as much as a junior corporate executive. Her schedule is usually booked up to three months in advance, and her mother has recently set a $40 an hour charge. The mortgage on the family residence has been paid off, and her mother now drives a new car. (Jo Beth herself never learned to drive.)

Is service to others the standard of a fulfilling life? Many view her as a therapist who soothes the fears and eases the doubts of her clients—none of whom ever turns around and sues for malpractice. Entrepreneurship? Her mother is even thinking that if business continues to be so good, they could found their own tax-exempt church. Prestige or status? Jo Beth would become the first ordained minister. Personal happiness or peace of mind? By their very nature, these are subjective judgments which can be made only by the person.

Would she have been any more successful if one of her marriages had survived, she didn't dress so oddly, and she had become a mother of two children and the owner of a late-model station wagon and a house full of contemporary furniture, plants, and pets? Her life might not have been any more secure or well spent in this role, but others would no doubt have been more comfortable since her lifestyle would not have forced them to examine their own values and basis of judgment.

The truth is that by any usual yardstick we can think of, Jo Beth is prospering—if only by a peculiar, accidental stroke of fortunate circumstances. Her life *is* a success, if you consider: An infant is born into the world with psychobiological damage and a subnormal threshold for stress. She grows up in an inadequate, hostile, and rejecting environment. She receives no intervention or remediation to interrupt her course and, doubly hurt, becomes an eccentric loner. As an adult, at last, she not only is at peace with her eccentricity, but has also found a way to turn it to her advantage.

One wonders how many oddly developing children end up either in reformatories or as freaks in carnival sideshows—"men of iron" or wild-eyed "snake women" leered at and exploited by their fellows, or passive, puppetlike, hypoactive young women in scant costumes who stare glassily ahead as their hyperactive male partners toss knives at them in tawdry road show reincarnations of vaudeville. Or as topless and nude dancers, prostitutes, drug addicts.

Jo Beth gets through most of her days by sleeping very late, making it a practice never to arise before four or five in the afternoon. But lions are known to sleep as much as twenty or twenty-two hours a day in hot weather, and so such self-regulated "somnolent detachment" is one acceptable form of adjustment to the environment. Blending surreptitiously into one's surroundings, in fact, is the most widely held criterion of survival or success throughout the animal world.

Long ago, bit by piece, she moved all her belongings out of the woodshed, where she had taken to sleeping after her first divorce, into the main house, where she now lives totally. Last year when the residence was renovated and the yard unearthed and landscaped, the old shelter was torn down, so the property in back of the house is now level and planted with a rose garden and a lawn.

In a darkened corner, during the trancelike state that precedes her readings, she often pictures herself as she was years ago, a lonely, tormented little girl who put on plays in a shack, only there was never any audience. The small gathering around her now truly believes she is guided by a higher energy, and that her "powers" are a gift, rather than a curse. It is a grown child's performance to make up for all the living room recitals that never were.

Every so often, she has a flash of what might have been possible in her life. She sees herself an outgoing, friendly, active young child playing among the rock piles in her grandmother's yard. Surrounded by kindly people, and not afraid of anything unless her grandmother has warned her. She chases a white cat out into the street and under a parked car . . .

Then the moment of memory is lost.

Along with the social isolation theory of mental illness, certain older homespun notions of physical "destiny" have also become disenfranchised and discredited in our ultra-scientific community; these folk-wisdoms recall some time-honored speculations on human behavior and motivation that are rooted in our earliest recorded past. In this century such intuitive conjectures have all but yielded to the supposedly more sophisticated, but ultimately untestable and unprovable, theories of psychoanalysis and its various branches. These schools all find the sources of disturbed behavior in penis envy, "fixation" at the oral or anal level, primary "object loss," or an over- or underdeveloped id, ego, or superego.

But back when man first emerged out of the primeval jungle, it was recognized that girth of shoulders, bundles of sinewy muscles, tallness, and keen visual acuity meant that—provided the spirits were favorable and barring some unforeseen but all-too-routine natural disaster—a person would grow up to be a hunter. Perhaps even a leader of other males if he were big, brawny, and pushy enough. If a small boy seemed to be weak or sickly or to possess some feminine traits, he was more likely to become a priest or a medicine man assuming he, too, survived into adulthood.

The possibility of physical destiny has become extremely unpopular in our democracy, where it has been relegated to the primitive, naive, or outright bedeviled as our technology has soared—and with it, our need to be omnipotent and above the wisdom of Mother Nature. Regardless of the facts of genetic endowment, we drive *all* our offspring to become doctors, lawyers, engineers. At the very least, we require of them these days computer expertise or "literacy." Most of the home computers that have been called "marvelous machines in search of a problem" are purchased in America by wishful parents.

Our software mania has recently led to the curious phenomenon of the computer camp. Children in shorts and T-shirts sit glassy-eyed in front of the terminals, keyboards, and other high tech apparatus alongside lakes and hiking trails, making push-button decisions on the fate of the world. And even though their young charges cannot read, spell, or write, a few specialized camps are offering computer training, felt to be immediately rewarding because it is tactile, for learning handicapped youngsters. It would seem as if the development of our brain through the millennia has enabled us not only to assume supremacy in the animal kingdom, but also to take to heart the responsibility for reversing the variants of nature.

The related popular belief in the survival of the fittest lived on in the gladiatorial contests of ancient Rome, in the Viking plunderers of the tenth century, and into the Middle Ages in crusades or "holy wars," which siphoned off the excessive energy and high spirits of fiery, cross-bearing youths. Later, the world was prey to pirates, knights-errant, duelists, legionnaires, warlords, samurai, matadors, mercenaries, cossacks, heavy-weight prizefighters, and five-star generals. Recently, the army of Argentinian soldiers that marched to doom in the Falkland Islands consisted of scared but idealistic young men. Under the shadows cast by their gray berets, most looked to be all of fifteen or sixteen years old.

There is a hint of the long-standing man-in-the-street ideas of "physical personality" in the recent studies that have found increased levels of serotonin, a nerve conductivity substance, in the brains of "powerful" leaders in monkey packs. While it is difficult to know to what extent such findings can be translated to human behavior, many researchers feel that similarly altered chemical levels may occur among dominant, aggressive, and/or charismatic people.

Other personality traits, such as extraversion, shyness, or withdrawal, long felt to be socially produced may well also turn out to have a physical basis, and to be more or less heightened or suppressed by tension and strain from the environment—much like the body's protective or immune mechanisms. And on a recent talk show, psychologist Joyce Brothers, who has made several fortunes by reeling off from memory the popular psychogenic descriptions of behavior, announced that she now wants, belatedly in life, to attend medical school because "Biochemisty is where it's at."

With noticeable exceptions (gang fights and world wars come to mind), most aggression-prone adolescents can no longer direct their rage and energy against large mammals such as bison or the members of other tribes—at least not without encountering possible legal consequences. Nor can they head west as they once could with assurance of unlimited expanses of virgin land. There are no more orange groves, and only one Alaska is left, and it isn't nearly spacious enough for all our modern frontiersmen. There is of course the moon, but while shooting up into space may appeal to impulsive young gamblers, it isn't likely that they would apply themselves long enough to acquire the technical background and knowledge required of present-day astronauts.

Yet there are some children with an excess of hormones or inner tension—mistrustful and sealed off from the adult world—who may not be able to improve, get better, or fit into our schools and communities, which seem to them as restricted as postage stamps. Not without superhuman effort on the part of parents and dedicated professionals who do not cease caring. The world, which has become too small, confined, and close for these youngsters, feels like a cage. The lack of viable alternatives to academic success and social "popularity" contributes to the stress.

The spirited, energetic boy who is cheerful and hardworking at home, where he repairs old furniture, and at grandmother's, where he drives the tractor lawn mower, finds he cannot stay seated at school. Violence (domestic and other kinds), school vandalism, property damage, joyriding, theft, the use of illegal drugs, hyperactivity, and learning disabilities have all become the new outposts or behavioral hinterlands. Many also become sexually promiscuous or engage in serious misconduct such as prostitution and arson—activities that stir excitement and mask their painful, depressive feelings.

For some time now, penologists have been aware of the great increase in violent crimes committed by children and youth. In some juvenile detention facilities, the floors and rooftops have been turned into beds. A few states like Vermont have recently lowered the age at which children can be tried for their serious acts with adult responsibility. Far from being idiosyncratic to the United States, outbreaks of school violence and assaults on teachers and students have been reported lately in low-crime Japan, as well as in Britain, France, Sweden, and Israel.

Usually the angry young person who acts out has been subjected to some degree of violence in his home life—whether in the form of constant heated arguments between the parents, psychological rejection and abandonment, or actual physical battering. There is a widespread fiction afoot that only people who are mentally ill and/or lower-class will violate the bodies of their children. But as we saw in previous chapters, it is relatively easy for the overworked, under-too-much-stress parent in our bullet-paced, expensive world—where survival has become a grueling daily battle against the odds—to turn into a child abuser. Modern stresses include not only the high cost of living but rampant joblessness, rootlessness, and family break-ups.

The increase in violence among children is a logical corollary of our lifestyle which should come as no surprise, yet the nationwide trends always seem a slight shock to news anchorpersons, judges, and the general public, including some parents. Cultural sanctions of "legitimate" force and institutionalized violence are part of our background and are seized upon by the industries that produce the entertainment that surrounds our impulsive children, giving them both a "double message" and a tacit permission, and making violence as American as cherry pie.

Many schools have gone back to corporal punishment, and each day we are finding "better," more devious, and less guilt-ridden ways of carrying out sentences of the death penalty. Our very system of law enforcement is largely a macho, masculine world in which police are reluctant to intervene in domestic violence against women and children. All this happens so consistently that it comes to seem like "normal" or appropriate behavior. The touchy, moody, restless, hyperkinetic Anglo-Saxon comic strip character Captain Easy, who is usually depicted with a guarded stance and ready fists, has been a national symbol, with good reason, as long as most of us can remember. Or substitute Li'l Abner and the violent world of Dogpatch.

Often children model their own violent behavior on the sort of adults who use the "kick in the ass" approach, which only deepens their emotional withdrawal even as it forces them to assume a false (and therefore neurotic) exterior of toughness and impenetrability. This process of "identification with the aggressor" has special appeal to young children, given the inflexible, eye-for-an-eye morality they all share regardless of their social or economic background. Modeled anger, rage, and hatred may at least give these youngsters a momentary feeling of power and a fleeting sense of authority over their damaged and out-of-control lives.

There is a serious question whether children should be queried on television news programs about their opinions of dangerous world crises, but recently a reporter on a major network interviewed a boy of twelve in the Korean community in Los Angeles for his reaction to the 1983 downing of a Korean passenger plane by a Russian missile. After the boy had expressed his dissatisfaction with the way the president had handled the situation, the reporter leaned in closer. Thrusting the microphone into the boy's small face, he asked what *he* would have done had he been at the helm instead. The youth's answer came as quickly and effortlessly as his shrug. "Make war," he said as though it were the most natural occurrence in the world.

As Patrick's story unfolds, no optimist with rose-colored social blinders who would like to bank on our current state of enlightenment, compassion, and social progress can deny that we are still exposing our defective, troublesome children on mountainsides—figuratively, of course, but sometimes no less inhumanely.

In time, we reap a crop of angry, alienated, disillusioned, and suspicious adolescents who live in tense, shrunken, and separate worlds. Only at this point, when it is almost too late, do we ask how on earth things have gone so wrong as to reach this sorry impasse of hurts and hurt-backs.

I first met Patrick, a modern-day Norseman warrior, when he was referred to the psychiatric department of the Youth Authority by his counselor for the punishable infraction of smoking a marijuana cigarette in his dormitory. I saw a rather stocky, medium-height young man of nineteen with a high forehead, sparse beard, loosely curling shoulder-length brown hair, tattooed arms, and soulful green eyes. In the incongruous prison setting, he had a pained, crucified look—like a young lead actor in a real-life version of *Jesus Christ Superstar*. Obviously in need of extensive dental work—his teeth were darkening around the edges—but a markedly handsome teenager just the same.

Though it was a sweltering hot afternoon in August, he wore a sweatshirt under an army field jacket, and knee-high swamp boots, as though this outfit were some sort of protective armor. Sitting sullenly across the office, his hands fumbling in his crotch, he displayed sudden, rotary eye movements, jerky head and neck contractions, mouth grimaces, and occasional rabbitty nose twitches. He had been "down" (in jail) for approximately seven months, four of them spent in Juvenile Hall awaiting sentencing on what should have been misdemeanor charges, then moved to the youth training center to serve out the remainder of his term of twenty-two months.

His counselor's immediate concern was the marijuana violation, but Patrick felt he had nothing to live for. He believed the other wards were putting "a rat and homosexual jacket" on him, he couldn't function around so many others packed like tinned sardines in the overcrowded double-bunked dormitories, he couldn't eat, and he was getting "paranoid" the way he always did when he was very upset. He couldn't get out of bed in the morning, clean his assigned area, and make his bed according to institutional procedure. Usually he fell asleep sometime in the early morning, with the result that he had become a "hard" sleeper.

He wanted a transfer to the medical/psychiatric correctional facility in the northern part of the state, where if nothing else he would at least have his own room. The medicine he was taking was causing him to feel agitated, tense, and "worn down"; he was fidgeting even more than usual despite the Dilantin and phenobarbital and was beginning to twitch uncontrollably all over his body, including his arms and legs. When he had truthfully informed the custody officers in Juvenile Hall of his self-destructive urges, he had wound up for five days in the suicidal observation ward in the infirmary which was run by them—in a bed with three of his limbs tied down and only one hand free. No mental health worker had ever stopped by to talk with him.

Behind the list of current symptoms and complaints lay a long and painful history of years of troubles. The youngest of four children in an intact middle-class family, Patrick was reported to have developed normally until the age of eighteen months, when he contracted a high fever and fell victim to infantile encephalitis. Serious behavior and learning difficulties soon followed. Unable to handle the additional stress of a difficult-to-rear child on top of all the other family dissensions, his mother turned to alcohol while his father buried himself in long hours of work in his real estate business.

By the third grade, at the age of nine, Patrick found himself in a private placement in the country known as Wayside Teen Ranch, almost a hundred miles from home. A pattern became established early on where he would spend a year in this placement, then return home during the summer recess to "fail" almost immediately, usually within a few weeks, and be returned to the Ranch in time for the next school semester.

When I asked him what sorts of things he would do on those visits that caused him to be sent back, a puzzled look crossed his face as he searched his memory. "Just a lot of crazy things like I broke dishes or mirrors," he came up with after a long blank spell.

"I'd get so mad I'd scream and shout or pound the walls and bust up my room. Then when no one was looking, I'd go eat spoons of sugar—it was like I couldn't make myself stop.

"And I didn't have a lot of friends. The Ranch was always better because there were a couple of grownups I knew liked me there and I wasn't scared of failing all the time. The other kids didn't call me crazy Kelly because I was in the retard class.

"I'd be so scared I'd be shaking each time I went home. I remember being scared when I put my suitcase down in the house, wondering how long I would last this time. To get back to your question, I never really knew exactly what happened because it would happen so quick, as soon as I got there. My Mom and Dad would start in yelling and fighting.

Usually about me, and who was to blame for the way I was. That kind of thing, and always putting me down.

"When she wasn't drinking, Mom would call me a selfish little snob who didn't care about anyone else, or an idiot or an asshole, and tell me I wasn't worth anything. I'd believe her because she was my Mom. And I'd be aching to go back to the Ranch but I'd be too scared to tell anyone or use the phone to call the school because I didn't want to seem ungrateful. Everyone at home was angry enough at me already. My big brother and little sisters too, because I guess I caused a lot of problems in their lives. They were all normal and I was sort of a big embarrassment for them. I tried not to let it bother me, but I suppose I was just one of those jealous kids.

"Don't get me wrong. It wasn't like life was any bed of roses at the Ranch either because they were very strict and watched every move you made and it wasn't all that great. When I first went there, I was the youngest and I was teased a lot because of my spasms—the way my face and neck get to twisting real ugly—and I couldn't read or write so I had to fight a lot at first, but at least everyone wasn't mad at me all the time. There were a lot of physical things I like you could always do when things got bad like swimming, backpacking and outdoor activities.

"At home I just felt boxed in and trapped. I had nowheres to go with all the feelings about how rotten and useless I was that would build up inside so I'd just sort of explode and do something I knew would get me sent back. Once I ran my arms through a window on purpose to cut them up. Or I'd eat about a pound of sugar and then I'd run away from home. I'd get out on the freeway and start to hitchhike but someone would always bring me back. After a while it happened so often the dudes at school started to call me Road-Dog.

"This last time when I left the Ranch I knew it was supposed to be for good because they don't keep kids over eighteen, but it wasn't any different at home. As soon as I got there I felt the same old panic having no one I could talk to like I had a couple of people I could rap with at the Ranch. I always felt like I was on trial at home and failing despite anything I did, and I *was*—failing, I mean. I didn't have any normal relationships and I was still uncoordinated and didn't think I could do any of those things like sports to make them proud of me. I'm not sniveling, but I never had one normal year out of my whole life. I was shaky about getting out because I had graduated from high school but I knew I didn't have any skills or a trade so I could earn a living. And then I thought, I ain't got no old lady out there. I thought about that a lot.

"Everybody at home was still mad at me. I got so tired of it, I got tired trying to hang on. I felt I was going a little crazy and there was nothing to stop me—nothing solid I could hold onto. I lost fifteen pounds the first month out because I didn't think I was entitled to any of their food. I felt like a stranger and the refrigerator was off limits. All the time I was thinking about taking a razor blade and splitting my throat." (Here Patrick made a violent gesture across his neck which showed the great rage and disappointment in himself he feels.) "I wanted to kill myself since I was no good to myself or anyone else—it was building up in my head. I was in a bad way where I just felt like giving up because everything in the world was my fault. Like I was one big failure. I mean, if I couldn't make my own parents love me, how could I make anyone else love me?

"I lasted about a month at home, which was as long as I had ever lasted there, and then I hitchhiked back to Santa Cruz with a trucker. It was the middle of the night when I knocked on Reverend Marty's door and his whole family stuck their heads out, but the next day the Rev said I had to go back and try to make things work out at home a little longer."

The incident that landed Patrick in the juvenile jail several weeks later was a seemingly spontaneous and rather arbitrary arrest for disturbing the peace, and malicious mischief. During the month at home, he had had a few odd jobs, mostly painting and yard work, but nothing that could sustain him for long. He let his hair grow down his back and hung around with a drug crowd because he "fit in." (As he put it colorfully, "If I made any friends, I made them in back alleys and bars.")

He started to smoke marijuana very heavily, used LSD, "crank" or Methedrine, and "bennies"—"anything to get high on"—and began having memory lapses. He forgot names as soon as he heard them, and couldn't concentrate on his train of thought long enough to hold a coherent or relevant conversation. Several of his old symptoms such as visual distortions, "mirror focus," and extreme clumsiness returned.

One night he had been downtown with some street-corner youths, all a few years younger, gotten drunk on beer and cheap wine, and smashed some bottles in the street. Just as a police car was driving past the dark, quiet shopping mall, one of the bottles had shattered the windshield of a parked car.

Random though it seemed, that incident symbolized Patrick's whole life—the difficulties he had always had in controlling his aggressive impulses, his poor choice of companions, his longing to be accepted and belong, and strong urges to retaliate and "get even" for the years of discouragement and anger at the world that put him in a losing situation. "Why, Lord, me?" he had agonized over and over. It also seemed to express his life in that the punishment—nearly two years in the custody of the Youth Authority in a closed setting—was clearly out of all reasonable proportion to the crime.

Though there had been a fairly steady stream of family discord and an occasional eruption into domestic violence in his family's suburban, Spanish-style home, his three siblings who were not similarly afflicted by neurological difficulties had managed to hold together, graduate from school with no obvious problems, and continue to do well thereafter. His older brother had been on the football team in high school and graduated from a state college with a degree in engineering. One sister married shortly after high school, and the other became a veterinarian's assistant.

Around the age of fifteen, Patrick had discovered alcohol and taken to it instantly, like the proverbial duck to water. For the first time in his life, his body felt calmer, more relaxed, and "right." With a few drinks in him, he wasn't excruciatingly shy and tongue-tied around girls the way he usually was because of his awkward attempts to cover his distressing feelings of inferiority and stupidity. When in the company of young women, he would confabulate wishful stories of academic and personal success, and strive to maintain a happy-go-lucky, "normal" emotional facade. Later, realizing that, even if a girl had agreed to go out with him to a movie or a restaurant, he couldn't live up to the false picture he had painted, he would feel ashamed.

Beer loosened him up, both physically and emotionally, and gave him a sense of confidence, well-being, and euphoria. By the time of his arrest he had become dependent on its hazy, effervescent effects—along with marijuana, when he could get it—much as he had once craved the inner "resolution" and sense of security sugar cubes or ice cream gave him.

(Patrick's early addiction to sweets and his later involvement in substance abuse calls to mind the prevalent candy, cigarette, soda, and coffee addictions and the nail biting and serious dental problems of most young persons in alcohol or drug treatment programs. These excesses have long been noticed by social workers, attorneys, and other persons who deal in their daily practices with the rapidly increasing group of hospitalized teenage offenders.

The old psychoanalytic notions, which have proved to have no heuristic or treatment value whatsoever, claimed that these young persons were more "oral dependent" than the average because of rather profound emotional deprivations—hence the overflowing ashtrays found in many inpatient adolescent treatment establishments, the candy wrappers, and the aluminum cans cascading, ghetto style, down the stairs.

The new research has challenged this traditional view—revealing, for example, that impulsive teenage boys are likely to become heavy drinkers when their poor self-image catches up with them on the brink of adulthood. Suddenly many immature, extraverted, and aggressive boys like Patrick show the true—submissive and dependent—core of their personality. The reasons lie mainly in their behavior chemistry; neurochemistry, in turn, depends on genetic factors.

And a pioneer study out of Denmark supports the theory that the offspring of alcoholics are particularly sensitive to the effects of alcohol because of genetically transmitted changes in their brains and central nervous systems; these youngsters have a "biological marker," or warning sign, that indicates a high risk for alcoholism. The fact that the brains of alcoholics' children respond in a different way to alcohol brings us full circle, back to the theory of genetically inherited predispositions toward certain aberrant and self-destructive behaviors.

Despite his alcoholism, the years at Wayside had not been futile as a constructive influence in molding Patrick's life and shaping the direction of his future. The regimen of strict supervision and the emphasis on self-responsibility for one's shortcomings had slowly but surely done their work of effecting prosocial changes in the wild, distractible third-grader who lit fires and fought at the drop of a hat.

Under the fears of failure and the feeling of not being good enough, Patrick the graduate wanted more than anything else to have "a nice job around decent people," and not to be always around "Satanic music" or bad types of people. His second wish was to have a girlfriend.

Only vocational preparation had been the one glaring gap in the otherwise excellent program of remediation, and he did not know how he could ever reach his goal. It was partly the excessive concentration on academic upgrading and "equality" which comes from our idealism of democracy, but mostly a simple lack of funds for extracurricular or "para-educational" projects, that had caused the staff to fail to involve their charges in these critical lessons in survival.

There was one glimmer of hope, in the person of the director of education at Wayside, who was known as Reverend Marty—even though he had no official or informal connection with any church or religious organization. During his own student days, he had been Patrick's first houseparent. After he had graduated from college with a degree in elementary education, he had become a teacher in the Learning Center at the Ranch. Three years later, he was promoted to supervisor of educational programs.

Except for several summers when he had disappeared on long-needed sabbaticals, Marty had pretty much stood by Patrick ever since the day the youngster had first appeared in his cottage—a rebellious, surly, defiant, deeply depressed and troubled nine-year-old with bitter, stinging tears just below the surface of his rage. For the first year or two of Patrick's stay, Marty had stuck by him through a lot more thick than thin.

Marty had never been on the surface an especially warm or physically affectionate counselor like some of the others. He did not cuddle the younger children or hold them on his lap, although his wife often did. But Patrick and the other boys knew they could trust him to be supportive within the limits of acceptable behavior, impartial, and fair—basically a responsible man who was sensitively involved with them and unafraid to show the degree of his commitment.

Like most of the staff, Marty lived with his family in a small house on the grounds of the school which had been converted from an old motel. Patrick's most treasured childhood memories were of spending a privileged Friday evening once a month with Marty and his family in their home. On those nights he would help his teacher carry in armloads of wood for the fireplace, and then sit down to dinner with the family. Afterwards they would play cards in the living room, or maybe Monopoly or Parcheesi. His two daughters, both a few years older than Patrick, attended the regular school in the neighborhood.

All the time he was growing up at the Ranch, Patrick's vision of happiness had been of being able to go to public school along with normal kids like Marty's daughters or his own siblings. In the nine years he lived in placement, he had never so much as set foot in the schoolyard, but he always strained to get a look inside it when he passed by in the school station wagon on trips into the nearby town.

More than anything, it seemed to him a joyful place. He had heard rumors about how the local school wasn't nearly so restrictive as the Learning Center—kids weren't supervised every minute, watched over as if by hawks, and graded on their behavior every fifteen minutes. Some of the better-functioning Wayside boys went to the public school in a bus that took them there each morning and returned late in the afternoons. But in all the time at the Ranch, Patrick was never considered sufficiently rehabilitated or behaviorally stable enough to attend an ordinary classroom.

The fun and freedom he had missed out on in his life—both at school and on nonexistent family outings—became his symbol for his loss. He would cut out and save every magazine picture of campers, fifth wheels, and Chinooks, whose small, compact worlds, safe from hurts, made them his favorites. His collection of toy vans represented the family fun he had never known and was his most prized possession. He kept those miniatures on a table next to his bed. Besides his high school diploma, they were the one thing he didn't give away to the younger boys when he left, but took home in a paper sack.

The worst part about leaving the Ranch had been the thought that he might never see Marty or his family again. In spite of his strapping size (his feet had hung over the edge of his cot for the last few years), Patrick did not feel grown up inside. He felt little, scared, and hopelessly unprepared for life—as indeed he was—cast out because of something arbitrary like a birthday into what he could only think of as the cold.

Over the years, Marty had become as indispensable to his sense of being okay in the world as his freedom to breathe, and this attachment had developed without his knowing about it at the time. Though he could not have put his feeling into words or otherwise expressed it, that seemingly unplanned, irrational episode at the mall contained in it the hope of seeing Marty again.

He wrote from the juvenile jail to his former teacher about his latest failure and continued need for contact. The letter was scrawled in a chicken-scratch combination of capital and small letters fused together, and the words that could be made out were full of misspellings; fackt, freind, woulent, dident, reson, whent, no (know), coodnent, in facked—but even the usually impassive guards whose job it was to read incoming and outgoing mail didn't have the heart to point out his illiteracy or the fact that the letter would probably never reach its destination. One of them readdressed the envelope so it would be deliverable.

In the harsh environment of Juvenile Hall, the strange lapses that Patrick had experienced whenever he was under unusual stress, since he was seven years old, returned. They indicate an underlying organic psychosis, which he describes this way: "Say you're just sitting there staring at your locker. I don't know if they're men or women, but suddenly I'll hear weird things like 'You're looking cute today,' or

'You're a cute mother fucker'—always insulting things like calling me a snitch or a queer. Or accusing me of things.

"At night I swear to God I'm not asleep but I'll be lying there feeling weird, cold and scared. I'll have these times where I'm sort of floating or levitating through the room. I can see myself looking down at my locker. I'll notice it's been broken into and I'll see someone piling all my stuff into the trash bin.

"For a while after I got home I was smoking a lot of weed and dropping acid. I'd dream about people dying, and how my sister Angie and her girlfriend would be blaming all these deaths on me—people I didn't even know—and then I'd think they were staring at me with Satanic eyes even when I wasn't sleeping.

"The first time I remember anything like this was before Wayside Ranch when we moved to a new house. I was so scared of the neighborhood and beginning a new school I started to stammer and mispronounce everything. It was right after my grandfather died. I couldn't sleep in the new room. I turned over in bed and seen him standing there in the living room crouched behind a chair. It scared the holy shit out of me—I remember I got really cold and something pulled my foot. I didn't know what to make of it, whether it was real or not, but the next day my grandmother said she thought she saw him too."[4]

Marty answered in the form of a proposal to the presiding judge of the juvenile court in which he outlined an alternative to two years incarceration in the Youth Authority. Patrick could live in a special apartment building in Santa Cruz for learning disabled young adults

[4] Organic mental disorders such as Patrick's are distinguished from environmentally produced or "functional" disturbances mainly on the basis of previously diagnosed or known dysfunctions of the brain. They are a heterogeneous group of symptoms which can be brought on in normal persons by various drugs such as hallucinogens, systemic infections, metabolic disorders like hypoglycemia, dehydration, salt or water imbalances, aging of the brain, or alcohol intoxication.

The perceptual disturbances which are common often result in various misinterpretations, illusions, and hallucinations that are strikingly similar to the ordinary, everyday experiences of many minimally brain dysfunctional children. The organic involvement may range from sensory misperceptions, confusion, anxiety, difficulty in sustaining attention, impulsivity, restlessness, and hyperactivity to disorientation, disordered stream of thought, memory loss, depression, impediments in speech, and sleep disturbances.

Hypnagogic or nighttime hallucinations, which are especially common in impulse-ridden children, may be associated with anxiety or unusual stress, but need not be. They are vivid images which are usually macabre and frightening occurring at the onset of sleep, in the transition of drowsiness from wakefulness to unconsciousness.

who needed assistance and guidance toward leading independent lives, and at the same time enroll in some trade training at a local junior college. The director of this privately funded program, which was still in an experimental stage, had agreed to accept Patrick on a month's trial with the stipulations that he work closely with his probation officer and not violate any of the conditions of his release, including weekly urine analysis testing for drugs and alcohol. Best of all, he would be able to see Reverend Marty and his family from time to time. The judge, the supervising probation officer, and the superintendent of the Youth Authority facility all in turn agreed to this exchange.

The grin that spread across his prematurely weathered face when the plan was revealed to him showed how badly Patrick, who was still a sugar craver, needed dental repairs, but the light in his eyes was no less radiant for this disfigurement. What the proposal meant most of all was that there was at least one person in the world who cared about him, who believed he was worthwhile and shouldn't be thrown away the way the nocturnal phantom had expressed his contempt when he had trashed all his belongings.

With the sense of renewal in knowing he had mattered enough to make a difference to another person, Patrick could struggle ahead with his often-interrupted life. He had flashes of backpacking hikes up into the mountains with the Reverend and the other boys, summer afternoons in the pool learning to swim and dive, and peaceful evenings in the cozy school living room. He recalled how his dormitory, which was known as Coyote Cottage, had once won every game in the annual summer competition with the other cottages, all of which had wildlife names like Condor, Hart, Buffalo, or Blackbird. That night he fell asleep untormented by the apparitions which had appeared to him regularly since his incarceration.

Back in Santa Cruz, Marty and his wife sat up late to talk about the arrangement. Though it was not the school's policy to maintain contact once a boy had graduated, they agreed they could do no less than accept partial responsibility for this errant but cherished boy for the next few months, until he learned a trade and could be out on his own.

Through the years, other youths who had left the program had continued to haunt Marty, but no other boy had ever presented him with so poignant a picture of the imitation or parody of normal development these children conveyed that was the most painful part of his work. No other youngster had seemed so much as Patrick to long to be normal. He felt optimistic that with prolonging his support, and overseeing his schooling in a trade where his low academic skills wouldn't matter—along with the community program, which would teach him to structure his time—the boy would have his chance.

Patrick would not leave the youth training center until the end of the week, but an hour after he learned of the plan for his parole he was packed and ready to depart.

It may seem a little discouraging and hardly worth all the effort that went into it that Patrick's fondest hope—what he looks forward to the most in his life—is yet another group living situation. "Like a regular family," he told his counselor and bunk mates excitedly at dinner that night. But when he left, his hair was brushed back neatly behind his ears, and he was wearing clean blue jeans, a colorful Hawaiian shirt that appeared to express his expectation, several gold chains around his neck, and his best silver hoop earring.

Totaled up, all his education, residential treatment, and incarceration have cost his parents and the state about the same amount as the special nuts and bolts on an MX missile or an F-15 fighter plane, or a fraction of one projectile on a nuclear submarine. The cost in dollars and cents, though, is not the important thing.

The primary goal of all this work has been to help him regain a sense of trust, purpose, direction, and the many choices that lie ahead. He will always be biochemically vulnerable and sometimes behave as reflexively as an amoeba, but he is still a sentient, living being. Like all creatures, he longs for a group where he will not be put down, be ostracized, or stand out like a lost sheep.

This is his wish for love and acceptance—his gentle rainbow glimpse of future lights off in the distance—and it includes a developing sense of himself as a particular person who has a range of opportunities awaiting—school, work, even marriage and children. On the deepest level, it is a physical sense of others who are there, and whom he can reach out to in times of need. One thing he has learned from his life is that a picket fence and a front yard do not necessarily make a home.

At nineteen his search for a family, which is tantamount to finding the hidden treasure of himself, is just beginning. Even so, Patrick is one of the lucky ones. For in this age of civilization, education, and affluence, there are far worse fates for many of the children of our man-made winter. Damaged youngsters who are passed over every day, placed in files in county offices to await the never-neverland of caring homes, children who have no Marties and no hope.

Once in a while these children grow up to express their painful lives, and the frustration, alienation, and self-estrangement they feel, through music, art or writing. Patrick is learning to play the guitar in anticipation of one day being able to write songs which will tell about his world, and capture the tears he could not express at the age of nine that first day at the Ranch. The thing that hurt him the most, inexplicably at the time, when the child care worker first showed him his bed and cubby area, was a big, tinseled, blue crepe paper banner under his window spelling out Welcome, Patrick.

Shirley Klein is a part-time poetess, full-time vocational rehabilitation counselor out in West Virginia born with cerebral palsy, a central nervous system affliction, who reaches out of her clumsy and contorted body through her poetry. She has written a book of poems called *Of Bitter Choice* in which she discusses her loneliness, hurt, and rejection and the normal experiences she will never know. Sometimes her arms wave out of control and her tongue sweeps her chin. People quickly avert their gaze and pretend she is not passing by in her wheelchair. But what they will never realize is that her shoulders ache in their cold nakedness as she sees others caressed by lovers she will never have.

The preface describes the choice which led to the title of her book. "It had been a difficult birth. The doctor had to use forceps. I lay like a piece of meat on the table as the doctor looked at my father with a wordless question; my father nodded yes. And, thus, I was consigned to life, a life challenged by cerebral palsy . . ."

"In my work," she closes, "I write of the unseen self behind the wheelchair, the unsure step, the wet chin, the awkward movement and the garbled speech. In so doing, I strive to speak for others who face the same hostile world I do, thereby confronting that world with a reality that will no longer be ignored or denied."

Claude, you who were once Baby Astronaughty, looking at a photograph of you as you are today, proud in your pink preppie shirt and only a little uncertain in the twist of your smile, I can hear the faint, tinkly, phantom music of the ice cream van that used to pass our house. It calls to me, like winds blowing, its tale of loss: all the carefree, normal happiness of childhood that was denied you. And I ache for you.

Do you remember how you cried that autumn years ago when we moved to the small apartment near a rocky beach and had to leave your wagon behind because there was no yard? My special boy, Shirley

Klein, has said it for me: ". . .we all drag wagons behind us. Big, red, empty wagons. Waiting for someone to fill them with some hope, dreams, love."

As Phoebe Snow said in song to her strange, autistic little daughter, her heart would break when the other children laughed at her, but then she would rally. She would tell her child that no matter how deep or withering the pain, she had to stand her ground, she had to stick around.

APPENDICES

APPENDICES

Appendix
1

The "For Parents Only" Questionnaire

This original checklist was the basis for the statistics cited in Chapter 1 and some of the questionnaire material in Chapter 3. Unlike the behavioral scales of Chapter 3, the "For Parents Only" Questionnaire is not designed as a diagnostic checklist. Parents might want to complete it, though, and bring it along for reference when discussing their child's problems with his pediatrician. As in the previous questionnaires, responses should be evaluated within the larger context of the total functioning of the child. The central question should always be: Is my child's behavior a problem for himself or others? If the answer is yes, this questionnaire can help in defining particular problem areas. A parent can star relevant items, or item-clusters, or circle them with a colored pencil.

1. Boy or girl _____
2. Eye color of child _____
   Parents _____
3. Hand preference _____
   Handedness of parents _____
   Preference shown for right or left hand by age _____
   Ambidextrous (used both hands equally) after two years? _____
   Many left-handers in extended family? _____
4. Other learning disabled, hyperactive, asthmatic, or allergic adults in family _____
   _____
   On mother's side? _____
   Father's side? _____

5. Only child? If not, birth order _____

6. More than one learning disabled child in immediate family?_____

7. Fetal or birth position _____

8. Length of gestation _____

9. Birth weight _____

10. Method of delivery _____
    Anesthesia used? _____
    Other drugs given? _____
    Any problems or concerns at birth? _____

11. Brief description of behavior and personality in infancy: _____
    _____
    _____
    _____

12. Large reaction to noise, cold, wetness, startle, pain, etc.? _____
    When and how first noted _____

13. Difficulty falling or remaining asleep _____
    Confused cycles of waking and sleep _____
    Night wakefulness _____ For how long? _____

14. Any nursing or feeding difficulties? (e.g., always hungry, poor sucking or swal-
    lowing, breast refusal) _____ Describe: _____
    _____

15. Much crying? _____ Persistent? _____

16. Breast or bottle-fed _____ Age weaned _____ Problems? _____

17. Solid foods started at age _____

18. Digestive problems _____
    Constipation _____
    Diarrhea _____
    Vomiting _____
    Gas _____
    Colic _____

19. Number of colds in first year _____
    Bronchitis? _____
    Croup? _____
    Noisy Breathing? _____
    Other respiratory problems? _____

20. Ear infections _____ Any complications? _____ Describe: _____
    _____

21. Eye problems in first two years _____ Describe: _____
    _____

22. Hearing problems? _____

23. Identifiable allergies? _____ Which? _____

24. Formula changes or food intolerances _____

25. Rashes _____
    Eczema _____
    Boils _____
    Impetigo _____
    Other sensitivity _____

26. Response to frustration or delay   Mild, easygoing _____
    Average _____ Severe, easy falling apart _____

27. Did you provide infant with
    _____ a lot of touch, cuddling and body contact
    _____ a moderate amount
    _____ very little

28. Response to touch and body stimulation _____
    _____

29. Any problems noted in early attachment and bonding? _____

30. Age at which child first
    _____ smiled
    _____ showed separation fear
    _____ reacted with fear to strangers

31. Ticklish, goosey, squirmy _____

32. Difficulty in diapering and dressing _____

33. Stiff, resisted cuddling _____ Or floppy, poor muscle tone _____

34. Definite preference for body position as infant? _____ Describe: _____
    _____

35. Self-abuse — head-knocking, hitting or scratching self, etc. _____
    Approximate age began _____ Stopped _____

36. Repetitive behaviors — rocking, bed-rocking, thumb sucking, bottom-clutching, hair
    twirling, "security" blanket, etc. _____ Began at age _____
    Stopped _____

37. Eye contact — Good, steady _____ Fairly steady _____
    Poor focus, jerky eye movements, nystagmus _____

38. Age at which child
    _____ held up head
    _____ crawled or crept
    _____ stood
    _____ walked

39. Number of accidents in first year _____ Second year
    and beyond _____

40. Ate unusual substances? _____ Describe: _____
    _____

41. Toucher — reached, broke, extremely clumsy _____ Stopped excessive
    touching at age _____

42. Temper tantrums? _____

43. Method(s) of discipline _____
    _____

44. Describe response to discipline or restraint: _____
    _____

45. Any unusual occurrences or observations in first two years? ____ Describe: ____
    _____

46. Excessive need for sameness? _____ Describe: _____
    _____

47. Rash, impulsive, no normal sense of danger? ____ Describe specific incidents ____
    _____

48. Difficulty with "cause-effect" reasoning _____ Describe _____
    _____

49. Never satisfied _____

50. Lacked stamina, tired easily _____

51. Lapses in activity, staring into space, hesitations, back-tracking _____

52. Seemed immature _____ How so? _____
    _____

53. Clung to early games and objects _____

54. Collected odd objects or junk _____

55. Took things apart _____

56. Intrusive—e.g., pounced and jumped on others _____

57. Couldn't carry tunes, remember songs or nursery rhymes _____
    Later memory problems? _____ Describe: _____
    _____

58. Difficulty with time and space _____ Describe: _____
    _____

59. Trouble with opposites—up/down, over/under, inside/outside, etc. _____

60. Receptive language:
    Pointed to objects at age _____
    Obeyed simple commands at age _____

61. Expressive language: First word at age _____ Two-word
    sentences at age _____ Three or more word sentences
    at age _____

62. Speech problems? e.g., garbled, hard to understand _____
    Describe: _____ Until age _____

63. Fine motor problems—e.g., uncoordinated, trouble building with blocks, coloring,
    drawing, cutting, stringing beads, lacing, buttoning _____ Describe
    specifically: _____
    _____

64. Gross motor difficulties—e.g., bike riding, swing pumping, hopping, skipping, running, keeping up with others physically _____ Describe specifically: _____

65. Cross-dominant (e.g., uses right eye to sight an object, left foot to kick, right hand to throw, or some other combination of eye, foot and hand preference) _____

66. Trouble with auditory discrimination or assimilation—e.g., can't distinguish "bed" from "bad," "pat" from "pet," difficulty with word endings, many mispronunciations _____

67. Sweets craver? _____ Began at age _____

68. Poor eater, picky _____ Anemia? _____
Other food problems _____

69. Fear of the dark _____
Nightmares or night terrors _____
Bed-wetting _____
Sleepwalking _____
Overtiredness _____
Always up early _____

70. Describe other early fears _____

71. Age toilet-trained: Bladder _____ Bowel _____
Problems with training? _____

72. First group situation (nursery school, play group, or day care) at age _____
If no nursery school, briefly describe home situation: _____

73. Briefly describe behavior and personality as preschooler: _____

74. Any dramatic or unusual changes noted between pre- and postschool behavior?

75. Response to first school or group situation _____

76. Describe any social academic, or physical problems at preschool age _____

77. Teachers' reports _____

78. Aggressive, reckless, outgoing behaviors in school _____ Or phobic, withdrawn behaviors _____

79. Unusually dependent on parent? _____

80. Age child began parallel play _____
Age began interactive play _____
Problems? _____

81. Home atmosphere: Strict _____ Permissive _____ In between _____
    Describe type and frequency of discipline in preschool years _____
    _____

82. When were difficulties or "difference" first noted? _____ Describe
    specific behaviors which made you suspicious and uneasy _____
    _____

    When did you first take child to doctor? _____
    When was difficulty first diagnosed? _____
    Reaction of doctor or other professionals _____
    _____

    Your own reaction _____
    _____

83. What has been child's worst problem? _____
    _____

    What has been your worst problem? _____
    _____

84. What would have helped the most in child's early years? _____
    _____

Appendix
2

A Potpourri
Home Curriculum

If you think back on your early years, you will probably realize that your most effective and memorable learning began with simple objects or ideas. Building on everyday activities and chance encounters, you can similarly help your child integrate his experiences into broad learning adventures. For example, he may learn from a footprint in the ground about the fossils or "stories" scientists find in rocks. Later he may learn about the earth's layers and how sediment is laid down in the sea, and that the seas first became filled with oxygen-releasing plants and bacteria and, gradually, larger forms. And always remember: children do *not* have to sit still in order to learn.

A handful of suggestions or points of departure to help the active child to assimilate a sweep of learning follow.

Coral gardens; tropical fish and aquariums; ant farms; balance scales; kaleidoscopes; models of ships; ties and knots; the study of bats, owls, and other nocturnal animals; echoes; animal "radar systems"; directions in space such as north and south, right and left (use small, different-colored flags); traffic lights; dust motes; cinders; spiders and webs; gliding birds and migration patterns; gutters; construction sights; desert animals and vegetation; tin-can telephones; wolves; whales; space modules and space colonies; bird calls and barking dogs (different ways to communicate); jet planes; lawn mowers (small motors); rainbows; thunder; ocean waves; animal oddities (walruses, sea cows, sloths, lizards, etc.); searchlights; nightingales; smoke signals; sign language; trains; aerial photographs; Eskimos; forests; phases of the moon; ice boxes; wood-burning stoves; compasses; weather vanes; coal; sheep dogs; solar panels; greenhouses; sand dunes; fog; neon lights; jumping fish; cacti; sharks; honeycombs; snail shells; ferns; butterflies; insects; seashells; crystals; snowflakes; igloos; rocks; sticks; leaves; acorns; candles; ice cubes; music boxes; maps; hurricanes; the special sensing cells on earthworms; velvet monkeys; marsupials such as kangaroos and koala bears; galaxies; glaciers; frogmen; fireflies; clouds; caterpillars; volcanoes; underwater plants; skyscrapers; knights; mouse holes; mountains; dolphins; blimps; steamboats and sailboats; rain and snow.

Growing plants and vegetables; hardware stores; swap meets; junkyards; secondhand and antique shops; fitting pieces of pipe plumbing; model making; comic strips; cooking lessons; supermarkets; campsites; Indian rock art; typing; any and all tools; tracing braille or other forms of raised, three-dimensional writing; flow pens for strong feedback; alphabet soup; making "ransom notes" out of junk mail letters; guesstimating (e.g., How may paper clips long is this?); hieroglyphics; finding numbers and letters in license plates; farms; dairies; mobile home parks; palm trees; television (children's classics and documentaries, reading *TV Guide* and sharing thoughts about programs); a home library shelf; reading to your child; billboards; menus; traffic and road signs; counting the number of forks, plates, etc., on the table; talking about or writing down descriptions of the things your child sees and experiences; magazine subscriptions; library cards; writing notes to your child; entering contests; posting a chores chart; telephone books; diaries and journals; writing letters and postcards; reading labels on jars, medicines, food cans, and household products; record album jackets; joke books; word games; recipes; blackboards and message centers; shopping lists; writing directions for finding a park or store or assembling a project; captions for snapshots in albums; catalogs; advertisements; making greeting cards with felt pens; telling time to the half-hour; naming the seasons, days of the week and months of the year; numerical concepts which use different-size buttons (first, middle, third, few, all, last, several, many, least, and none); matching numerals to a group of objects up to 10; identifying circles, squares, triangles, cones, rectangles, and other shapes; recognizing and counting with pennies, nickels, and dimes; reading a calendar; spatial relationships (inside, between, top, bottom, over, under, and so on); time (before, after) and other relationships (different, same); measuring (using a ruler or tape measure); playing "store" with labels and prices; hopscotch; letting your child count the freckles on his nose by dotting them with a magic marker.

Exploring questions like those in the children's section of the newspaper: What keeps a kite up in the air? What makes a light bulb burn out? How are smells produced? How does an elevator work? How does blood travel around the body? What makes the wind blow?

It may comfort the more academically minded parent to know that there are published word lists containing all of the words most commonly found in children's first books or preprimers. The most famous is *The Basic Sight Word Test* by Edward Dolch[1], which lists a total of 220 beginning words, but some of the other word lists (e.g., the one found in *Principles and Practices of Teaching Reading* by Arthur Heilman)[2] pare the elementary words that a child needs to know in order to read down to as few as 100. All of the lists contain the words most frequently encountered in reading, such as "a," "an," "I," "my," "the," "then," "this," "but," "who," "what," "where," "when," and "why." If your child recognizes these "core words" by sight, you can fill in the other words for him until he learns them on his own.

[1] Garrard Publishing Company, 1942
[2] Charles E. Merrill Publishing Company, 1967

Appendix
3

A Sample Weekday Schedule

7:00–7:30	Wake-up time and premeal grooming. This should include washing face and hands, brushing teeth, combing hair, toileting, and dressing. Pajamas should be put in appropriate place (e.g., hamper), bathroom should be tidied, bed should be made.
7:30–7:45	Breakfast (should always include protein—e.g., egg, cottage cheese, meat, milk if not allergic—and whole-grain toast, muffin, or cereal).
7:45–	Post-breakfast chores such as wiping table, washing and drying dishes, sweeping, planning of day's activities or school.
10:00–10:30	Protein snack (peanuts, peanut or almond butter on half a slice of whole-wheat toast, hard-cooked eggs, cup of bean or lentil soup, meat, or cheese).
11:00–11:30	Quiet time—relaxation techniques, table projects, music, reading, stretching or breathing exercises, etc.
11:30–12:00	Help child prepare his own lunch.
12:00–12:45	Lunch and clean up.
12:45–2:30	Leisure indoor or outdoor activities, or school, outing, or shopping.
2:30–3:30	Various physical chores, such as mopping, vacuuming, dusting, cleaning, tidying, laundry, taking out garbage; or any assigned outdoor duties, such as watering lawn, cleaning garage.
3:30–4:00	Protein snack or half regular dinner. Relaxation techniques.
4:00–5:00	Homework if in school; otherwise, quiet activity.

5:30–6:00   Premeal grooming and wind-down.

6:30–7:00   Dinner—should include protein, no dessert.

7:00–8:00   Quiet activities—e.g., board games, checkers, cards, story time, face-to-face talking (things you need to say to each other; include any problems in the day's events and/or worries about the next day), or "house meeting."

8:00–8:30   Bath and protein snack. Set out next day's clothes. Bedtime hugs, reassurances, and kisses.

Appendix
4

Books for Do-It-Yourself Diagnosis and Treatment

Ayers, A. Jean. *Sensory Integration and Learning Disorders*. Western Psychological Services, 12031 Wilshire Boulevard, Los Angeles, Ca. 90025, 1972.

Davis, Adele. *Let's Have Healthy Children*. Harcourt, Brace & World, New York, 1959.

Dufty, William. *Sugar Blues*. Warner Books, New York, 1976.

Frostig, Marion. *Movement Education: Theory and Practice*. Follett Educational Corp., Chicago, 1970.

Janov, Arthur. *Imprints*. Coward-McCann, New York, 1983.

Kaufman, B. *Son-Rise*. Harper & Row, New York, 1976.

Klein, Shirley. *Of Bitter Choice*. To order send $2 to Shirley Klein, 2715 Fairlawn, Lot 32, Dunbar, W.Va. 25064.

Lawick-Goodall, Jane. *In the Shadow of Man*. Houghton Mifflin, Boston, 1971.

Leboyer, Frederick. *Birth without Violence*. Knopf, New York, 1978.

Levy, Harold. *Square Pegs, Round Holes*. Little, Brown, Boston, 1973.

Liedloff, Jean. *The Continuum Concept*. Knopf, New York, 1977.

Liepemann, Lisa. *Your Child's Sensory World*. Dial, New York, 1973.

Massie, Robert and Suzanne. *Journey*. Knopf, New York, 1975.

Oppenheimer, Jess (TV writer-producer). "All About Me." *Journal of Learning Disabilities*, January 1968.

Prudden, Bonnie. *Fitness from Six to Twelve*. Harper & Row, New York, 1972.

Simonson, O. Carl, and others. *Getting Well Again*. J. P. Tarcher, 9110 Sunset Boulevard, Los Angeles, Ca. 90069, 1978.

Smith, Lendon. *Feed Your Kids Right*. McGraw-Hill, New York, 1979.

Smith, Lendon. *Improving Your Child's Behavior Chemistry*. Prentice-Hall, Englewood Cliffs, N.J., 1976.

"Books Talk." Library of Congress Talking Books program. For a free copy, send a postcard with your name and address to Consumer Information Center, Dept. 578L, Pueblo, Colo. 91009.

"Creative Food Experiences for Children." Published by CSPI (Center for Science in the Public Interest). Order from Nutrition Action Reports, P.O. Box 7226, Washington, D.C. 20044.

National Dairy Council, Nutrition-Education Materials. Free catalog, 6300 North River Road, Rosemont, Ill. 60018.

Appendix

5

Famous Dyslexics, School Failures, and/or Left-Handed Geniuses

Albert Einstein
Thomas Edison
Leonardo da Vinci
Michelangelo
Benjamin Franklin
Hans Christian Andersen
Pablo Picasso
Thomas Carlyle
Niels Bohr
Winston Churchill

Vincent van Gogh
Nelson Rockefeller
General George S. Patton
Clarence Darrow
Carl Sandburg
Cole Porter
Babe Ruth
Reggie Jackson
Bruce Jenner
Captain Bligh

Queen Victoria

Appendix
6

Glossary of Clinical Terms

Attention deficit disorder — A medical/psychiatric diagnosis applied to children with mild to moderate neurological (developmental) impairment. The key symptoms are short attention span and impulsivity. Excessive motor activity and reckless, supercharged behavior ("hyperactivity") may or may not accompany the basic attentional difficulties.

Biofeedback techniques — Procedures which supply information on the state of various physiological activities such as heart rate, blood pressure, brain wave pattern, or skin temperature. This information is usually presented in an auditory or visual mode. It is intended to enable the patient who is hooked up to the recording apparatus to gain some voluntary control over the physiologic processes associated with his "free-floating" anxiety or psychosomatic illness.

Biological marker — A visible spot, line, or other identification on genes which is evidence for a family-linked trait, tendency, or behavioral pattern. Recently, researchers have found such identifying features which predispose children of alcoholics to alcoholism, and children of manic-depressives to manic-depressive illness.

Borderline personality disorder — A disturbance in social behavior, mood, and self-image which in children is often accompanied by impulsivity and unpredictable behavior. Emotional lability (marked ups and downs) may also be present, as well as intense anger and lack of control of anger. Although not psychotic, the person may be temporarily out of touch with reality.

Cerebral cortex — The "thinking" or reasoning portion of the brain in man, also known as the "new brain" or "neocortex." This largest brain division occupies the upper part of the cranial cavity and is divided into two roughly symmetrical halves called the right and left hemispheres. While it has long been considered to be the seat of consciousness and higher mental processes, we now know that the brain "thinks" as an integrated whole, in concert with all its other parts.

Clinical ecology — A branch of science and medicine which investigates the relationship between man and his environment. It is especially concerned with the sources, alleviation, and treatment of environmentally caused physical and mental diseases such as pollution-related sensitivities and illnesses.

Conduct disorder — A persistent pattern of inappropriate aggression and violation of the rights of others, property, or social rules. Chronic feelings of emptiness, boredom, restlessness, and low self-esteem typically accompany this disorder. Conduct problems have been linked to early attentional difficulties, overly harsh parental discipline, large family size, frequent shifting of parent figures, emotional neglect, and school failure.

Confabulation — Fabrication, exaggeration, or embellishment which compensates for underlying feelings of inadequacy, ineptness, and low self-regard. Many learning-disabled children are prone to express wishes of great power, prowess, and popularity through these verbal fantasies.

Developmental or maturational lag — A delay in the attainment of normal physical, neurological, intellectual, or social maturity. Usually slowness is found in more than one of these areas in the developmentally immature child.

Dyslexia — A general term for any and all developmental difficulties in reading. Visual system problems such as inability to control eye movements, to scan visually, or to "track" printed words may be implicated. Often the dyslexic child reads or writes words backwards, sees double or "scrambled" letters and words, confuses right and left, reverses numbers and letters, writes illegibly, and is generally disorganized and forgetful.

EEG (electroencephalography — The recording and printout of the electrical activity of the brain (brain waves) by means of electrodes applied to the scalp. This procedure is sometimes useful in detecting and diagnosing disturbances in brain functioning which manifest themselves in puzzling behavior problems such as fits or rage and unprovoked aggression. Abnormal EEG (electroencephalography) patterns are often associated with poor impulse control.

Epilepsy — A disturbance in the electrical rhythms of the brain which is diagnosed by the clinical technique of electroencephalography. Typical symptoms are convulsive episodes with loss of consciousness ranging from transient to prolonged, persistent irritability and explosiveness, abnormal motor activity, or sensory disturbances. Epilepsy is of two kinds: biological (genetic) epilepsy, with which the person is born, and secondary or acquired epilepsy, which is associated with head injury, concussion, or other trauma.

Expressive speech — Spoken words, sentences, and expressions which develop in young children subsequent to the acquisition of "receptive speech," or verbal understanding.

Fine motor coordination — Skill in using the hands and fingers. The manipulative abilities include manual dexterity, finger dexterity, arm-hand steadiness, and aiming ability.

Gate theory — The hypothesis that stimulation of large (myelinated or "sheathed") fibers in the sensory nerves which run from the surface of the body to the brain will tend to block or "gate" the perception of pain, whereas stimulation of small fibers with little or no sheathing insulation in these same nerves will tend to heighten the brain's sensitivity to pain and injury.

Gross motor coordination — Ability to use the arms, legs, and other body parts in a smooth, harmonious fashion.

Hyperkinesis — Excessive involuntary motor activity marked by distractibility, a feeling of inner tension, rashness, and abnormally great reaction to environmental stimuli, to the point where the child cannot inhibit his response.

Hypnagogic hallucinations — Visual and/or auditory images, distortions, and illusions which are usually frightening and morbid associated with the drowsiness preceding sleep. Some researchers believe minimal brain dysfunctional children are more prone than the average to these nocturnal misperceptions.

Hypoactivity — Abnormally restricted activity and lack of interest believed to be brought on in some neurologically impaired children by the same basic limbic system defect in screening which also produces hyperactivity. Too many electrical messages have been permitted to reach the sensory cortex. While most affected children react to the constant overload of stimuli by panic behavior or "fight," a lesser number respond by withdrawal or "flight."

Infantile autism — A severe childhood handicap which involves a disturbance in many areas of functioning. The child appears rigid, emotionally detached, and underreactive to the physical environment, as though any and all incoming stimuli are too painful. While ritualistic, repetitive, and obsessional behaviors are often marked, speech and communication skills do not develop. This lack of responsiveness was once thought to be the result of neglect and poor parenting, but recent studies support the view that this profound handicap results from hereditary or biochemical factors—specifically, a malfunctioning "filtering" system in the reticular and limbic structures of the brain. By definition, this diagnosis is always made within the first thirty months of life.

Laterality — The tendency to prefer the organs (hand, foot, ear, eye) of the same side of the body. In humans, this preference is related inversely to the dominant hemisphere of the brain—i.e., the left side of the brain controls movement on the right side of the body, and the right half of the brain controls the left side of the body.

Learning disability — The equivalent term in education for medical conditions of mild to moderate brain dysfunction. Learning handicaps are those attentional, perceptual, or perceptual-motor problems which restrict the improvement in skills of children with average or above-average intelligence.

Left-brain/right-brain theory — The concept that the two halves of the brain are specialized for different functions. Specifically, the left side is believed to control verbal and analytical reasoning and learning, and the right side spatial-temporal operations. Recent research which has shown that the brain responds as a functional whole has largely dispelled this idea that the two brain hemispheres operate independently.

Limbic system — A group of brain structures also known as the "old brain" or reptilian brain located between the spinal cord and the cortex. This division of the brain regulates many autonomic functions such as breathing, heartbeat, and body temperature. Since it also functions as a screening device to modulate all incoming sensory stimuli, it is of great importance in emotional response and behavior.

Magical thinking — The belief that one's own thoughts, wishes, words, or deeds will bring about desirable or undesirable consequences in a manner which transcends normal logic or cause and effect reasoning. While this disconnected, wishful ideation is believed to be an early and primitive stage in cognitive development for all children, many neurologically impaired children show persistence of the magical pattern until very late in childhood.

Mirror focus — A perceptual malfunctioning or brain "short circuit" in which objects such as words on the printed page are seen backwards or in reverse.

Mirror motion — The tendency for the organs on one side of the body to mimic the activity on the other side. Normally this impulse becomes inhibited in children by around the age of seven, but the "neurological" child finds it very difficult, if not impossible, for example, to rapidly turn one hand palm up then down without simultaneously moving the other hand in imitation.

Mixed cerebral dominance (cross dominance) — Variants in the usual pattern of right-eye, right-hand, right-foot (or left-eye, left-hand, left-foot) coordination. For example, a child may be right-eyed, left-handed, and right-footed, or show some other combination of eye, hand, and foot preference. These divergences, which are considered "soft" neurological signs, are often associated with clumsiness, hyper-activity, perceptual-motor difficulties, mirror motion, and exaggerated response to stress.

Myelinization — The process in fetuses and infants of gradually developing a protective, fatty sheath around nerve cells in the peripheral and central nervous systems. This outer coating acts as an insulator and conductor (speeder) of electrical messages or nerve impulses.

Nystagmus — Slight, involuntary movements of the eyeball including unsteadiness, inability to focus, vertical or horizontal shifting, rotary motion, or darting or "dancing" eyes. Some educators believe that this uncontrolled visual activity is the prime cause of reading disability or dyslexia.

Organic personality — A constellation of psychological traits and behaviors associated with transient or permanent dysfunction of the brain. Key symptoms are irritability, explosiveness, memory deficit, and decreased control over impulses. In severe cases, speech difficulties and a degree of disorientation (confusion about time, place, or person) may also be present. This pattern is milder in symptomatology than organic psychosis, and does not involve the gross loss of normal reality testing, a clouded state of consciousness, and the bizarre symptoms such as delusions and hallucinations, all characteristic of a psychotic state. Observant physicians and parents often note a touch of the "organic personality pattern" in neurological children.

Organic psychosis — A heterogeneous group of major mental disorders associated with an identifiable source of brain dysfunction such as alcohol or drug intoxication and withdrawal, senile dementia, metabolic deficiencies like hypoglycemia, encephalitis (inflammation of the brain), or head injury. Memory impairment, disorientation, hal-lucinations, diminished cognitive capacity, and anxiety and depression—all secondary reactions to reduced or lost primary brain functions—are the most prominent symptoms.

Paranoid ideation — Persistent and unfounded suspiciousness, especially the idea that one is being singled out for unfair treatment, harassment, or persecution.

Patterning — Physical and sensory methods designed to recover brain functions which have been impaired by birth trauma or later accident. These techniques consist of repetitive manipulation of body parts on the theory that damaged areas of the brain can relearn underdeveloped or lost capabilities.

Perceptual or central processing dysfunction — A general term officially adopted by the U.S. Office of Education to describe a variety of childhood handicaps in learning and cognition which require programs of special remedial instruction.

Play therapy — A technique of psychotherapy for use with children which attempts to bring buried feeling and unconscious need to awareness by indirect or "projective" means. The therapist observes as the child manipulates dolls, dollhouses, blocks, and other toys, draws pictures, builds structures, and so on, on the theory that he will "give" or attribute his emotion to the dolls and other objects in his imagination. It is assumed that the child himself and his immediate family members are always the central characters in the fantasies and play dramas.

Psychosis — A general term for any bizarre or unusual behavior, whether of organic (body) or emotional origin. The primary symptom is a loss of contact with reality—i.e., a disturbance or alteration in the individual's habitual relationship to the external world.

Receptive speech — The ability to understand what is said, manifested in young children by obeying simple commands and pointing to objects when they are named.

Reticular activating system (RAS) — A group of structures at the base of the brain and deep in the brain stem, also known as the reticular formation, which may have either an arousing (excitatory) or inhibitory effect on the cortex.

Schizophrenic disorders — Severe forms of mental illness characterized by withdrawal, greatly restricted (blunted or flat) affect, loosening of associations (disconnected and frequently shifting thoughts and ideas), idiosyncratic and eccentric thinking, and an autistic loss of contact with the real environment. Delusions (false or mistaken beliefs) and hallucinations (imaginary visual, auditory, gustatory, or olfactory images and sensations) are often present.

Sequencing — The ability to organize or arrange material in a given order of succession or a continuous series. Simple examples of this skill, which is often impaired in minimal brain dysfunction children, are to follow a three-part command, and to repeat the days of the week or months of the year in consecutive order.

Social isolation hypothesis — The theory that mental illness results from intense loneliness and emotional estrangement brought about by the lack of close and fulfilling relationships with significant others.

"Soft" neurological signs — General or nonlocalized indicators of body problems. Finger or other sensory "agnosia" (loss of sensation), difficulty in walking along a narrow line, mirror motion, right-left confusion, word and letter reversals, slurring and articulation errors, and mixed or cross dominance in eye, hand, and foot preference are among the most common minimal cerebral symptoms. In general, they reflect some degree of disturbance in balance, coordination, or bodily "rhythm."

Thought disorder — A disturbance in the content or form of thinking which may involve delusions (especially of being controlled or persecuted), illogical ideas, loose associations, concretism, neologisms (coining of new and bizarre words and phrases), or idiosyncratic preoccupation and perseveration.

Visual-motor system — The coordinated functioning or "teamwork" of eye and hand movements. Educators cite difficulties in the smooth, simultaneous operation of eye and hand as the most frequent cause of learning handicaps in children.

Index

361